본 교재 『HALF 모의고사』는 압박감을 느끼는 실전의 상황에 대비하고자 지금까지 권혁민 하프모의고사에서 가장 오답률이 높았고 실전에 가장 가까운 문제들로 구성하였습니다.

우리가 실전에서 원하는 점수를 얻지 못하는 이유는 다양합니다.

그 이유 중에 가장 수험생이 많이 이야기 해주시는 부분이 "읽히지 않았다." 입니다.

왜 일까요?

그것은 시간에 대한 압박도 있겠지만 평소에 내가 공부하는 문제풀이 혹은 모의고사의 수준이 실제 시험과의 괴리로 인해 실전보다 쉬운 지문만을 연습하다가 **당일 난이도 + 타과목에 대한 압박 + 개인적인 불안** 등이 겹쳐져 영어지문 자체가 읽히지 않는 것입니다.

이에 본 교재 『HALF 모의고사』는 실전보다 높은 난이도의 가장 잘 선별된 지문 문제만을 수록해 두었기에 우리 수험생들이 실전에서 흔들리지 않고 제 실력을 발휘할 수 있는 좋은 실전적 문제임을 알려드립니다.

저는 많은 것을 바라지 않았습니다. 우리 친구들이 당일 쌓은 실력을 그대로만 발휘하길 바랄뿐입니다.

부디 이 교재가 그런 역할을 해주길 바라며 이 교재가 나오기까지 큰 버팀목이 되어준 웅비출판사 대표님 및 임직원 여러분에게 감사드립니다.

저자 권혁민

[문제편]

01회	하프 모의고사	8
02회	하프 모의고사	13
03회	하프 모의고사	17
04회	하프 모의고사	21
05회	하프 모의고사	27
06회	하프 모의고사	32
07회	하프 모의고사	38
08회	하프 모의고사	44
09회	하프 모의고사	49
10회	하프 모의고사	54
11회	하프 모의고사	60
12회	하프 모의고사	65
13회	하프 모의고사	71
14회	하프 모의고사	76
15회	하프 모의고사	82
16회	하프 모의고사	87
17회	하프 모의고사	92
18회	하프 모의고사	98
19회	하프 모의고사	103
20회	하프 모의고사	108

[해설편]

01회	하프 모의고사 해설	114
02회	하프 모의고사 해설	123
03회	하프 모의고사 해설	130
04회	하프 모의고사 해설	138
05회	하프 모의고사 해설	145
06회	하프 모의고사 해설	153
07회	하프 모의고사 해설	162
08회	하프 모의고사 해설	171
09회	하프 모의고사 해설	179
10회	하프 모의고사 해설	187
11회	하프 모의고사 해설	195
12회	하프 모의고사 해설	202
13회	하프 모의고사 해설	209
14회	하프 모의고사 해설	217
15회	하프 모의고사 해설	224
16회	하프 모의고사 해설	233
17회	하프 모의고사 해설	240
18회	하프 모의고사 해설	250
19회	하프 모의고사 해설	258
20회	하프 모의고사 해설	266

권혁민 ONEPACK 하프 모의고사

권혁민 ONEPACK

문제

24시간에 끝내는 One Pack

하프모의고사

01 하프 모의고사

01 밑줄 친 단어의 의미와 가장 가까운 것은?

> She is known for her devotion to the <u>cause</u> of women's rights in the 19th century.

① reason ② objective ③ agent ④ origin

02 글의 흐름상 빈칸에 들어갈 단어를 순서대로 고른 것은?

> Often described as the _____ rags to riches tale, the story of steel magnate Andrew Carnegie's rise begins in 1835 in a small one-room home in Dunfermline, Scotland. Born into a family of _____ laborers, Carnegie received little schooling before his family emigrated to America in 1848. Arriving in Pennsylvania, he soon got a job in a textile mill, where he earned only $1.20 per week.

① quintessential – destitute
② exceptive – devout
③ interesting – meticulous
④ deleterious – impoverished

03 밑줄 친 부분 중 어법상 가장 옳지 않은 것은?

> I ① <u>convinced</u> that making pumpkin cake ② <u>from scratch</u> would be ③ <u>even</u> easier than ④ <u>making</u> cake from a box.

04 밑줄 친 부분 중 어법상 가장 옳지 않은 것은?

> When you find your tongue ① <u>twisted</u> as you seek to explain to your ② <u>six-year-old</u> daughter why she can t go to the amusement park ③ <u>that has been</u> advertised on television, then you will understand why we find it difficult ④ <u>wait</u>.

05 영작이 올바른 문장을 고르시오.

① 만일 그 물품이 내일까지 배달되지 않으면 그들은 그것에 대해 불평을 할 것이다.
   ⇨ If the item should not be delivered tomorrow, they would complain about it.
② 그는 그의 학급의 어느 다른 야구선수 보다 더욱 능숙하다.
   ⇨ He was more skillful than any other baseball players in his class.
③ 바이올리니스트가 공연을 끝내자마자 관객들은 일어나서 갈채를 보냈다.
   ⇨ Hardly has the violinist finished his performance before the audience stood up and applauded.
④ 제과업자들은 밀의 소비 장려를 요구하며 거리로 나오도록 요구되어 왔다.
   ⇨ Bakers have been made come out, asking for promoting wheat consumption.

06 글의 제목으로 가장 적절한 것을 고르시오.

> When we think of the people who make our lives miserable by spreading malicious viruses, most of us imagine an unpopular teenager boy, brilliant but geeky, venting his frustrations from the safety of a suburban bedroom. Actually, these stereotypes are just that — stereotypes — according to Sarah Gordon, an expert in computer viruses and security technology. Since 1992, Gordon has studied the psychology of virus writers. "A virus writer is just as likely to be the guy next door to you," she says. The virus writers Gordon has come to know have varied backgrounds; while predominantly male, some are female. Some are solidly academics, while others are athletic. Many have friendships with members of the opposite sex, good relationships with their parents and families; most are popular with their peers. They don't spend all their time in the basement. One virus writer volunteers in his local library, working with elderly people. One of them is a poet and a musician, another is an electrical engineer, and others work for a university quantum physics department.

① Unmasking Virus Writers
② Virus Writers: Gender and Class
③ Underground Virus Writers
④ Mysterious Activities by Virus Writers

07 다음 글의 내용으로 가장 적절한 것은?

> The evolution of intelligence among early large mammals of the grasslands was due to the interaction between the hunting carnivores and the herbivores that they hunted. The interaction resulting from the differences between predator and prey led to a general improvement in brain functions; however, certain components of intelligence were improved far more than others. The kind of intelligence favored by the interaction is defined by attention. Herbivores and carnivores develop different kinds of attention related to escaping or chasing. For both, arousal attunes the animal to what is ahead. Perhaps it does not experience forethought as we know it, but the animal does experience something like it. The predator is searchingly aggressive, inner-directed, but aware in a sense closer to human consciousness than, say, a hungry lizard's instinctive snap at a passing beetle. The herbivore prey is of a different mind. It is wary rather than searching, and expectant rather than anticipating.

① Climate was important in establishing the proper relation between predator and prey.
② Lizards are more vigilant to their prey than mammals.
③ Prey species pay attention not to be caught, which developed certatin functions of their brains.
④ The interaction between carnivores and herbivores developed brutality in the mammals.

08 주어진 글 다음에 이어질 글의 순서로 가장 적절한 것은?

Two major techniques for dealing with environmental problems are conservation and restoration. Conservation involves protecting existing natural habitats. Restoration involves cleaning up and restoring damaged habitats. The best way to deal with environmental problems is to prevent them from happening. Conserving habitats prevents environmental issues that arise from ecosystem disruption.

(A) To solve the problem, the city built a sewage-treatment complex. Since then, the harbor waters have cleared up. Plants and fish have returned, and beaches have been reopened.

(B) For example, parks and reserves protect a large area in which many species live. Restoration reverses damage to ecosystems. Boston Harbor is one restoration success story.

(C) Since the colonial period, the city dumped sewage directly into the harbor. The buildup of waste caused outbreaks of disease. Beaches were closed. Most of the marine life disappeared and as a result, the shellfish industry shut down.

① (A) – (B) – (C)
② (B) – (C) – (A)
③ (C) – (A) – (B)
④ (C) – (B) – (A)

09 다음 빈칸에 들어갈 말로 가장 적절한 것을 고르시오.

Naturally, people eat many different kinds of meals and choose them with the intention of communicating the right message to the right audience. One would not reheat half-eaten leftovers when trying to impress a potential lover, just as one would not spend a fortune on extravagant ingredients for a hurried everyday meal eaten in solitude. Every meal has, in a sense, its own coded message. This is not to say, however, that it is always readily perceived or interpreted correctly by others. What may be intended as cozy informality to someone preparing a meal might be interpreted as laziness by an invited guest. Equally, a meal of roast beef offered to a vegetarian might be construed as a calculated insult. As with all language, there can be _____. Despite this, an outsider observing or commenting on an eating event can usually decode the intended message without too much difficulty.

① usefulness
② borrowing
③ miscommunication
④ correspondence

10 빈칸 (A), (B)에 들어갈 말로 가장 적절한 것은?

Since the concept of a teddy bear is very obviously not a genetically inherited trait, we can be confident that we are looking at a cultural trait. However, it is a cultural trait that seems to be under the guidance of another, genuinely biological trait: the cues that attract us to babies (high foreheads and small faces). Cute, baby-like features are inherently appealing, producing a nurturing response in most humans. Teddy bears that had a more baby-like appearance — however slight this may have been initially — were thus more popular with customers. Teddy bear manufacturers obviously noticed which bears were selling best and so made more of these and fewer of the less popular models, to maximize their profits. In this way, the selection pressure built up by the customers resulted in the evolution of a more baby-like bear by the manufacturers.

↓

Due to its inherent attraction and __(A)__ considerations, the teddy bear has been transformed to the present baby-like appearance, showing that a cultural trait can be __(B)__ by a biological trait.

	(A)	(B)		(A)	(B)
①	commercial	guided	②	commercial	replaced
③	intellectual	guided	④	intellectual	represented

02 하프 모의고사

01 다음 밑줄 친 단어의 의미와 가장 가까운 것은?

> He would only make himself ridiculous by quoting poetry to them which they could not understand. They would think that he was airing his superior education.

① concealing
② refreshing
③ jilting
④ showing off

02 다음 밑줄 친 단어의 의미와 가장 가까운 것은?

> Severe droughts, floods and heat waves rocked the world last year as greenhouse gas levels climbed, boosting the odds of some extreme weather events.

① chances
② solutions
③ dangers
④ symptoms

03 다음 빈칸에 들어갈 단어로 가장 적절한 것은?

> The ultimate value of any hypothesis lies in its predictive or explanatory power, which means that additional facts must be _____ from an adequate hypothesis.

① deducible
② vulnerable
③ conductible
④ inseparable

04 다음 밑줄 친 부분 중, 어법상 틀린 것은?

> We are constantly losing land to new ① housing developments, and I have seen the lands ② on which I grew up ③ playing slowly ④ to shrink away.

05 다음 빈칸에 들어갈 알맞은 것은?

It is a widely known fact that heat makes gases _____.

① expand
② to expand
③ being expanded
④ to be expanded

06 어법상 가장 적절한 것은?

① The roof of the house needs being painted.
② One hour's delay will not bother me.
③ I ask only that I am treated with respect.
④ I bought this blue dress of my sister at the department store.

07 다음 글의 빈칸에 들어갈 말로 가장 적절한 것을 고르시오.

City dwellers are accustomed to speed and change, and little disturbed by the unusual. They are, however, more _____ than their rural neighbors. City life affords more opportunities for wrongdoing, and crime is more prevalent in cities than in rural regions. The absence of many restraints tends to increase the crime rate in large cities. The city, with its almost limitless potentialities for the welfare and happiness of its inhabitants, also contains possibilities of evil greater than ever before. In addition, city dwellers know more about world affairs than do rural dwellers because of their readier access to newspapers, books, magazines, etc. Their knowledge of other peoples and other cultures tends to break down ancient prejudices, but it also weakens the hold of traditions and ideals which have a steady influence on character.

① isolated
② competitive
③ restless
④ self-centered

08 다음 글의 제목으로 가장 적절한 것은?

> The problem that judges face is not that there are too many rules. A legal system is made up of rules, and the task of judges is to help interpret the rules in particular situations. Judges are prevented from doing this work well when they are required to pick one of the multiple aims of sentencing, like retribution, and prevented from balancing it with other important aims, like rehabilitation. They are forbidden from exercising judgment when rigid sentencing rules deny them the discretion to interpret the circumstances, to make this punishment fit this crime and this individual. But it's not only rigid rules like mandatory sentencing laws that discourage the wisdom to balance and interpret. Sometimes good principles, coupled with the best of intentions, can have the same effect. Principles are valuable guidelines, and we'd be lost without them. We admire principled people. We want our politicians to act on principle and not out of narrow self-interest. Protect human rights. Protect national security. Defend free speech. Our codes of professional ethics are all about the good principles that should guide doctors, lawyers, and architects. Respect for client and patient autonomy. Loyalty. Trust. "Unprincipled" is an epithet. But like rules, good principles, unleavened by judgment, can be dangerous. They can make us dumb to the nuances of context. A good principle can blind us to other good principles with which it needs to be balanced. In policy making, the results can be disastrous. In the everyday work of doctors, the results are bad practice.

① The Danger of a Good Principle
② The Great Principle of Humanity
③ Good Principles vs. Bad Principle
④ Principles that Judges Have to Stick to

09 다음 글의 밑줄 친 부분 중, 문맥상 낱말의 쓰임이 적절하지 않은 것은?

Good writers are not passive; they don't simply record ① immediate responses. They look closely, ask questions, analyze, make connections, and think. Learning to see with a writer's eye ② benefits not just those who write for a living but all professionals. In any career you choose, success depends on keen observation and in-depth analysis. A skilled physician detects minor symptoms in a physical or follows up on a patient's complaint to ask questions that lead to a diagnosis others might miss. A successful stockbroker observes ③ overlooked trends and conducts research to detect new investment opportunities. A passerby might assume a busy store must be successful, but a retail analyst would observe what merchandise people are purchasing and how they are paying for it. If all the shoppers are buying discount items and paying with credit cards, the store could be ④ earning money on the sales.

10 다음 글의 내용과 일치하지 않는 것은?

Western civilization arose in the Near East and spread eventually to North America and other continents. For two thousand years, however, it has been intimately associated with Europe. A mere peninsula of Asia, Europe is, except for Australia, the smallest of the continents. Its population, even counting offshoots overseas, has never been more than a minority of mankind. Yet it had played a towering role in the world. The extraordinary length and irregularity of its coastline—a veritable lacework of bays, inlets, channels, and internal seas—and a rich system of riverways brought Europeans close to one another and gave them access to the rest of the world. Although it is situated in the same latitudes as Canada, Europe has a moderate climate and a fairly regular rainfall. The resources of the continent are sufficiently modest to exact effort and forethought and sufficiently ample to regard them. They have neither the luxuriance that makes man lazy and improvident nor the barrenness that makes him niggardly and takes away his hope.

① Western civilization originated from the Near East.
② Natural conditions in Europe were good for shipping.
③ European populations grew rapidly with Western civilization.
④ Europe had resources that were neither too plentiful nor too scarce.

03 하프 모의고사

01 다음 밑줄 친 단어의 의미와 가장 가까운 것은?

> His promise of <u>unyielding</u> support for the policy, however, is a cause of concern, rather than an act of reassurance for many people, who aptly regard the policy as a failure.

① opinionated ② implead ③ denounce ④ insulate

02 다음 빈칸에 들어갈 표현으로 적절한 것을 고르시오.

> The poet just wants to sit and meditate, _____ against a post.

① while his back leaning
② with his back is leaning
③ while his back to lean
④ with his back leaning

03 (A), (B), (C) 각 빈칸 문맥에 맞는 말로 가장 적절한 것은?

> Ishan works for a large PR and advertising company, he is responsible for sourcing images from photographic agents. He reports to the creative director who is very supportive and encouraging when Ishan wants to discuss work issues face to face, but appears uncaring and combative when he communicates with Ishan via e-mail. This is because when the creative director writes e-mails, he does not __(A)__ the 'softer' elements of the conversation that take place when he is discussing the issues face to face. His e-mails are written in a list style, setting out the tasks that must be completed to 'fix' the situations, whereas when he meets with Isahn he will __(B)__ the difficulties and will even makes jokes about the problems to lighten the atmosphere. This more __(C)__ approach is not reflected in his written style, and even though Ishan knows he means no harm, his e-mail imply impatience and anger about the situation which makes Ishan worry, and question whether he should have raised the issue in the first place.

	(A)	(B)	(C)
①	exclude	acknowledge	relaxed
②	exclude	ignore	aggressive
③	include	acknowledge	aggressive
④	include	acknowledge	relaxed

04 다음 글의 밑줄 친 부분 중, 어법상 틀린 것은?

> A space rock ① <u>big enough to</u> cause widespread damage will hit the Earth only about once ② <u>every 1,000 year</u>, but experts say the destruction would be ③ <u>so extreme</u> that nations should develop a joint defense ④ <u>against space rocks</u>.

05 어법상 가장 적절한 것은?

① Ken could be a very attractive man but he pays no attention to his clothes.
② The researchers agreed, at principle, to exchange their findings.
③ Your method seems as odd to us as ours do to you.
④ She was a glad girl and liked to hang out with her classmates.

06 다음 글의 요지로 적절한 것을 고르시오.

> You've got a vocabulary list to learn for your French class. What's the best way to study? You might be tempted to stare at the words for a long time — reading, then reading again. And again. After this exercise — with more staring, followed by more reading — you might hope the words and translations should have been copied into your head like songs into an iPod. There may be a better way to remember: More testing! We often think of testing as a way to measure how much information a person remembers, but research shows that testing can be a powerful study strategy as well. In a recent experiment, researchers found that students who were quizzed as they studied scored higher on vocabulary tests than the students who only read and reread. That's not too surprising — teachers have told students for thousands of years that self-testing is a good study strategy.

① Memory recall is a useful skill to have a conversation with foreigners.
② Small quizzes involve recovering stored information from memory.
③ Quizzing yourself while studying beats staring at words for word acquisition.
④ The translation process starts by pronouncing words a person wants to memorize.

07 다음 빈칸에 들어갈 말로 가장 적절한 것을 고르시오.

A remarkable feature of sugar is the ways in which, over the course of time, it has been employed _____. When thoroughly mixed together, sugar and ground almonds with a bit of oil becomes a kind of modeling clay. When heated, refined white sugar liquefies. Properly handled as it dries, it can be dyed, spun, blown, artistically cast, or painted. Its uses in these ways have long existed in China, India, and the Middle East. Once sugar spread from the Old World to the New, its production expanded explosively, and it was put to such uses in many other places. Hence, there is no single center of origin for the artistic uses of sugar, even though the baker-sculptors of Egypt, Italy, Germany, and the United Kingdom, and the candy makers of Mexico and Indonesia, among others, are justly famous. Spun and sculpted sugar figures — some classic, some comical — seem to have become popular wherever artistic individuals happened to work in or near kitchens.

① medically
② collectively
③ aesthetically
④ competitively

08 글의 흐름으로 보아, 주어진 문장이 들어가기에 가장 적절한 곳은?

The adjustment of the rods to dim light is caused by the production of a chemical called rhodopsin or "visual purple."

Have you ever gone from a bright sunny afternoon into a dark motion picture theatre? Once inside, you are not surprised to find that you're practically blind for a while. (①) After about 5 minutes, you'll find your sight returning, with colors becoming more visible as your cones adapt to the darkness. (②) Over the course of approximately 30 minutes, your rods attain their full sensitivity. (③) Slight improvements in your dim-light vision may continue for a considerable length of time after that. (④) The amount of this substance in your rods determines how sensitive they are to light. Exposure to bright light fades rhodopsin out of the eye and causes it to become temporarily less sensitive to light.

* rod 간상체(명암을 식별하는 시세포) ** cone 원추체(색채 시각을 담당하는 시세포)

09 주어진 글 다음에 이어질 글의 순서로 가장 적절한 것은?

It was believed prior to the 1970s that chimpanzees were primarily vegetarian and that they might occasionally eat a small animal or bird but would not deliberately and systematically kill larger animals for meat.

(A) Together they try to steer the prey to a congenial spot for capture. A successful hunt is often followed by sharing with the resultant meat.

(B) However, as Goodall witnessed, they not only eat and relish meat but also hunt for meat. In particular, they hunt monkeys, which are not easy to catch for the larger and more terrestrial chimps.

(C) Hunting such prey requires cooperation and coordination, foresight and planning. The hunters usually divide the assignment between those who will give chase through the branches and those who will pursue along the ground below.

① (A) – (C) – (B) ② (B) – (A) – (C)
③ (B) – (C) – (A) ④ (C) – (A) – (B)

10 다음 빈칸에 들어갈 말로 가장 적절한 것을 고르시오.

It's crucial to maintain integrity by _____. Many people misunderstand that. They think they can do whatever they want when it comes to the small things because they believe that as long as they don't have any major lapses, they're doing well. But that's not the way it works. Webster's New Universal Unabridged Dictionary describes integrity as "adherence to moral and ethical principles; soundness of moral character; honesty." Ethical principles are not flexible. A little white lie is still a lie. Theft is theft — whether it's $1, $1,000, or $1 million. Integrity commits itself to character over personal gain, to people over things, to service over power, to principle over convenience, to the long view over the immediate. Nineteenth-century clergyman Phillips Brooks maintained, "Character is made in the small moments of our lives." Anytime you break a moral principle, you create a small crack in the foundation of your integrity. And when times get tough, it becomes harder to act with integrity, not easier.

* lapse : 실수, 과실

① taking care of the little things
② showing loving care for strangers
③ taking credit for the work of others
④ checking your biases and being fair

04 하프 모의고사

01 다음 밑줄 친 단어의 의미와 가장 가까운 것은?

> However, many still feel China is an imperious country that is sometimes impossible to communicate with.

① drawl
② insolent
③ quaint
④ eccentric
⑤ mawkish

02 다음 빈칸에 들어갈 표현으로 적절한 것을 고르시오.

> The health of American children is _____ — they move too little and eat too much junk. But there was promising news this week when America's Centres for Disease Control and Prevention (CDC) announced that obesity rates were flat for most children and _____ for those aged two to five.

① mediocre – dropped
② paramount – plagued
③ reversible – stagnated
④ solid – multiplied

03 다음 밑줄 친 부분 중 문법적으로 어색한 부분을 고르시오.

> Difficulties with culture shock ① are often related to an ② individual's ability ③ to speak the language of ④ the country which he or she is living.

04 다음 빈칸에 들어갈 말로 적절한 것을 고르시오.

> Holmes compares himself to Dupin and Lecoq, _____ them as really existing historical figures.

① having treated
② being treated
③ treating
④ having been treated

05 다음 우리말 영작이 올바르지 않는 문장을 고르시오.

① 우리가 그녀를 격려하는 것은 쉽다.
⇨ She is easy for us to encourage.
② 나의 딸에게는 그녀의 친구와 점심을 먹을 만큼의 충분한 돈이 있다.
⇨ My daughter has enough money to have lunch with her friend.
③ 우리는 지하철을 타고 집으로 가는 것이 현명한 것이라 생각한다.
⇨ We think the sensible thing would be to take a subway home.
④ 바닥에서 자고 있는 내 아들을 보아라.
⇨ Look at the asleep my son on the floor.

06 밑줄 친 부분에 들어갈 표현으로 가장 적절한 것을 고르시오.

> Tom : Frankly, I don't think my new boss knows what he is doing.
> Jack : He is young, Tom. You have to give him a chance.
> Tom : How many chances do I have to give him? He's actually doing terribly.
> Jack : _____
> Tom : What? Where?
> Jack : Over there. Your new boss just turned around the corner.

① Speak of the devil
② I wish you good luck
③ Keep up the good work
④ Money makes the mare go

07 빈칸 (A), (B)에 들어갈 말로 가장 적절한 것은?

> Mitterer and de Ruiter used a color categorization paradigm to study the relationship between "world knowledge" and color categories. First, half of the observers saw typically orange objects (e.g., carrot) in a good orange and typically yellow objects (e.g., banana) in a hue midway between orange and yellow. The other half saw typically orange objects in the intermediate hue and typically yellow objects in a good yellow. Later, observers were asked to categorize a color-neutral object (e.g., sock) colored somewhere between yellow and orange as either yellow or orange. The researchers found that if the observers had seen typically yellow objects in the intermediate hue, this hue was subsequently categorized as yellow. The reverse was true for the observers who had seen typically orange objects in the intermediate hue.

> After observers were ___(A)___ a typically yellow or orange object in an intermediate hue, they thought the intermediate hue of a color-neutral object ___(B)___ the category of the previous object's typical color.

	(A)	(B)
①	exposed to	matched
②	exposed to	narrowed
③	reminded of	changed
④	reminded of	determined

08 주어진 글 다음에 이어질 글의 순서로 가장 적절한 것은?

The difficulty in determining whether con-elation equals causation causes an enormous number of misunderstandings. Until a specific mechanism demonstrating how A causes B is identified, it's best to assume that any correlation is accidental, or that both A and B relate independently to some third factor.

(A) A more likely explanation is that cancer diagnoses and milk consumption both have a positive correlation with increased age: On average, milk drinkers live longer than non-milk drinkers, and the older you are, the more likely you are to develop cancer.

(B) This does not, however, mean that drinking milk actually causes people to live longer: It could be that people who drink milk have better access to high-quality health care or eat more healthily than those who do not.

(C) An example that highlights this is the correlation between drinking milk and cancer rates, which some support groups use to argue that drinking milk causes cancer.

① (A) – (C) – (B)
② (B) – (A) – (C)
③ (B) – (C) – (A)
④ (C) – (A) – (B)

09 왜 일부 검찰과 경찰들은 "CSI effect"에 대해 걱정하는가?

> Solving "cold case" homicides relies more on the emergence of new witnesses than on the DNA analyses and other forensic techniques celebrated in crime dramas. Funded by the U.S. Justice Department's National Institute of Justice, the report adds to existing evidence that old-fashioned investigative work, rather than the latest forensic technologies, matters the most in homicide cases. Most of these people were shooting victims. That doesn't leave a lot of DNA from the murderer. Delays in receiving DNA results often lead detectives to discount DNA's impact in solving murders. That is a concern because some prosecutors and police officials have worried about a CSI effect (named after the popular police-drama television series) that may affect murder trials. Jurors may have come to expect complex forensic techniques to solve cases, instead of the often messy real-life details of investigations that center on interviews with witnesses. If anyone ever wanted to do a show about a real-life homicide investigation, I can guarantee it would be a lot less exciting and conclusive than a TV show.

① Jurors may expect more scientific proof of guilt than what witnesses say.
② The judge may place a lower value on circumstantial evidence.
③ Jurors are asked to make an inference of guilt from indirect evidence.
④ Prosecutors feel pressured when eyewitness testimony is necessary.

10 다음 빈칸에 들어갈 말로 가장 적절한 것을 고르시오.

Some types of persuasive communications are believed in the end to be self-persuasive. If a particular communication provokes thoughts in the person that are in the direction of supporting the communication, then the person will move towards being influenced by the message. Conversely, if the message provokes anti-thoughts, then the person will move against it. So, the precise wording or style of a persuasive message does matter. _____ are also very important. For example, one is far more likely to persuade an intelligent audience with a balanced presentation that produces both sides of the argument than with a one-sided case. However, no matter how well contrived and persuasive a communication might be, if the receiver of it is already set to produce counter-arguments, then it is much less likely to succeed. Generally speaking, what is crucial is how much involvement a person has in an issue. Changing attitudes is no easy matter, particularly if they are well entrenched in the way that prejudiced attitudes are.

① The varieties of message sources used in integrated communications
② The simple and direct actions of the message sender
③ Cultural barriers which block the free flow of the message
④ The characteristics of the intended receiver of the message

05 하프 모의고사

01 밑줄 친 단어의 의미와 가장 가까운 것은?

> Their guest did not protract his stay that evening above an hour longer.

① weird
② grotesque
③ outlandish
④ dawdle

02 다음 빈칸에 들어갈 단어로 적절한 것을 고르시오.

> The well-born young Athenian who gathered around Socrates found it quite _____ that their hero was so intelligent, so brave, so honorable — so ugly.

① paradoxical
② charitable
③ deliberate
④ turbulent

03 (A), (B), (C) 각 빈칸 문맥에 맞는 말로 가장 적절한 것은?

> The equipment of the kitchen can seem unimportant compared to the history of food itself. It is all very well fussing over the details of table settings and jelly moulds, but what does this matter compared to a basic hunger for bread? Perhaps this explains why kitchen tools have been so ___(A)___ in histories of food. Culinary history has become a hot subject over the past two decades. But the focus of these new histories, with a few notable exceptions, has ___(B)___ been ingredients rather than technique: what we cooked rather than how we cooked it. There have been books on potatoes, cod and chocolate and histories of cookbooks, restaurants and cooks. The kitchen and its tools are more or less ___(C)___ — and as a result, half the story is missing. This matters: we change the texture, the taste, the nutritional content and the cultural associations of ingredients simply by using different tools and techniques to prepare them.

	(A)	(B)	(C)
①	neglected	scarcely	focused
②	emphasized	overwhelmingly	absent
③	neglected	overwhelmingly	absent
④	emphasized	scarcely	focused

04 다음 글의 밑줄 친 부분 중, 어법상 틀린 것은?

① Far better it is to dare mighty things, ② even though checked by failure, than ③ taking to rank with those poor spirits ④ who neither enjoy much nor suffer much.

05 다음 빈칸에 들어갈 표현으로 적절한 것을 고르시오.

The second is the intellectuals; and if their attachment to ideas is passionate, and not only passionate but programmatic, they are almost certain to abuse _____.

① whatever they acquire power
② what they acquire every power
③ whatever power they acquire
④ the power whatever they acquire

06 다음 글의 주제로 가장 적절한 것은?

Historians' approaches to the past vary enormously, but some common disciplinary features unite them. There are limits to what historians can study: they can study only parts of the past that left evidence behind and for which evidence has survived. The dominant type of evidence has been documentary: government archives, private papers, newspapers and published materials have long been the most consulted forms of source. The range has recently broadened, and many historians are now happy to use artefacts, buildings, visual evidence, oral testimony and many other non-written sources. However, regardless of the type of evidence, the point is that without evidence, historians cannot function. So all studies of history are driven by the discovery of evidence from the period being studied, and its analysis and interpretation. Historians aim to describe what happened, explain how and why it happened, and link past events to wider contexts and the passage of time.

① ways historians search for historical evidence
② importance of evidence in historical research
③ difficulty of using evidence from the past properly
④ contributions of historians to exploring current problems

07 carpa에 관한 다음 글의 내용과 일치하지 않는 것은?

A carpa is a popular improvised show of the nineteenth and twentieth centuries, often performed in a tent on a street corner or vacant lot in Mexico City. Itinerant performers move their collapsible stages from one town to the next, performing shows consisting of songs and comedy to a lower-and middle-class audience. Plots are based on recent events or current topics of interest, and the mood of the performances is determined by the subject matter. The audience and performers are able to directly relate to each other in this relaxed informal performance setting. Performers support themselves by charging a small entrance fee for their shows. Now most carpa troupes have been absorbed into variety shows or circuses. As Mexico City becomes larger and more cosmopolitan, remaining carpa performances are in more obscure corners of the city.

① This show is often held on street corners and vacant lots in Mexico City.
② It will perform a show composed of songs and comedies to audiences in the middle and lower classes.
③ The plot of events long ago is reconstructed and shown.
④ The audience and performers interact in a comfortable atmosphere.

08 다음 빈칸에 들어갈 말로 가장 적절한 것은?

A good image of what we mean by decision making is of a person pausing at a fork in the road, and then choosing one path — to reach a desired goal or to avoid an unpleasant outcome. The most important evolutionary situations that selected our basic decision-making capacities probably involved physical approach or avoidance — which waterhole, field, fruit tree, cave, stranger, mate, and so forth, to approach and which to avoid. In prehistoric times, bad decisions were punished in a dramatic manner; as the philosopher Willard van Orman Quine commented, "Creatures inveterately wrong in their inductions have a pathetic but praiseworthy tendency to die before reproducing their kind." In other words, animals, including humans, that make bad predictions of the future and consequently bad decisions tend to die before they can pass their genes on to the next generation; this is one reason that we, and other animals, _____.

① often choose to follow others
② are unreliable decision makers
③ want to try every option available
④ are good at making survival decisions

09 다음 빈칸에 들어갈 말로 가장 적절한 것을 고르시오.

The human species is unique in its ability to expand its functionality by inventing new cultural tools. Writing, arithmetic, science — all are recent inventions. Our brains did not have enough time to evolve for them, but I reason that they were made possible because _____. When we learn to read, we recycle a specific region of our visual system known as the visual word-form area, enabling us to recognize strings of letters and connect them to language areas. Likewise, when we learn Arabic numerals we build a circuit to quickly convert those shapes into quantities — a fast connection from bilateral visual areas to the parietal quantity area. Even an invention as elementary as finger-counting changes our cognitive abilities dramatically. Amazonian people who have not invented counting are unable to make exact calculations as simple as, say, 6 — 2. This "cultural recycling" implies that the functional architecture of the human brain results from a complex mixture of biological and cultural constraints.

① our brains put a limit on cultural diversity
② we can mobilize our old areas in novel ways
③ cultural tools stabilize our brain functionality
④ our brain regions operate in an isolated manner

10 빈칸 (A), (B)에 들어갈 말로 가장 적절한 것은?

> Consider the website Pandora, which allows users to identify a favorite song or singer and devises a kind of default music station on the basis of that choice. The website has many virtues, and it is a lot of fun. But there is a risk to learning and self-development in any situation in which people are defaulted into a kind of echo chamber, even if they themselves took the initial step to devise it. The same might be said about Netflix, which assembles a set of suggestions, based on users' previous choices (and evaluations). Netflix's kind of fine-tuning, which allows a great deal of precision in the resulting suggestions, obviously offers a great convenience, because people see what they are highly likely to enjoy. The question is whether the conveniences come at a cost, in the form of inevitable self-narrowing, simply because the relevant suggestions are based on previous choices and do not encourage people to branch out.

> Both Pandora and Netflix have the ability to serve their users with music or movies __(A)__ to their initial or previous choices, which can have the effect of __(B)__ the scope of their experiences to what the world has to offer in music or movies.

	(A)	(B)		(A)	(B)
①	similar	limiting	②	similar	expanding
③	superior	defining	④	superior	limiting

06 하프 모의고사

01 밑줄 친 단어의 의미와 가장 가까운 것은?

> The town had been <u>besieged</u> for two months but still resisted the aggressors.

① surrounding   ② ensuing
③ far-reaching   ④ fawning

02 빈칸에 들어갈 문장으로 가장 적절한 것은?

> Many people are risk-averse because they consider the negative consequences of failure to outweigh the reward of success. Our culture of looking down on failure makes us even less likely to risk our necks. _____. Progress and innovation are inextricably entwined with risk and failure.

① But we should not underestimate the importance of experimenting and taking risks, especially in these turbulent economic times
② But many organizations suffer from 'corporate anorexia nervosa' and have an unfavorable climate for enterprising people
③ That is why we need a paradigm shift marking a transition to a future
④ That is why combinatoric innovation is not an efficient process

03 다음 우리말 영작이 올바르지 않는 문장을 고르시오.

① 중국은 자신들의 고대유산과 자신들이 문화와 역사에 기여한 데 대해 자긍심을 갖고 있다.
⇨ China prides itself on its ancient legacy, and its contributions to culture and history.

② 아무리 좋은 아이디어라도 그것을 실행에 옮길 예산이나 인적 자원이 없다면 실패할 수 있다.
⇨ The best ideas can fail if there's no budget or human resources to carry out them.

③ 영국은 부유한 나라이지만, 소수이긴 해도 무시할 수 없는 만큼의 아이들이 비참한 환경에서 살아가고 있다.
⇨ Britain is a rich country, but a sizable minority of its children live in squalor.

④ 십대 아이들이 학교에서 최선을 다해 공부하기 위해서는 하루에 적어도 9시간의 수면이 요구된다.
⇨ Teens require at least nine hours of sleep a day in order for them to do their best in school.

04 다음 중 옳은 문장을 고르시오.

① Despite the bus being empty, he came and sat in front of me.
② The question of whether computers can have minds is rapid becoming a significant issue.
③ They suggested me to take more exercise.
④ He seems to master Chinese when young.

05 영작이 올바른 문장을 고르시오.

① 근본적인 문제는 농부들이 그들의 작물에 대해 충분한 돈을 지불받지 못한다는 사실이다.
⇨ The basic problem is that farmers do not pay enough for their crops.

② 대학 교육비가 너무 빠른 속도로 증가해서 이제 많은 사람들이 감당할 수 있는 수준을 넘어섰다.
⇨ The cost of a college education has risen so rapid that it is now beyond the reach of many people.

③ 만약 소화에 문제가 있다면 이런 종류의 약이 정말로 효과가 있다.
⇨ This type of medicine really works very good if you have got anything the matter with your digestion.

④ 거의 모든 학생들이 그 회의에 참석했다.
⇨ Almost all the students were present at the meeting.

06 다음 글의 주제로 가장 적절한 것은?

> Many of us labor under a self-limiting myth that contributes to our "invisibility" — the "myth of craftsmanship," the idea that good work speaks for itself. Organization survivors know that, in fact, good work speaks for itself only if you give it a voice. Recent years have seen the rise of what has been called the "entrepreneurial economy": "championing" a product, an idea, or a career, and giving it a powerful voice. In any contact-dependent endeavor, success requires both effective performance and effective self-promotion — making your competence and your ability to contribute visible. If you can't do that, you will be passed over for promotion during succession planning time, or when the company is determining which individuals to keep during layoffs. Even if you're an ace at keeping your boss up to speed, remember that in today's fluid business climate, he or she might be gone tomorrow. You need to cover all your bases and stand out in the eyes of your boss's boss.

① difficulties in making your competence visible
② relationships between recognition and job satisfaction
③ tendency to exaggerate one's business accomplishment
④ importance of self-promotion in surviving in the workplace

07 다음 글의 내용으로 가장 적절하지 않은 것은?

Driving an electric car confers a badge of greenery, or so the marketing departments of their makers would have you believe. Yet a report which analyzes the life cycle of car emissions (i.e., all the way from those created by the mining of materials for batteries, via the ones from the production of fuel and the generation of electricity, to the muck that actually comes out of the exhaust) presents a rather different picture. A battery-powered car recharged with electricity generated by coal-fired power stations, it found, is likely to cause more than three times as many deaths from pollution as a conventional gas-driven vehicle. Even a battery car running on the average mix of electrical power generated in America is much more hazardous than the conventional alternative.

① Mining the materials for car batteries creates pollution.
② America generates electricity by burning coal.
③ Electric cars in America produce three times more pollution than conventional cars.
④ Electric cars are marketed as environmentally friendly.

08 주어진 글 다음에 이어질 글의 순서로 가장 적절한 것을 고르시오.

In discussions of design, the terms convergence and divergence are often mentioned. These concepts are used to capture two basic approaches in design thinking.

(A) This, however, does not mean that the whole design process is a continuous convergence from the broad initial situation to the narrow final solution. Rather, a design process is driven by the will to learn as much as possible about different opportunities existing in a particular situation.

(B) It creates a deeper understanding and a more detailed and narrowly focused proposal. Since the final outcome is usually an artifact, a system, or a specification, the design process always ends in a convergence phase with the focus on one specific solution.

(C) Divergence is an approach where the designer expands her thinking to cover broader issues, find more alternatives, and explore more opportunities. It is a process that creates more information and options. Convergence is about focusing on a specific solution or a synthesis of several ideas.

① (A) – (B) – (C) ② (A) – (C) – (B)
③ (B) – (A) – (C) ④ (C) – (B) – (A)

09 다음 빈칸에 들어갈 말로 가장 적절한 것을 고르시오.

What we dream in sleep are unintended fleeting thoughts that randomly pass through the mind. Compared to dreaming, when we are awakened, most of our thoughts and actions are deliberate. And, even the thoughts that enter our mind unconsciously still have relevance to something that matters to us, which is not the case with most of our dreams. This is not to be oblivious to the idea that sometimes our dreams represent our deeper subconscious psyche. However, most dreams do not even remotely relate to our lives. Thus, in my opinion, abstract arts, as compared to rhythmic arts or imitative arts, resemble the state of dreaming as compared to the state of being awake, and the greatest majority of abstract arts _____ despite the fact that many of them might be very pleasant to look at.

① should be approached with caution and deliberate consideration
② are the expression of feelings rather than the depiction of reality
③ lack any substance that could be articulated in a meaningful way
④ are characterized by resolving a series of conceptual ambiguity

10 다음 빈칸 (A), (B)에 들어갈 말로 가장 적절한 것은?

> Facts are ideas whose accuracy is clearly and amply documented and affirmed by knowledgeable people, like "The house was painted on November 18, 1999." Opinions are ideas that have not yet been sufficiently documented and are therefore still open to dispute. Obvious indicators of opinion are sentences that include words such as: "generally, it is thought, or I believe that." Despite the clarity and simplicity of these definitions, the task of distinguishing facts from opinions can be difficult. One reason is that not every statement of fact is factual. The most obvious example is a lie — for example, a child saying she didn't eat the cookies when she did, or a criminal swearing he is innocent. In addition to lies, there are honest ___(A)___ . A person might misread a memo and tell a colleague a meeting is scheduled for three o'clock today when it is actually scheduled for tomorrow. Or an art expert might declare a painting to be the work of a master and only later discover it is a brilliant forgery. Another reason is that opinions are often stated as if they were facts. Consider these statements: "The death penalty constitutes cruel and unusual punishment," or "The cause of children committing crimes is irresponsible parenting." Each statement appears to be factual because of the way it is stated. Yet informed people continue to disagree about each. Therefore, each statement is an opinion. This is not to say that either of these statements is false, only that neither issue has been ___(B)___ .

	(A)	(B)		(A)	(B)
①	mistakes	settled	②	mistakes	included
③	prejudices	ignored	④	prejudices	settled

07 하프 모의고사

01 다음 밑줄 친 단어의 의미와 가장 가까운 것은?

> He was <u>exasperated</u> by the delay of the airplane.

① evacuated
② pacified
③ infuriated
④ threatened

02 다음 빈칸에 들어갈 단어로 적절한 것을 고르시오.

> It is hard to say which _____ the above-mentioned factors is most responsible for the distortion and misunderstanding of his philosophy.

① by
② with
③ in
④ of

03 다음 빈칸에 들어갈 말로 적절한 것을 고르시오.

> Ms. Kane was appointed head librarian because of her organizational abilities and her plans for improving the library's services. At first, the other staff members appreciated her ideas and enthusiasm. But after several weeks of working with her, they began to resent her frequent memos and meetings. The more they learned about her management style, the less the liked it. As one librarian said to another, familiarity breeds _____. The library staff welcomed Ms. Kane and her ideas at first, but after they got to know her better their respect for her changed to dislike and scorn.

① loyalty
② contempt
③ affinity
④ fraternity

04 다음 빈칸에 들어갈 알맞은 것은?

> One of the three shops the building contained was for rent; _____ was an all-night restaurant; the third was a garage.

① other
② other thing
③ the other
④ another

05 다음 우리말 영작이 올바르지 않는 문장을 고르시오.

① 이 식민지의 이야기는 그 이웃 식민지의 이야기보다 덜 흥미롭다.
⇨ The story of this colony is of less interest than that of the neighbor colony.
② 그러나 이것은 그들이 그 주식에 돈을 쏟아 붓는 것을 제지하지 못했다.
⇨ This, however, has deterred them from pouring money into the stock.
③ 그들은 다른 사람들이 당연하게 여기는 모든 것들을 그녀가 갖기를 원한다.
⇨ They want her to have everything other people take for granted.
④ 과거의 나쁜 행실을 거론하며 그 여자아이를 비난하는 것은 온당치 못하다.
⇨ It's not fair to hold the girl's past bad behavior by her.

06 다음 글의 주제로 가장 적절한 것은?

We argue that the ethical principles of justice provide an essential foundation for policies to protect unborn generations and the poorest countries from climate change. Related issues arise in connection with current and persistently inadequate aid for these nations, in the face of growing threats to agriculture and water supply, and the rules of international trade that mainly benefit rich countries. Increasing aid for the world's poorest peoples can be an essential part of effective mitigation. With 20 percent of carbon emissions from (mostly tropical) deforestation, carbon credits for forest preservation would combine aid to poorer countries with one of the most cost-effective forms of abatement. Perhaps the most cost-effective but politically complicated policy reform would be the removal of several hundred billions of dollars of direct annual subsidies from the two biggest recipients in the OECD — destructive industrial agriculture and fossil fuels. Even a small amount of this money would accelerate the already rapid rate of technical progress and investment in renewable energy in many areas, as well as encourage the essential switch to conservation agriculture.

① reforming diplomatic policies in poor countries
② increasing global awareness of the environmental crisis
③ reasons for restoring economic equality in poor countries
④ coping with climate change by reforming aid and policies

07 주어진 글 다음에 이어질 글의 순서로 가장 적절한 것을 고르시오.

Clearly, schematic knowledge helps you — guiding your understanding and enabling you to reconstruct things you cannot remember.

(A) Likewise, if there are things you can't recall, your schemata will fill in the gaps with knowledge about what's typical in that situation. As a result, a reliance on schemata will inevitably make the world seem more "normal" than it really is and will make the past seem more "regular" than it actually was.

(B) Any reliance on schematic knowledge, therefore, will be shaped by this information about what's "normal." Thus, if there are things you don't notice while viewing a situation or event, your schemata will lead you to fill in these "gaps" with knowledge about what's normally in place in that setting.

(C) But schematic knowledge can also hurt you, promoting errors in perception and memory. Moreover, the types of errors produced by schemata are quite predictable: Bear in mind that schemata summarize the broad pattern of your experience, and so they tell you, in essence, what's typical or ordinary in a given situation.

① (C) – (B) – (A)
② (B) – (A) – (C)
③ (B) – (C) – (A)
④ (C) – (A) – (B)

08 phainopepla nitens에 관한 다음 글의 내용과 일치하지 않는 것은?

> Phainopepla nitens are medium-sized, crested birds with white wing patches that show in flight. Males are all black, and females and juvenile males are gray-brown. Both the male and the female have red eyes, but these are more noticeable in the female than the male. Phainopepla nitens leave the hot desert during the summer months, and return to Death Valley in October when the weather cools a bit. Around January, serious courting gets under way. During the courting time lasting for up to four months the male builds a nest. If the female likes his craftsmanship, the male and the female mate. Although phainopepla nitens eat insects, their most favorite food is the berry of the parasitic mistletoe that grows on the mesquite trees, so this is where the nesting usually takes place. The baby grows to be ready to leave the nest in five weeks. When the weather starts to warm up, these birds fly to a cooler climate where the courting, nest building, and egg laying start once again. * mistletoe: 겨우살이

① 암수 모두 빨간색 눈을 가지고 있다.
② 10월에 Death Valley 로 되돌아온다.
③ 가장 좋아하는 먹이는 곤충이다.
④ 태어난 지 5주가 지나면 새끼는 둥지를 떠날 준비가 된다.

09 다음 빈칸에 들어갈 말로 가장 적절한 것을 고르시오.

> When a writer becomes an advocate for a particular point of view, he or she "selects" for reporting only the bits of evidence that support that position. This kind of selectivity involves an ignorance of evidence, either willful or unconscious, that favors opposing points of view. Ignoring evidence is not always willful, however; sometimes it is a product of limited awareness or limited resources, and thus is unintentional. For example, before the rise of feminist perspectives in the social sciences, many researchers did not see the pervasiveness of sexism in everyday life. Thus, evidence bearing on sexism was often missed in studies of a wide range of social relations. Many other forms of ignorance and unrecognized bias infect all research. While it would be great if every social scientist had some way to recognize the impact of such bias on his or her own research, there is no automatic safeguard. Social scientists are only human, and they can't designate evidence as relevant if _____.

① there's too little evidence to prove their argument
② other experts are strongly critical of their research
③ their unrecognized biases persuade them to ignore it
④ their findings are of considerable interest to investors

10 다음 글의 내용과 일치하지 않는 것을 고르시오.

Think of how Wi-Fi has made computing so much more convenient. It has untethered users from troublesome cable connections to the internet, allowing them to wander around the home or office with laptop or tablet in hand, surfing the web, making free phone calls, sending files wirelessly to printers, video to television sets, and many more things. But what if Wi-Fi radio beams travelled not just a few hundred feet but stretched for several miles — and were unimpeded by trees, terrain and walls so that they could penetrate all the nooks and crannies within buildings? That is the promise of "white-space" wireless. "White-space" is technical slang for television channels that were left vacant in one city so as not to interfere with TV stations broadcasting on adjacent channels in a neighbouring city. In the early days of television, America's broadcasting authorities reserved 50 or so channels for TV stations. But because of worries about interference, no metropolitan area has ever come close to using all 50 channels at its disposal. In rural areas, vacant channels (ie, white-space) have frequently amounted to 70% or more of the total bandwidth available for television broadcasting. With the recent switch from analogue to digital television, much of this protective white-space is no longer needed. Unlike analogue broadcasting, digital signals do not "bleed" into one another — and can therefore be packed closer together. The attraction of white-space is that the frequencies used for television broadcasting (54MHz to 806MHz) were chosen in the first place for the distance they could travel and their ability to penetrate obstacles. They were also good at transmitting information quickly. Where Wi-Fi can shuttle data at 160-300 megabits per second, white-space can do so at 400-800 megabits per second.

① Wi-Fi is supported by many applications and devices as a wireless network technology.
② Wi-Fi allows an electronic device to send data wirelessly in the unlimited distances over a computer network.
③ Wi-Fi exchanges data over a computer network by using radio waves.
④ A device that can use Wi-Fi connects to a network resource such as the internet via a wireless network access point.

08 하프 모의고사

01 다음 밑줄 친 단어의 의미와 가장 가까운 것은?

> No one wants to be gulled by a sensational press, but the torrent of public figures who have been made to eat their own words on television erodes the very possibility of trust between the public and an individual reporter.

① decay
② upbraid
③ convert
④ deceive

02 다음 빈칸에 들어갈 단어로 적절한 것을 고르시오.

> Luxury goods makers have long valued Chinese consumers not just because of their huge appetite for luxury goods but also for their willingness to pay more than their Western _____.

① cooperators
② conspirators
③ co-workers
④ counterparts

03 다음 밑줄 친 부분 중 문법적으로 어색한 부분을 고르시오.

> It is terrific ① that generations ② of little girls will grow up, ③ known that women can ④ run for president.

04 다음 중 어법상 옳지 않은 문장을 고르시오.

① If I were you, I wouldn't return the call.
② However good a letter may express the thoughts of a writer, it cannot carry the full warmth of his personality.
③ She and her family have been here since 1993.
④ You'd better get your visa extended before it expires.

05 다음 중 문법적으로 옳지 않은 것은?

① Teenagers spend a lot of time thinking about what others think of them.
② The news that she was promoted was music to her husband's ears.
③ Women were looked upon as being housewives rather than breadwinners.
④ Her books have published in 15 languages and sold in over 20 countries.

06 다음 글의 빈칸 (A), (B)에 들어갈 말로 가장 적절한 것은?

Young people today lack self-confidence, which is evident in their awareness of appearance. Many young people wear brand-name clothes to boost their confidence. It is hard for them to feel good about themselves without those brand names.   (A) , some girls believe they would look 10 pounds heavier in a pair of $15 jeans. A survey published by Boston Magazine showed that 31 out of 100 teen girls' clothes were all brand names. "They make me look thinner and give me confidence," was the common reason given.   (B) , this belief in name brands actually contributes to the lack of self-confidence. According to Simon David Buckingham, who wrote Unorganization: Life Styles for the Next Millennium, when people buy designer goods, they can hide behind an image created by someone else, because these purchasers don't have the independence and originality to create their own lifestyle.

	(A)	(B)
①	In fact	In addition
②	In fact	However
③	Therefore	Accordingly
④	Therefore	Similarly

07 (A), (B), (C) 각 빈칸 문맥에 맞는 말로 가장 적절한 것은?

The Atitlán Giant Grebe was a large, flightless bird that had evolved from the much more widespread and smaller Pied-billed Grebe. By 1965 there were only around 80 birds left on Lake Atitlán. One immediate reason was easy enough to spot: the local human population was cutting down the reed beds at a furious rate. This __(A)__ was driven by the needs of a fast growing mat-making industry. But there were other problems. An American airline was intent on developing the lake as a tourist destination for fishermen. However, there was a major problem with this idea: the lake __(B)__ any suitable sporting fish! To compensate for this rather obvious defect, a specially selected species of fish called the Large-mouthed Bass was introduced. The introduced individuals immediately turned their attentions to the crabs and small fish that lived in the lake, thus __(C)__ with the few remaining grebes for food. There is also little doubt that they sometimes gobbled up the zebra-striped Atitlán Giant Grebe's chicks.

	(A)	(B)	(C)
①	accommodation	lacked	competing
②	accommodation	supported	cooperating
③	destruction	lacked	competing
④	destruction	supported	cooperating

08 다음 글의 내용과 일치하지 않는 것을 고르시오.

Followers are a critical part of the leadership equation, but their role has not always been appreciated. For a long time, in fact, "the common view of leadership was that leaders actively led and subordinates, later called followers, passively and obediently followed." Over time, especially in the last century, social change shaped people's views of followers, and leadership theories gradually recognized the active and important role that followers play in the leadership process. Today it seems natural to accept the important role followers play. One aspect of leadership is particularly worth noting in this regard: Leadership is a social influence process shared among all members of a group. Leadership is not restricted to the influence exerted by someone in a particular position or role; followers are part of the leadership process, too.

① For a length of time, it was understood that leaders actively led and followers passively followed.
② People's views of subordinates were influenced by social change.
③ The important role of followers is still denied today.
④ Both leaders and followers participate in the leadership process.

09 주어진 문장이 들어갈 위치로 가장 적절한 것은?

The same thinking can be applied to any number of goals, like improving performance at work.

The happy brain tends to focus on the short term. (①) That being the case, it's a good idea to consider what short-term goals we can accomplish that will eventually lead to accomplishing long-term goals. (②) For instance, if you want to lose thirty pounds in six months, what short-term goals can you associate with losing the smaller increments of weight that will get you there? (③) Maybe it's something as simple as rewarding yourself each week that you lose two pounds. (④) By breaking the overall goal into smaller, shorter-term parts, we can focus on incremental accomplishments instead of being overwhelmed by the enormity of the goal in our profession.

10 빈칸에 들어갈 말로 가장 적절한 것은?

About 20 years ago, a delicate seaweed named Caulerpa taxifolia was brought from its native habitat in the Pacific Ocean to a zoo in Germany, where it was used to decorate saltwater aquarium exhibits, a seemingly harmless action. The seaweed was such a success that samples were sent to other institutions, including the Oceanographic Museum in Monaco. Within about five years of its introduction there, an unfortunate accident took place. The seaweed was accidentally flushed into the Mediterranean when exhibit tanks were cleaned. This might seem harmless, but considering it so would ignore the tremendous power of the species to act as _____. Once freed in the Mediterranean, Caulerpa quickly changed its growth pattern and adapted to its new habitat. This may have occurred through a mutation or through hybridization with native seaweeds. Whatever the exact genetic explanation, today Caulerpa grows about six times larger in the Mediterranean than it does in its native Pacific Ocean. Over the past two or three years, Caulerpa has spread to the Adriatic, and it now appears to threaten the entire Mediterranean with its ability to choke out competing seaweeds. It grows on rocks, sand, and mud. It grows so widely and quickly that it blankets competing native seaweeds, excluding them and it appears to be toxic to local animals that feed on seaweeds.

① biological invaders
② trade barriers
③ germ carriers
④ protective filters

09 하프 모의고사

01 다음 밑줄 친 단어의 의미와 가장 가까운 것은?

> Riding a roller coaster can be a joy ride of emotions: the nervous anticipation as you're strapped into your seat, the questioning and regret that comes as you go up, up, up, and the <u>sheer</u> adrenaline rush as the car takes that first dive.

① utter ② scary ③ occasional ④ manageable

02 밑줄 친 부분의 의미와 가장 가까운 것은?

> Justifications are accounts in which one accepts responsibility for the act in question, but denies the <u>pejorative</u> quality associated with it.

① derogatory ② extrovert ③ mandatory ④ redundant

03 (A), (B), (C) 빈칸의 문맥에 맞는 낱말로 가장 적절한 것은?

> A broody hen, which sits on her eggs, needs to incubate her eggs for 21 days before they hatch. The eggs are protected under her against a featherless patch of skin on her breast called a brood patch. Though it is normally a feathered area on her body, the hormones of broodiness cause her to lose feathers on her belly, creating __(A)__ contact with the skin and acting to incubate the eggs. She turns the eggs several times each day so that the embryo inside the egg does not stick to the shell membrane. She will become very __(B)__, having her feathers stand on end and making a shrieking sound if approached too closely. Broody hens will leave the nest unattended for short periods of time only in search of food and water and to eliminate waste. Care should be taken not to position water and food too closely to the nest, as it could attract attention to the nest site and will __(C)__ her needed exercise.

	(A)	(B)	(C)
①	direct	protective	decrease
②	direct	protective	increase
③	direct	tolerant	decrease
④	indirect	tolerant	increase
⑤	indirect	tolerant	decrease

04 밑줄 친 부분 중 어법상 가장 옳지 않은 것은?

Inventor Elias Howe attributed the discovery of the sewing machine ① <u>for</u> a dream ② <u>in which</u> he was captured by cannibals. He noticed as they danced around him ③ <u>that</u> there were holes at the tips of spears, and he realized this was the design feature he needed ④ <u>to solve</u> his problem.

05 다음 우리말 영작이 올바른 문장을 고르시오.

① 그는 노파에게 공손하게 사과했다.
　⇨ He politely apologized the old lady.
② 나의 한 친구는 이 소설을 읽는 것을 즐겼다.
　⇨ A friend of mine enjoyed to read this novel.
③ 그녀는 부모님 댁을 격주로 주말에 방문한다.
　⇨ She visits her parents every other weekends.
④ 운동을 하는 좋은 방법은 자전거를 타는 것이다.
　⇨ A good means of exercise is riding a bicycle.

06 다음 글의 주제로 가장 적절한 것은?

As the digital revolution upends newsrooms across the country, here's my advice for all the reporters. I've been a reporter for more than 25 years, so I have lived through a half dozen technological life cycles. The most dramatic transformations have come in the last half dozen years. That means I am, with increasing frequency, making stuff up as I go along. Much of the time in the news business, we have no idea what we are doing. We show up in the morning and someone says, "Can you write a story about (pick one) tax policy/immigration/climate change?" When newspapers had once-a-day deadlines, we said a reporter would learn in the morning and teach at night—write a story that could inform tomorrow's readers on a topic the reporter knew nothing about 24 hours earlier. Now it is more like learning at the top of the hour and teaching at the bottom of the same hour. I'm also running a political podcast, for example, and during the presidential conventions, we should be able to use it to do real-time interviews anywhere. I am just increasingly working without a script.

① a reporter as a teacher
② a reporter and improvisation
③ technology in politics
④ fields of journalism and technology

07 다음 빈칸에 들어갈 단어로 적절한 것을 고르시오.

Nobel Prize-winning psychologist Daniel Kahneman changed the way the world thinks about economics, upending the notion that human beings are rational decision-makers. Along the way, his discipline-crossing influence has altered the way physicians make medical decisions and investors evaluate risk on Wall Street. In a paper, Kahneman and his colleagues outline a process for making big strategic decisions. Their suggested approach, labeled as "Mediating Assessments Protocol," or MAP, has a simple goal: To put off gut-based decision-making until a choice can be informed by a number of separate factors. "One of the essential purposes of MAP is basically to _____ intuition," Kahneman said in a recent interview with The Post. The structured process calls for analyzing a decision based on six to seven previously chosen attributes, discussing each of them separately and assigning them a relative percentile score, and finally, using those scores to make a holistic judgment.

① improve ② delay
③ possess ④ facilitate

08 글의 흐름으로 보아, 주어진 문장이 들어가기에 가장 적절한 곳을 고르시오.

Languages, too, have adapted over time to serve the needs of a particular population in their environment.

Language disappearance only superficially resembles species extinction. Animal species are complex, have evolved over long periods of time, possess unique traits, and have adapted to a specific ecological environment. (①) An extinct dodo bird can be stuffed by taxidermists and displayed in a museum after all its kind are dead and gone. (②) But a stuffed dodo is no substitute for a thriving dodo population. (③) They have been shaped by people to serve as repositories for cultural knowledge, efficiently packaged and readily transmittable across generations. (④) Like dodo birds in museums, languages may be preserved in dictionaries and books after they are no longer spoken. But a grammar book or dictionary is but a dim reflection of the richness of a spoken tongue in its native social setting.

09 주어진 글 다음에 이어질 글의 순서로 가장 적절한 것을 고르시오.

Who could deny that the human body is a miracle? Imagine: each of us is safely housed within a bundle of blood, bone, and guts nurturing a little glow of life while suspended in a sea of constant change and danger.

(A) In other words, traditional housing approaches were specific to the culture, climate, and environment. Consider the igloo, a building using the thermal mass of ice to enclose heat and resist snow, or the ancient Egyptians' ventilation domes that produced interior cooling amid burning desert heat.

(B) Housing, likewise, originally developed slowly within particular human cultures and in response to specific climates and environments. Each culture around the world crafted a unique style of housing from the fabric of their surroundings.

(C) The miracle becomes even more amazing when you consider the long, slow, evolutionary process of give and take that produced the human body. Our bodies developed with nature, within it, as part of it, over time.

① (A) – (C) – (B)   ② (B) – (A) – (C)
③ (C) – (B) – (A)   ④ (C) – (A) – (B)

10 다음 글의 내용으로 적절한 것은?

> There are many different types of headaches. Tension or muscle headaches are experienced as a dull band of pain on both sides of the head. They may be caused by poor posture, eyestrain, or emotional conflicts such as grief or depression. Tension headache is the most common type of headache and is typically treated with over-the-counter medications. A migraine headache tends to produce a throbbing pain, often quite severe, and is generally localized on one side of the head. Often accompanied by nausea, vomiting, and dizziness, migraines affect more than 23 million people in North America. Women are three times more likely than men to have an attack. Migraines are associated with increased blood flow in the arteries and veins which surround the brain. About one-third of migraine sufferers will report the presence of an "aura" between five and 30 minutes before the migraine begins. This aura may involve visual experiences such as wavy lines or flashing lights or visual or auditory hallucinations. The presence of aura may indicate neurological problem, and you should seek medical attention.

① Women have more migraine headaches than men because they suffer more depression.
② Migraine headaches accompanied by an "aura" have the potential to be devastating.
③ Migraine headaches can be cured by taking over-the-computer medications.
④ One can relieve a migraine headache by rectifying a poor posture

10 하프 모의고사

01 다음 밑줄 친 단어의 의미와 가장 가까운 것은?

> Twenty years of Fascist talk of "Rome's fated hills" and "ineluctable destines," of "unavoidable events" and "plows tracing furrows in the ground," have in the end left no trace in contemporary Italian.

① mutable
② inexorable
③ dismissive
④ potent

02 다음 빈칸에 들어갈 표현으로 적절한 것을 고르시오.

> He had been elected by a wide margin, promising to _____ the imbalances of an ever more economically divided city.

① stimulate
② preserve
③ rectify
④ agitate

03 다음 빈칸에 들어갈 표현으로 적절한 것을 고르시오.

> The Yazoo Basin _____ the finest agricultural land in Mississippi, but floods and poor drainage have always caused problems in this area.

① contains
② contains of
③ containing
④ containing of

04 다음 우리말을 영어로 바꾼 것 중 잘못된 것은?

① 우리는 보다 나은 해결책을 찾고 있는 John을 격려했다.
  ⇨ We have encouraged John committed to finding a better solution.
② 그는 부모의 반대에도 불구하고 꿈을 결코 포기하지 않았다.
  ⇨ He never ever gave up his dream despite his parents' objection.
③ 그가 예전에 일을 했던 것처럼 지금도 열심히 일을 하면 좋을 것 같다.
  ⇨ I wish he were working now as hard as he did before.
④ 너희들은 농구를 하는 거보다 등산을 하는 편이 더 나을 것 같다.
  ⇨ You may as well climb the mountains than play basketball.

05 (A), (B), (C)의 각 네모 안에서 어법에 맞는 표현으로 적절한 것은?

Exactly how, when, why, and where the first maps came to be created is difficult to discover. Much of what was drawn in prehistoric and early historical times (A) [has/have] not survived, so what we find today may not be wholly representative of what was once there. There are other problems for the modern observer. Maps (B) [make/made] in prehistoric times cannot be accompanied by a title that explains the meaning of the drawing or that describes its content. However, we may be sure that in early times, just like today, maps were created for a variety of purposes and (C) [took/taken] a variety of forms. It may also be clear that, contrary to popular belief, of all the purposes to which maps have been put through the ages, the least important single purpose has been to find the way. Sea charts did not come into existence until the European Middle Ages, and topographical maps were not normally carried about by land travelers until the 18th century.

① have – make – taken
② have – made – took
③ has – made – taken
④ has – made – took

06 (A), (B), (C) 각 빈칸 문맥에 맞는 말로 가장 적절한 것은?

I noticed that the wavelike motion of fish's fins and bodies was similar to the twisting patterns of seaweeds. Seaweeds can be quite ___(A)___ if you pull on them. I discovered this when I caught hold of their stalks while snorkeling near reefs or rocks. As a surge from a wave washed me away from where I wanted to be, I grabbed on to seaweeds to anchor myself. Often they broke. Yet even in the wildest storms, these same weeds were able to stay ___(B)___ and survive. The surge of huge waves couldn't break or dislodge most plants from their grip on the ocean floor. It became apparent to me that they were adapting their shapes to the path of least resistance to ___(C)___ the onrush of water. Although at first it appeared that the weed fronds were moving chaotically, long observation showed me that all the plants were generally bending to a particular swirling pathway.

	(A)	(B)	(C)
①	sturdy	afloat	check
②	sturdy	intact	relieve
③	fragile	afloat	check
④	fragile	intact	relieve

07 다음 글의 내용으로 가장 적절한 것은?

From Boston to Los Angeles, from New York City to Chicago to Dallas, museums are either planning, building, or wrapping up wholesale expansion programs. These programs already have radically altered facades and floor plans or are expected to do so in the not-too-distant future. In New York City alone, six major institutions have spread up and out into the air space and neighborhoods around them or are preparing to do so. The reasons for this confluence of activity are complex, but one factor is a consideration everywhere—space. With collections expanding, with the needs and functions of museums changing, empty space had become a very precious commodity. Probably nowhere in the country is this more true than at the Philadelphia Museum of Art, which has needed additional space for decades and which received its last significant facelift ten years ago. Because of the space crunch, the Art Museum has become increasingly cautious in considering acquisitions and donations of art, in some cases passing up opportunities to strengthen its collections. Deaccessing—or selling off—works of art has taken on new importance because of the museum's space problems. And increasingly, curators have been forced to juggle gallery space, rotating one masterpiece into public view while another is sent to storage. Despite the need for additional gallery and storage space, however, "the museum has no plan, no plan to break out of its envelope in the next fifteen years", according to Philadelphia Museum of Art's president.

① 대부분의 박물관들이 더 많은 공간을 필요로 하는 이유는 Changing needs 때문이다.
② 대부분의 박물관들이 더 많은 공간을 필요로 하는 이유는 More curators 때문이다.
③ 대부분의 박물관들이 더 많은 공간을 필요로 하는 이유에 Changing functions 때문이다.
④ 대부분의 박물관들이 더 많은 공간을 필요로 하는 이유에 Enlarged collections 때문이다.

08 다음 글의 빈칸 (A), (B)에 들어갈 말로 가장 적절한 것은?

Before language develops, emotions and touch are the primary means by which parent and child communicate. (A) , it would not be surprising if preverbal infants had some basic understanding of other people's emotional, nonverbal communications, which research has indicated is indeed the case. For example, infants as young as 14 months understand that emotions are often "about" a particular event (e.g., someone is scared of a dog) and are very adept at identifying what a person is emoting about. In addition, by 18 months, infants begin to appreciate that two people can have a different emotional response about the exact same object (e.g., you like peas, but I hate them). (B) , 14-month-old infants are still highly egocentric and assume that everyone has the same emotional responses to a particular object or event.

	(A)	(B)		(A)	(B)
①	Consequently	In contrast	②	Consequently	Similarly
③	Nevertheless	Similarly	④	Nevertheless	For instance

09 빈칸 (A), (B)에 들어갈 말로 가장 적절한 것은?

When you hear someone tell you outright that they need help after just informing you of her tendency toward seizures, it is a bit hard to imagine that you wouldn't notice or be aware that she was in trouble. Nevertheless, the presence of others can prevent us from helping. This is because of a powerful effect that groups can have on us, known as diffusion of responsibility. For a victim to receive help, someone needs to decide that it will be his or her responsibility to act. When you are responsible, the moral thing to do is to help. When you are the only witness, the burden clearly rests on your shoulders. But when others are present, it is easy to imagine that someone else should or has already taken action. In fact, even being primed to think about being part of a group can make people feel less personally accountable and less likely to donate money or stay to help out an experimenter.

⬇

If there are multiple ___(A)___ in a situation where help is needed, the likelihood of them feeling responsible for taking action ___(B)___.

	(A)	(B)		(A)	(B)
①	victims	diminishes	②	victims	disappears
③	witnesses	increases	④	witnesses	diminishes

10 다음 빈칸에 들어갈 말로 가장 적절한 것은?

About ten thousand years ago, farming was discovered and proved to be a more efficient and dependable way to provide calories than the nomadic lifestyle of hunter-gatherers. For the first time, a few individuals were able to accumulate surplus food, and with it possessed the resources to hire others to do their bidding. Instead of having to roam across the landscape in search of nutrition, farmers could settle in villages and then cities, accumulating property. It was agriculture that made the division of labor possible, and thus created the conditions for civilized living. The downside has been that it also made possible the exploitation of labor. This pattern has repeated itself throughout history whenever a new technological development has allowed some enterprising individuals to get an edge over the rest of the population. It happened again in the Middle Ages when a few knights arrayed in expensive armor were able to force defenseless farmers to share their produce. It happened when the first factories using mechanical looms put thousands of independent cottage industries out of business, and then hired the unemployed weavers as factory hands. In each case, a minority who happened to be well positioned to exploit the new way of doing things was able to benefit, and as a result opened a wide gap in the ownership of resources. The minority in power then used political and legal means to institutionalize and protect its predominance — until a new political or technological revolution came along to challenge solid _____.

① myths
② prejudices
③ inequalities
④ hypotheses

11 하프 모의고사

01 다음 밑줄 친 단어의 의미와 가장 가까운 것은?

> Your insouciant attitude indicates that you do not understand the seriousness.

① indifferent
② sarcastic
③ impeccable
④ impassioned

02 다음 빈칸에 들어갈 단어로 가장 적절한 것은?

> Alcoholics Anonymous takes its name from the fact that it's a _____ group — people use only their first names and do not identify one another as members of the group.

① obstinate
② advisory
③ remedial
④ confidential

03 다음 빈칸에 들어갈 표현으로 가장 적절한 것은?

> If you think about the calories of the cake, you _____ the cake.

① will regret to eat
② regret eating
③ will regret eating
④ regret to eat

04 다음 문장에서 문법적으로 어색한 부분을 고르시오.

> The magicians, ① having discovered Minecoo Aniello's great wealth, concretely ② laid a plan ③ of robbing him ④ of his good fortune.

05 다음 우리말 영작이 올바르지 않은 문장을 고르시오.

① 공식적인 반대가 없어서, 휴가를 허락받았다.
 ⇨ There being no official objection, leave was granted.

② 바로 떠나면, 당신은 그 기차를 잡을 수 있다.
 ⇨ Leaving immediately, the train can be caught for you.

③ 팔짱을 낀 채, 그녀는 화난 목소리로 말했다.
 ⇨ She spoke in an angry voice, with her arms folded.

④ 그들의 치아로 판단해 볼 때, 그들은 다양한 음식을 먹었다.
 ⇨ Judging from their teeth, they had a variety of diets.

06 다음 글의 빈칸 (A), (B)에 들어갈 말로 가장 적절한 것은?

> Some people are more susceptible to pain than others. For example, women experience painful stimuli more intensely than men. These gender differences are associated with the production of particular hormones. __(A)__, certain genes are linked to the experience of pain, so that we may inherit our sensitivity to pain. However, the experience of pain is not determined by biological factors alone. For example, women report that the pain experienced in childbirth is moderated to some degree by the joyful nature of the situation. __(B)__, even a minor stimulus can produce the perception of strong pain if it is accompanied by anxiety like a visit to the dentist. Clearly, then, pain is a perceptual response that depends heavily on our emotions and thoughts.

	(A)	(B)
①	In addition	In contrast
②	In addition	As a result
③	Therefore	Similarly
④	Nevertheless	In contrast

07 다음 빈칸에 들어갈 말로 가장 적절한 것은?

Bees have their choice of flora according to color. Lord Avenbury once made an experiment to see if the color of flowers attracted bees. Placing honey on slips of paper of different shades, he found that the insects which visited them seemed to have a marked preference for blue, after which came white, yellow, red, green and orange. This finding should be considered for our beekeeping planning. If pollination is the prime consideration of taming bees and if the crop is identified, the color of other floras in the vicinity should be considered while planning. Let us consider beekeeping near a mustard field. Mustard gives tiny yellow flowers full of nectar and pollen. For better yield of mustard seeds, pollination is necessary. But if there is plenty of blue-colored wild flora in the vicinity, bees may prefer the blue flowers to mustard. Although we shall get honey and other products, the objective for pollination of mustard may be _____.

① defeated
② disclosed
③ protected
④ promoted

08 다음 글의 내용으로 가장 적절하지 않은 것은?

> Genetic research has produced both exciting and frightening possibilities. Scientists are now able to create new forms of life in the laboratory due to the development of gene splicing. On one hand, the ability to create life in the laboratory could greatly benefit mankind. For example, because insulin is very expensive to obtain from natural sources, scientists have developed a method to manufacture inexpensively in the laboratory. Another beneficial application of gene splicing is in agriculture. Scientists foresee the day when new plants will be developed using nitrogen from the air instead of from fertilizer; therefore food production could be increased. In addition, entirely new plants could be developed to feed the world's hungry people. Not everyone is excited about gene splicing, however. Some people feel that it could have terrible consequences. A laboratory accident, for example, might cause an epidemic of an unknown disease that could wipe out humanity. As a result of this controversy, the government has made rules to control genetic experiments. Still many people feel that these rules are not strict enough even though the scientific community may feel that they are too strict.

① Food production capacity with gene splicing is sufficient to meet the demands.
② Nitrogen in the atmosphere may be used for expediting the growth of plants in future.
③ The regulations of gene splicing are relevant to risks associated with the fall of mankind.
④ It is possible to produce insulin chemically identical to the naturally produced form.

09 다음 글의 밑줄 친 부분 중, 문맥상 낱말의 쓰임이 적절하지 않은 것은?

Laughter resulting from humor shows itself when people find themselves in an ① <u>unfavorable</u> situation, for which they generally would have felt anger and/or fear, and the detection of incongruent elements allows them to watch it from a different perspective. In this instance, thus, laughter comes from the release of energies generally associated with negative feelings, but that in the specific situation, thanks to the ② <u>consistency</u> of perspective, can be expressed as laughter of relief. Humor, in this perspective, represents a defense mechanism that allows people to ③ <u>better</u> handle difficult and stressful life situations. Freud even describes this humor as "the highest of the defense mechanisms." This self-defense mechanism — differently from the ability to understand jokes, which is very widespread — does not ④ <u>present</u> itself in every human being. Actually, some individuals are able to see the funny and positive side of a certain situation, while others, even in the same circumstances, react showing negative feelings.

10 주어진 글 다음에 이어질 글의 순서로 가장 적절한 것은?

A mnemonic device that uses imagery is known as 'the method of place.' Here you form an association between something you want to remember and a particular location on a familiar walk.

(A) You continue in this manner until you have developed an image connecting each point in your speech to a landmark. Then, When it's time to present the speech, you simply imagine that you're taking that familiar walk.

(B) As you pass the first familiar landmark on that walk, you develop an image that somehow connects that familiar landmark to the first point in your speech. For example, the image of a tree with a nest of baby birds could help you remember that you have to begin providing healthy foods when children are young.

(C) Let's say that you have to present a speech about healthy eating habits in one of your classes and that your speech consists of seven main ideas. You simply imagine yourself taking a very familiar walk.

① (A) – (C) – (B) ② (B) – (A) – (C)
③ (B) – (C) – (A) ④ (C) – (B) – (A)

12 하프 모의고사

01 밑줄 친 단어의 의미와 가장 가까운 것은?

> Don's few personal <u>effects</u> were in a suitcase under the bed.

① belongings
② outcomes
③ influences
④ impacts

02 다음 밑줄 친 단어의 의미와 가장 가까운 것은?

> What companies will ultimately choose is still <u>up in the air</u>, but for now the technology is being tested to demonstrate its viability.

① uncertain
② approachable
③ complicated
④ meticulous

03 다음 빈칸에 들어갈 단어로 가장 적절한 것은?

> Named after Vulcan, the Roman god of fire, volcanoes are best known for their _____ power. But they can also be havens for life, as _____ for plants and animals during ice ages.

① blazing – obstacles
② proficient – heritages
③ destructive – refuges
④ beneficial – charms

04 다음 빈칸에 들어갈 표현으로 가장 적절한 것은?

> Other possible contributors to the increased suicide _____ economic hardship and isolation.

① is risk
② risk is
③ being risk
④ risk are

05 다음 문장에서 문법적으로 어색한 부분을 고르시오.

> You will not always ① get along with everyone that you ② encounter, but it is imperative that you ③ are able to tolerate each other and ④ focus on the common goal.

06 (A), (B), (C)의 각 네모 안에서 어법에 맞는 표현으로 가장 적절한 것은?

> After physicist Richard Feynman won a Nobel prize for his work, he visited his old high school and looked up his records. He was surprised to find that his grades were not as good as he had remembered (A) [them/it] and that his IQ was 124, not much above average. Dr. Feynman saw that winning the Nobel prize was one thing, but winning it with an IQ of only 124 was really something. Most of us would assume that the winners of Nobel prizes have exceptionally high IQs. Feynman confided that he always assumed that he (B) [did/was]. If Feynman had known he was just a bit above average in the IQ department, he would not have launched the unique research experiments (C) [that/what] would win him the greatest recognition the scientific community can give.

	(A)	(B)	(C)
①	them	did	that
②	them	did	what
③	it	was	that
④	it	did	what

07 글의 흐름으로 보아, 주어진 문장이 들어가기에 가장 적절한 곳은?

As the heart begins beating, the head of the chicken is moved up and down in a manner that mimics the movement that will be used later for pecking the ground.

It was for quite some time thought that when chickens hatched and immediately began pecking the ground for food, this behavior must have been instinctive. In the 1920s, a Chinese researcher named Zing-Yang Kuo made a remarkable set of observations on the developing chick egg that overturned this idea. (①) He found that rubbing heated Vaseline on a chicken egg caused it to become transparent enough so that he could see the embryo inside without disturbing it. (②) In this way, he was able to make detailed observations of the chick's development, from fertilization to hatching. (③) One of his observations was that in order for the growing embryo to fit properly in the egg, the neck is bent over the chest in such a way that the head rests on the chest just where the developing heart is encased. (④) Thus the "innate" pecking behavior that the chicken appears to know miraculously upon birth has, in fact, been practiced for more than a week within the egg.

08 빈칸 (A)와 (B)에 들어갈 말로 가장 적절한 것은?

Psychologist Michelene Chi asked physics professors and some Ph.D. students from the physics department and several undergraduate students to solve several physics problems. As expected, the professors and Ph.D. students were better at solving the physics problems than were the undergraduates. Interestingly, however, the physics experts were not necessarily faster than the undergraduates. Sure, once the professors and Ph.D.s got going on a problem, they were quicker to compute a solution. But Chi also found that the professors and Ph.D.s were slower than the undergraduates to begin to solve the problems. The experts paused before they ever put pencil to paper. They spent a few moments assessing the underlying structure of the problem and figuring out the best physics principle to use. The undergraduates, on the other hand, jumped right into problem-solving, which often got them in trouble. By rushing to start the problem, the undergraduates got distracted by irrelevant problem details, which led them astray.

The above experiment indicates that a big difference between success and failure in difficult problem-solving situations is the ___(A)___ taken to think about a problem at the ___(B)___ stage.

	(A)	(B)		(A)	(B)
①	time	final	②	time	initial
③	perspective	halfway	④	perspective	initial

09 다음 글의 내용으로 가장 적절하지 않은 것은?

> Narcissistic individuals feel superior to others, fantasize about personal successes, and believe they deserve special treatment. When they feel humiliated, they often lash out aggressively or even violently. Unfortunately, little is known about the origins of narcissism. Such knowledge is important for designing interventions to curtail narcissistic development. We demonstrate that narcissism in children is cultivated by parental overvaluation: parents believing their child to be more special and more entitled than others. In contrast, high self-esteem in children is cultivated by parental warmth: parents expressing affection and appreciation toward their child. These findings show that narcissism is partly rooted in early socialization experiences, and suggest that parenttraining interventions can help curtail narcissistic development and reduce its costs for society.

① Narcissistic children may have difficulty in socializing with other children.
② The parental attention to their children is not always harmful to the life of children.
③ Thanks to the parental intervention, all narcissistic children can become normal.
④ Making children narcissistic depends on the parenting method of parents.

10 다음 빈칸에 들어갈 말로 가장 적절한 것은?

I was counseling a man who had been in a long and painful relationship with a woman who constantly found fault with him and laid the blame for her unhappiness. "She is not doing it to you," I suggested to him, "She is doing it for you." "How's that?" he asked. "You 'hired' your girlfriend to magnify every self-hating thought you have had about yourself and play it back to you in such an intense and obvious way that you would have to examine your self-worth until you recognize and practice it," I told him. If others are continually annoying you with criticism, do not fight back or run away. Instead, say "thank you" to them. They are your best teachers, not because they are correct in their fault-finding, but because they are serving as a mirror of your own internal critic. They have come to show you how hard you are on yourself so that you can begin to love yourself and heal a long pattern of internal self-abuse. Criticism cannot disturb you unless you agree with it. If you are clear and confident about who you are and what you do, negative feedback will not be a big factor in your psyche. If you harbor internal doubts about yourself or your abilities, _____, someone will likely voice those doubts. If you argue or seek revenge, you have missed the gift of the experience. If you look inside and ask yourself, "Is this really true?," then you are on your way to higher ground. If it is true, you can correct it. If not, you can forget it. Your critic is your friend. Do not fight with your critic.

① most of all
② however
③ therefore
④ similarly

13 하프 모의고사

01 다음 밑줄 친 단어의 의미와 가장 가까운 것은?

> Brown and his wife are always bickering.

① hugging　　② dancing　　③ joking　　④ arguing

02 다음 빈칸에 알맞은 것은?

> We tried everything to _____ him, but the injured man remained unconscious.

① rectify　　② mitigate　　③ resuscitate　　④ freeze

03 다음 빈칸에 들어갈 표현으로 적절한 것을 고르시오.

> Even though the giraffe is very tall, this coloring _____ when it stands on the shade of a tree. Thus it is protected from enemies.

① makes hard to see　　② makes it hard to see
③ making easy to see　　④ makes it easy to see

04 다음 중 옳은 문장을 고르시오.

① It is difficult that we master English in one or two years.
② Social competence is a skill we often take it for granted.
③ All you have to do now is recover from the operation.
④ He has given me many useful advices on my study.

05 다음 우리말 영작이 올바르지 않는 고르시오.

① 당신은 단지 많은 채소를 먹는 것만으로도 당신이 건강을 유지할 수 있다고 생각할지도 모른다.
   ⇨ You might think that just eating a lot of vegetables will keep you perfectly healthy.
② 학문적 지식이 늘 당신이 옳은 결정을 하도록 이끌어 주진 않는다.
   ⇨ Academic knowledge isn't always that leads you to make right decisions.
③ 다치는 것에 대한 두려움은 그가 무모한 행동에 가담하는 것을 막지 못했다.
   ⇨ The fear of getting hurt didn't prevent him from engaging in reckless behaviors.
④ Julie의 주치의는 그녀에게 가공식품을 많이 먹는 것을 멈추라고 말했다.
   ⇨ Julie's doctor told her to stop eating so many processed foods.

06 다음 글의 제목으로 가장 적절한 것은?

> The public plays almost no expressive or even approving role in selecting "big pictures" of photojournalism (the exception being some contests to name "photo of the year"). Editors do not poll the public before displaying images of the day's news and selecting those worthy of more extensive coverage and comment. The Pulitzer Prize, too, is voted upon by journalistic elites. Photographers and journalists (through prize committees), editors (through selection), and political and editorial elites (through notation and commentary) impose greatness and thus fame on images. Historians and textbook companies, by reemploying or "quoting" such images for discussion or simply illustration, reaffirm that they are "great." Obviously, after repeatedly viewing and absorbing such observations, members of the public are likely to agree with this verdict, even if they may be less than susceptible to the pictures' affecting their beliefs or actions. Elites, thus, largely set the agenda of greatness and establish the criteria for which images are judged great.

① Elites Determine Great Images
② The Prized Picture: Making Sense out of Life
③ Fearless Photographers Take Big Pictures
④ Spoken Image: Photography and Language

07 다음 글에서 전체 흐름과 관계없는 문장은?

I have met several art therapists and doctors who can pinpoint illnesses people have by asking patients to draw how they see themselves and how they feel about their life. ① Folding a sheet of paper twice to make four quarters, these doctors and therapists have the patients use colored pencils to draw and color in their face, body, family, and anything else that they feel is relevant on different parts of the page. ② This can give an experienced health practitioner information about their patients' lives, what emotions they are dealing with, and what tests may need to be done, as well as the possible causes of a patient's "dis-ease." ③ In counselling, the relationship between the therapist and client is extremely important as this helps to facilitate the process of change and can enable clients to reach a greater understanding of themselves. ④ The different quarters can also relay information about the patient's past, present, and future. This kind of intuitive drawing technique is particularly powerful with children, as it also gives them an opportunity to express themselves and understand what is going on in their lives.

08 다음 글의 내용과 일치하는 것은?

Soils of farmlands used for growing crops are being carried away by water and wind erosion at rates between 10 and 40 times the rates of soil formation, and between 500 and 10,000 times soil erosion rates on forested land. Because those soil erosion rates are so much higher than soil formation rates, that means a net loss of soil. For instance, about half of the top soil of Iowa, the state whose agriculture productivity is among the highest in the U.S., has been eroded in the last 150 years. On my most recent visit to Iowa, my hosts showed me a churchyard offering a dramatically visible example of those soil losses. A church was built there in the middle of farmland during the 19th century and has been maintained continuously as a church ever since, while the land around it was being farmed. As a result of soil being eroded much more rapidly from fields than from the churchyard, the yard now stands like a little island raised 10 feet above the surrounding sea of farmland.

① A churchyard in Iowa is higher than the surrounding farmland.
② Iowa's agricultural productivity has accelerated its soil formation.
③ The rate of soil formation in farmlands is faster than that of soil erosion.
④ Iowa has maintained its top soil in the last 150 years.

09 빈칸 (A)와 (B)에 들어갈 말로 가장 적절한 것은?

International maritime codes specify that more maneuverable vessels must keep out of the way of less maneuverable vessels. The captains of more maneuverable vessels, such as power-driven boats, are responsible for avoiding less steerable vessels, such as sailing ships, and ships engaged in fishing, and vessels not under command. It is easier for powerboats to avoid hitting sailing ships than vice versa. Aviation codes are based on the same principle. The right of way of the sky ranks craft in order of the ease with which they can be controlled. Airplanes in normal operation, which are the most easily maneuvered aircraft, have the lowest priority in right of way. Airplanes refueling other aircraft, which are less easily maneuvered, have a greater right of way than airplanes in normal operation. Balloons, which are still less maneuverable than airplanes refueling other aircraft, have a higher priority right of way. Finally, aircraft in distress have the highest priority right of way of all, since an aircraft in distress is very difficult or impossible to control.

↓

On the sea or in the sky, the responsibility of giving way usually falls on the party who has less difficulty in __(A)__ the vehicle because it is easier for that party to __(B)__ an accident.

	(A)	(B)		(A)	(B)
①	controlling	report	②	controlling	avoid
③	leaving	investigate	④	leaving	report

10 다음 빈칸에 공통으로 들어갈 말로 가장 적절한 것은?

A San Francisco-based polygrapher told me about a polygraph exam he had given to a 45-year-old bank vice-president who was a suspect in an embezzlement investigation. When initially run through the polygraph exam, the bank vice-president's heart rate, blood pressure, and other physiological levels were quite high. This is normal for both innocent and guilty people, because such an exam is almost always threatening. _____, the polygrapher suspected that the bank vice-president was lying or holding back information, because his physiological levels went even higher when he was asked about some of the details of the embezzlement. With repeated questions, the vice-president finally broke down and confessed to embezzling $74,000 over a 6-month period. In line with standard procedures, after the bank vice-president had signed a written confession, he was then polygraphed again to be certain that his confession was itself not deceptive. When connected to the monitoring device the second time, his overall physiological levels were extremely low. His hands were no longer sweaty. His heart rate and blood pressure were extraordinarily low. You can appreciate the irony of this situation. This man had come into the polygrapher's office a free man, safe in the knowledge that polygraph evidence was not allowed in court. _____, he confessed. Now, his professional, financial, and personal lives were on the brink of ruin. He was virtually assured of a prison term. Despite these realities, he was relaxed and at ease with himself. Indeed, when a policeman came to handcuff and escort him to jail, he warmly shook the polygrapher's hand and thanked him for all he had done.

① Moreover ② Therefore
③ As a result ④ Nevertheless

14 하프 모의고사

01 밑줄 친 단어의 의미와 가장 가까운 것은?

> She owes her election to having <u>tapped</u> deep public disillusionment with professional politicians.

① drained
② utilized
③ struck
④ extracted

02 다음 밑줄 친 표현과 의미와 가장 가까운 것은?

> She is <u>on the fence</u> about going to see the Mona Lisa at the Louvre Museum.

① anguished
② enthusiastic
③ apprehensive
④ undecided

03 다음 빈칸에 들어갈 말로 적절한 것을 고르시오.

> The seasoned burglars were extremely careful not to leave any footprints, but this time they _____ and were immediately apprehended.

① missed out
② broke through
③ slipped up
④ backed off

04 다음 글의 밑줄 친 부분 중, 어법상 어색한 것은?

When people face real adversity — disease, unemployment, or the disabilities of age — affection from a pet takes on new meaning. A pet's continuing affection becomes crucially important for ① those enduring hardship because it reassures them that their core essence has not been damaged. Thus pets are important in the treatment of ② depressed or chronically ill patients. In addition, pets are ③ used to great advantage with the institutionalized aged. In such institutions it is difficult for the staff to retain optimism when all the patients are declining in health. Children who visit cannot help but remember ④ what their parents or grandparents once were and be depressed by their incapacities. Animals, however, have no expectations about mental capacity. They do not worship youth. They have no memories about what the aged once ⑤ was and greet them as if they were children. An old man holding a puppy can relive a childhood moment with complete accuracy. His joy and the animal's response are the same.

05 다음 중 옳은 문장을 고르시오.

① I found my wife laying unconscious beside the kitchen table.
② The rent for our new apartment is higher than our old apartment.
③ Last week, Fred has had a broken leg and a sprained wrist.
④ As a parent, I can imagine how hard it is for him to see his son die slowly.

06 다음 우리말 영작이 올바른 문장을 고르시오.

① 그 경기는 비 때문에 연기되었다.
   ⇨ The game was postponed on account of rain.
② 제시가 많이 도와줬기 때문에 나는 가까스로 그 경기에서 승리했다.
   ⇨ With a lot of help from Jesse, I managed winning the game.
③ 바쁘지 않으면 기꺼이 너를 도와줄 텐데.
   ⇨ I would help you willingly but that I was busy.
④ 나는 너와 그것에 대해 논의하고 싶다.
   ⇨ I want to discuss about it with you.

07 다음 글의 주제로 적절한 것은?

Forget splashy news articles about initial public offerings, the latest tech gizmo, Google buses or ever-climbing real estate prices. For San Francisco, that was so 2014. So far, the city's biggest news stories in 2015 have read like one unbelievable horror story come to life. There were nine homicides in January, including four young men gunned down in a car in Hayes Valley and a mother killed by a stray bullet in front of her three children in broad daylight in the Bayview. Last weekend saw a spate of home invasions — none of them believed to be related. In one, an assailant forced her way into an Ocean View home, covered the head of a 26-year-old woman with a towel and then tied her up with extension cords. The assailant made off with jewelry, cell phones and money. Masked men rammed a sport utility vehicle into a museum at the site of the original Wells Fargo Bank and fled with Gold-Rush era nuggets. Then there was a shocking discovery made by kayakers in Lake Merced: a mysterious decomposing body found floating facedown among the reeds. T. S. Eliot, in his poem The Waste Land, wrote that "April is the cruelest month", but it's hard to imagine a month more cruel in San Francisco than January.

① News articles reflect the ways in which a society has changed.
② San Francisco has witnessed an unprecedented number of horrible crimes so far this year.
③ It is clear that there is a growing disrespect for life in San Francisco.
④ T. S. Eliot should have written that the cruelest month is January, not April.

08 다음 글의 내용으로 가장 적절한 것은?

> Unlike many other real assets, such as farmland or property, art is movable, which is handy for buyers who do not plan to tell the taxman about it. It can be a relatively discreet way of investing, too: Christie's arranged $916m of private purchases in 2014, compared with just $266m in 2009. Even so, the risks of investing in art are high. Prices are volatile and the market is idiosyncratic — no two pieces are interchangeable. "Especially at the top it's based on the passions and whims of a small group of collectors," says Orlando Rock from Christie's. The most popular genres and the most expensive pieces skew art's overall performance as an asset. Last year 0.5% of transactions accounted for nearly half the value of all fine art sold at auction. According to Arts Economics, a research firm, the value of works of art that cost more than €200,000 is growing five times faster than the cheaper stuff. And although contemporary art has had a great year, prices for Old Masters are stagnant and Chinese decorative art is losing value.

① Rising prices of art in recent years must have scared off lots of speculators.
② The works of art are difficult to hide from tax collectors.
③ The demand for art works can vary depending on their genre.
④ The more expensive the works of art are, the faster they decrease in value.

09 빈칸 (A)와 (B)에 들어갈 말로 가장 적절한 것은?

"Why, in country after country that mandated seat belts, was it impossible to see the promised reduction in road accident fatalities?" John Adams, professor of geography at University College London, wrote in one of his many essays on risk. "It appears that measures that protect drivers from the consequences of bad driving encourage bad driving. The principal effect of seat belt legislation has been a shift in the burden of risk from those already best protected in cars, to the most vulnerable, pedestrians and cyclists, outside cars." Adams started to group these counterintuitive findings under the concept of risk compensation, the idea that humans have an inborn tolerance for risk. As safety features are added to vehicles and roads, drivers feel less vulnerable and tend to take more chances. The phenomenon can be observed in all aspects of our daily lives. Children who wear protective gear during their games have a tendency to take more physical risks. Hikers take more risks when they think a rescuer can access them easily.

According to John Adams, the phenomenon that safety measures ___(A)___ careless driving may be accounted for by the notion that a greater sense of security ___(B)___ people to take more risks.

	(A)	(B)
①	contribute to	tempts
②	contribute to	forbids
③	discourage	tempts
④	discourage	forces

10 다음 빈칸에 들어갈 말로 가장 적절한 것을 고르시오.

It turns out that the brain is modular, its neurons wired together into circuits that perform complex tasks. Some regulate heart rate and body temperature, and others enable us to write poetry or figure out Sudoku puzzles. Blocked into different regions of the brain, every circuit seems to _____. As a child grows, certain brain structures associated with particular functions have periods of intense activity and development, while others remain relatively quiet. Then the quiet structures awaken and begin to develop rapidly, while previously active structures hit the end of their growth spurts. In the middle of a growth spurt, the brain's various structures are like a room full of preschoolers. While two in one corner drift to sleep, three in another will act up. When those three go to sleep, others will wake up and fuss.

① be similar in function
② have its own timetable
③ have different components
④ be connected to one another

15 하프 모의고사

01 밑줄 친 단어의 의미와 가장 가까운 것은?

> The elegant Princess ingrid has long complained about Duchess Sarah Norton's <u>common</u> accent.

① vulgar
② recognizable
③ trivial
④ frequent

02 다음 밑줄 친 표현의 의미와 가장 가까운 것은?

> He never takes responsibility for his problems and always tries to <u>pass the buck</u>.

① foot the bill
② break even
③ ignore others
④ blame someone else

03 다음 빈칸에 들어갈 표현으로 가장 적절한 것은?

> The asteroid that occurred in what is now the Yucatan at the end of the Cretaceous period, 66 million years ago, was probably 10km or more across. That impact is widely thought to have brought with it a _____ which killed off well over half the species on the planet.

① natural selection
② genetic diversity
③ mass extinction
④ global warming

04 다음 문장들 중 어법상 가장 적절한 것은?

① It is much more easy to edit document on a word processor than on a typewriter.
② The students were all obedient and did what the teacher had told them to do.
③ The computer has made it possible the phenomenal leap in human proficiency.
④ It is Mr. Brown's responsibility of maintenance all computer files on current projects.

05 다음 우리말을 영어로 옮긴 것 중 틀린 것을 고르시오.

① 그를 설득하지 못한다면 정보를 얻을 수 없을 것이다.
⇨ Unless you persuade him, you won't get information.
② 그는 누가 들을까봐 내게 작은 소리로 말했다.
⇨ He talked to me in whispers lest he should be heard.
③ 나는 그를 도울 수도 없고, 또한 돕고 싶지도 않다.
⇨ I cannot help him, and I don't want to help him, too.
④ 잘못을 저지르지 않는 사람은 하나도 없다.
⇨ There is no one but commits errors.

06 주어진 글 다음에 이어질 글의 순서로 가장 적절한 것은?

> Some teachers are eager to make immigrant students blend in with others as quickly as possible. They rarely consider the transitional phase these children and families experience while struggling to adjust to the new environment.

> (A) Some Muslim girls in the local school wore the traditional headscarves(hijab), while others did not. Some girls expressed to their teachers their wish that they could remove their headscarves like their friends. The teachers encouraged them to remove their scarves at school, suggesting they could replace them before returning home.
> (B) Rather than accelerating the mainstreaming process, this overzealous approach of the teachers can sometimes have the opposite result. An example of such a negative outcome occurred during the conduct of one set of workshops, which included several Muslim families.
> (C) Shortly thereafter, some of the girls who removed their headscarves were no longer in school. Hence the teachers' eagerness to accelerate the acculturation process only served to abolish the opportunity completely.

① (C) – (B) – (A) ② (B) – (A) – (C)
③ (B) – (C) – (A) ④ (C) – (A) – (B)

07 다음 빈칸에 들어갈 말로 가장 적절한 것은?

Life has rules and only the foolish person refuses to follow these rules at all. However, sometimes we expand this "rule" approach to life to such a degree that we get locked into patterns that are no longer applicable to life and our creative juices get squeezed out. Therefore, one way to enhance our creativity is to challenge the rules. In the movie IQ, Walter Matthau played the part of Einstein. Meg Ryan was Einstein's niece. At one point in the movie, Einstein said to his niece, "Question everything!" That's good advice. Every advance in history came from someone who challenged the rules. Columbus discovered America because he challenged the rules of navigation. Martin Luther started the Reformation because he challenged the rules of the church. Einstein discovered the theory of relativity because he challenged the rules of Newtonian physics. Sometimes creativity arises out of the awareness that we do not have to _____.

① imagine a future without any form of conflict
② be under pressure to improve our own creativity
③ be a genius to make valuable contributions to science
④ do things in the same way they have always been done

08 다음 글의 빈칸에 들어갈 말로 가장 적절한 것은?

Contemporary Western athletes speak in their own terms about time _____. Tennis great Jimmy Connors has described transcendent occasions when his game rose to a level where he felt he'd entered a "zone." At these moments, he recalls, the ball would appear huge as it came over the net and seem suspended in slow motion. In this rarified air, Connors felt he had all the time in the world to decide how, when, and where to hit the ball. In truth, of course, his seeming eternity lasted only a fraction of a second. Basketball chatter is also laced with mystical-sounding references to "getting into zones" where time stands still. Players describe unexplainable occasions when everyone around them seems to move in slow motion. During these moments they report a feeling of being able to move around, between, and through their opponents at will.

① limit   ② waste
③ pressure   ④ expansion

09 다음 글의 빈칸 (A), (B)에 들어갈 말로 가장 적절한 것은?

The principle of distinctiveness suggests that we make attributions about people based on whether their particular characteristics and actions are associated with specific outcomes unique to the situation. Distinctiveness is the extent to which things occur only with each other and not with other things.   (A) , if a student, who has a habit of submitting his assignments late, seems well liked by peers and professors but is clearly treated harshly by one of the professors, then the student seems to cause a distinctive reaction from this professor. If the professor in question is consistently harsh with many other students, then the behavior is not distinctive to the late-assignment student; rather it is low in distinctiveness, and you will tend to consider the professor a harsh person. If,   (B) , you see this professor being friendly with all students except the student with the late assignments, then the student seems to be unique or distinctive in eliciting this response from the professor. In this case, the professor's behavior is high in distinctiveness and you are more likely to attribute the cause to the late student having done something to upset this professor.

	(A)	(B)
①	For example	instead
②	For example	consequently
③	On the contrary	instead
④	On the contrary	consequently

10 다음 글의 주제로 가장 적절한 것은?

> A chef does not turn off the oven when the meal is half done. Even microwaves take some time to cook. Far too often we lose patience with the process and quit too soon, missing out on what we could have gained. In these fast times, we run the risk of cutting the harvest short. Watching the corn grow can be a very anxious process. We want it safely in the barn now. Yesterday would be even better. Our lives are one big hurry. We rush through our childhood, red lights, and a courtship as if channel surfing. We speed-read directions, come late to and leave early from meetings, and choose a church because its worship service is precisely one hour long. Our addiction to speed gets us things we'd not have without it, but it also guarantees we'll never see things we long for most. For example, going into debt to purchase a car, clothes, and vacation can keep us from qualifying for a house or the kind of home we dream about. Haste in a relationship can ruin long-term fulfillment, because we go too fast too soon or wind up with someone who is less than our dreams. The unwillingness to persevere with an organization through its trying times can cut us out of potential rewards when the tide changes. Waiting for the harvest is not fun for most of us, but when we plant seed and then run off to some other plot of ground without reaping our harvest, we've wasted a portion of our lives.

① ways to cure shopping addiction
② myths that waste energy in the kitchen
③ disadvantages of moving too fast in life
④ effects of late-life debt use on quality of life

16 하프 모의고사

01 다음 밑줄 친 단어의 의미와 가장 가까운 것은?

> They all failed to understand my gestures; some were simply stolid, some thought it was a jest and laughed at me.

① tremulous
② apathetic
③ wayward
④ diffident

02 다음 밑줄 친 부분과 의미와 가장 가까운 것은?

> This sort of thing will cut no ice the international market.

① back
② have no influence
③ advocate
④ support

03 다음 문장에서 문법적으로 어색한 부분을 고르시오.

> Just as a planet ① circling the sun cannot help ② following Kepler's laws, so a program ③ obeying an invariant cannot help but ④ behaving in a predictable way.

04 다음 빈칸에 들어갈 단어로 가장 적절한 것은?

> Videotape was not new in 1963, but the technology was unwieldy, and the machines were huge, neither terribly reliable nor easily _____.

① portable
② noticeable
③ vulnerable
④ reversible

05 다음 우리말을 영어로 옮긴 것 중 틀린 것을 고르시오.

① 나는 그처럼 아량 있는 사람을 본 적이 없다.
   ⇨ I've never met such an understanding man as him.
② 무엇 때문에 너는 공무원이 되기로 결심을 했느냐?
   ⇨ What made you decide to become a public servant?
③ 인간이 항상 환경의 지배를 받는 것은 아니다.
   ⇨ Men are not always influenced by environment.
④ Brian은 자신의 건강이 좋지 않다고 주장하고 있다.
   ⇨ Brian insist that his health be in bad shape.

06 다음 글의 주제로 가장 적절한 것은?

> Robert Schuman's works for the piano are acknowledged as brilliant masterworks. However, his large scale orchestral works have always suffered by comparison to those of contemporaries such as Mendelssohn and Brahms. Perhaps this is because Schuman's works should be measured with a different yardstick. His works are often considered poorly orchestrated, but they actually have an unusual aesthetic. He treats the orchestra as he does the piano: one grand instrument with a uniform sound. This is so different from the approach of most composers that, to many, it has seemed like a failing rather than a conscious artistic choice.

① The greatness of Schuman's piano works
② The difference between piano works and orchestral music
③ The reassessment of Schuman's musical works
④ The influence of Schuman's performances

07 글의 흐름으로 보아, 주어진 문장이 들어가기에 가장 적절한 곳은?

> Only a few analysts noted the large number of "undecided" respondents a week before the election.

Public opinion polls are snapshots of opinions and preferences at a specific moment in time and as expressed in response to a specific question. Given that definition, it is fairly easy to understand situations in which the polls are wrong. (①) For example, opinion polls leading up to the 1980 presidential election showed President Jimmy Carter defeating challenger Ronald Reagan. (②) Those voters shifted massively to Reagan at the last minute, and Reagan won the election. (③) The famous photo of Harry Truman showing the front page of the newspaper that declared his defeat in the 1948 presidential election is another tribute to the weakness of polling. (④) Again, the poll that predicted his defeat was taken more than a week before Election Day. Truman won the election with 49.9 percent of the vote. *tribute 증거

08 다음 빈칸에 들어갈 말로 가장 적절한 것을 고르시오.

What does curiosity mean, and why is it so important? We think of curiosity as exploration: being inquisitive, seeking to learn and understand. Some associate curiosity with being nosy. After all, aren't we being nosy if we are curious about another person, asking personal questions? We believe there is a difference between the two. Nosy people ask questions and proceed to weigh the answers provided. Their intention is not to learn about the other person, but to compare, perhaps wanting to determine who is better or worse. In contrast, true curiosity _____. It is about exploring and learning with the goal of greater understanding, which is free from setting values. When curious people ask a question, their only intention is to better understand, whether it is another person, an idea, a place, an origin, or anything that creates an interest in further exploration.

① grows with age
② overcomes fear
③ holds no judgment
④ comes from confidence

09 주어진 글 다음에 이어질 글의 순서로 가장 적절한 것을 고르시오.

Mass customization is a strategy that allows manufacturers or retailers to provide individualized products to consumers. Today's apparel supplier must look for new ways to offer customers top-quality goods at highly competitive prices.

(A) The customer then receives the finished product in a very short time. This technological strategy is used today by some fashion firms. This type of customization is often limited, however, to a small number of customers.

(B) Based on the exact image, body scanning software then defines and captures all the measurements necessary for actually producing the garment or shoe. This data is forwarded online to the manufacturer, whose production technologies ensure an exact fit.

(C) Consumers desire products that can be personalized through fit preferences, color selection, fabric choices, or design characteristics. A solution to the fit preference is a body or foot scanner that takes a customer's measurements digitally, creating what is referred to as digital twin.

① (A) – (C) – (B)
② (B) – (A) – (C)
③ (B) – (C) – (A)
④ (C) – (B) – (A)

10 다음 글의 내용으로 가장 적절한 것은?

If You're Bitten, Trap the Spider

In the rare case you do get bitten, it's a good idea to trap the spider so you can identify the species in case treatment is needed. Isolate your leggy little tourist — along with fruit, if that's where you found it — in a plastic bag or container. Put that package in the fridge to slow the cold-blooded arachnid down. This makes it easier to brush it into a jar or other container, wearing rubber gloves if you like. "Do this quickly and with confidence." If you're too uncomfortable, you can put the whole shebang in the freezer, which will kill the spider, leaving an intact specimen for identification. If you're bitten, an ice pack on the area will usually suffice for treatment, but experts suggest seeking medical attention if you experience symptoms such as "increasing pain, nausea, vomiting, sweating, dilated pupils, uncontrollable muscle spasms, and loss of consciousness." If a Spider Is in Your Food, Don't Set It Free. In case the spider is a non-native species that got into your house via your food, don't release it outside. The animal could harm the native environment. If you found the spider elsewhere in your house, you can put it outside. If the spider did arrive in your food, "although it pains me to say this [as an arachnologist], the best course of action is to probably to kill the eight-legged cargo," the experts say.

* arachnid 거미류의 절지동물 ** arachnologist 〈동물〉 거미학자

① It is not necessary to treat a spider as dangerous until you know better.
② Alien spiders in your imported fruits may disturb the local ecosystem.
③ Most of the known spiders are venomous enough to be harmful to humans.
④ It is important to receive immediate medical attention when you're bitten by spiders.

17 하프 모의고사

01 밑줄 친 단어의 의미와 가장 가까운 것은?

> This isn't terribly important and maybe I'm just a bit <u>dense</u>, but if someone could clarify, I'd really appreciate it.

① crowded
② heavy
③ opaque
④ stupid

02 다음 빈칸에 들어갈 단어로 가장 적절한 것은?

> Snapchat's primary value proposition is a _____ mobile message that disappears after a few seconds to protect message privacy.

① transient
② ubiquitous
③ tailored
④ bilateral

03 다음 빈칸에 들어갈 단어로 가장 적절한 것은?

> Impulsive children interrupt others, are impatient about waiting their turn, blurt out answers before hearing the entire question, or _____ other people's conversations.

① butt in on
② listen in on
③ stand up for
④ look up to

04 다음 빈칸에 들어갈 표현으로 적절한 것을 고르시오.

> Our news is free of charge, but just as the popularity of our news grows, _____.

① so too have our costs of operation
② our costs of operation do so too
③ so too do our costs of operation
④ our costs of operation have so too

05 (A), (B), (C)의 각 네모 안에서 어법에 맞는 표현으로 가장 적절한 것은?

> Like life in traditional society, but unlike other team sports, baseball is not governed by the clock. A football game is comprised of exactly sixty minutes of play, a basketball game forty or forty-eight minutes, but baseball has no set length of time within which the game must be completed. The pace of the game is therefore leisurely and (A) [unhurried/unhurriedly], like the world before the discipline of measured time, deadlines, schedules, and wages paid by the hour. Baseball belongs to the kind of world (B) [which/in which] people did not say, "I haven't got all day." Baseball games do have all day to be played. But that does not mean that they can go on forever. Baseball, like traditional life, proceeds according to the rhythm of nature, specifically the rotation of the Earth. During its first half century, games were not played at night, which meant that baseball games, like the traditional work day, (C) [ending/ended] when the sun set.

	(A)	(B)	(C)
①	unhurried	in which	ended
②	unhurried	which	ending
③	unhurriedly	which	ended
④	unhurriedly	which	ending

06 다음 글의 요지로 적절한 것을 고르시오.

> Some health-screening efforts have gone too far. A recent study found that yearly mammograms do not prolong the lives of low-risk women ages 40 to 59. Following more than 89,000 women for 25 years in a randomized controlled trial (the gold standard of science), the study is methodologically impressive. As hard as it is for our pro-screening culture to believe, the data are clear. We are taxing far too many women not only with needless and sometimes humiliating X-rays but also with unnecessary follow-up surgery. In this era of rising medical prices, cutting waste should be the top priority, especially when that waste pulls doctors away from the important work of caring for sick patients. A 2012 Institute of Medicine report concludes that Americans spend as much as one-third of their health care dollars on tests, medicine, procedures and administrative burdens that do not improve health outcomes. Reducing overdiagnosis and overtreatment will require broadening medicine's focus beyond hunting and killing disease to sound research and education on appropriate care.

① Excessive screening can cause unintended harm, stress and waste.
② Advances in modern medicine will help reduce growing healthcare costs.
③ A health-screening test used to detect tumors is rarely problematic.
④ The risks of chasing indolent diseases can only be detected by a screening test.

07 다음 빈칸에 들어갈 말로 가장 적절한 것을 고르시오.

> If we can't have everything we want today, what do we do? We are forced to make choices. We must choose some goods and services and not others. Sometimes this kind of choosing can be visibly painful. Have you ever watched children in a toy store with a gift certificate in hand? It can take them all day before they make a choice. And instead of bubbling with excitement over the toy they bought, they usually appear frustrated over not being able to walk away with everything! Life is like that. _____ governs us. Because we cannot have everything all at once, we are forever forced to make choices. We can use our resources to satisfy only some of our wants, leaving many others unsatisfied.

① Scarcity   ② Morality
③ Knowledge   ④ Reputation

08 다음 글의 제목으로 가장 적절한 것은?

> Trish and Andrea enjoyed a good relationship as business partners until Andrea began to feel victimized by the amount of time she needed to devote to a project. Overwhelmed by the prospect of what lay ahead, she sent Trish an e-mail demanding a larger share of the profits. Trish was shocked and hurt by the message and by the impersonal way it was delivered. Rather than let herself become overwhelmed by hurt and disappointment, she reminded herself that she and Andrea were friends and that she didn't understand what was so troubling. Trish made an appointment to discuss the matter leisurely with Andrea in a comfortable setting that favored communication. When the two met, Trish was relaxed and genuinely interested in knowing why Andrea felt resentful when she hadn't in the past. Face to face, with Trish showing genuine interest and regard, Andrea relaxed and was able to tell Trish that their project had become more than she could handle. Andrea felt reassured by Trish's support and their interaction as they discussed possible solutions that would enable Andrea to continue working on the project. The discussion ended with each feeling greater excitement about working together and more appreciation for one another.

① Emotionally Intelligent Communication Turns Mad into Glad
② Nonverbal Cues That Convey Confidence at Work
③ How to Peacefully Break Up with Your Business Partner
④ Leaving a Never-Ending Conversation Without Being Rude

09 다음 글의 내용으로 가장 적절한 것은?

> The general tendency is away from conflicts that are clearly one side against the other toward multiplayer conflicts in which several groups, ranging from the local to the international, kaleidoscopically compete against one another as much as they participate in a two-way fight. Fragmentation is not new, but its effects are radically catalyzed by the speed and interconnectivity of contemporary globalization driven by the information revolution. The information revolution encourages fragmentation because it simultaneously has the power to bring powerful networks together and to break them up. Consider the Arab Spring, in which a disparate range of people and of interests were drawn together by the simple and powerful desire to rise up against oppressive regimes. But, once formed, the information revolution catalyzed the fragmentation of those networks once they started to disagree with one another, thus reforming new groups. Look at how the Arab Spring became the Arab Winter; comrades in arms have been split by factional and religious differences. Fragmentation profoundly affects any armed conflict that may well start as a relatively polarized fight, as people are drawn together under one cause — be it toppling Bashar Assad in Syria or Moammar Gadhafi in Libya — but soon fight among each other as much as with the original enemy. These confusing, complex, multilayered patterns are replicated by each of the factions' regional and international backers. The convoluted evolution of who backs whom with the mutating factions in Syria over the past three years, and now in Iraq, makes that clear.

① Libyans and Syrians had a clear enemy to be defeated at the beginning of the revolution.
② The consequences of the Arab Spring differ depending on the forms of political systems.
③ The people who participated in the Arab Spring fought for constitutional monarchy to protect minorities.
④ The group which was firmly in control of networks took absolute power in the Middle East.

10 다음 빈칸에 들어갈 말로 가장 적절한 것은?

The "hygiene hypothesis," which proposes that kids today live in overly sanitized environments thanks to things like bleach and hand sanitizers, has been long used to explain the rise in children's allergies. The thought was that urban immune systems do not get exposed to enough bacteria and other microbes that prepare the immune system to be _____. This hypothesis is partly based on studies showing that children raised on farms have fewer allergies and asthma attacks. Playing outside, digging for worms, planting vegetables, and essentially coming into contact with plenty of dirt and livestock are actually good things. Not just good — essential! Bacteria, viruses, parasites, and fungi play a critical role in developing and maintaining a healthy gut and immune system. Another explanation for the rise in allergies has been called the "old friends hypothesis," because allergic children lack a diversity of these friendly microbes in their guts. To evaluate these theories, scientists compared microbial samples from an urban apartment to those from a rural farm. Shockingly, they found that the two environments actually had similar numbers of microbes. What differed, however, was the diversity of bacteria. The microbial sample from the urban apartment was limited, while the microbial sample from the farm was rich with varied microbes. A study of an Amazonian indigenous tribe free of chronic illness — isolated entirely from modern life — revealed the most diverse number of microbes ever documented in humans. A healthy gut is filled with diverse microbes: the more kinds, the better. Biodiversity makes the difference between balance and dysregulation.

① healthy
② infected
③ changed
④ inefficient

18 하프 모의고사

01 다음 밑줄 친 단어의 의미와 가장 가까운 것은?

> The flowers delivered yesterday have already withered.

① wilted ② wavered
③ wandered ④ writhed

02 다음 빈칸에 들어갈 표현으로 가장 적절한 것은?

> Natural instincts are either disregarded or treated as nuisances, as _____ traits to be suppressed or at all events to be brought into conformity with external standards. Since conformity is the aim, what is distinctively individual in a young person is _____ or regarded as a source of mischief or anarchy.

① obnoxious – brushed aside ② beneficent – bottled up
③ profane – sanctified ④ ghastly – encouraged

03 다음 빈칸에 들어갈 표현으로 적절한 것을 고르시오.

> This is to confirm our understanding and agreement in regard of the long-term lease by us of one refrigerator truck from you. If you are at one with our understanding, as attached, please confirm _____.

① by letter, fax or email ② by a letter, a fax or an email
③ by a letter, fax or email ④ by a letter, fax, or an email

04 다음 빈칸에 들어갈 표현으로 적절한 것을 고르시오.

> Relationship is more valuable than money; ___(A)___ may give us more comfort in life, but ___(B)___ gives us satisfactions which no amount of money can buy.

	(A)	(B)
①	this	that
②	that	this
③	these	those
④	those	these

05 다음 중 어법상 어색한 문장을 고르시오.

① When questioned, she denied being a member of the group.
② Allowed unusual privileges, the prisoner seemed to enjoy his captivity.
③ Through now frail, they were quit capable of looking after themselves.
④ Considering works of art, the collections of china were admitted into the country without customs duties.

06 다음 우리말 영작이 올바르지 않는 문장을 고르시오.

① 구독자에게 제공된 이 보고서에 들어 있는 그 어떤 정보도 개인에 맞춘 재정 자문을 포함하고 있지 않다
  ⇨ None of the information contained in these reports provided to the subscribers constitute personalized financial advice.
② 가격이 오르고 있는 치즈와 밀가루 비용 때문에 돈이 궁한 피자 제조업자에게는 자금이 힘든 때이다.
  ⇨ It is a tough time for pizza makers, who are strapped by rising cheese and flour costs.
③ 치솟는 석유 가격이 가장 큰 석유 소비국인 미국의 수요 붕괴의 원인이 되고 있다.
  ⇨ The surging oil price is leading to demand destruction in the largest consumer of oil - the United States.
④ 나는 이 집과 지금 이후로 이 집에서 살게 될 모든 사람들에게 신의 은총이 내리기를 하늘에 기도한다.
  ⇨ I pray heaven to bestow the vest of blessing on this house and all that shall hereafter inhabit it.

07 다음 글의 제목으로 가장 적절한 것은?

On the national level of culture, we assume that people of the same national background share many things that bind them in a common culture: language, values, norms, and traditions. Thus, we expect Germans to differ from Hmong based on differing national cultures. However, cultures can be formed on other levels, such as generation, gender, race, and region, among others. For example, in many parts of the country, regionalisms exist. People who live in the middle of the United States (in states such as Kansas, Illinois, Iowa, Nebraska, Indiana, and Wisconsin) are often referred to as "Midwesterners." People who live in Vermont, New Hampshire, Maine, Massachusetts, Rhode Island, and Connecticut are called "New Englanders." Both Midwesterners and New Englanders have their own unique way of looking at things, but the two regions also share a great deal in common — namely, pragmatic thinking and an independent spirit.

① Culture Is Multilayered
② Culture Shapes Our Behavior
③ Diversity Makes Us Stronger
④ We Are All the Same Within!

08 다음 빈칸에 들어갈 말로 가장 적절한 것은?

Here's a curious paradox. If perfection is a state beyond improvement, then isn't every moment, by definition, perfect? After all, any given "now," any given moment of reality is what it is in the sense that it cannot be anything other than what it is. Take this moment, right now: this moment is already here, and, as such, as theoretically imperfect as it may be, it is — at present — beyond any _____. While you could take the lessons of this moment and try to make the next moment better, this very moment is beyond improvement. It is too late to add anything to this moment to make it better. And if this moment, this slice of reality, is beyond improvement, then it's the only way it can be (the best it can be — perfect).

① doubt
② argument
③ evaluation
④ modification

09 빈칸 (A)와 (B)에 들어갈 말로 가장 적절한 것은?

Martin Buber taught that there are two kinds of relationships: I–Thou and I–It. As an example of the difference between the two, imagine heading to work on a daily route that includes a stop at one of the corporate coffee chain stores. You place the same order each morning, get the same stuff, throw down the money and pick up the change. This automatic, mechanical, "It's early! I'm sleepy!" interaction with the person behind the counter is the kind of relationship Buber would call I–It. Then, one day, instead of a muffin, you order a whole wheat bagel with no-fat cream cheese. The barista smiles and comments, "On a diet?" and you are taken by surprise, to the point of embarrassment. Here you thought that the counter clerk did not even recognize you, let alone remember what you eat. The dull routine has broke; you discover that, unbeknownst to yourself, your presence makes a difference. Leaving the shop, instead of dragging with fatigue as usual, you realize your mood has lifted a little, thanks to the reaction you received. Buber would say that this exchange was I–Thou.

⬇

The kind of relationship Martin Buber would call I–It is characterized by __(A)__ interaction, and in the kind of relationship he would call I–Thou, we feel we are perceived as a(n) __(B)__ .

	(A)	(B)
①	informal	loyal customer
②	informal	authoritative figure
③	symbolic	stereotypical image
④	impersonal	particular person

10 다음 글의 내용으로 가장 적절한 것은?

> The zoo is not a window on nature but rather a prism that bends the light according to the culture it is set in. And our view of nature accords us a clearer view of ourselves. We have always defined man in comparison to other animals. We thought we were the only tool users, but Jane Goodall and others dispelled that notion. Today, our place as the only true language users is being questioned. But human beings are not defined by what we do with our hands or our vocal cords but by what we do with our hearts. Arguments can be made for preserving nature because it may hold medical and technological secrets that could cure cancer or provide more efficient solar energy. Arguments can be made that we must preserve the fragile web of life because changing one small thread could alter the whole world. But the best argument for putting so much energy into preserving nature is for the sheer, breathtaking, poetic beauty of the diversity of life. This is an argument that is at once selfish and altruistic. Throughout history, zoos have entertained and educated; now they have a staggering opportunity before them: to tip the global balance back in favor of nature. To work toward the restoration of harmony in the living world. Zoos, which have provided so much joy to people, can now breathe life back into moribund populations of wild creatures.

① It is worthwhile to preserve nature if only for the sake of the diversity of life itself.
② Human beings are unquestionably the only species that can use language, if not tools in general.
③ Nature must be studied mainly because it will certainly yield knowledge we can use for our well-being.
④ Confining wildlife in zoos for entertainment and education is now facing adamant objections.

19 하프 모의고사

01 밑줄 친 단어의 의미와 가장 가까운 것은?

> One goal of this symposium is to canvass modern scientific thought and research approaches regarding the three main categories of selection that Darwin addressed during his career.

① scrutinize ② portray
③ emulate ④ represent

02 다음 밑줄 친 부분의 풀이가 잘못된 것을 고르시오.

① The arrest of their leader touched off a riot. [= stopped]
② Bill takes the part of his sister. [= supports]
③ They are ready to meet us halfway. [= compromise with]
④ Her good advice is lost on him. [= doesn't influence]

03 다음 빈칸에 들어갈 표현으로 가장 적절한 것은?

> Pressure to publish in leading academic journals encouraged researchers to cut corners and pursue trendy fields of science instead of doing more important work. The problem was _____ by editors who were not active scientists but professionals who _____ studies that were likely to make a splash.

① exacerbated – favored
② ameliorated – preferred
③ obscured – snubbed
④ remedied – misrepresented

04 다음 문장들 중 어법상 가장 적절한 것은?

① The virus that caused several hundred cases of flu is similar with one that causes a flu-like illness in swine.
② In opposition to President Carter's Foreign policy was the House Majority Leader and the Chairman of the Ways and Means Committee.
③ We have, in fact, two kinds of morality side by side: one which we preach but do not practice and another which we practice but do not preach.
④ Many of the old plantation gardens around Chalreston were planted a century or more ago and have been carefully tended and improved ever since.

05 다음 우리말 영작이 올바르지 않은 문장을 고르시오.

① 난민들은 식량도 쉴 곳도 없다.
   ⇨ The refugees had neither food nor shelter.
② 그는 용감함에도 불구하고 그 일을 하는 데 머뭇거렸다.
   ⇨ Brave man as he was, hesitated to do it.
③ 네가 시키는 대로 해라, 그렇지 않으면 벌을 받을 것이다.
   ⇨ Do what you are told, or you will be punished.
④ 모형 비행기는 제어 전선 혹은 무선 송신기 둘 중 하나에 의해 조종될 수 있다.
   ⇨ Model airplanes can be guided both by control wires or by radio transmitters.

06 다음 글의 요지로 가장 적절한 것을 고르시오.

Circumstantial evidence is evidence not drawn from the direct observation of a fact. If, for example, there is evidence that a piece of rock embedded in a wrapped chocolate bar is the same type of rock found in the candy factory, and that rock of this type is found in few other places, then there is circumstantial evidence that the stone found its way into the candy during manufacture and suggests that the candy-maker was negligent even though there is no eyewitness evidence that this is true. Despite a popular notion to look down on the quality of circumstantial evidence, it is of great usefulness if there is enough of it and if it is properly interpreted. Each circumstance, taken singly, may mean little, but a whole chain of circumstances can be as conclusive as direct evidence.

① A manufacturer's negligence can be shown by direct evidence only.
② Enough circumstantial evidence is as persuasive as direct evidence.
③ Circumstantial evidence can be very useful in science.
④ Circumstantial evidence can be accepted by the court.

07 다음 빈칸에 들어갈 말로 가장 적절한 것을 고르시오.

Security should be thought of as an art; it cannot be accomplished through the old "tools and techies" model. An organization should not believe itself to be secure simply because it spends millions on security devices every year. The fact is that having an infinite budget and a large variety of security resources can often be more of a detriment than a benefit in many organizations. Organizations with vast resources at their command are very likely to try to solve security problems by implementing new security toys. I use the word "toy" because a security device, no matter how expensive or complex, is nothing more than a toy if it does not function within a greater security framework. Security cannot be handled exclusively through expensive equipment, as many of us have been led to believe. Security is not a technology; it is a thought process and a methodology. Security within our technologies is nothing until security is _____.

① in danger
② made simple
③ up to standard
④ within our minds

08 주어진 글 다음에 이어질 글의 순서로 가장 적절한 것은?

Prior to the Second World War, nation-states regulated their economic and fiscal affairs primarily as domestic matters; however, in the post-war era we have witnessed a huge expansion and intensification of economic interdependence.

(A) The resulting destabilization of these national economies hastened the 'Asian Economic Crisis' and sparked a global recession. Increasingly, national institutions cannot handle emerging economic, political, and social problems; this has prompted an urgent call for effective international regulatory institutions.

(B) As a result, the global economy is acutely vulnerable to disruption by the malfunction of any single nation-state's fiscal-political system; a serious malfunction can trigger a chain reaction known commonly as the 'domino effect.'

(C) Such a disruptive event occurred in 1997 when Thailand, with a relatively small national economy, suffered a financial collapse which touched off sufficient uncertainty among investors that they pulled their money out of neighbouring Malaysia, Indonesia, and South Korea.

① (C) – (B) – (A)   ② (B) – (A) – (C)
③ (B) – (C) – (A)   ④ (C) – (A) – (B)

09 글의 흐름으로 보아, 주어진 문장이 들어가기에 가장 적절한 곳을 고르시오.

To meet what it needs, a solution adopted by psychologists was not to attempt to examine the mind's workings.

One of the major obstacles in getting psychology recognized as a branch of science was the abstract nature of the mind. (①) In order to establish its scientific credentials, psychologists needed to adopt scientific methodology, including observation and experimentation. (②) Because we only have direct access to our own minds, our observation of mental processes is introspective and necessarily subjective, but science demands an objective approach. (③) Instead, it was to observe how they manifest themselves in behavior. (④) Not only can behavior of humans be watched, but the behavioral response of a human being to a specific situation can be examined under strict laboratory conditions. Thanks to this objective scientific approach, behaviorism and its theories of stimulus and response dominated experimental psychology until the mid-20th century.

10 다음 글의 내용과 일치하지 않는 것은?

Within the context of the overall murder rate, the death penalty cannot be said to be widely or routinely used in the United States; in recent years the average has been about one execution for about every 700 murders committed, or 1 execution for about every 325 murder convictions. It is noted that the death penalty is sought and applied more often in some jurisdictions, not only between states but within states. A 2004 Cornell University study showed that while 2.5% of murderers convicted nationwide were sentenced to the death penalty, in Nevada 6% were given the death penalty. Texas gave only 2% of murderers the death sentence, less than the national average. Texas, however, executed 40% of those sentenced, which was about 4 times higher than the national average. California had executed only 1% of those sentenced. Only 1.4% of those executed since 1976 have been women. African-Americans make up 42% of death row inmates while making up only 12% of the general population. On the other hand, others note that this is lower than the 50% of the total prison population which is African-American and that whites are in fact twice as likely as African-Americans to receive the death penalty, and are also executed more quickly after sentencing.

① The percentage of those sentenced to the death penalty based on area
② The percentage of death row inmates based on race
③ The percentage of those sentenced to the death penalty based on occupation
④ The percentage of those executed based on gender

20 하프 모의고사

01 다음 밑줄 친 단어의 의미와 가장 가까운 것은?

> Cloth which is <u>diaphanous</u> is very fine or thin.

① sheer
② consensus
③ sensible
④ sagacious

02 다음 밑줄 친 표현과 의미가 가장 가까운 것은?

> He <u>goes off the deep end</u> about the unexpected result.

① falls from the cliff
② feels disheartened deeply
③ loses his self-restraint
④ acts with consideration

03 다음 빈칸에 들어갈 표현으로 가장 적절한 것은?

> Our society has developed a taboo against the use of words associated with group hatred, as a way to _____ said hatred.

① unfetter
② ennoble
③ transfuse
④ stigmatize

04 다음 빈칸에 들어갈 표현으로 가장 적절한 것은?

> Good medical practice is always characterized by _____ and diagnostic elegance, aimed not at saving money but at what would be best for the patient, since too much testing and treating can be harmful.

① pharmaceutical innovation
② emotional reservations
③ intellectual rigor
④ therapeutic parsimony

05 다음 문장들 중 어법상 적절하지 않은 것은?

① With the blood flowing form the wound, he shouted to us to come on.
② Nobody thought he would last 15 rounds, but he went the full distance.
③ Three years of seesaw fighting, in which many civilians died, resulted in a stalemate.
④ Whether happiness is relative or absolute depends on if it is about money or mentality.

06 다음 우리말 영작이 올바르지 않은 문장을 고르시오.

① 요즈음 자동차가 많아져서 대도시에서는 어떤 때는 걷는 것이 빠를 때가 있다.
   ⇨ Nowadays motorcars are so numerous that in a large city it sometimes takes less time to walk than to ride.
② 사람들은 흔히 책이 너무 비싸다고 불평하는데, 책값은 다른 물건만큼 오르지 않았다.
   ⇨ People often complain that books are too expensive, but their prices have not risen as much as other commodities.
③ 아무리 부유해도 행복을 살 수는 없다.
   ⇨ No matter how rich he is, he can't buy happiness.
④ 영어를 배우는 목적은 단지 그 말을 배우는 것뿐만 아니라, 영미의 문화를 이해하는 것이다.
   ⇨ The purpose of studying English is not only to learn the language itself, but to understand English and American culture.

07 다음 글의 주제로 가장 적절한 것은?

> In organizations, there is no simple cause-and-effect relationship between introducing a management technique and getting an improved business result. This contrasts with other spheres of activity where simple causal relationships do seem to operate. Hit the nail with the hammer, and it goes into the wood. Show a dog food, and it salivates. This kind of simple cause-and-effect logic can be misleading if applied to the complex world of organizations, where it is difficult to trace single effects to single causes. Uncontrollable outside factors can sink a wonderfully designed team (a hurricane just swept the entire inventory out to sea) or rescue one whose design was so bad that failure seemed assured (the firm that was competing for the contract just went belly-up). In organizations, multiple causes are operating at the same time and interacting with each over an extended period of time.

① complex causal relationship in organizations
② benefits of a fair relationship in organizations
③ strategies to maximize profits of organizations
④ new technologies introduced to manage a business

08 빈칸 (A)와 (B)에 들어갈 말로 가장 적절한 것은?

Gift giving is one of the most mysterious areas of shopping. Irrational behavior is almost the norm in this area of consumer spending and it is tolerated, expected, and even encouraged. Gift giving is less about shopping and more about the emotions of the shopper. This helps to explain the extreme nature of gift shopping and the illogical nature of the whole process. From the consumer's point of view, shopping for gifts is an emotional process that one gets caught up in. It is an area where the laws of supply, demand, and price go out the window as anxious shoppers do their utmost to bring pleasure to another person, and thereby, to themselves. The shopper shopping for gifts is the most susceptible of all shoppers. Smart retailers are ready to take advantage of the defenseless and emotionally vulnerable gift buyer. Meanwhile, the shopper knows he is vulnerable, but he is also unwilling to defend himself. Pleasing the recipient and conveying the intended emotional message are often more important than the price.

When shopping for gifts, consumers exhibit a(n) __(A)__ consumption pattern because they are driven usually by __(B)__.

	(A)	(B)		(A)	(B)
①	strategic	supply	②	strategic	demand
③	unreasonable	emotion	④	unreasonable	supply

09 다음 빈칸에 들어갈 말로 가장 적절한 것은?

> A point to keep in mind when thinking about paranormal, supernatural, and pseudo-scientific beliefs is that letting go of them is not necessarily a _____.
> Not only can thinking skeptically be safer and more economical over the course of a lifetime, it doesn't have to be any less fun, either. Whatever I may have lost by not believing in things like astrology and ghosts, I am confident that I more than make up for it by embracing reality with great enthusiasm. All scientific discoveries to date and all the mysteries still to be solved excite me, and I find plenty of reason for optimism and hope, even amid harsh realities. I understand that it may feel comforting or stabilizing to believe that invisible forces influence us, but it can also be comforting and stabilizing to realize that as humans we are smart enough and strong enough to face up to the universe as it really is and get on with our lives.

① must
② reality
③ sacrifice
④ pleasure

10 다음 글의 내용과 일치하지 않는 것은?

> For decades, Ebola haunted rural African villages like some mythic monster that every few years rose to demand a human sacrifice and then returned to its cave. It reached the West only in nightmare form, a Hollywood horror that makes eyes bleed and organs dissolve and doctors despair because they have no cure. But 2014 is the year an outbreak turned into an epidemic, powered by the very progress that has paved roads and raised cities and lifted millions out of poverty. This time it reached crowded slums in Liberia, Guinea and Sierra Leone; it traveled to Nigeria and Mali, to Spain, Germany and the U.S. It struck doctors and nurses in unprecedented numbers, wiping out a public-health infrastructure that was weak in the first place. One August day in Liberia, six pregnant women lost their babies when hospitals couldn't admit them for complications. Anyone willing to treat Ebola victims ran the risk of becoming one.

① Ebola has not been an intimidating epidemic in Africa for a long time.
② The dangers of Ebola were unjustifiably exaggerated in the West.
③ Ebola became a threatening epidemic as poverty was widespread in Africa.
④ Some Liberian women miscarried their babies as hospitals were unable to admit them.

권혁민 ONEPACK

해설

24시간에 끝내는 One Pack
하프모의고사

01 하프 모의고사 해설

01 밑줄 친 단어의 의미와 가장 가까운 것은?

> She is known for her devotion to the <u>cause</u> of women's rights in the 19th century.

① reason ② objective ③ agent ④ origin

[해설] **cause** [kɔːz] 몡 ① 원인이 되는 사람[것]; […의] 원인, 불씨 ② [행동·감정의] 근거, 이유, 동기, 까닭(= reason) ③ [법률] 소송 (사건), 소송의 원인[이유] ④ 목적, 대의명분, 목표, 주의, 주장, 신조(= objective)

[Remark] cause가 '근거, 이유, 동기, 까닭'으로 쓰일 경우는 for을 쓰지만 '목적, 대의명분, 목표, 주의, 주장, 신조'로 해석 될 경우는 for을 쓰지 않는다.

[어휘] **devotion** 전념, 헌신, 열애, 경주, 심취[to, for] **origin** 기원, 근원, 출처(= source) 원천; 발생, 발단(= derivation), 유래; 처음, 시작, 출발점(= beginning) 가문, 혈통(= ancestry); 태생(= parentage) **agent** (일정한 권한을 가진) 대리인[점]; 주선인, 중개인[물]; (공공 기관의) 직원

[해석] 그녀는 19세기 여성의 권리라는 대의명분에 대한 그녀의 헌신으로 알려져 있다.

[정답] ②

02 글의 흐름상 빈칸에 들어갈 단어를 순서대로 고른 것은?

> Often described as the _____ rags to riches tale, the story of steel magnate Andrew Carnegie's rise begins in 1835 in a small one-room home in Dunfermline, Scotland. Born into a family of _____ laborers, Carnegie received little schooling before his family emigrated to America in 1848. Arriving in Pennsylvania, he soon got a job in a textile mill, where he earned only $1.20 per week.

① quintessential – destitute
② exceptive – devout
③ interesting – meticulous
④ deleterious – impoverished

[해설] 첫 문장에서 가난뱅이에서 부자가 된 이야기라고 설명했으므로 두 번째 빈칸에는 카네기가 가난한 가정 출신이라는 것을 알 수 있다. 따라서 '빈곤한'을 의미하는 **impoverished**가 적절하다. 첫 번째 빈칸에는 가난뱅이에서 부자가 된 이야기는 일반적으로 흔히 들을 수 있다는 점에서 '전형적인'이 가능하다.

[어휘] **quintessential** 본질적인, 전형적인, 정수의(= essential, imperative, required) **destitute** [사람·생활 등이] 가난한, 극빈의, 빈곤한, [사람 등이] […을] 가지지 않은, 없는[of] **exceptive** 예외의, 예외적인, 반대하기 좋아하는 **devout** 경건한, 독실한, [기도 등이] 경건한 마음을 나타내는, 성실한, 열성적인(= dedicated, devoted, pious, reverent) **meticulous** 작은 일에 신경을 쓰는, 주의 깊은, 정확한(= scrupulous, punctilious, punctual, alert, wary)

[해석] 종종 전형적인 가난뱅이에서 부자가 된 이야기로 묘사되는 철강왕 **Andrew Carnegie**의 출세 이야기는 1835년 Scotland의 Dunfermline에 있는 작은 단칸방에서 시작된다. 빈곤한 노동자의 가정에서 태어나 Carnegie는 그의 가족이 미국으로 1848년 이민 가기 전까지 교육을 거의 받지 못했다. Pennsylvania에 도착하여, 그는 곧 섬유 공장에 일자리를 얻었는데 그곳에서 그는 주당 $1.20 밖에 벌지 못했다.

[정답] ①

03 밑줄 친 부분 중 어법상 가장 옳지 않은 것은?

I ① <u>convinced</u> that making pumpkin cake ② <u>from scratch</u> would be ③ <u>even</u> easier than ④ <u>making</u> cake from a box.

[해설] ①에서 convince는 '~을 확신시키다'를 의미하는 동사로 확신 시킬 대상인 '목적어'가 온 다음에 of/that와야 한다. 헌데 위 지문처럼 that절까지 밑줄이 없고 convince까지만 밑줄이 있는 것으로 보아 convince를 수동태로 바꿔서 that이하를 표현할 수 있다. convinced that을 was/am convinced that절로 고쳐야 한다. ②에서 from scratch '~을 맨 처음부터, 무에서부터'의 관용표현이다. He built up the business from scratch.(그는 그 사업을 무에서 이루었다.) ③에서 비교급인 easier를 수식하기 위해 even이 바르게 쓰였다.

[원팩더하기] 비교급 약속 틀인 '비교급 than'바로 앞에 위치하고 <u>very</u>는 비교급 수식불가!! (원급만 수식가능)
– 훨씬 : even, much, still, far, a lot, a great deal
– 다소 : rather, somewhat
– 약간 : a bit, a little, slightly
– 배수 : two times, three times(once, twice-원급만 가능)
• His room is <u>much bigger than</u> mine./비교급 강조 표현 – 비교급 앞 위
• The U.S has <u>two times more</u> people <u>than</u> Japan./twice more (×)//<u>twice as</u> many people as (○)

④에서 that 명사절의 주어로 사용된 making pumpkin cake from scratch와 making cake from a box를 비교하는 것이므로 뒤에 오는 making cake from a box 역시 동명사가 와서 두개의 형태가 일치한 것으로 올바른 표현이다.

[원팩더하기] 통고/알림/확신동사 ⇨ A of B (A에게 B를 알리다)
– apprise/inform/notify A of B 통지하다
– assure/convince A of B 확신시키다
– remind A of B A에게 B를 상기시키다
– accuse A of B B라는 이유로 A를 고발, 비난하다
※ <u>통고·확신동사는 that절을 목적어로 취할 때 반드시 그 사이에 간접목적어가 필요하다.</u>
• The experience <u>convinced</u> him [that he was right.]

[해석] 호박 케이크를 맨 처음부터 만드는 것이 박스에 담긴 믹스로 케이크를 만드는 것보다 훨씬 더 쉬울 것이라고 나는 확신했다.

[정답] ①

04 밑줄 친 부분 중 어법상 가장 옳지 않은 것은?

When you find your tongue ① twisted as you seek to explain to your ② six-year-old daughter why she can t go to the amusement park ③ that has been advertised on television, then you will understand why we find it difficult ④ wait.

[해설] ④에서 wait에만 밑줄이 있다면 이를 확인 할 수 있는 자리는 목적보어에 해당하는 동사원형 내지는 문장에서 동사자리일 것이다. 하지만 wait를 동사로 본다면 it을 주어로 봐야하는데 그렇다면 waits로 써야하므로 이는 잘못된 접근이다. wait의 앞의 문장을 보면 동사 다음에 why 즉 의문사는 명사절이고 명사절 속에 find + it + 형용사의 구조가 있는 것으로 보아 가목적어, 진목적어의 구조를 생각할 수 있기에 wait는 to wait으로 고쳐야 한다. 참고로 find, consider, think, believe, think의 동사는 3, 5형식 구분이 중요하다. 이들 동사 뒤에 동사가 있으면 3형식이고 동사가 없으면 5형식임을 기억해두자. then you will understand why we find it difficult to wait.의 문장에서 find 뒤로 동사가 없으므로 이때 find는 5형식구조 중에 가목적어, 진목적어로 쓰인 구조가 된다. ①에서 find는 가목적어, 진목적어를 취할 수 있는 동사이기도 하고 지금처럼 분사를 목적격 보어로 취할 수 있는 타동사이다. 목적어인 your tongue이 스스로 꼬일 수 없기에 수동의 의미가 있으므로 목적격 보어는 과거분사인 twisted가 바르다. ②에서 수량형용사가 측정단위 명사와 쓰이는데 뒤에 명사가 오는 한정 용법으로 사용될 경우, 측정단위 명사는 단수형으로 온다. 수량 형용사인 six가 측정단위 명사인 year와 사용되었는데 뒤에 old boy라는 명사와 함께 와서 한정 용법으로 사용되었다. 따라서 year라는 단수형태가 바르다. ③에서 that 이하가 선행사 amusement park를 수식하는 관계대명사절이다. 관계대명사 that은 동사인 was advertised의 주어 역할을 하는 주격 관계대명사로 바르게 쓰였다.

[해석] 당신이 TV에서 광고된 놀이공원에 그녀가 왜 갈 수 없는지를 당신의 여섯 살 된 딸에게 설명하려고 시도하면서 당신의 혀가 꼬이는 것을 발견하면, 그렇다면 당신은 왜 우리가 기다리는 것을 힘들다고 느끼는지 이해하게 될 것이다.

[정답] ④

05 영작이 올바른 문장을 고르시오.

① 만일 그 물품이 내일까지 배달되지 않으면 그들은 그것에 대해 불평을 할 것이다.
 ⇨ If the item should not be delivered tomorrow, they would complain about it.

② 그는 그의 학급의 어느 다른 야구선수 보다 더욱 능숙하다.
 ⇨ He was more skillful than any other baseball players in his class.

③ 바이올리니스트가 공연을 끝내자마자 관객들은 일어나서 갈채를 보냈다.
 ⇨ Hardly has the violinist finished his performance before the audience stood up and applauded.

④ 제과업자들은 밀의 소비 장려를 요구하며 거리로 나오도록 요구되어 왔다.
 ⇨ Bakers have been made come out, asking for promoting wheat consumption.

[해설] ①에서 미래에 발생할 가능성이 매우 희박한 일을 가정할 때 가정법 미래를 사용한다. 가정법 미래는 「If + 주어 + should / were to + 동사원형, 주어 + 조동사(과거형) + 동사원형」의 형태가 온다. tomorrow를 보아 가정법 미래가 쓰여야 하며, 그 형태가 바르게 사용되었다. ②에서 최상급 대용표현으로 「주어 + 비교급 + than any other + 단수명사」가 사용된다. 따라서 players라는 복수명사가 아닌 player라는 단수명사가 와야 한다. players ⇨ player ③에서 '~하자마자 ~하다'의 표현으로 「Hardly + had + 주어 + p.p.~, when/before + 주어 + 과거시제~」가 온다. 따라서 has가 아니라 had가 되어야한다. has ⇨ had ④에서 사역동사 make가 능동태로 사용된 문장에서 목적격보어로는 원형 부정사가 온다. 그러나 수동태가 될 경우 원형부정사로 쓰인 목적격 보어는 to부정사의 형태가 된다. have been made라는 수동태가 왔으므로 목적격 보어인 come out은 to부정사가 되어야 한다. come out ⇨ to come out

[정답] ①

06 글의 제목으로 가장 적절한 것을 고르시오.

> When we think of the people who make our lives miserable by spreading malicious viruses, most of us imagine an unpopular teenager boy, brilliant but geeky, venting his frustrations from the safety of a suburban bedroom. Actually, these stereotypes are just that — stereotypes — according to Sarah Gordon, an expert in computer viruses and security technology. Since 1992, Gordon has studied the psychology of virus writers. "A virus writer is just as likely to be the guy next door to you," she says. The virus writers Gordon has come to know have varied backgrounds; while predominantly male, some are female. Some are solidly academics, while others are athletic. Many have friendships with members of the opposite sex, good relationships with their parents and families; most are popular with their peers. They don't spend all their time in the basement. One virus writer volunteers in his local library, working with elderly people. One of them is a poet and a musician, another is an electrical engineer, and others work for a university quantum physics department.

① Unmasking Virus Writers
② Virus Writers: Gender and Class
③ Underground Virus Writers
④ Mysterious Activities by Virus Writers

[해설] 글의 전반부에서 우리가 일반적으로 추측하는 바이러스 유포자의 유형에 대해 언급한 후 실제로는 그런 유형은 고정관념일 뿐, 실제 바이러스 유포자는 이웃집 남자처럼 평범하고 다양한 배경을 가지고 있다고 저자는 말한다. 따라서 바이러스 유포자들이 과연 어떤 사람인지 그 정체를 밝히는 글이라 볼 수 있다.
① 바이러스 유포자들의 정체 밝히기 ② 바이러스 유포자 : 성과 계층 ③ 지하의 바이러스 유포자들
④ 바이러스 유포자들의 신비한 행동

[어휘] **miserable** 비참한 **malicious** 사악한 **geeky** 괴짜의 **vent** 발산하다 **frustration** 불만 **suburban** 평범한 **stereotype** 고정관념 **psychology** 심리 **come to** ~하게 되다 **varied** 다양한 **predominantly** 대부분 **solidly** 확고하게 **academic** 학구적인 **athletic** 스포츠맨다운 **volunteer** 자원 봉사로 하다 **electrical engineer** 전기 기술자 **quantum physics** 양자물리학 **unmask** 정체를 드러내다

[해석] 우리가 악성 바이러스를 퍼뜨려 우리의 생활을 비참하게 만드는 사람들에 대해서 생각할 때, 우리 대부분은 안전한 교외의 침실에서 자신의 불만을 표출하는 똑똑하지만 괴짜이고 인기 없는 십대 소년을 상상한다. 컴퓨터 바이러스와 보안 기술 전문가인 Sarah Gordon에 따르면 실제로 이런 고정관념은 단지 고정관념일 뿐이다. 1992년부터 Gordon은 바이러스 유포자들의 심리를 연구해 왔다. "바이러스 유포자들은 단지 당신의 이웃에 사는 남자와 꼭 같을 가능성이 있다"고 그녀는 말한다. Gordon이 알게 된 바로는 바이러스 유포자들은 다양한 배경을 가지고 있다. 대부분이 남성이지만 일부는 여성이다. 일부는 매우 학구적이고, 반면에 다른 사람들은 운동을 좋아한다. 많은 사람들이 다수의 이성 친구와 친구 관계이며 그들의 부모 그리고 가족과 좋은 관계를 유지하고 있다. 대부분은 자신들 또래에서 인기가 있다. 그들은 모든 시간을 지하실에서 보내지 않는다. 한 바이러스 유포자는 지역 도서관에서 나이든 사람과 일하며 자원봉사를 한다. 그들 중 하나는 시인이며 음악가이다. 다른 사람은 전기 기술자이다. 그리고 다른 사람들은 대학의 양자역학학과에서 일한다.

[정답] ①

07 다음 글의 내용으로 가장 적절한 것은?

> The evolution of intelligence among early large mammals of the grasslands was due to the interaction between the hunting carnivores and the herbivores that they hunted. The interaction resulting from the differences between predator and prey led to a general improvement in brain functions; however, certain components of intelligence were improved far more than others. The kind of intelligence favored by the interaction is defined by attention. Herbivores and carnivores develop different kinds of attention related to escaping or chasing. For both, arousal attunes the animal to what is ahead. Perhaps it does not experience forethought as we know it, but the animal does experience something like it. The predator is searchingly aggressive, inner-directed, but aware in a sense closer to human consciousness than, say, a hungry lizard's instinctive snap at a passing beetle. The herbivore prey is of a different mind. It is wary rather than searching, and expectant rather than anticipating.

① Climate was important in establishing the proper relation between predator and prey.
② Lizards are more vigilant to their prey than mammals.
③ Prey species pay attention not to be caught, which developed certatin functions of their brains.
④ The interaction between carnivores and herbivores developed brutality in the mammals.

[해설] 육식동물은 초식동물을 쫓고 초식동물은 육식동물에게 잡히지 않으려고 하는 것이 상호작용이고, 그것은 두 동물의 회피나 추적과 관계된 서로 다른 종류의 주의력을 발달시킨다고 했으므로 뇌의 기능의 발달을 언급한 ③이 옳은 진술이다. ① 기후는 포식자와 먹이 사이의 적절한 관계를 확립하는 데 중요했다. ② 도마뱀은 포유류보다 자신의 먹이에 더 경계를 늦추지 않는다. ③ 피식자 종(초식동물)은 잡히지 않기 위해 주의를 기울인다. 그것 때문에 그들 뇌의 어떤 기능이 발달했다. ④ 육식동물과 초식동물 사이의 상호작용은 포유류의 잔인성을 발달 시켰다.

[어휘] evolution 진화, 발전 intelligence 지능, 정보 mammal 포유동물 carnivore 육식동물 herbivore 초식동물 predator 약탈자 prey 먹이 favor 찬성하다 define 정의하다 attention 주의 arousal 각성 attune 적응시키다 snap 덥석 물기 brutality 잔인성, 무자비 vigilant 방심 않는

[해설] 초원의 초기 대형 포유류들 사이에서 지능의 진화는 사냥하는 육식동물들과 그것들에게 사냥 당하는 초식동물들 사이의 상호 작용 때문이었다. 포식자와 먹이 사이의 차이로 인한 그 상호작용은 뇌 기능의 전반적인 향상을 가져왔다. 하지만 지능의 어떤 요소들은 다른 요소들보다 훨씬 더 향상되었다. 상호작용으로 유리하게 된 지능의 종류는 주의력에 의해 정의된다. 초식동물과 육식동물은 회피나 추적과 관계된 서로 다른 종류의 주의력을 발달시킨다. 초식동물과 육식동물 둘 다에게 흥분상태는 그 동물 앞에 놓인 상황에 적응시킨다. 아마도 육식동물은 우리가 알고 있는 그런 신중함을 경험하지는 않지만 그와 비슷한 어떤 것을 경험한다. 포식자는 면밀하게 공격적이고 내부 지향적이다. 하지만 그것은 가령 배고픈 도마뱀이 지나가는 딱정벌레를 본능적으로 잡아채는 것보다 인간의 의식에 더 가까운 의미에서 인식력이 있다. 초식동물인 먹이는 생각이 다르다. 그것은 탐색적이기 보다는 신중하고, 예상하기 보다는 기다린다.

[정답] ③

08 주어진 글 다음에 이어질 글의 순서로 가장 적절한 것은?

> Two major techniques for dealing with environmental problems are conservation and restoration. Conservation involves protecting existing natural habitats. Restoration involves cleaning up and restoring damaged habitats. The best way to deal with environmental problems is to prevent them from happening. Conserving habitats prevents environmental issues that arise from ecosystem disruption.

> (A) To solve the problem, the city built a sewage-treatment complex. Since then, the harbor waters have cleared up. Plants and fish have returned, and beaches have been reopened.
>
> (B) For example, parks and reserves protect a large area in which many species live. Restoration reverses damage to ecosystems. Boston Harbor is one restoration success story.
>
> (C) Since the colonial period, the city dumped sewage directly into the harbor. The buildup of waste caused outbreaks of disease. Beaches were closed. Most of the marine life disappeared and as a result, the shellfish industry shut down.

① (A) – (B) – (C) ② (B) – (C) – (A)
③ (C) – (A) – (B) ④ (C) – (B) – (A)

[해설] 주어진 글은 환경의 보존과 복원에 대해 이야기 하고 있다. 이에 대한 구체적인 예시를 제시하는 (B)가 연결될 수 있고, (B)에서 복원의 예시로 제시된 보스턴 항구의 사례에 대한 구체적인 설명인 (A), (C)가 이후에 연결될 수 있다. (C)에서 보스턴 항구의 문제가 설명되고 (A)에서 그 문제에 대한 해결책이 제시되므로 (B) – (C) – (A)가 올바른 순서이다. 또한 (B)에서 Boston Harbor가 처음 등장하고, (C)에서 the city와 the harbor라는 언어적 단서가 제시되어 (C)가 (B)에 이어짐을 알 수 있다. 또한 (A)에 있는 the problem, the harbor를 통해 (A)가 (C)에 이어짐도 알 수 있다.

[어휘] deal with 다루다 conservation 보존 restoration 복원 natural habitat 자연 서식지 restore 복원하다 arise from ~에서 발생하다 ecosystem 생태계 disruption 파괴 sewage-treatment complex 폐수처리장 reserve 보호구역 reverse 반전시키다 dump 투기하다 buildup 축적 outbreak 발생 marine life 해양생물 shellfish 조개

[해석] 환경 문제를 다루는 두 가지 주요 기술은 보존과 복원이다. 보존은 현존하는 자연 서식지를 보호하는 것과 관련이 있다. 복원은 깨끗이 청소하는 것과 손상된 서식지를 회복하는 것과 관련이 있다. 환경 문제를 다루는 최상의 방법은 문제가 생기는 것을 막는 것이다. 서식지를 보존하는 것은 생태계 파괴로부터 발생하는 환경 문제를 막는다. (B) 예를 들어 공원과 보호구역은 많은 종들이 사는 거대한 지역을 보호한다. 복원은 생태계에 대한 파괴를 되돌려 놓는다. 보스턴 항구는 하나의 성공적 복원 이야기의 예이다. (C) 식민지 시대부터, 시는 폐수를 항구에 직접 투기했다. 축적된 오물은 질병을 초래했다. 해변은 폐쇄되었다. 대부분의 해양 생물들이 사라졌고 그 결과 갑각류 산업은 문을 닫았다. (A) 이 문제를 해결하기 위해 시는 폐수처리 복합시설을 세웠다. 그 이후 항구의 바닷물은 깨끗해졌다. 식물과 어류가 돌아오고, 해변은 재개장되었다.

[정답] ②

09 다음 빈칸에 들어갈 말로 가장 적절한 것을 고르시오.

Naturally, people eat many different kinds of meals and choose them with the intention of communicating the right message to the right audience. One would not reheat half-eaten leftovers when trying to impress a potential lover, just as one would not spend a fortune on extravagant ingredients for a hurried everyday meal eaten in solitude. Every meal has, in a sense, its own coded message. This is not to say, however, that it is always readily perceived or interpreted correctly by others. What may be intended as cozy informality to someone preparing a meal might be interpreted as laziness by an invited guest. Equally, a meal of roast beef offered to a vegetarian might be construed as a calculated insult. As with all language, there can be _____. Despite this, an outsider observing or commenting on an eating event can usually decode the intended message without too much difficulty.

① usefulness
② borrowing
③ miscommunication
④ correspondence

[해설] 어떤 사람에게 음식을 제공할 때, 그 음식 자체가 메시지를 전달한다는 내용의 글이다. 때로는 음식을 통해 의도한 의미가 아닌 다른 의미가 전달되기도 한다고 했으므로, 빈칸에 ③ '잘못된 전달'이 가장 적절하다.
① 유용성 ② 차용 ④ 유사성

[어휘] **intention** 의도 **leftovers (pl.)** 남은 음식 **potential** 장래에 ~의 가능성이 있는 **extravagant** 사치스러운 **ingredient** 재료 **in solitude** 혼자서 **coded** 암호화된 **cozy** 다정한, 안락한 **informality** 약식 (행위) **roast** 구운 **vegetarian** 채식주의자 **calculated** 계산된 **comment on** ~에 대해 의견을 말하다 **construe** 해석하다 **decode** 해독하다

[해석] 당연히, 사람들은 많은 다른 종류의 음식을 먹으며, 적절한 청중에게 적절한 메시지를 전달하려는 의도를 갖고 그것들을 선택한다. 혼자 허둥대며 먹는 일상의 음식을 위해서 사치스러운 재료에 많은 돈을 쓰지 않는 것처럼, 장래에 연인이 될 가능성이 있는 사람에게 감명을 주기 위해 노력할 때, 반쯤 먹다 남은 음식을 다시 데우지는 않을 것이다. 어떤 의미에서 모든 음식은 그 자체의 암호화된 메시지를 갖고 있다. 그러나 이것이 언제나 다른 사람에게 쉽게 인식되거나 올바르게 해석된다는 말을 하려는 것이 아니다. 식사를 준비하는 사람에게는 다정한 약식 행위로 의도될 수 있는 것이 초대받은 손님에게는 나태함으로 해석될 수도 있다. 마찬가지로, 채식주의자에게 제공된 구운 소고기 식사는 계산된 모욕으로 해석될 수도 있다. 모든 언어에서처럼, 잘못된 전달이 있을 수 있다. 그럼에도 불구하고, 식사하는 것을 관찰하거나 그에 대해서 의견을 말하는 외부인은 보통 아주 큰 어려움 없이 의도된 메시지를 해독할 수 있다.

[정답] ③

10 빈칸 (A), (B)에 들어갈 말로 가장 적절한 것은?

Since the concept of a teddy bear is very obviously not a genetically inherited trait, we can be confident that we are looking at a cultural trait. However, it is a cultural trait that seems to be under the guidance of another, genuinely biological trait: the cues that attract us to babies (high foreheads and small faces). Cute, baby-like features are inherently appealing, producing a nurturing response in most humans. Teddy bears that had a more baby-like appearance — however slight this may have been initially — were thus more popular with customers. Teddy bear manufacturers obviously noticed which bears were selling best and so made more of these and fewer of the less popular models, to maximize their profits. In this way, the selection pressure built up by the customers resulted in the evolution of a more baby-like bear by the manufacturers.

Due to its inherent attraction and ___(A)___ considerations, the teddy bear has been transformed to the present baby-like appearance, showing that a cultural trait can be ___(B)___ by a biological trait.

	(A)	(B)		(A)	(B)
①	commercial	guided	②	commercial	replaced
③	intellectual	guided	④	intellectual	represented

정답 ①

02 하프 모의고사 해설

01 다음 밑줄 친 단어의 의미와 가장 가까운 것은?

> He would only make himself ridiculous by quoting poetry to them which they could not understand. They would think that he was airing his superior education.

① concealing
② refreshing
③ jilting
④ showing off

[해설] air [ɛər] 동 방송하다, 드러내 보이다, ~을 공표하다, 퍼뜨리다, 쇄신하다 = show off
[영영] air : make public
[어휘] ridiculous 우스운, 우스꽝스러운 quote 인용하다 superior 상급의, 우수한 conceal 숨기다, 감추다 refresh 상쾌하게 하다, 재충전하다, 기운을 차리다 jilt 버리다
[해석] 그들이 이해할 수 없는 시를 그들에게 인용함으로써 그는 단지 자신을 우스꽝스럽게 만들 뿐이었다. 그들은 그가 고급교육을 받았다는 것을 자랑하고 있다고 생각했다.

[정답] ④

02 다음 밑줄 친 단어의 의미와 가장 가까운 것은?

> Severe droughts, floods and heat waves rocked the world last year as greenhouse gas levels climbed, boosting the odds of some extreme weather events.

① chances
② solutions
③ dangers
④ symptoms

[해설] the odd [adz] 명 가능성, 불평등, 가망, 확률 = chance, probability, difference
[영영] the odd : the likelihood of a thing occurring rather than not occurring
[어휘] drought 가뭄 flood 홍수 heat wave 장기간의 rock 요동치게 하다 greenhouse 온실 extreme 극단적인 solution 용해
[해석] 온실가스 수치가 상승하여 몇몇 극단적인 날씨 현상이 발생할 확률을 끌어올림에 따라 작년에 극심한 가뭄 홍수 무더위가 세계에 불어 닥쳤다.

[정답] ①

02 하프 모의고사 해설 **123**

03 다음 빈칸에 들어갈 단어로 가장 적절한 것은?

> The ultimate value of any hypothesis lies in its predictive or explanatory power, which means that additional facts must be _____ from an adequate hypothesis.

① deducible
② vulnerable
③ conductible
④ inseparable

[해설] 가설의 궁극적인 가치는 예측력이나 설명력에 있다고 한 다음 계속적 용법의 관계대명사절에서 이 말의 의미를 설명하고 있다. 적절한 가설이라면 추가적인 사실들을 추론해 낼 수 있을 것이다.

[어휘] **ultimate** 궁극의, 최종적인 **hypothesis** 가설 **predictive** 예언[예보]하는 **explanatory** 설명적인, 해석의 **adequate** 적당한, 충분한 **vulnerable** 비난[공격] 받기 쉬운, 약점이 있는 **conductible** 전도성의, 전도되는 **inseparable** 불리할 수 없는, 불가분의 **deducible** 추론할 수 있는

[해석] 어떤 가설의 궁극적인 가치는 가설의 예측력이나 설명력에 있다. 이것은 (부가적으로) 더해지는 사실들이 적절한 가설에서 추론될 수 있어야 한다는 것을 의미한다.

[정답] ①

04 다음 밑줄 친 부분 중, 어법상 틀린 것은?

> We are constantly losing land to new ① <u>housing</u> developments, and I have seen the lands ② <u>on which</u> I grew up ③ <u>playing</u> slowly ④ <u>to shrink</u> away.

[해설] ①에서는 '주택 건설' '주택 개발'이란 뜻의 명사로 쓰였다. ②에서는 **which**의 선행사는 **the lands**이며, '땅 위에서 자란 것'이므로 전치사 **on**을 쓴 것이다. 더불어 **on which** 뒤에 완전한 문장이 이어짐을 확인할 수 있다. ③에서는 관계사절 속에서 보어의 역할을 하는 현재분사이며, **play** 동사는 자동사로 쓰였다. ④에서는 **have seen**의 목적어는 **the lands**부터 **playing**까지다. ④는 목적보어인데, 지각동사 **see**의 목적보어는 **to**부정사가 아닌 원형동사이여야 하므로 **to shrink**를 **shrink**로 고쳐야 한다.

[해석] 우리는 새로운 주택 개발로 끊임없이 땅을 잃고 있으며, 나는 내가 놀며 자랐던 땅들이 서서히 줄어드는 것을 보아왔다.

[정답] ④

05 다음 빈칸에 들어갈 알맞은 것은?

It is a widely known fact that heat makes gases _____.

① expand
② to expand
③ being expanded
④ to be expanded

[해설] 사역동사 make의 목적보어로는 동사원형이 와야 하며, expand가 '팽창하다'라는 뜻의 자동사로 쓰일 수 있으므로 ①이 정답이다.

[해석] 기체를 가열하면 팽창한다는 사실은 널리 알려져 있다.

[정답] ①

06 어법상 가장 적절한 것은?

① The roof of the house needs being painted.
② One hour's delay will not bother me.
③ I ask only that I am treated with respect.
④ I bought this blue dress of my sister at the department store.

[해설] ①에서는 사물이 주어로 쓰인 동사 need, want 등의 뒤에 능동의 동명사가 오면 수동의 의미를 갖는다. 따라서 being painted를 painting으로 고쳐야 한다. ②에서는 사물의 경우 일반적으로 소유격 표현을 쓰지 않으나, 시간, 무게, 거리 등을 나타낼 때에는 소유격 표현이 가능하다. ③에서는 제안, 요구, 주장, 명령의 뜻을 가진 동사의 목적어로 쓰인 that절 안의 동사는 '(should) 동사원형'으로 써야 한다. 주어진 문장에서 동사 ask가 요구의 의미이므로, 이것이 이끄는 that절속의 동사는 ('should) 동사원형'이 되어야 한다. am을 be 혹은 should be로 고친다. ④에서는 인칭대명사의 소유격과 한정사(관사, 지시형용사, 소유격, 부정형용사 등)는 하나의 명사를 중복해서 수식할 수 없으므로 이중소유격의 형태로 나타내야 한다. 따라서 my sister를 my sister's로 고친다.

[해석] ① 그 집의 지붕은 페인트칠을 해야 한다. ② 한 시간 지연되는 것이 나에게 폐를 끼치지는 않을 것이다. ③ 나는 단지 존경심을 갖고 나를 대우해주기를 요구할 뿐이다. ④ 나는 내 여동생의 이 파란 드레스를 백화점에서 구입했다.

[정답] ②

07 다음 글의 빈칸에 들어갈 말로 가장 적절한 것을 고르시오.

City dwellers are accustomed to speed and change, and little disturbed by the unusual. They are, however, more _____ than their rural neighbors. City life affords more opportunities for wrongdoing, and crime is more prevalent in cities than in rural regions. The absence of many restraints tends to increase the crime rate in large cities. The city, with its almost limitless potentialities for the welfare and happiness of its inhabitants, also contains possibilities of evil greater than ever before. In addition, city dwellers know more about world affairs than do rural dwellers because of their readier access to newspapers, books, magazines, etc. Their knowledge of other peoples and other cultures tends to break down ancient prejudices, but it also weakens the hold of traditions and ideals which have a steady influence on character.

① isolated
② competitive
③ restless
④ self-centered

해설 첫 문장과 대조되는 빈칸 문장 이후의 뒷받침하는 내용을 단서로 활용한다. 범죄율이 증가하고, 해악의 가능성이 커졌으며, 전통과 이상의 영향력이 약해진 현실 속에서 도시인들이 느낄 수 있는 것은 '불안감(restless)'일 것이다. ① 분리[격리]된, 고립된 ② 경쟁의, 경쟁 상대를 이용하는 ④ 자기 본위의, 자기중심의, 이기적인.

어휘 dweller 거주자, 주민 be accustomed to ~에 익숙하다 disturbed 동요되는, 교란되는 rural 시골의, 지방의 afford 제공하다 wrongdoing 비행, 위법행위 prevalent 만연한, 널리 행해지는 absence 부재, 결석 restraint 제한, 억제 limitless 무제한의 potentiality 가능성, 잠재력 inhabitant 주민 contain 포함하다 evil 악, 해악 affair 일, 사건 ready 쉬운 access to ~에 접근, ~의 입수[획득] prejudice 편견 hold 영향력, 지배력 steady 꾸준한, 안정된

해석 도시 거주자들은 속도와 변화에 익숙하며 특이한 것을 별로 동요되지 않는다. 그러나 그들은 시골에 사는 이웃사람들보다 더 불안감을 느낀다. 도시 생활은 비행의 더 많은 기회를 제공하며, 범죄는 시골 지역보다 도시에서 더 만연한다. 많은 제한이 없는 것이 대도시에서의 범죄율을 증가시키는 경향이 있다. 도시는 주민들의 복지와 행복을 위한 거의 무제한의 가능성이 있지만 또한 전보다 더 큰 해악의 가능성을 가지고 있다. 게다가 신문과 서적, 잡지 등을 더 가까이하기 쉽기 때문에 시골에 사는 사람들보다 세상사에 대해 더 많이 알고 있다. 다른 민족들과 다른 문화권에 대한 그들의 지식은 옛 편견들을 무너뜨리는 경향은 있지만, 성격에 꾸준히 영향을 미치는 전통과 이상의 영향력을 또한 약화시키기도 한다.

정답 ③

08 다음 글의 제목으로 가장 적절한 것은?

The problem that judges face is not that there are too many rules. A legal system is made up of rules, and the task of judges is to help interpret the rules in particular situations. Judges are prevented from doing this work well when they are required to pick one of the multiple aims of sentencing, like retribution, and prevented from balancing it with other important aims, like rehabilitation. They are forbidden from exercising judgment when rigid sentencing rules deny them the discretion to interpret the circumstances, to make this punishment fit this crime and this individual. But it's not only rigid rules like mandatory sentencing laws that discourage the wisdom to balance and interpret. Sometimes good principles, coupled with the best of intentions, can have the same effect. Principles are valuable guidelines, and we'd be lost without them. We admire principled people. We want our politicians to act on principle and not out of narrow self-interest. Protect human rights. Protect national security. Defend free speech. Our codes of professional ethics are all about the good principles that should guide doctors, lawyers, and architects. Respect for client and patient autonomy. Loyalty. Trust. "Unprincipled" is an epithet. But like rules, good principles, unleavened by judgment, can be dangerous. They can make us dumb to the nuances of context. A good principle can blind us to other good principles with which it needs to be balanced. In policy making, the results can be disastrous. In the everyday work of doctors, the results are bad practice.

① The Danger of a Good Principle
② The Great Principle of Humanity
③ Good Principles vs. Bad Principle
④ Principles that Judges Have to Stick to

[해설] 좋은 원칙이라는 이유로 다른 중요한 목적들과 균형을 이루지 못하고 상황에 따라 판단이 변화하지 않는 원칙의 위험성에 대해 쓴 글이다. 그러므로 이 글의 제목으로는 ①'좋은 원칙의 위험성'이 가장 적절하다. ② 인간성의 위대한 원칙 ③ 좋은 원칙 대 나쁜 원칙 ④ 판사가 고수해야 하는 원칙들

[어휘] sentence ~에게 판결을 내리다 retribution 처벌, 징벌 rehabilitation 갱생, 사회 복귀 rigid 엄격한, 완고한 discretion (자유) 재량, 판단[선택·행동]의 자유, 결정권 mandatory 의무적인, 강제적인 security 안보, 안전 autonomy 자율권, 자치권 dumb 우둔한, 말을 못 하는 nuance 미묘한 차이, 뉘앙스 context 맥락, 상황, 사정 practice (의사·변호사 등의) 업무, 영업

[해석] 판사들이 직면하는 문제는 규정이 너무 많다는 것이 아니다. 법체계는 규정들로 구성되어 있고 판사의 임무는 특정 상황에서 그 규정들을 해석하는 것을 돕는 것이다. 판사들은 자신들이 처벌과 같은 판결의 다양한 목적들 중 하나를 선택할 필요가 있을 때, 그리고 그 목적을 갱생과 같은 다른 중요한 목적들과 균형을 이루지 못할 때 이 일(규정을 해석하는 일)을 잘하지 못하게 된다. 판사들은 엄격한 양형 규정으로 인해서, '이' 처벌은 '이' 범죄에 적합하고 '이' 개인에게 적합하도록 하는 상황을 해석하는 재량권이 인정되지 않을 때 제대로 판결을 하지 못하게 된다. 하지만 균형을 이루고 해석하는 지혜를 좌절시키는 것은 의무적인 양형 법률과 같은 엄격한 규정들뿐만이 아니다. 때때로 가장 좋은 의도와 결부된 좋은 원칙들도 같은 결과를 가져올 수 있다. 원칙은 가치 있는 지침이며, 그것들이 없으면 우리는 길을 잃게 될 것이다. 우리는 원칙에 입각한 사람들을 존경한다. 우리는 정치가들이 편협한 사리 추구에서가 아니라 원칙에 따라 행동하기를

원한다. 인권을 보호하라. 국가 안보를 보호하라. 표현의 자유를 지켜라. 우리의 직업윤리 규범은 모두 의사, 변호사, 그리고 건축가들을 인도해야 하는 좋은 원칙들에 관한 것이다. 고객과 환자의 자율권에 대한 존중. 충성. 신뢰. '원칙이 없는'이란 말은 욕설이다. 하지만 규정들처럼 판단에 의해 영향을 받지 않는 좋은 원칙들은 위험할 수 있다. 그것들은 우리를 맥락의 미묘한 차이에 우둔하게 할 수 있다. 좋은 원칙은 우리로 하여금 균형을 이룰 필요가 있는 다른 좋은 원칙들을 못 보게 할 수 있다. 정책을 만드는 데 있어서 그 결과는 재앙이 될 수 있다. 의사들의 일상의 일에서 그 결과는 잘못된 의료 행위이다.

[정답] ①

09 다음 글의 밑줄 친 부분 중, 문맥상 낱말의 쓰임이 적절하지 않은 것은?

Good writers are not passive; they don't simply record ① <u>immediate</u> responses. They look closely, ask questions, analyze, make connections, and think. Learning to see with a writer's eye ② <u>benefits</u> not just those who write for a living but all professionals. In any career you choose, success depends on keen observation and in-depth analysis. A skilled physician detects minor symptoms in a physical or follows up on a patient's complaint to ask questions that lead to a diagnosis others might miss. A successful stockbroker observes ③ <u>overlooked</u> trends and conducts research to detect new investment opportunities. A passerby might assume a busy store must be successful, but a retail analyst would observe what merchandise people are purchasing and how they are paying for it. If all the shoppers are buying discount items and paying with credit cards, the store could be ④ <u>earning</u> money on the sales.

[해설] 모든 쇼핑객이 구매하는 것이 할인 품목이고 신용카드로 지불한다면 그 가게는 제품 판매에서 돈을 잃을 수 있으므로 ④ earning을 losing 정도로 바꿔야 한다.

[어휘] passive 수동적인 immediate 즉각적인 analyze 분석하다 benefit ~에게 이롭다; 이익 keen 예리한, 날카로운 observation 관찰 in-depth 심층적인 physician 의사, 내과의사 detect 찾아내다, 발견하다 complaint 질환, 병, 고충, 불평 diagnosis 진단(법) overlook 간과하다, 빠뜨리고 보다 passerby 지나가는 사람 assume 추측하다, 추정하다 retail 소매(의) merchandise 상품, 제품

[해석] 훌륭한 작가들은 수동적이지 않고 즉각적인 반응을 그냥 기록만 하지는 않는다. 그들은 '자세히 살피고', '질문하고', '분석하고', '연관시키고', 그리고 '생각한다'. 작가의 눈으로 보는 것을 배우는 것은 글쓰기를 업으로 삼는 사람들뿐만 아니라 모든 전문직 종사자들에게 도움이 된다. 여러분이 선택하는 그 어떤 직업에서든 성공은 예리한 관찰과 심층적인 분석에 달려 있다. 노련한 의사는 신체검사에서 가벼운 증상을 찾아내거나 환자의 푸념에 대해 더 알아보고 다른 사람들이 놓칠 수 있는 진단으로 이끄는 질문을 한다. 성공한 증권 중개인은 간과된 경향을 관찰하고 연구해서 새로운 투자 기회를 찾아낸다. 행인은 붐비는 가게는 틀림없이 번창한다고 추측할 수 있지만, 소매 분석가는 사람들이 어떤 상품을 구매하고 있는지, 그리고 그것에 대해 어떻게 지불하고 있는지 관찰할 것이다. 모든 쇼핑객이 할인 품목을 구매하면서 신용 카드로 지불하고 있다면, 그 가게는 판매할 때 돈을 벌고(→ 잃고)있을 수 있다.

[정답] ④

10 다음 글의 내용과 일치하지 않는 것은?

Western civilization arose in the Near East and spread eventually to North America and other continents. For two thousand years, however, it has been intimately associated with Europe. A mere peninsula of Asia, Europe is, except for Australia, the smallest of the continents. Its population, even counting offshoots overseas, has never been more than a minority of mankind. Yet it had played a towering role in the world. The extraordinary length and irregularity of its coastline—a veritable lacework of bays, inlets, channels, and internal seas—and a rich system of riverways brought Europeans close to one another and gave them access to the rest of the world. Although it is situated in the same latitudes as Canada, Europe has a moderate climate and a fairly regular rainfall. The resources of the continent are sufficiently modest to exact effort and forethought and sufficiently ample to regard them. They have neither the luxuriance that makes man lazy and improvident nor the barrenness that makes him niggardly and takes away his hope.

① Western civilization originated from the Near East.
② Natural conditions in Europe were good for shipping.
③ European populations grew rapidly with Western civilization.
④ Europe had resources that were neither too plentiful nor too scarce.

[해설] European populations grew rapidly with Western civilization. ⇨ 그 인구는 비록 후손들까지 합쳐도 소수민족보다 많은 적이 없었다.//본문의 내용과 일치하지 않는다. ① Western civilization originated from the Near East. ⇨ 서구 문명이 근동 지역에서 일어나 결국 북아메리카와 다른 대륙으로 퍼졌다.(○) ② Natural conditions in Europe were good for shipping. ⇨ 해안선의 특히 길고 불규칙적인 것은 진짜 세공으로 다듬어진 만들, 입구, 해협 그리고 육지로 둘러싸인 풍부한 강줄기들은 유럽인을 다른 것들과 밀접하게 하였으며 세계의 나머지와 접근할 수 있게 했다. ④ Europe had resources that were neither too plentiful nor too scarce. ⇨ 대륙의 자원들은 땀 흘린 노력과 기대치에 합당한 만큼의 적당량을 얻기에 충분하다고 간주되고 있다.

[어휘] offshoot (씨족의) 분파, 분가 irregularity 불규칙 veritable 실제의, 진실의 lacework 레이스 세공 inlet 후미, 입구 luxuriance 무성, 풍부 improvident 경솔한, 부주의한 barrenness 불모, 메마름 niggardly 인색한, 쩨쩨한, 빈약한 moderate (기후 등이) 알맞은, 온화한 modest 적당한, 겸손한 ample 충분한, 넓은 forethought 깊은 생각, 신중

[해석] 서구 문명이 근동 지역에서 일어나 결국 북아메리카와 다른 대륙으로 퍼졌다. 그러나 2000년간 그것은 즉시 유럽과 관련이 되었다. 아시아의 하나의 반도에 속하는 유럽은 호주를 제외하고 가장 작은 대륙이다. 그 인구는 비록 후손들까지 합쳐도 소수민족보다 많은 적이 없었다. 하지만 그것은 세계에서 큰 역할을 했다. 해안선의 특히 길고 불규칙적인 것은 진짜 세공으로 다듬어진 만들, 입구, 해협 그리고 육지로 둘러싸인 풍부한 강줄기들은 유럽인을 다른 것들과 밀접하게 하였으며 세계의 나머지와 접근할 수 있게 했다. 유럽은 비록 캐나다와 같은 경도에 있지만 유럽은 온화한 기후와 다소 일정한 강우량을 갖고 있다. 대륙의 자원들은 땀 흘린 노력과 기대치에 합당한 만큼의 적당량을 얻기에 충분하다고 간주되고 있다. 그것은 게으르게 하거나 경솔하게 할 만큼 충분하지도 않고 인색하게 만들거나 희망을 빼앗아갈 만큼 메마르지도 않다.

[정답] ③

03 하프 모의고사 해설

01 다음 밑줄 친 단어의 의미와 가장 가까운 것은?

> His promise of <u>unyielding</u> support for the policy, however, is a cause of concern, rather than an act of reassurance for many people, who aptly regard the policy as a failure.

① opinionated ② implead
③ denounce ④ insulate

[해설] unyielding [ənjíːldiŋ] 형 완고한, 굽히지 않는, 단호한, 단단한 = opinionated
[영영] unyielding : ① stubbornly unyielding ② resistant to physical force or pressure
[어휘] implead, denounce 기소하다, 고소하다 insulate 격리시키다
[해석] 하지만 정책에 대하여 그가 굽히지 않는 지지를 약속하는 것이 그 정책을 실패로 간주하는 많은 사람들에게는 확신을 주기보다는 걱정거리가 되고 있다.

[정답] ①

02 다음 빈칸에 들어갈 표현으로 적절한 것을 고르시오.

> The poet just wants to sit and meditate, _____ against a post.

① while his back leaning ② with his back is leaning
③ while his back to lean ④ with his back leaning

[해설] while은 접속사로 절이 와야 하므로, ①과 ③은 빈칸에 들어갈 수 없는 반면, with는 전치사로 뒤에 절이 올 수 없으므로 ②도 빈칸에 들어갈 수 없다. ④의 with his back leaning은 '분사구문의 부대상황(with + 목적어 + 현재분사)'으로 빈칸에 적절하다.

> [원팩더하기] With 부대상황
> With + 목 + 분사 [ing/p.p/형용사/부사(구)]
> – with 목적어 (being) 형용사/부사(구)
> • With that presentation (being) satisfactory, we ~
>   그 발표가 만족스러워서, 우리는~
> • With many children (being) at school, we can't~
>   많은 아이들이 학교에 있어서, 우리는 ~할 수 없다.

[해석] 그 시인은 등을 기둥에 기댄 채, 그냥 앉아서 명상하기를 원한다.

[정답] ④

03 (A), (B), (C) 각 빈칸 문맥에 맞는 말로 가장 적절한 것은?

> Ishan works for a large PR and advertising company, he is responsible for sourcing images from photographic agents. He reports to the creative director who is very supportive and encouraging when Ishan wants to discuss work issues face to face, but appears uncaring and combative when he communicates with Ishan via e-mail. This is because when the creative director writes e-mails, he does not ___(A)___ the 'softer' elements of the conversation that take place when he is discussing the issues face to face. His e-mails are written in a list style, setting out the tasks that must be completed to 'fix' the situations, whereas when he meets with Isahn he will ___(B)___ the difficulties and will even makes jokes about the problems to lighten the atmosphere. This more ___(C)___ approach is not reflected in his written style, and even though Ishan knows he means no harm, his e-mail imply impatience and anger about the situation which makes Ishan worry, and question whether he should have raised the issue in the first place.

	(A)	(B)	(C)
①	exclude	acknowledge	relaxed
②	exclude	ignore	aggressive
③	include	acknowledge	aggressive
④	include	acknowledge	relaxed

[해설] (A) 광고 제작 감독이 대면하면서 일할 때의 호의적인 모습과는 달리 | 이메일로 연락할 때는 호전적이게 되는 이유는 대면하면서 일할 때의 더 부드러운 요소가 이메일에서는 포함되어 있지 않기 때문이다. 따라서 '포함하다'의 뜻인 include가 적절하다. exclude는 '배제하다'라는 뜻이다. (B) 광고 제작 감독이 대면하면서 일할 때 호의적으로 대하려고 하는 모습을 설명하는 문장이므로, '인정하다'를 의미하는 acknowledge가 적절하다. ignore는 '무시하다'라는 뜻이다. (C) 이메일로 연락할 때에는 반영되지 않는, 대면해서 일할 때의 접근 방식이므로 '여유 있는'을 의미하는 relaxed가 적절하다. aggressive는 '공격적인'이라는 뜻이다.

[어휘] PR 홍보 (public relations) source (특정한 곳에서 무엇을) 공급받다 agent 대리인 supportive 도움을 주는 encouraging 호의적인, 격려하는 uncaring 배려심이 없는 combative 호전적인 via ~을 통하여 element 요소 set out ~을 제시하다, 진열하다 lighten 가볍게 하다 atmosphere 분위기 reflect 반영하다 imply 암시하다 impatience 조바심, 조급함 raise (문제를) 거론하다, 제기하다

[해석] Ishan은 큰 홍보 및 광고 회사를 위해 일하는데, 거기서 그는 사진 대리인으로부터 이미지를 공급받는 업무를 맡고 있다. 그는 대면하면서 업무상 사안에 대해 논의하고 싶어 할 때는 매우 도움을 주고 호의적이지만 이메일을 통해 연락할 때는 배려심이 없고 호전적으로 보이는 광고 제작 감독에게 업무 보고를 한다. 이것은 그 광고 제작 감독이 이메일을 쓸 때는, 사안에 대해 대면하여 논의할 때 일어나는 대화의 '더 부드러운' 요소를 포함하지 않기 때문이다. 그의 이메일은 나열식으로 쓰여 있어서 상황을 '해결'하기 위해 완수되어야 하는 과업들은 제시하고 있는 반면, Ishan과 만날 때 그는 으레 어려움을 인정하며 분위기를 가볍게 하기 위해 그 문제에 대해 농담도 한다. 이러한 더 여유 있는 접근 방법은 그의 글쓰기 방식에는 반영되어 있지 않은데, Ishan은 그가 악의가 없다는 것을 알지만 그의 이메일은 Ishan을 근심하게 하는 상황에 대한 조바심과 분노를 암시하고 있으며, 우선 그가 그 문제를 거론했어야 했는지를 문제시한다.

[정답] ④

04 다음 글의 밑줄 친 부분 중, 어법상 틀린 것은?

> A space rock ① <u>big enough to</u> cause widespread damage will hit the Earth only about once ② <u>every 1,000 year</u>, but experts say the destruction would be ③ <u>so extreme</u> that nations should develop a joint defense ④ <u>against space rocks</u>.

[해설] every가 '~마다'의 의미로 쓰일 때 뒤에는 복수형 명사가 온다. 예를 들어서 '4년 마다'를 표현할 때에는 every four years나 every fourth year를 쓴다. 물론 '1년마다'를 표현할 때에는 every one year라 써야 한다. 따라서 ②의 '1,000년마다'의 표현을 쓰기 위해 every 1,000 year를 every 1,000 years로 고쳐야 적절하다. ③의 so는 뒤의 결과의 내용을 이끄는 that절과 연결되는 so~that구문을 쓴 것이라서 so 자리에 very, much, too등은 쓸 수 없다.

[해석] 광범위한 피해를 입힐 수 있을 만큼 큰 우주석이 대략 1,000년에 한 번씩 지구에 떨어질 것이다. 그러나 전문가들은 그 파괴력이 너무나 대단해서 국가들은 우주석을 막을 연합방어책을 마련해야 한다고 말한다.

[정답] ② every 1,000 year ⇨ every 1,000 years

05 어법상 가장 적절한 것은?

① Ken could be a very attractive man but he pays no attention to his clothes.
② The researchers agreed, at principle, to exchange their findings.
③ Your method seems as odd to us as ours do to you.
④ She was a glad girl and liked to hang out with her classmates.

[해설] ①에서는 '가정법 + but[except, save] + 직설법' 구문이 쓰인 문장이다. 앞 문장의 '주동사의 과거형 + 동사원형'의 구조를 통해 가정법 과거의 문장임을 알 수 있는데, 이것은 현재 사실의 반대를 가정하는 것이므로 이어지는 접속사 but 다음에 문장에는 직설법 현재시제가 온 것이다. ②에서는 동사 agreed와 목적어 to exchange their findings 사이에 at principle이 삽입되어 있다. '원칙적으로'라는 의미를 나타낼 경우 principle은 전치사 in과 함께 쓰인다. 따라서 at principle을 in principle로 고친다. ③에서는 소유대명사 ours는 our method를 의미하므로 대동사 do는 단수형 does가 되어야 한다. ④에서는 glad가 한정적 용법의 형용사로 쓰일 경우 사람을 수식할 수 없다. 따라서 한정적 용법이 가능한 happy나 bright 등의 형용사로 바꾸어야 한다. hang out with는 '~와 친하게 지내다'라는 의미의 숙어표현이다.

[해석] ① 켄은 매우 매력적인 사람이 될 수도 있지만, 그는 옷에 신경을 쓰지 않는다. ② 연구원들은 그들의 연구 결과를 교환하는 데 원칙적으로 합의했다. ③ 우리의 방법이 너희에게 이상하게 보이는 만큼 너희의 방법도 우리에게 이상하게 보인다. ④ 그녀는 명랑한 소녀였고 학급 친구들과 어울리는 것을 좋아했다.

[정답] ①

06 다음 글의 요지로 적절한 것을 고르시오.

You've got a vocabulary list to learn for your French class. What's the best way to study? You might be tempted to stare at the words for a long time — reading, then reading again. And again. After this exercise — with more staring, followed by more reading — you might hope the words and translations should have been copied into your head like songs into an iPod. There may be a better way to remember: More testing! We often think of testing as a way to measure how much information a person remembers, but research shows that testing can be a powerful study strategy as well. In a recent experiment, researchers found that students who were quizzed as they studied scored higher on vocabulary tests than the students who only read and reread. That's not too surprising — teachers have told students for thousands of years that self-testing is a good study strategy.

① Memory recall is a useful skill to have a conversation with foreigners.
② Small quizzes involve recovering stored information from memory.
③ Quizzing yourself while studying beats staring at words for word acquisition.
④ The translation process starts by pronouncing words a person wants to memorize.

[해설] 이 글은 단어를 학습하는 데 있어 단어를 오랫동안 바라보는 것 보다는 시험이 강력한 학습전략이 될 수 있으며 이를 뒷받침 해주는 실험에서 시험을 보는 학생들이 어휘시험에서 반복해서 단어를 읽기만 했던 학생들보다 더 높은 성적을 받았다고 했으므로 이 글의 요지로 ③ '공부하면서 스스로 퀴즈를 내는 것은 단어 습득을 위한 단어들을 보는 것을 이긴다.'이 적절하다. ① 기억을 불러오는 것은 외국인과 대화를 할 때 유용한 기술이다. ② 작은 퀴즈는 메모리에서 저장된 정보를 복구하는 것을 포함한다. ④ 번역 과정은 사람이 외우고 싶은 단어를 발음하는 것으로 시작한다.

[어휘] tempt 관심 끌다, 마음을 끌다 stare 응시하다(at) measure 판단하다, 평가하다 conduct 행하다, 처리하다 quiz ~에게 질문하다, 테스트를 하다

[해석] 당신은 불어수업 시간에 배워야할 어휘 목록을 갖고 있다. 가장 좋은 공부 방법은 무엇인가? 당신은 오랫동안 그 단어들을 읽고 또 읽으면서 뚫어지게 보고 싶은 마음이 들지도 모른다. 그리고 이 과정을 되풀이 한다. 더 보고 더 읽는 연습을 하고 나면 노래가 아이팟에 들어가듯 단어와 해석이 머릿속에 복사되었기를 기대할지도 모른다. 기억하는 데 더 좋은 방법이 있을지도 모른다. 시험을 더 많이 보는 것이다. 우리는 종종 시험을 한 사람이 얼마나 많은 양의 정보를 기억하고 있는지 측정하는 방법으로 생각한다. 하지만 시험은 강력한 학습전략이 될 수도 있다. 최근 실시된 실험 에서 연구자들은 공부하면서 시험을 보았던 학생들이 어휘 시험에서 반복해 서 읽기만 한 학생들보다 더 높은 성적을 받았다는 것을 알게 되었다. 이것은 그리 놀랄 일은 아니다. 선생님들은 아주 오랫동안 자가 평가가 훌륭한 학습전략이라고 학생들에 말해왔다.

[정답] ③

07 다음 빈칸에 들어갈 말로 가장 적절한 것을 고르시오.

A remarkable feature of sugar is the ways in which, over the course of time, it has been employed _____. When thoroughly mixed together, sugar and ground almonds with a bit of oil becomes a kind of modeling clay. When heated, refined white sugar liquefies. Properly handled as it dries, it can be dyed, spun, blown, artistically cast, or painted. Its uses in these ways have long existed in China, India, and the Middle East. Once sugar spread from the Old World to the New, its production expanded explosively, and it was put to such uses in many other places. Hence, there is no single center of origin for the artistic uses of sugar, even though the baker-sculptors of Egypt, Italy, Germany, and the United Kingdom, and the candy makers of Mexico and Indonesia, among others, are justly famous. Spun and sculpted sugar figures — some classic, some comical — seem to have become popular wherever artistic individuals happened to work in or near kitchens.

① medically
② collectively
③ aesthetically
④ competitively

[해설] 설탕은 약간의 기름이 들어가서 분말 아몬드와 섞이면 조형 점토가 되어 여러 가지 예술적인 방식으로 사용될 수 있으며, 중국, 인도, 그리고 중동에서 그런 용도로 오래 전부터 사용되어 오다가, 신세계에서도 그렇게 사용되기 시작했으며, 설탕 조각상은 예술적인 기질을 가진 사람들이 부엌이나 부엌 근처에서 일하는 곳이면 어디든 인기가 있었다는 내용의 글이다. 글 전체적으로 설탕이 예술적으로 사용되었다는 것을 말하고 있으므로, 빈칸에 들어갈 말로는 ③ '미적으로'가 가장 적절하다. ① 의학적으로 ② 집단적으로 ④ 경쟁적으로

[어휘] **feature** 특징, 특성 **employ** 사용하다, 이용하다 **thoroughly** 완전히, 철저히 **ground almond** 분말 아몬드 **modeling clay** 조형 점토 **refined** 정제된 **properly** 적절하게 **spin** 실을 잣다 **cast** 주조하다 **Old World** 구세계(유럽, 아시아, 아프리카를 가리킴) **New World** 신세계(과거에 남북 아메리카를 가리키던 말) **expand** 확대되다 **explosively** 폭발적으로 **hence** 이런 이유로 **sculptor** 조각가 **sculpt** 조각하다 **figure** 인물 상(像), 조상(彫像) **liquefy** 액화되다

[해석] 설탕의 놀랄 만한 특징은 시간이 흐름에 따라 그것이 미적으로 사용되어 온 방식이다. 한데 완전히 섞이면, 약간의 기름이 들어간 설탕과 분말 아몬드는 일종의 조형 점토가 된다. 가열이 되면 정제된 백설탕은 액화된다. 마를 때 적절히 처리해 주면, 그것을 염색하거나, 실로 만들거나, 바람을 불어 모양을 만들거나, 예술적으로 주조하거나, 혹은 색칠할 수 있다. 이런 방식으로 그것을 사용하는 것은 중국, 인도, 그리고 중동에서 오래 전부터 존재해 왔다. 설탕이 일단 구(舊)세계에서 신(新)세계로 퍼지자, 그것의 생산이 폭발적으로 확대되었고, 그것은 많은 다른 곳에서 그런 용도로 쓰였다. 이런 이유로, 이집트, 이탈리아, 독일, 그리고 영국의 빵으로 조각을 하는 제빵사와 다른 곳들 중에서도 멕시코와 인도네시아의 사탕 제조업자가 당연히 유명함에도 불구하고, 설탕의 예술적 사용에 대한 기원의 중심이 단 한 곳에만 있는 것은 아니다. 실로 만들어지고 조각된 설탕 조각상은 (어떤 것들은 고전적이고, 어떤 것들은 익살스러운데) 예술적인 기질을 가진 사람들이 부엌이나 부엌 근처에서 우연히 일했던 곳이면 어디에서든지 인기가 있었던 것처럼 보인다.

[정답] ③

08 글의 흐름으로 보아, 주어진 문장이 들어가기에 가장 적절한 곳은?

> The adjustment of the rods to dim light is caused by the production of a chemical called rhodopsin or "visual purple."

Have you ever gone from a bright sunny afternoon into a dark motion picture theatre? Once inside, you are not surprised to find that you're practically blind for a while. (①) After about 5 minutes, you'll find your sight returning, with colors becoming more visible as your cones adapt to the darkness. (②) Over the course of approximately 30 minutes, your rods attain their full sensitivity. (③) Slight improvements in your dim-light vision may continue for a considerable length of time after that. (④) The amount of this substance in your rods determines how sensitive they are to light. Exposure to bright light fades rhodopsin out of the eye and causes it to become temporarily less sensitive to light.

* rod 간상체(명암을 식별하는 시세포) ** cone 원추체(색채 시각을 담당하는 시세포)

[해설] 주어진 문장은 '간상체의 조정이 로돕신이라는 화학물질의 생성에 의해 일어난다.'라는 내용으로, 그 물질의 양이 간상체가 빛에 얼마나 민감한가를 결정한다는 내용 앞에 오는 것이 자연스럽다. 따라서 정답은 ④이다.

[어휘] **adjustment** 조정, 수정 **chemical** 화학물질 **visual purple** 시홍(붉은색의 감광색소) **motion picture** 영화 **practically** 거의, 사실상 **adapt to** ~에 적응하다 **approximately** 대략, 거의 **sensitivity** 감수성, 감응성 **substance** 물질 **exposure** 노출

[해석] 화창한 오후의 밝은 곳으로부터 어두운 영화관으로 들어가 본 적이 있는가? 일단 안에 들어가면, 여러분은 잠시 눈이 거의 안 보이게 되는 것을 발견하더라도 놀라지 않는다. 약 5분 후에 여러분은 시력이 돌아오는 것을 발견할 것이며, 원추체가 어둠에 적응하게 되면서 색깔을 점차 볼 수 있게 된다. 대략 30분 동안에 걸쳐 간상체는 완전한 감수성을 갖게 된다. 그 이후에 상당한 시간 동안 어두침침한 빛에서의 시력이 조금씩 나아지는 것이 지속될 수도 있다. 어두침침한 빛에 맞추어 간상체가 조정되는 것은 로돕신 또는 '시홍'이라 불리는 화학물질의 생성 때문에 일어난다. 간상체에 있는 이 물질의 양이 그것이 빛에 얼마나 민감한가를 결정한다. 밝은 빛에의 노출은 눈으로부터 로돕신을 서서히 없애고, 그것(눈)을 빛에 일시적으로 덜 민감해지게 한다.

[정답] ④

09 주어진 글 다음에 이어질 글의 순서로 가장 적절한 것은?

It was believed prior to the 1970s that chimpanzees were primarily vegetarian and that they might occasionally eat a small animal or bird but would not deliberately and systematically kill larger animals for meat.

(A) Together they try to steer the prey to a congenial spot for capture. A successful hunt is often followed by sharing with the resultant meat.
(B) However, as Goodall witnessed, they not only eat and relish meat but also hunt for meat. In particular, they hunt monkeys, which are not easy to catch for the larger and more terrestrial chimps.
(C) Hunting such prey requires cooperation and coordination, foresight and planning. The hunters usually divide the assignment between those who will give chase through the branches and those who will pursue along the ground below.

① (A) – (C) – (B) ② (B) – (A) – (C)
③ (B) – (C) – (A) ④ (C) – (A) – (B)

[해설] 침팬지가 채식주의여서 고기를 얻기 위해 더 큰 동물을 죽이지는 않았을 것이라고 믿었다는 내용을 반박하며, 침팬지가 고기를 먹고 즐기고 사냥하기도 하며, 특히 원숭이를 사냥한다는 (B)가 이어진다. 원숭이를 잡기가 쉽지 않아서 침팬지는 두 부류로 추격의 임무를 나눈다는 (C)가 이어진 다음, 함께 사냥감을 잡기에 알맞은 장소로 몰아넣으며 사냥이 성공한 후에는 고기를 나눈다는 (A)가 오는 것이 적절하다. 그러므로 글의 자연스러운 순서는 ③ '(B) – (C) – (A)'이다.

[어휘] terrestrial 땅 위에 사는, 육생의 congenial 알맞은, 마음에 prior to ~이전에 primarily 본래, 주로 vegetarian 채식주의(자)의 deliberately 의도적으로 systematically 체계적으로 steer 몰다, 조종하다 capture 잡기, 포획, 생포 resultant 결과로서 생기는 witness 목격하다 coordination 조정, 조화 foresight 예측력, 예지 assignment 임무, 과제, 할당 chase 추격, 추구 relish 즐기다, 맛있게 먹다 드는

[해석] 침팬지들은 본래 채식주의였으며, 때때로 작은 동물이나 새를 먹었을지도 모르지만, 고기를 얻기 위해 의도적으로 그리고 체계적으로 더 큰 동물들을 죽이지 않았을 것이라고 1970년대 이전에는 믿었다. (B) 하지만 Goodall이 목격한 대로 그들은 고기를 먹고 즐길 뿐만 아니라 고기를 얻기 위해 사냥도 한다. 특히 그들은 원숭이를 사냥하는데, 몸집이 더 크고 땅 위에 살 때가 더 많은 침팬지들이 원숭이를 잡기는 쉽지 않다. (C) 그런 사냥감을 사냥하는 것은 협동과 조정, 예측력과 계획을 필요로 한다. 사냥꾼들은 보통 나뭇가지 사이로 추격하는 부류와 아래에 있는 땅을 따라 뒤쫓는 부류 사이에 임무를 나눈다. (A) 그들은 함께 사냥감을 잡기에 알맞은 장소로 몰아넣으려고 한다. 성공한 사냥 후에는 그 결과로서 생기는 고기를 나누어 먹는다.

[정답] ③

권혁민 하프 모의고사

10 다음 빈칸에 들어갈 말로 가장 적절한 것을 고르시오.

It's crucial to maintain integrity by _____. Many people misunderstand that. They think they can do whatever they want when it comes to the small things because they believe that as long as they don't have any major lapses, they're doing well. But that's not the way it works. Webster's New Universal Unabridged Dictionary describes integrity as "adherence to moral and ethical principles; soundness of moral character; honesty." Ethical principles are not flexible. A little white lie is still a lie. Theft is theft — whether it's $1, $1,000, or $1 million. Integrity commits itself to character over personal gain, to people over things, to service over power, to principle over convenience, to the long view over the immediate. Nineteenth-century clergyman Phillips Brooks maintained, "Character is made in the small moments of our lives." Anytime you break a moral principle, you create a small crack in the foundation of your integrity. And when times get tough, it becomes harder to act with integrity, not easier.

* lapse : 실수, 과실

① taking care of the little things
② showing loving care for strangers
③ taking credit for the work of others
④ checking your biases and being fair

[해설] 작은 선의의 거짓말도 역시 거짓말이고 작은 액수의 도둑질도 도둑질이어서 도덕적 원칙에 작은 틈이 생기면 상황이 어려워질 때 진실성을 지키기가 더 어려워지므로 진실성을 유지하기 위해서는 작은 일에 주의를 기울여야 한다는 내용이다. 따라서 빈칸에 들어갈 가장 적절한 것은 ① '작은 일에 주의를 기울임'이다. ② 낯선 사람에 대한 애정 어린 보살핌을 보여주는 것 ③ 다른 사람들의 일에 대한 공로를 인정받는 것 ④ 편견을 확인하고 공정한 태도를 취하는 것

[어휘] crucial 중요한 integrity 진실성, 정직 adherence to ~에 대한 고수 soundness 온전함 white lie 선의의 거짓말 commit oneself to ~에 헌신하다 clergyman 성직자

[구조분석] They think they can do whatever they want when it comes to the small things because they believe that as long as they don't have any major lapses, they're doing well.: whatever는 anything that이라는 의미로 선행사를 포함한 관계사이다. when it comes to는 '~에 있어서는'이라는 의미이다. as long as는 '~인 한'이라는 의미로 종속절을 이끈다.

[해석] 작은 일에 주의를 기울임으로써 진실성을 유지하는 것이 중요하다. 많은 사람들이 그 점을 오해한다. 그들은 어떤 큰 실수가 없는 한 자기들이 잘 하고 있는 거라고 믿기 때문에 작은 일에 있어서 자기들이 원하는 무엇이든지 할 수 있다고 생각한다. 그러나 그것은 일이 돌아가는 방식이 아니다. Webster's New Universal Unabridged Dictionary는 진실성을 '도덕적이고 윤리적인 원칙을 고수하는 것; 도덕적 인격의 온전함; 정직'이라고 설명한다. 윤리적 원칙은 유연하지 않다. 작은 선의의 거짓말도 거짓말이다. 훔친 것이 1달러이든, 1,000달러이든, 또는 백만 달러이든 도둑질은 도둑질이다. 진실성은 개인적인 이익보다는 인격을 위해, 사물보다는 사람을 위해, 권력보다는 봉사를 위해, 편리함보다는 원칙을 위해, 즉각적인 것보다는 장기적인 관점을 위해 헌신한다. 19세기의 성직자인 Phillips Brooks는 "인격은 우리 삶의 작은 순간들에서 만들어진다."라고 주장했다. 어떤 도덕적 원칙을 어길 때마다 진실성의 기초에 작은 틈을 만든다. 그리고 어려운 시절이 왔을 때 진실성을 갖고 행동하기가 더 쉬워지는 것이 아니라 더 어려워진다.

[정답] ①

04 하프 모의고사 해설

01 다음 밑줄 친 단어의 의미와 가장 가까운 것은?

> However, many still feel China is an imperious country that is sometimes impossible to communicate with.

① drawl
② insolent
③ quaint
④ eccentric
⑤ mawkish

[해설] imperious [impíəriəs] 형 오만한, 고압적인, 도도한 = insolent, disdainful, peremptory, pompous, assuming
[영영] imperious : having or showing arrogant superiority to and disdain of those one views as unworthy
[어휘] drawl 꾸물거리다, 늑장부리다 quaint, eccentric 기괴한, 기이한, 별난 mawkish 역겨운, 별나게 감상적인
[해석] 하지만 중국을 고압적이고 때로는 소통 불가의 국가로 느끼는 사람이 많다.

[정답] ②

02 다음 빈칸에 들어갈 표현으로 적절한 것을 고르시오.

> The health of American children is _____ — they move too little and eat too much junk. But there was promising news this week when America's Centres for Disease Control and Prevention (CDC) announced that obesity rates were flat for most children and _____ for those aged two to five.

① mediocre – dropped
② paramount – plagued
③ reversible – stagnated
④ solid – multiplied

[해설] 움직이지 않고 몸에 안 좋은 음식을 먹는다고 했으므로 아이들의 건강상태는 그리 좋지 않다고 볼 수 있다. 따라서 첫 번째 빈칸에는 mediocre가 적절하며, 그 다음 문장이 but으로 연결되어 있으므로 앞 문장과는 반대되는 내용이 와야 한다. 이번 주 미국 질병통제예방센터가 발표한 뉴스는 희망적이라고 했으므로 아이들의 건강과 관련된 비만율이 떨어졌다고 해야 옳다. 따라서 두 번째 빈칸에는 dropped가 적절하다.
[어휘] mediocre 보통 밖에 안 되는, 썩 좋지는 않은 junk 쓸모없는 물건, 정크푸드 flat 일률적인, 균일의 paramount 최고의, 지상의 reversible 뒤집을 수 있는 stagnate 지체되다, 침체되다 solid 견고한, 튼튼한
[해석] 미국 어린이들의 건강은 썩 좋지 않다. 아이들은 너무 움직이지 않으며 건강에 좋지 않은 음식을 너무 많이 섭취한다. 하지만 이번 주에 발표된 뉴스는 희망적인데 미국 질병통제예방센터(CDC)는 대부분의 아이들의 비만율이 변동이 없으며 2세부터 5세까지의 어린이들의 비만율은 떨어졌다고 발표했다.

[정답] ①

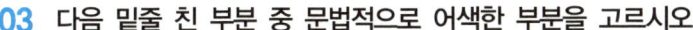

03 다음 밑줄 친 부분 중 문법적으로 어색한 부분을 고르시오.

Difficulties with culture shock ① are often related to an ② individual's ability ③ to speak the language of ④ the country which he or she is living.

해설 ④에서 선행사 the country 다음 절(he or she is living)이 따르므로 관계대명사가 필요한데 동사 live는 자동사이므로 목적어가 필요 없다. 따라서 관계대명사가 아닌 관계부사를 써야 한다. ①에서 relate + 목적어 + to(with)의 수동태형태이다. ③에서 ability와 같은 명사는 to 부정사가 뒤에서 꾸며준다.

해석 문화적 충격과 관련된 어려움들은 종종 그가 살고 있는 국가의 언어를 말하는 개인의 능력과 관계가 있다.

정답 ④

04 다음 빈칸에 들어갈 말로 적절한 것을 고르시오.

Holmes compares himself to Dupin and Lecoq, _____ them as really existing historical figures.

① having treated ② being treated
③ treating ④ having been treated

해설 빈칸 다음에 목적어 them이 주어져 있기 때문에 수동형으로는 쓸 수 없으므로 ②와 ④가 정답에서 먼저 제외된다. and treats를 분사구문의 형태로 바꾼 ③ treating이 정답이다. treat A as B는 'A를 B로 생각하다, 간주하다'라는 뜻이다.

어휘 compare 비교하다, 견주다, 비유하다 existing 현존하는, 현재 있는

해석 홈즈(Holmes)는 자기 자신을 뒤팽(Dupin)과 르코크(Lecoq)에 비유하며, 그들을 실제 현존하는 역사적인 인물로 생각한다.

정답 ③

05 다음 우리말 영작이 올바르지 않은 문장을 고르시오.

① 우리가 그녀를 격려하는 것은 쉽다.
  ⇨ She is easy for us to encourage.
② 나의 딸에게는 그녀의 친구와 점심을 먹을 만큼의 충분한 돈이 있다.
  ⇨ My daughter has enough money to have lunch with her friend.
③ 우리는 지하철을 타고 집으로 가는 것이 현명한 것이라 생각한다.
  ⇨ We think the sensible thing would be to take a subway home.
④ 바닥에서 자고 있는 내 아들을 보아라.
  ⇨ Look at the asleep my son on the floor.

해설 ④에서 asleep은 서술형용사로서, 전치 수식을 할 수 없으므로 asleep을 전치 수식이 가능한 현재분사 sleeping으로 고친다. ①에서 easy는 [어렵다, 쉽다]의 뜻을 가진 형용사로, 사람을 주어로 할 수 없고 'It be + 난이형용사 + to 동사원형~' 구문으로만 사용한다. 이때 to 동사원형의 목적어가 가주어 자리로 이동 할 수 있다. ②에서 형용사 enough는 앞, 뒤에서 식이 모두 가능하다. ③에서 문맥상 '현명한 것'이라는 의미가 되어야 하므로 '분별력 있는, 현명한'이라는 뜻의 형용사 sensible은 적절하다. home은 그 자체로 '집으로'라는 뜻의 부사로도 쓰인다.

> 원팩더하기 enough
> 형용사 – 명사 앞, 뒤에서 수식(enough money)
> 부사 – 형, 부 뒤에서 수식 (foolish enough to say~)
> that절과 결합 불가, enough to 동사원형 / enough N 가능

정답 ④

06 밑줄 친 부분에 들어갈 표현으로 가장 적절한 것을 고르시오.

> Tom : Frankly, I don't think my new boss knows what he is doing.
> Jack : He is young, Tom. You have to give him a chance.
> Tom : How many chances do I have to give him? He's actually doing terribly.
> Jack : _____
> Tom : What? Where?
> Jack : Over there. Your new boss just turned around the corner.

① Speak of the devil
② I wish you good luck
③ Keep up the good work
④ Money makes the mare go

해설 where? 단서이다. 어떤 사람에 대해 얘기하는데 그 사람이 나타날 때 Speak of the devil '호랑이도 제 말 하면 나타난다더니'라는 표현을 찾는 문제이다. Keep up the good work. 지금처럼 계속 잘 해봐! 'Money makes the mare go' 돈이 있으면 망아지도 움직이게 한다. 돈만 있으면 뭐든 할 수 있다

어휘 chance 기회, 가능성, 우연 terribly 끔찍하게, 지독히, 매우 speak of 에 대해서 말하다 devil 악마 keep up 계속하다 mare 암말

해석 Tom : 솔직히 신임 상사는 자신이 무엇을 하고 있는지 모르는 것 같아.
Jack : Tom, 그는 어리잖아. 그에게 기회를 줘야 해.
Tom : 얼마나 많은 기회를 그에게 줘야 하지? 그가 사실 끔찍하게 하고 있어
Jack : 호랑이도 제 말 하면 온다더니.
Tom : 뭐? 어디?
Jack : 저기. 너의 새로 온 상사가 금방 모퉁이를 돌았어.

정답 ①

07 빈칸 (A), (B)에 들어갈 말로 가장 적절한 것은?

Mitterer and de Ruiter used a color categorization paradigm to study the relationship between "world knowledge" and color categories. First, half of the observers saw typically orange objects (e.g., carrot) in a good orange and typically yellow objects (e.g., banana) in a hue midway between orange and yellow. The other half saw typically orange objects in the intermediate hue and typically yellow objects in a good yellow. Later, observers were asked to categorize a color-neutral object (e.g., sock) colored somewhere between yellow and orange as either yellow or orange. The researchers found that if the observers had seen typically yellow objects in the intermediate hue, this hue was subsequently categorized as yellow. The reverse was true for the observers who had seen typically orange objects in the intermediate hue.

After observers were ___(A)___ a typically yellow or orange object in an intermediate hue, they thought the intermediate hue of a color-neutral object ___(B)___ the category of the previous object's typical color.

	(A)	(B)
①	exposed to	matched
②	exposed to	narrowed
③	reminded of	changed
④	reminded of	determined

[해설] 사람들은 사물의 전형적인 색에 대한 지식을 가지고 있기 때문에, 중간 색조를 띤 사물에 노출된 후에 색 중립적인 사물의 중간 색조를 보았을 때 그 사물의 색조가 그 이전 사물의 전형적인 색의 범주와 부합한다고 인식한다는 내용의 글이므로 (A)는 exposed to(~에 노출되다), (B)는 matched(잘 어울리는, 필적하는, 대등한)가 적절하다.

[어휘] hue 색조, 빛깔 intermediate 중간의 remind A of B ~에게 ~을 생각하게 하다 narrowed 좁은, 편협한

[해석] Mitterer와 de Ruiter는 '세상에 대한 지식'과 색 범주들의 관계를 연구하기 위해 색 범주화 패러다임을 사용했다. 우선, 관찰자들의 절반은 완전한 주황색인 전형적인 주황색 사물(예를 들어, 당근)과 주황색과 노란색 사이의 중간 색조를 띤 전형적인 노란색 사물(예를 들어, 바나나)을 보았다. 나머지 절반은 중간 색조를 띤 전형적인 주황색 사물과 완전한 노란색인 전형적인 노란색 사물을 보았다. 이후에 관찰자들은 노란색과 주황색 사이의 어딘가의 색을 띤 색 중립적인 사물(예를 들어, 양말)을 노란색이나 주황색 중 하나로 분류하라고 요구받았다. 연구자들은 관찰자들이 중간 색조를 띤 전형적인 노란색 사물을 보았으면 나중에 이 색조가 노란색으로 분류되었다는 것을 발견했다. 중간 색조를 띤 전형적인 주황색 사물을 보았던 관찰자들에게 있어서는 그 반대였다.

⇨ 관찰자들이 중간 색조를 띤 전형적인 노란색 혹은 주황색 사물에 노출된 후, 그들은 색 중립적인 사물의 그 중간 색조가 이전 사물의 전형적인 색의 범주와 부합한다고 생각했다.

[정답] ①

08 주어진 글 다음에 이어질 글의 순서로 가장 적절한 것은?

The difficulty in determining whether con-elation equals causation causes an enormous number of misunderstandings. Until a specific mechanism demonstrating how A causes B is identified, it's best to assume that any correlation is accidental, or that both A and B relate independently to some third factor.

(A) A more likely explanation is that cancer diagnoses and milk consumption both have a positive correlation with increased age: On average, milk drinkers live longer than non-milk drinkers, and the older you are, the more likely you are to develop cancer.

(B) This does not, however, mean that drinking milk actually causes people to live longer: It could be that people who drink milk have better access to high-quality health care or eat more healthily than those who do not.

(C) An example that highlights this is the correlation between drinking milk and cancer rates, which some support groups use to argue that drinking milk causes cancer.

① (A) – (C) – (B)
② (B) – (A) – (C)
③ (B) – (C) – (A)
④ (C) – (A) – (B)

[해설] 주어진 글은 인과관계가 드러나기 전까지는 두 변인이 서로 우연히 관련이 있게 되었거나 다른 요인과 독립적으로 연관되어 있다고 보는 것이 타당하다고 설명한다. 이것을 뒷받침하기 위해 우유 섭취와 암 발병률의 상관관계를 사례로 제시하는 내용인 (C)가 이어지고 두 요인이 나이라는 제3의 요인과 각각 독립적으로 관련이 있다고 설명하는 내용인 (A)가 (C)에 이어지는 것이 적절하다. 그러나 우유 마시기가 더 오래 사는 것을 직접 초래하는 것은 아니며 우유를 마시는 사람들의 또 다른 건강관리 습관이라는 제3의 요인과 관련이 있을 가능성이 있다는 (B)가 (A)에 이어지는 것이 자연스럽다.

[어휘] determine 결정하다 correlation 상관관계 causation 인과관계 misunderstanding 오해 mechanism 체계 demonstrate 보여 주다 accidental 우연적인 factor 요인 cancer 암 diagnosis 진단(pl, diagnoses) access 이용, 접근 rate ~율, 비율

[해석] 상관관계가 인과관계와 같은 것인지 아닌지를 결정하는 데 있어서의 어려움은 매우 많은 오해를 초래한다. 어떻게 A가 B를 초래 하는지를 보여 주는 특정한 체계가 명확히 밝혀질 때까지는 어떠한 상관관계도 우연적인 것이라고 가정하거나 A와 B가 둘 다 어떤 제3의 요인과 독립적으로 관련되어 있다고 가정하는 것이 최선이다. (C) 이것을 가장 잘 보여 주는 한 예가 우유를 마시는 것과 암 발병률 간의 상관관계인데 몇몇 옹호 집단은 우유를 마시는 것이 암을 '초래 한다'고 주장하기 위해 이것을 이용한다. (A) 더 그럴듯한 한 가지 설명은 암 진단과 우유 소비 모두가 증가한 나이와 양의 상관관계가 있다는 것이다. 즉, 평균적으로 우유를 마시는 사람들은 우유를 마시지 않는 사람들보다 더 오래 살고 아울러 사람들이 나이가 들수록 암이 발병할 가능성도 더 커진다는 것이다. (B) 그러나 이것이 실제로 우유를 마시는 것이 사람들을 더 오래 살게 한다는 것을 의미하지는 않는다. 다시 말해 우유를 마시는 사람들이 그렇지 않은 사람들에 비해 질이 높은 의료 서비스를 더 잘 이용하거나 더 건강에 좋게 먹을 가능성이 있다는 것이다.

[정답] ④

09 왜 일부 검찰과 경찰들은 "CSI effect"에 대해 걱정하는가?

Solving "cold case" homicides relies more on the emergence of new witnesses than on the DNA analyses and other forensic techniques celebrated in crime dramas. Funded by the U.S. Justice Department's National Institute of Justice, the report adds to existing evidence that old-fashioned investigative work, rather than the latest forensic technologies, matters the most in homicide cases. Most of these people were shooting victims. That doesn't leave a lot of DNA from the murderer. Delays in receiving DNA results often lead detectives to discount DNA's impact in solving murders. That is a concern because some prosecutors and police officials have worried about a CSI effect (named after the popular police-drama television series) that may affect murder trials. Jurors may have come to expect complex forensic techniques to solve cases, instead of the often messy real-life details of investigations that center on interviews with witnesses. If anyone ever wanted to do a show about a real-life homicide investigation, I can guarantee it would be a lot less exciting and conclusive than a TV show.

① Jurors may expect more scientific proof of guilt than what witnesses say.
② The judge may place a lower value on circumstantial evidence.
③ Jurors are asked to make an inference of guilt from indirect evidence.
④ Prosecutors feel pressured when eyewitness testimony is necessary.

[해설] 범죄 과학 드라마인 CSI의 영향으로 "배심원들은 사고 경위 대신에 복잡한 범죄과학기술을 기대하게 되었는지도 모른다."라고 했으므로 검찰과 경찰이 CSI의 효과에 대해 우려하고 있는 것으로 ① '배심원들은 목격자들이 말하는 것보다 더 많은 과학적 유죄의 증거를 기대할 수 있다.'이 정답이다. ② 판사는 정황 증거에 대해 더 낮은 가치를 두게 될 것이다. ③ 배심원들은 간접적인 증거로부터 죄책감을 추론하도록 요청받는다. ④ 검찰은 목격자 증언이 필요할 때 압박감을 느낀다.

[어휘] cold case (범죄 수사의) 미해결 사건, 오리무중의 사건 homicide 살인 witness 증인, 목격자 forensic 법의학적인, 범죄 과학 수사의 old-fashioned 옛날식의, 구식의 investigative 연구의, 조사의 prosecutor 검찰관 conclusive 결정적인, 확실한

[해설] '미해결 살인사건'의 해결은 범죄 드라마를 통해 널리 알려진 DNA 분석과 다른 범죄과학 기술보다는 새로운 증거들의 출현에 더 많이 의존한다. 미국 법무부 소속 국립사법연구소에서 자금 지원을 받은 보고서는 최신 범죄과학 기술보다는 구식의 수사 업무가 살인 사건에 가장 중요하다는 기존의 증거를 강화시켜준다. (살인 사건에 연루된) 대부분의 사람들은 총격 희생자들이었다. 그런 사건에서 살인자들은 많은 DNA를 남기지 않는다. DNA 검사결과를 넘겨받는 것이 지연되면 종종 수사관들이 살인사건을 해결하는 데 있어 DNA의 영향을 무시하게 된다. 그것은 문제이다. 몇몇 검찰관들과 경찰관들은 살인 사건 공판에 영향을 줄 수도 있는 (유명한 수사 드라마에서 이름을 딴) CSI 영향에 대해 우려해왔기 때문이다. 배심원들은 사건을 해결하는데 있어 목격자들의 인터뷰에 중심을 두고 있는 복잡한 수사사건의 사고 경위 대신에 복잡한 범죄과학 기술을 기대하게 되었는지도 모른다. 누구든 실제 살인 사건 수사에 대한 드라마를 보기를 원한다면 TV 드라마보다 훨씬 재미없고 (증거들이) 결정적이지 않을 것이라고 나는 장담할 수 있다.

[정답] ①

10 다음 빈칸에 들어갈 말로 가장 적절한 것을 고르시오.

> Some types of persuasive communications are believed in the end to be self-persuasive. If a particular communication provokes thoughts in the person that are in the direction of supporting the communication, then the person will move towards being influenced by the message. Conversely, if the message provokes anti-thoughts, then the person will move against it. So, the precise wording or style of a persuasive message does matter. _____ are also very important. For example, one is far more likely to persuade an intelligent audience with a balanced presentation that produces both sides of the argument than with a one-sided case. However, no matter how well contrived and persuasive a communication might be, if the receiver of it is already set to produce counter-arguments, then it is much less likely to succeed. Generally speaking, what is crucial is how much involvement a person has in an issue. Changing attitudes is no easy matter, particularly if they are well entrenched in the way that prejudiced attitudes are.

① The varieties of message sources used in integrated communications
② The simple and direct actions of the message sender
③ Cultural barriers which block the free flow of the message
④ The characteristics of the intended receiver of the message

[해설] 빈칸 다음에 이어진 예를 보면, 편파적인 주장보다는 논쟁의 양편을 균형 있게 제시하는 것에 더 설득력 있게 끌리게 될 청중이 있는 한편, 이미 반대 의사가 굳어져 있어서 아무리 설득력 있는 의사 전달을 해도 변하지 않는 사람도 있다고 했으므로, 빈칸에는 ④ '그 메시지를 받도록 의도된 사람의 특성'이 들어가는 것이 가장 적절하다. ① 통합 통신에 사용되는 메시지 소스의 종류 ② 메시지 발송인의 단순하고 직접적인 작업 ③ 메시지의 자유로운 흐름을 차단하는 문화적 장벽

[어휘] **provoke** 떠올리게[일으키게] 하다 **precise** 정확한 **case** 주장 **counter-argument** 반론, 반박 **contrive** 고안하다 **entrenched** (태도 등이) 확립된

[해석] 설득력 있는 의사 전달의 일부 유형은 결국 자기 설득적이라고 믿어진다. 특정한 의사소통이 그 의사를 지지하는 쪽의 생각들을 그 사람에게 떠올리게 한다면, 그 사람은 그 메시지에 의해 영향을 받는 쪽으로 움직일 것이다. 반대로, 그 메시지가 반대의 생각을 떠올리게 한다면, 그 사람은 그것에 반대하는 쪽으로 움직일 것이다. 그래서 설득적 메시지의 정확한 언어 표현이나 문체는 정말 중요하다. 또한 그 메시지를 받도록 의도된 사람의 특성도 매우 중요하다. 예를 들어, 편파적인 주장보다는 논쟁의 양편 모두를 제시하는 균형 잡힌 발표로 지적인 청중을 설득할 가능성이 훨씬 더 크다. 그러나 어떤 메시지가 아무리 잘 고안되고 설득력이 있더라도 그 메시지를 받는 사람이 이미 반론을 제시하기로 정해져 있다면, 성공할 가능성은 훨씬 더 적다. 일반적으로 말하자면, 중요한 것은 어떤 사람이 어떤 사안에 얼마나 많이 연루되어 있느냐이다. 태도를 바꾼다는 것은 쉽지 않은 문제인데, 편견을 가진 태도가 확립되어 있는 방식으로 태도가 견고하다면 특히 그러하다.

[정답] ④

05 하프 모의고사 해설

01 밑줄 친 단어의 의미와 가장 가까운 것은?

> Their guest did not protract his stay that evening above an hour longer.

① weird
② grotesque
③ outlandish
④ dawdle

[해설] protract [proutrǽkt] 동 …을 연장하다, 오래 끌게 하다 = dawdle, procrastinate, loiter
[영영] protract : lengthen in time; cause to be or last longer
[어휘] weird, grotesque, outlandish 기괴한, 기이한, 별난
[해석] 그들의 손님은 그날 밤 그의 집에 머무는 것을 한 시간 이상 끌지 않았다.

[정답] ④

02 다음 빈칸에 들어갈 단어로 적절한 것을 고르시오.

> The well-born young Athenian who gathered around Socrates found it quite _____ that their hero was so intelligent, so brave, so honorable — so ugly.

① paradoxical
② charitable
③ deliberate
④ turbulent

[해설] 자기들이 숭배하는 영웅적인 인물이 내적으로는 intelligent, brave, honorable 하지만, 외모가 ugly하다면 겉과 속이 서로 다른 모습을 동시에 갖추고 있다고 생각할 수 있다. '역설적인, 모순된'의 ① paradoxical이 정답이다.
[어휘] honorable 명예로운, 존경할 만한, 고결한 paradoxical 역설적인, 모순된, 불합리한, 기묘한 charitable 자비로운, 관대한, 자선의 deliberate 계획적인, 고의의, 생각이 깊은, 신중한 turbulent 몹시 거친, (바람, 파도가) 사나운, 떠들썩한, 소란스런
[해석] 소크라테스 주변에 모인 훌륭한 집안 출신의 아테네의 젊은이들은 그들의 영웅이 매우 지적이고, 무척 용감하고, 대단히 존경할만 했지만, 너무 못생겼다는 것은 아주 역설적이라고 생각했다.

[정답] ①

03 (A), (B), (C) 각 빈칸 문맥에 맞는 말로 가장 적절한 것은?

> The equipment of the kitchen can seem unimportant compared to the history of food itself. It is all very well fussing over the details of table settings and jelly moulds, but what does this matter compared to a basic hunger for bread? Perhaps this explains why kitchen tools have been so ___(A)___ in histories of food. Culinary history has become a hot subject over the past two decades. But the focus of these new histories, with a few notable exceptions, has ___(B)___ been ingredients rather than technique: what we cooked rather than how we cooked it. There have been books on potatoes, cod and chocolate and histories of cookbooks, restaurants and cooks. The kitchen and its tools are more or less ___(C)___ — and as a result, half the story is missing. This matters: we change the texture, the taste, the nutritional content and the cultural associations of ingredients simply by using different tools and techniques to prepare them.

	(A)	(B)	(C)
①	neglected	scarcely	focused
②	emphasized	overwhelmingly	absent
③	neglected	overwhelmingly	absent
④	emphasized	scarcely	focused

[해설] (A) 역사적으로 음식 자체는 중요시되어 왔지만, 주방 도구는 중요시되지 않았다고 했으므로, '무시된'이라는 뜻의 neglected를 써야 한다. emphasized는 '강조된'이라는 뜻이다. (B) 요리의 역사는 음식 재료를 어떻게 요리하느냐보다는 음식 재료 자체에 주로 초점이 맞춰져 왔다고 했으므로, '압도적으로'라는 뜻의 overwhelmingly를 써야 한다. scarcely는 '거의 ~ 아닌'이라는 뜻 이다. (C) 요리에 대한 책의 주제는 주로 요리 재료, 식당, 요리사 등이었다고 했고 주방과 주방 도구에 대한 것은 상대적으로 없었으므로, '없는'이라는 뜻의 absent를 사용해야 한다. focused는 '초점이 맞춰진'이라는 뜻이다.

[어휘] all very well 아주 그럴듯한, 대단히 좋아 보이는 mould 모형, 틀 subject 주제, 과목, 실험 대상 notable 눈에 띄는 ingredient 재료 cod 대구 texture (음식이 입안에서 느껴지는) 질감 nutritional 영양의 association 연관, 제휴 prepare (음식을) 조리하다, 준비하다 fuss 법석[야단/호들갑]을 떨다 culinary 요리의

[해석] 음식 자체의 역사에 비해 주방 도구는 중요해 보이지 않을 수 있다. 상차림과 젤리 모형들의 세부 사항에 관해 야단법석을 떠는 것이 아주 그럴듯해 보이지만, 이것이 빵에 대한 기본적인 갈망에 비해 뭐 그리 중요한가? 이는 아마 음식의 역사에서 왜 주방 도구가 그토록 무시되어 왔는지를 설명해 줄지 모른다. 요리의 역사는 지난 이십년간 인기 주제가 되어 왔다. 하지만 이 새로운 역사의 초점은, 눈에 띄는 몇 가지를 제외하고, 기술보다는 재료, 즉 그것을 '어떻게' 요리 했느냐보다는 '무엇'을 요리했느냐에 압도적으로 맞춰져 왔다. 감자, 대구와 초콜릿, 그리고 요리책, 식당 및 요리사의 역사에 관한 책들은 있어 왔다. 주방과 그 도구들은 거의 없고, 결과적으로 이야기의 절반 이 빠져 있다. 이것은 중요한 점이다. 즉 우리는 단순히 식재료를 조리하기 위해 여러 다른 도구와 기술을 사용하는 것만으로도 식재료의 질감, 맛, 영양 성분, 그리고 문화적 연관성을 바꾼다.

[정답] ③

04 다음 글의 밑줄 친 부분 중, 어법상 틀린 것은?

① Far better it is to dare mighty things, ② even though checked by failure, than ③ taking to rank with those poor spirits ④ who neither enjoy much nor suffer much.

[해설] 비교급의 접속사 than이 연결하는 것은 문법적으로 동일해야 한다. 따라서 ③의 taking은 앞 문장의 진주어 역할을 하는 to dare와 병치되는 것이어야 하기 때문에 taking을 to take로 고쳐야 적절하다. ①에서 far는 비교급 better의 강조부사로 쓴 것으로 이와 같이 비교급을 강조하는 자리에 much, still, a lot, even, far 등은 쓸 수 있지만 very는 쓸 수 없다. ②의 even though는 '비록'의 뜻의 종속접속사인데 even tough는 though, although의 접속사로도 쓸 수 있지만 even although의 형태로는 쓸 수 없다.

[해석] 비록 실패에 의해 좌절을 하더라도 큰일을 감행하는 것이, 별로 즐거워하지도 않으며, 별로 괴로워하지도 않는 불쌍한 사람들과 자리를 같이 차지하고 있는 것보다는 훨씬 좋다.

[정답] ③ taking ⇨ to take

05 다음 빈칸에 들어갈 표현으로 적절한 것을 고르시오.

The second is the intellectuals; and if their attachment to ideas is passionate, and not only passionate but programmatic, they are almost certain to abuse _____.

① whatever they acquire power
② what they acquire every power
③ whatever power they acquire
④ the power whatever they acquire

[해설] 빈칸은 abuse의 목적어가 들어갈 자리이며 ①와 ②는 둘 다 whatever와 what 뒤의 주어 + 동사의 구조가 있는 것을 통해 whatever와 what은 acquire 뒤에 power의 목적어가 있기 때문에 what과 whatever가 목적어 역할을 할 수 없어서 틀린 구조가 된다. ④는 the power의 명사와 whatever S + V의 명사절이 연결어구 없이 중복되어 있기 때문에 틀린 구조가 된다. 따라서 ③가 적절한 정답이 된다. 이 문장의 whatever power는 '어떤 힘을'의 뜻으로 이는 acquire의 목적어 역할을 하는 명사절 접속사이다.

[해석] 두 번째는 지식인들이다. 만일 그들의 사상에 대한 애정이 강렬하며 그것이 단지 강렬할 뿐 아니라 계획적이기도 하다면 그들이 얻게 된 무슨 권력이든지 그들은 거의 틀림없이 남용하게 될 것이다.

[정답] ③

06 다음 글의 주제로 가장 적절한 것은?

Historians' approaches to the past vary enormously, but some common disciplinary features unite them. There are limits to what historians can study: they can study only parts of the past that left evidence behind and for which evidence has survived. The dominant type of evidence has been documentary: government archives, private papers, newspapers and published materials have long been the most consulted forms of source. The range has recently broadened, and many historians are now happy to use artefacts, buildings, visual evidence, oral testimony and many other non-written sources. However, regardless of the type of evidence, the point is that without evidence, historians cannot function. So all studies of history are driven by the discovery of evidence from the period being studied, and its analysis and interpretation. Historians aim to describe what happened, explain how and why it happened, and link past events to wider contexts and the passage of time.

① ways historians search for historical evidence
② importance of evidence in historical research
③ difficulty of using evidence from the past properly
④ contributions of historians to exploring current problems

[해설] 모든 역사학자들의 연구는 증거에 기반하고 있다는 공통점을 지닌다는 내용의 글이므로, 글의 주제로 가장 적절한 것은 ② '역사 연구에 있어 증거의 중요성'이다. ① 역사학자들이 역사적 증거를 찾는 방법들 ③ 과거로부터 증거를 적절히 활용하는 것의 어려움 ④ 현재의 문제를 탐구하는 데 있어 역사학자들의 공로

[어휘] **archive** 공적(公的)기록, 공문서 **testimony** 증거, 증언 **enormously** 대단히, 엄청나게 **disciplinary** 학문의, 학과의 **leave ~ behind** ~을 뒤에 남기다, ~을 놓아 둔 채 잊고 오다 **dominant** 지배적인, 우세한 **documentary** 기록의, 문서로 이루어진 기록물 **consult** 참고하다, 상의하다 **artefact** 인공물 **oral** 구두의 **interpretation** 해석 **passage** (시간의) 흐름, 경과

[해석] 과거에 대한 역사학자들의 접근법은 매우 다양하지만, 몇 가지 공통된 학문적인 특징이 그것들을 묶어 준다. 역사학자들이 연구할 수 있는 것에는 제한이 있는데, 증거를 뒤에 남겼고 증거가 존속되어 온 과거 시기의 일부만을 연구할 수 있는 것이다. 증거의 주요한 유형은 기록물 형태였는데, 예컨대 정부 기록문서, 개인 서류, 신문, 출판물이 오랫동안 가장 많이 참조된 형태의 자료였다. 최근 그 범위는 확대되었는데, 많은 역사학자들이 이제는 인공물, 건물, 시각적 증거물, 구두 증언과 글로 쓰이지 않은 많은 다른 자료를 기꺼이 사용하고 있다. 그러나 증거의 유형과 무관하게 중요한 점은 증거가 없으면 역사학자들은 제대로 기능할 수 없다는 것이다. 그러므로 모든 역사 연구는 연구되는 시기로부터의 증거를 발견하고, 그것을 분석하고 해석함으로써 추진된다. 역사학자들은 어떤 일이 일어났는지 기술하고, 그 일이 어떻게, 왜 일어났는지 설명하고, 과거의 사건을 더 넓은 맥락과 시간의 흐름과 연결 짓는 것을 목표로 한다.

[정답] ②

07 carpa에 관한 다음 글의 내용과 일치하지 않는 것은?

A carpa is a popular improvised show of the nineteenth and twentieth centuries, often performed in a tent on a street corner or vacant lot in Mexico City. Itinerant performers move their collapsible stages from one town to the next, performing shows consisting of songs and comedy to a lower-and middle-class audience. Plots are based on recent events or current topics of interest, and the mood of the performances is determined by the subject matter. The audience and performers are able to directly relate to each other in this relaxed informal performance setting. Performers support themselves by charging a small entrance fee for their shows. Now most carpa troupes have been absorbed into variety shows or circuses. As Mexico City becomes larger and more cosmopolitan, remaining carpa performances are in more obscure corners of the city.

① This show is often held on street corners and vacant lots in Mexico City.
② It will perform a show composed of songs and comedies to audiences in the middle and lower classes.
③ The plot of events long ago is reconstructed and shown.
④ The audience and performers interact in a comfortable atmosphere.

해설 줄거리는 최근의 사건이나 흥미있는 시사문제에 기반을 둔다(Plots are based on recent events or current topics of interest)고 하였다. 그러므로 ③이 글의 내용과 일치하지 않는다.

어휘 itinerant 이리저리 이동하는 improvised 즉흥적인, 즉흥적으로 만든 vacant lot 공터 collapsible 접을 수 있는 consist of ~로 구성되다 plot 줄거리 current topic 시사문제 subject matter (책·연설·그림 등의) 주제[소재] relate to ~와 교감[공감]하다 charge 청구[요구]하다, 부과하다 troupe 공연단, 극단 cosmopolitan 국제적인, 세계적인 obscure 외진, 어두운, 모호한

해석 carpa는 19세기와 20세기의 인기 있는 즉흥쇼인데, 멕시코시티의 길모퉁이나 공터의 텐트 안에서 자주 공연된다. 이리저리 이동하는 공연자들은 자신들의 접이식 무대를 이 마을 저 마을로 옮겨가며 하류와 중류층의 관객에게 노래와 코미디로 구성되는 쇼를 공연한다. 줄거리는 최근의 사건이나 흥미있는 시사문제에 기반을 두고, 공연의 분위기는 그 주제에 의해 결정된다. 관객과 공연자들은 이런 편안한, 격식을 차리지 않는 공연 상황에서 서로서로 직접 교감할 수 있다. 공연자들은 자신들의 쇼에 대한 적은 입장료를 받아서 생계를 유지한다. 현재 대부분의 **carpa** 공연단이 버라이어티 쇼나 서커스로 흡수되었다. 멕시코시티가 더 커지고 더욱 국제적으로 되어감에 따라서 남아 있는 **carpa** 공연은 그 도시의 더 외진 모퉁이에(서 행해지고) 있다.

  ③

08 다음 빈칸에 들어갈 말로 가장 적절한 것은?

A good image of what we mean by decision making is of a person pausing at a fork in the road, and then choosing one path — to reach a desired goal or to avoid an unpleasant outcome. The most important evolutionary situations that selected our basic decision-making capacities probably involved physical approach or avoidance — which waterhole, field, fruit tree, cave, stranger, mate, and so forth, to approach and which to avoid. In prehistoric times, bad decisions were punished in a dramatic manner; as the philosopher Willard van Orman Quine commented, "Creatures inveterately wrong in their inductions have a pathetic but praiseworthy tendency to die before reproducing their kind." In other words, animals, including humans, that make bad predictions of the future and consequently bad decisions tend to die before they can pass their genes on to the next generation; this is one reason that we, and other animals, _____.

① often choose to follow others
② are unreliable decision makers
③ want to try every option available
④ are good at making survival decisions

[해설] 현명치 못한 결정을 내리는 사람이나 동물은 자손을 번식시키기 전에 죽게 되므로, 현재 살아있는 우리는 생존과 관련된 결정을 잘한 조상들의 유전자를 물려받은 존재들일 것이다. 따라서 빈칸에 들어갈 말로 가장 적절한 것은 ④ '살아남기 위한 결정을 내리는 데 능숙한'이다. ① 흔히 다른 사람들을 추종하는 것을 선택하는 ② 신뢰할 수 없는 의사 결정자인 ③ 이용 가능한 모든 선택사항을 시도하기를 원하는

[어휘] **inveterately** 만성적으로 **pathetic** 불쌍한 **pause** 잠시 멈추다 **fork** 분기점 **evolutionary** 진화의 **capacity** 능력 **avoidance** 기피, 회피 **waterhole** 물웅덩이 **cave** 동굴 **mate** 짝, 친구 **prehistoric** 선사시대의 **philosopher** 철학자 **comment** 언급하다 **induction** 귀납적 결론 **praiseworthy** 칭찬할 만한 **reproduce** 번식하다 **prediction** 예측 **gene** 유전자 **generation** 세대

[해석] 의사 결정이 의미하는 바를 잘 보여주는 이미지는 원하는 목표에 도달하거나 불쾌한 결과를 피하고자 길의 분기점에서 잠시 멈춘 후 하나의 길을 선택하는 사람에 대한 것이다. 우리의 기본적인 의사 결정 능력을 선택한 진화의 가장 중요한 상황은, 아마도 어떤 물웅덩이, 들판, 과일나무, 동굴, 낯선 사람, 짝 등에 접근하고, 어떤 것들을 피해야 하는지와 같은 물리적인 접근이나 기피를 포함했을 것이다. 선사시대에는 현명하지 못한 결정은 극적인 방식으로 처벌받았다. 즉, 철학자 Willard van Orman Quine이 언급한 것처럼, "만성적으로 귀납적 결론을 잘못 내리는 생물은 자신의 종족을 번식하기 전에 죽는, 불쌍하지만 칭찬할 만한 경향을 지니고 있다." 바꾸어 말하면, 사람을 포함하여, 미래에 대해 잘못된 예측을 해서 그 결과 현명하지 못한 결정을 내리는 동물은, 자신들의 유전자를 다음 세대에 전달할 수 있기 전에 죽는 경향이 있는데, 이것이 우리, 그리고 다른 동물들이 살아남기 위한 결정을 내리는 데 능숙한 한 가지 이유이다.

[정답] ④

09 다음 빈칸에 들어갈 말로 가장 적절한 것을 고르시오.

The human species is unique in its ability to expand its functionality by inventing new cultural tools. Writing, arithmetic, science — all are recent inventions. Our brains did not have enough time to evolve for them, but I reason that they were made possible because _____. When we learn to read, we recycle a specific region of our visual system known as the visual word-form area, enabling us to recognize strings of letters and connect them to language areas. Likewise, when we learn Arabic numerals we build a circuit to quickly convert those shapes into quantities — a fast connection from bilateral visual areas to the parietal quantity area. Even an invention as elementary as finger-counting changes our cognitive abilities dramatically. Amazonian people who have not invented counting are unable to make exact calculations as simple as, say, 6 — 2. This "cultural recycling" implies that the functional architecture of the human brain results from a complex mixture of biological and cultural constraints.

① our brains put a limit on cultural diversity
② we can mobilize our old areas in novel ways
③ cultural tools stabilize our brain functionality
④ our brain regions operate in an isolated manner

[해설] 인간이 새로운 것을 발명하여 그 기능을 확장하는 것은 인간의 뇌에 이미 존재하는 영역을 새로운 방식으로 연결 짓는 것이라는 내용이 빈칸 뒤에 이어지므로, 빈칸에 들어갈 말로 ②가 가장 적절하다. ① 우리의 뇌가 문화적 다양성에 제한을 가하기 ③ 문화적 도구가 우리의 뇌 기능을 안정시켜 주기 ④ 우리의 뇌 영역이 독립적인 방식으로 작동하기

[어휘] **constraint** 제약 **functionality** 기능성, 기능 **arithmetic** 산수, 계산 **Arabic numeral** 아라비아 숫자 **calculation** 계산 **architecture** 구조, 건축 **constraint** 제약 **bilateral** 양측의 **parietal** 정수리(부분)의

[해석] 인간은 새로운 문화적 도구를 발명함으로써 자신의 기능성을 확장하는 능력에 있어서 독특하다. 쓰기, 산수, 과학, 이 모든 것은 최근에 발명된 것이다. 우리의 뇌가 그것들을 위해 진화할 충분한 시간이 없었으나, 나는 우리가 우리의 오래된 영역들을 새로운 방식으로 동원할 수 있기 때문에 그것들이 가능하게 되었으리라고 추론한다. 우리가 읽는 것을 배울 때, 우리는 시각적인 단어-형태 영역이라고 알려진 우리의 시각 시스템의 특정 영역을 재활용하는데, 이것이 우리가 일련의 문자를 인식하고 그것들을 언어 영역에 연결할 수 있게 해 준다. 마찬가지로, 우리가 아라비아 숫자를 배울 때 우리는 그러한 모양들을 빠르게 수량으로 변환하는 회로를 만드는데, 이것은 양측의 시각 영역을 정수리 부분의 수량 영역과 빠르게 연결하는 것이다. 손가락으로 헤아리기와 같은 기본적인 발명조차도 우리의 인지 능력을 극적으로 변화시킨다. 수를 세는 것을 발명하지 않은 아마존 사람들은, 예를 들어, 6 빼기 2처럼 간단한 것을 정확하게 계산할 수 없다. 이러한 '문화적 재활용'은 인간의 두뇌의 기능적 구조가 생물학적, 문화적 제약의 복잡한 혼합물로부터 생겨난 것이라는 것을 암시한다.

 ②

10 빈칸 (A), (B)에 들어갈 말로 가장 적절한 것은?

Consider the website Pandora, which allows users to identify a favorite song or singer and devises a kind of default music station on the basis of that choice. The website has many virtues, and it is a lot of fun. But there is a risk to learning and self-development in any situation in which people are defaulted into a kind of echo chamber, even if they themselves took the initial step to devise it. The same might be said about Netflix, which assembles a set of suggestions, based on users' previous choices (and evaluations). Netflix's kind of fine-tuning, which allows a great deal of precision in the resulting suggestions, obviously offers a great convenience, because people see what they are highly likely to enjoy. The question is whether the conveniences come at a cost, in the form of inevitable self-narrowing, simply because the relevant suggestions are based on previous choices and do not encourage people to branch out.

Both Pandora and Netflix have the ability to serve their users with music or movies __(A)__ to their initial or previous choices, which can have the effect of __(B)__ the scope of their experiences to what the world has to offer in music or movies.

	(A)	(B)		(A)	(B)
①	similar	limiting	②	similar	expanding
③	superior	defining	④	superior	limiting

[해설] 좋아하는 노래나 가수를 선택하면 그것에 기반을 두고 그와 유사한 노래들로 자동 설정되는 Pandora와 이용자의 선택이나 평가에 기반을 두고 시청할 것 같은 프로그램을 모아서 제안해 주는 Netflix는 이용자의 경험을 협소하게 하여 새로운 분야로 진출해 보라고 장려하지 않는다고 했으므로, 요약문의 빈칸 (A)에는 similar가, (B)에는 limiting이 가장 적절하다.

[어휘] devise 만들다, 고안하다 echo chamber (에코 효과를 내는) 반향실 fine-tuning 미세 조정 branch out 새로운 분야로 진출하다 default (컴퓨터에서) 자동적으로 주어지는 설정; 자동으로 설정하다

[해석] 이용자가 좋아하는 노래나 가수를 확인할 수 있게 하고, 그 선택에 근거하여 자동 설정되어 주어지는 일종의 음악 방송 프로그램을 만드는 웹사이트 Pandora를 생각해 보라. 그 웹사이트는 많은 장점을 가지고 있고, 그것은 매우 재미있다. 그러나 비록 사람들 자신이 그것을 만드는 최초의 조치를 취하기는 했지만, 그들에게 일종의 반향실이 자동 설정으로 주어지는 그 어떤 상황에서든지 학습과 자기 계발에 대한 위험 요소가 있다. 이용자의 이전의 선택 사항 (및 평가)을 바탕으로 일련의 (시청) 제안을 모아주는 Netflix에 대해서도 같은 말을 할 수 있을 것이다. 결과적인 (시청) 제안에서 상당한 정확성을 허용하는 Netflix의 일종의 미세 조정은 분명히 커다란 편리함을 제공하는데, 사람들이 자신이 즐길 가능성이 매우 높은 것을 보기 때문이다. 문제는 그 편리함이 불가피한 자기 협소화의 형태로 대가를 치러야 얻을 수 있는 것인지 여부인데, 다만 관련된 (시청) 제안은 이전의 선택에 근거하고 사람들에게 새로운 분야로 진출해 보라고 장려하지 않기 때문이다.

⇨ Pandora나 Netflix는 이용자에게 그들이 처음 또는 이전에 선택한 것과 비슷한 음악이나 영화를 제공해주는 능력을 갖고 있는데, 그것은 세상이 음악이나 영화에서 제공하려고 가지고 있는 것에 대한 그들의 경험의 범위를 제한하는 효과를 가질 수 있다.

[정답] ①

06 하프 모의고사 해설

01 밑줄 친 단어의 의미와 가장 가까운 것은?

> The town had been besieged for two months but still resisted the aggressors.

① surrounding
② ensuing
③ far-reaching
④ fawning

[해설] besiege [bisíːdʒ] 동 포위하다, 에워싸다, 몰아대다, 괴롭히다 = surround, harass
[영영] besiege : ① surround so as to force to give up ② cause to feel distressed or worried ③ harass, as with questions or requests
[어휘] ensuing 뒤이어(결과로) 일어나는(= subsequent) far-reaching 광범위한(= far-flung) fawning 아첨하는
[해석] 그 도시는 두 달 간 포위되어 있었으나 여전히 저항했다./침략자(aggressor)들에게

[정답] ①

02 빈칸에 들어갈 문장으로 가장 적절한 것은?

> Many people are risk-averse because they consider the negative consequences of failure to outweigh the reward of success. Our culture of looking down on failure makes us even less likely to risk our necks. _____. Progress and innovation are inextricably entwined with risk and failure.

① But we should not underestimate the importance of experimenting and taking risks, especially in these turbulent economic times
② But many organizations suffer from 'corporate anorexia nervosa' and have an unfavorable climate for enterprising people
③ That is why we need a paradigm shift marking a transition to a future
④ That is why combinatoric innovation is not an efficient process

[해설] Many people로 시작하며 현재의 사회적인 통념을 먼저 제시하는 글이다. 이런 경우 대개 이후에 이 통념과 반대되는 의견이 서술되어 글이 전개되는 경우가 많다. 빈칸 이전에서는 실패를 두려워하여 위험을 회피하고, 실패를 경시하여 위험을 무릅쓰지도 않는다는 기존 현상에 대한 부정적인 견해가 서술되었고, 빈칸 이후에서는 진보와 혁신이 위험과 실패와 불가분하게 얽혀있다. 즉 위험과 실패가 있어야 진보와 혁신이 있을 수 있다는 의견이 서술되면서 빈칸 이전과 반대되는 내용이 이어진다. 따라서 빈칸에는 위험을 회피하지 말고 이 위험을 무릅써야 한다는 어조의 글이 나와야 하므로 ①이 적절하다. ② 하지만 많은 기관들이 '기업의 거식증'으로부터 고통 받고 있고, 기업가들에게 호의적이지 않은 분위기를 가지고 있다. ③ 이것이 바로

우리가 미래로의 전환을 나타내는 패러다임의 변화가 필요한 이유이다. ④ 이것이 바로 조합 혁신이 효율적인 과정이 아닌 이유이다.

어휘 risk-averse 위험을 회피하려 하는 outweigh ~보다 더 크다[대단하다] inextricably 밀접하게 entwine 꼬다, 휘감다, 뒤엉키다, 얽히다

해설 많은 사람들이 위험을 회피하려 하는데 그들이 실패의 부정적인 결과가 성공의 보상보다 더 크다고 여기기 때문이다. 실패를 경시하는 우리의 문화는 우리가 위험을 무릅쓸 가능성을 심지어 더 적게 만들었다. 하지만 우리는, 특히 이러한 격동의 경제 시대에서, 실험하는 것과 위험을 감수하는 것의 중요성을 과소평가해서는 안 된다. 진보와 혁신은 위험과 실패와 불가분하게 얽혀있다.

정답 ①

03 다음 우리말 영작이 올바르지 않은 문장을 고르시오.

① 중국은 자신들의 고대유산과 자신들이 문화와 역사에 기여한 데 대해 자긍심을 갖고 있다.
⇨ China prides itself on its ancient legacy, and its contributions to culture and history.

② 아무리 좋은 아이디어라도 그것을 실행에 옮길 예산이나 인적 자원이 없다면 실패할 수 있다.
⇨ The best ideas can fail if there's no budget or human resources to carry out them.

③ 영국은 부유한 나라이지만, 소수이긴 해도 무시할 수 없는 만큼의 아이들이 비참한 환경에서 살아가고 있다.
⇨ Britain is a rich country, but a sizable minority of its children live in squalor.

④ 십대 아이들이 학교에서 최선을 다해 공부하기 위해서는 하루에 적어도 9시간의 수면이 요구된다.
⇨ Teens require at least nine hours of sleep a day in order for them to do their best in school.

해설 ①에서는 pride oneself on ~은 '~을 자랑스럽게 여기다'라는 의미인데, 이 표현에서는 pride가 동사로 쓰였다. 명사 pride를 사용하여 같은 의미를 갖는 표현을 만들 수 있는데, 이 경우에는 take pride in ~으로 한다. ②에서는 동사와 부사로 이루어진 이른바 '2어 동사'의 경우, 목적어가 대명사일 때엔 해당 목적어가 반드시 동사와 부사 사이에 들어가야 한다. carry out them을 carry them out으로 고친다. ③에서는 대명사 its는 Britain을 가리키며, 부분을 나타내는 표현인 a sizable minority of 뒤에 복수명사 children이 왔으므로 동사는 복수형 live로 썼다. ④에서는 a day에서 부정관사 A를 per의 의미로 쓰였으며, for them은 부정사의 의미상 주어로 나타낸 것이다.

정답 ②

04 다음 중 옳은 문장을 고르시오.

① Despite the bus being empty, he came and sat in front of me.
② The question of whether computers can have minds is rapid becoming a significant issue.
③ They suggested me to take more exercise.
④ He seems to master Chinese when young.

해설 ①에서는 Despite는 전치사이므로 동명사 being이 목적어로 왔다. 이 동명사의 의미상 주어가 the bus인데, 동명사의 의미상 주어가 명사인 경우에는 소유격으로 나타내지 않으므로 옳은 표현이다. ②에서는 2형식 동사 become 다음에 명사보어가 온 완전한 문장이므로 rapid는 동사를 수식하는 부사 rapidly가 되어야 한다. ③에서는 동사 suggest는 'suggest + 목적어 + to부정사'의 형태로 쓰지 않는다. that절을 목적어로 취하는 형태로 쓸 수 있으므로, They suggested to me that I should take more exercise로 고쳐야 한다. ④에서 뒤에 과거를 나타내는 부사구 'when young'이 나와 있으므로 to 동사원형의 시제를 과거로 써야 한다. 따라서 to master를 to have mastered로 고친다.

해석 ① 버스가 텅 비었음에도 불구하고, 그는 와서 내 앞에 앉았다. ② 컴퓨터가 지성을 가질 수 있는가 하는 문제는 빠른 속도로 중요한 이슈가 되어가고 있다. ③ 그들은 내게 운동을 더 할 것을 권했다. ④ 그는 어렸을 때 중국어를 완전히 익힌 것 같다.

정답 ①

05 영작이 올바른 문장을 고르시오.

① 근본적인 문제는 농부들이 그들의 작물에 대해 충분한 돈을 지불받지 못한다는 사실이다.
  ⇨ The basic problem is that farmers do not pay enough for their crops.
② 대학 교육비가 너무나 빠른 속도로 증가해서 이제 많은 사람들이 감당할 수 있는 수준을 넘어섰다.
  ⇨ The cost of a college education has risen so rapid that it is now beyond the reach of many people.
③ 만약 소화에 문제가 있다면 이런 종류의 약이 정말로 효과가 있다.
  ⇨ This type of medicine really works very good if you have got anything the matter with your digestion.
④ 거의 모든 학생들이 그 회의에 참석했다.
  ⇨ Almost all the students were present at the meeting.

해설 ①에서는 농부들이 작물에 대해 돈을 지급받아야 하므로, farmers와 pay는 수동관계에 있다. 따라서 pay를 be paid로 고쳐야 한다. ②에서는 so ~ that의 결과표시부사절인데 so와 that 사이에는 형용사/부사 둘 다 올 수 있는데 so 앞의 동사가 따라 형용사, 부사가 결정된다. rise는 1형식 완전자동사이므로 부사가 와야 한다. rapid ⇨ rapidly ③에서는 동사 works를 수식하는 역할을 해야 하므로 부사가 필요하다. 형용사 good을 부사 well로 고친다. have got something the matter with는 '~에 무언가 탈이 있다'라는 의미의 관용표현이다. ④에서는 all the students, all students 모두 가능한 표현이며, 부사 almost는 형용사 all을 수식하는 역할을 하고 있다.

정답 ④

06 다음 글의 주제로 가장 적절한 것은?

> Many of us labor under a self-limiting myth that contributes to our "invisibility" — the "myth of craftsmanship," the idea that good work speaks for itself. Organization survivors know that, in fact, good work speaks for itself only if you give it a voice. Recent years have seen the rise of what has been called the "entrepreneurial economy": "championing" a product, an idea, or a career, and giving it a powerful voice. In any contact-dependent endeavor, success requires both effective performance and effective self-promotion — making your competence and your ability to contribute visible. If you can't do that, you will be passed over for promotion during succession planning time, or when the company is determining which individuals to keep during layoffs. Even if you're an ace at keeping your boss up to speed, remember that in today's fluid business climate, he or she might be gone tomorrow. You need to cover all your bases and stand out in the eyes of your boss's boss.

① difficulties in making your competence visible
② relationships between recognition and job satisfaction
③ tendency to exaggerate one's business accomplishment
④ importance of self-promotion in surviving in the workplace

[해설] 일을 잘하면 자연스럽게 인정받고 눈에 띄게된다는 것은 근거 없는 믿음이며, 직장에서 자신의 업적을 적극적으로 홍보하고 눈에 띄도록 노력하지 않으면 승진하기도 어렵고 심지어 해고를 당할 수도 있다는 내용의 글이므로, 글의 주제로 ④ '직장에서 생존하는 데 있어서 자신을 홍보하는 것의 중요성'이 가장 적절하다. ① 여러분의 역량을 눈에 띄게 하는 것의 어려움 ② 인정과 직업 만족의 관계 ③ 자신의 사업상의 성취를 과장하는 경향

[어휘] myth 근거 없는 믿음 invisibility 눈에 보이지 않음 craftsmanship (훌륭한) 솜씨 speak for itself 자명하다, 분명하다 entrepreneurial 기업가의 champion ~을 위해 싸우다, 옹호하다 contact-dependent 접촉에 의존하는 endeavor 노력 pass over 제외[누락]시키다 succession 승계 layoff 일시적 해고 up to speed 최신 정보[지식]를 갖춘 fluid 유동적인 cover all one's bases 모든 것을 감안하다

[해석] 우리들 중 많은 사람들은 우리가 '눈에 보이지 않는 것'에 기여하는 스스로 제한하는 근거 없는 믿음, 즉 잘한 일은 자명하다는 생각인 '(훌륭한) 솜씨에 대한 근거 없는 믿음' 아래에서 노력한다. 조직에서 살아남은 사람들은, 잘한 일은 여러분이 그것을 소리 내어 말할 때에만 자명하다는 것을 안다. 최근 몇 년 동안 '기업가적 경제'라고 불리고 있는 것들의 증가가 보이고 있는데, 이것은 제품, 아이디어, 혹은 경력을 위해 '싸우고' 그것을 강력한 목소리로 주장하는 것이다. 접촉에 의존하는 어떤 노력에서든 성공은 효율적인 수행과 효율적인 자기 홍보 둘 다를 요구하는데, 이것은 여러분의 역량과 여러분의 기여하는 능력을 눈에 보이도록 하는 것이다. 여러분이 그것을 할 수 없다면 승계를 계획하는 시기나 회사가 일시적 해고를 하는 동안 어떤 직원을 계속 데리고 있을 것인가를 결정할 때, 여러분은 승진에서 제외될 것이다. 여러분이 자신의 상사가 최신 정보를 갖추도록 하는 것을 탁월하게 잘한다 할지라도 오늘날의 유동적인 사업 풍조에서 그들(여러분의 상사)도 내일이면 사라질 수 있다는 것을 기억하라. 여러분은 모든 것을 감안하면서 여러분의 상사의 상사 눈에도 띄어야 한다.

[정답] ④

07 다음 글의 내용으로 가장 적절하지 않은 것은?

Driving an electric car confers a badge of greenery, or so the marketing departments of their makers would have you believe. Yet a report which analyzes the life cycle of car emissions (i.e., all the way from those created by the mining of materials for batteries, via the ones from the production of fuel and the generation of electricity, to the muck that actually comes out of the exhaust) presents a rather different picture. A battery-powered car recharged with electricity generated by coal-fired power stations, it found, is likely to cause more than three times as many deaths from pollution as a conventional gas-driven vehicle. Even a battery car running on the average mix of electrical power generated in America is much more hazardous than the conventional alternative.

① Mining the materials for car batteries creates pollution.
② America generates electricity by burning coal.
③ Electric cars in America produce three times more pollution than conventional cars.
④ Electric cars are marketed as environmentally friendly.

[해설] 전기 자동차는 휘발유 자동차에 비해 오염물질로 인한 사망자를 3배 이상 많이 발생시킨다는 내용이 있을 뿐, ③의 내용은 없다. 3배 이상 많은 사망자수와 3배 이상의 오염물질을 같은 내용으로 볼 수 없다. ① 자동차 배터리에 사용할 원료를 채광 하는 것은 오염을 유발한다. ② 미국에서는 석탄을 태워 전기를 생산한다. ③ 미국에서의 전기 자동차는 전통적인 방식의 자동차보다 3배 이상의 오염 물질을 배출한다. ④ 전기 자동차는 환경 친화적이라고 홍보되고 있다.

[어휘] **confer** 수여하다, 베풀다 **analyze** 분석하다, 검토하다 **emission** (빛·열·향기 따위의) 발산, 배기가스, 배출물질 **muck** 폐기물, 오염물질 **exhaust** (엔진의) 배기가스, 배출, 배기 **hazardous** 위험한, 모험적인 **conventional** 전통적인, 안습적인 **alternative** 대안, 다른 방도

[해석] 전기 자동차를 운전하는 것은 친환경을 상징한다. 아니, 전기 자동차 회사의 마케팅 부서가 당신이 그렇게 생각하도록 만들 것이다. 하지만 자동차 배출물 질의 생애주기(다시 말해, 배터리를 만드는 원료의 채광과정에서 발생하는 유해가스에서부터 연료의 생산과 전기의 발전에서 만들어지는 유해가스와 실제로 자동차 배기가스에서 나오는 오염물질에 이르는 모든 것)를 분석한 연구 보고서는 상당히 다른 결론을 보여준다. 그 보고서에 따르면, 석탄을 사용하는 화력발전소가 생산하는 전기를 충전하는 전지 자동차는 오염물질로 인한 사망자를 기존의 휘발유 자동차의 3배 이상 만들어낸다. 심지어 미국에서 생산되는 전기를 평균적으로 섞어서 사용하는 전지 자동차의 경우도 기존 방식의 자동차보다 훨씬 더 위험하다.

 ③

08 주어진 글 다음에 이어질 글의 순서로 가장 적절한 것을 고르시오.

In discussions of design, the terms convergence and divergence are often mentioned. These concepts are used to capture two basic approaches in design thinking.

(A) This, however, does not mean that the whole design process is a continuous convergence from the broad initial situation to the narrow final solution. Rather, a design process is driven by the will to learn as much as possible about different opportunities existing in a particular situation.

(B) It creates a deeper understanding and a more detailed and narrowly focused proposal. Since the final outcome is usually an artifact, a system, or a specification, the design process always ends in a convergence phase with the focus on one specific solution.

(C) Divergence is an approach where the designer expands her thinking to cover broader issues, find more alternatives, and explore more opportunities. It is a process that creates more information and options. Convergence is about focusing on a specific solution or a synthesis of several ideas.

① (A) – (B) – (C)
② (A) – (C) – (B)
③ (B) – (A) – (C)
④ (C) – (B) – (A)

[해설] 주어진 글에서 언급한 두 개념에 대한 설명이 시작되는 (C)가 먼저 나오고, (C)의 후반부에 언급된 수렴의 개념을 계속 설명하는 (B)가 그다음에 나오며, (B)의 마지막에 언급된 디자인 과정은 수렴 단계로 끝난다는 내용에 제한 조건을 두는 내용의 (A)가 마지막에 나와야 한다. 따라서 이어질 글의 순서로 (C) – (B) – (A)가 가장 적절하다.

[어휘] convergence 수렴 divergence 발산 initial 초기의 proposal 제안 artifact 인공물 specification 자세한 설명서, 명세서 synthesis 통합

[해석] 디자인을 토론할 때, 수렴과 발산이라는 용어가 자주 언급된다. 이 개념들은 디자인 사고에 있어서 두 가지 기본적인 접근을 포착하기 위해 사용된다. **(C)** 발산은 디자이너가 더 넓은 문제를 다루고, 더 많은 대안을 발견하며, 더 많은 기회를 탐구하기 위해 자기 사고를 확장하는 접근법이다. 그것은 더 많은 정보와 선택 사항을 만들어 내는 과정이다. 수렴은 특정한 해결책이나 몇몇 아이디어의 통합에 집중하는 것에 관한 것이다. **(B)** 그것은 더 깊은 이해와 더 세부적이고 좁게 집중된 제안을 만들어 낸다. 최종 결과가 보통 인공물, 체제나 자세한 설명서이므로, 디자인 과정은 항상 하나의 특정한 해결책에 관해 집중하는 수렴 단계로 끝난다. **(A)** 그러나 이것이 모든 디자인 과정이 넓은 초기의 상황에서 좁은 마지막 해결책으로의 계속된 수렴임을 의미하지는 않는다. 오히려, 디자인 과정은 특별한 상황에 존재하는 다양한 기회에 관해 가능한 한 많이 배우려는 의지에 의해 움직인다.

[정답] ④

09 다음 빈칸에 들어갈 말로 가장 적절한 것을 고르시오.

> What we dream in sleep are unintended fleeting thoughts that randomly pass through the mind. Compared to dreaming, when we are awakened, most of our thoughts and actions are deliberate. And, even the thoughts that enter our mind unconsciously still have relevance to something that matters to us, which is not the case with most of our dreams. This is not to be oblivious to the idea that sometimes our dreams represent our deeper subconscious psyche. However, most dreams do not even remotely relate to our lives. Thus, in my opinion, abstract arts, as compared to rhythmic arts or imitative arts, resemble the state of dreaming as compared to the state of being awake, and the greatest majority of abstract arts _____ despite the fact that many of them might be very pleasant to look at.

① should be approached with caution and deliberate consideration
② are the expression of feelings rather than the depiction of reality
③ lack any substance that could be articulated in a meaningful way
④ are characterized by resolving a series of conceptual ambiguity

[해설] 우리가 깨어 있을 때 무의식조차 우리가 중요시하는 것과 관련이 있지만, 대부분 꿈은 우리 삶과 조금도 관련이 없고 추상 예술은 깨어있는 상태에 대비되는 꿈꾸는 상태와 유사하다고 했으므로, 빈칸에 들어갈 말로 ③ '의미 있는 방식으로 설명될 수 있는 어떤 실체도 없다'가 가장 적절하다. ① 조심스럽고 신중하게 고려하여 접근되어야 한다 ② 실제의 묘사라기 보다는 감정의 표현이다 ④ 일련의 개념적 모호성을 해소하는 것으로 특징지어진다

[어휘] **oblivious** 의식하지 못하는 **fleeting** 순식간의 **deliberate** 의도적인 **unconsciously** 무의식적으로 **have relevance to** ~와 관련이 있다 **subconscious** 잠재의식의 **psyche** 마음 (상태), 정신 **not even remotely** 조금도 ~하지 않다 **imitative** 모방적인

[해석] 우리가 잠을 자면서 꿈을 꾸는 것은 우리의 마음을 임의로 통과하는 의도하지 않은 순식간의 생각이다. 꿈을 꾸고 있을 때에 비해, 깨어 있을 때는 우리의 생각과 행동 대부분이 의도적이다. 그리고 무의식적으로 우리의 마음속에 들어오는 생각조차도 우리에게 중요한 것과 여전히 관련이 있는데, 이는 대부분의 우리의 꿈에는 해당하지 않는다. 이 말은 때때로 꿈이 우리의 더 깊은 잠재의식을 나타낸다는 개념을 (우리가) 의식하지 못하고 있다는 것이 아니다. 하지만 대부분의 꿈은 조금도 우리의 삶과 관련이 없다. 그래서 내 의견으로는 율동 예술이나 모방 예술에 비해 추상 예술은 깨어 있는 상태에 대비되는 꿈꾸는 상태와 유사해서, 그들 중 많은 수가 보기에는 아주 좋을 수도 있다는 사실에도 불구하고 대부분의 추상 예술에는 의미 있는 방식으로 설명될 수 있는 어떤 실체도 없다.

[정답] ③

10 다음 빈칸 (A), (B)에 들어갈 말로 가장 적절한 것은?

> Facts are ideas whose accuracy is clearly and amply documented and affirmed by knowledgeable people, like "The house was painted on November 18, 1999." Opinions are ideas that have not yet been sufficiently documented and are therefore still open to dispute. Obvious indicators of opinion are sentences that include words such as: "generally, it is thought, or I believe that." Despite the clarity and simplicity of these definitions, the task of distinguishing facts from opinions can be difficult. One reason is that not every statement of fact is factual. The most obvious example is a lie — for example, a child saying she didn't eat the cookies when she did, or a criminal swearing he is innocent. In addition to lies, there are honest ___(A)___. A person might misread a memo and tell a colleague a meeting is scheduled for three o'clock today when it is actually scheduled for tomorrow. Or an art expert might declare a painting to be the work of a master and only later discover it is a brilliant forgery. Another reason is that opinions are often stated as if they were facts. Consider these statements: "The death penalty constitutes cruel and unusual punishment," or "The cause of children committing crimes is irresponsible parenting." Each statement appears to be factual because of the way it is stated. Yet informed people continue to disagree about each. Therefore, each statement is an opinion. This is not to say that either of these statements is false, only that neither issue has been ___(B)___.

	(A)	(B)		(A)	(B)
①	mistakes	settled	②	mistakes	included
③	prejudices	ignored	④	prejudices	settled

[해설] (A) 메모를 잘못 읽어서 동료에게 잘못된 정보를 전달하거나 처음에는 대가의 작품이라고 공언했지만 나중에 대단한 위작이라는 것이 밝혀지는 것은 그 앞에 제시된 의도적인 거짓말과는 다른 '실수'이므로 빈칸에 들어갈 말로 mistakes가 가장 적절하다. (B) 의견은 논란의 여지가 있고, 제시된 두 개의 진술이 지식이 있는 사람들이 동의하지 않기 때문에 '합의되지' 않았다고 할 수 있으므로 빈칸에 들어갈 말로 settled가 가장 적절하다. ② 실수 - 포함되지 ③ 편견 - 무시되지 ④ 편견 - 합의되지

[어휘] amply 충분히 document 증명하다, 기록하다 affirm 지지하다, 단언하다 sufficiently 충분히 open to dispute 논쟁의 여지가 있는 indicator 지표 swear 맹세하다 declare 공언하다, 발표하다 forgery 모조(작), 위조(품) constitute ~이 되다 commit 저지르다, 범하다

[해석] 사실은 '그 집이 1999년 11월 18일에 페인트 칠 되었다.'처럼 그 정확성이 식견이 있는 사람들에 의해 분명하고 충분히 증명되며 뒷받침되는 생각이다. 의견은 아직 충분히 증명되지 않았으며 그러므로 여전히 논쟁의 여지가 있는 생각이다. 의견의 분명한 지표는 '일반적으로, 생각된다, 혹은 ~을 나는 믿는다.'와 같은 단어들을 포함하는 문장들이다. 이런 명확하고 간단한 정의에도 불구하고, 사실과 의견을 구별하는 과제는 어려울 수 있다. 한 가지 이유는 사실이라는 모든 진술이 사실인 것은 아니기 때문이다. 가장 분명한 사례는 거짓말인데, 쿠키를 먹고 먹지 않았다고 말하는 아이 또는 자신이 무죄라고 맹세하는 범죄자가 그 예이다. 거짓말 외에도 정직한 실수가 있다. 어떤 사람은 메모를 잘못 읽고 동료에게 회의가 실제로는 내일로 예정되어 있는데 오늘 세 시로 예정되어 있다고 말할지도 모른다. 혹은 예술 전문가가 어떤 그림을 대가의

작품이라고 공언하고 나중에서야 그것이 대단한 위작이라는 것을 발견한다. 다른 이유는 의견이 흔히 사실인 것처럼 진술되기 때문이다. '사형은 잔인하고 이상한 벌이된다.' 또는 '아이가 범죄를 저지르는 원인은 무책임한 육아 때문이다.'라는 이런 진술들을 생각해 보라. 각 진술은 그것이 진술되는 방식 때문에 사실인 것처럼 보인다. 하지만 지식이 있는 사람들은 각각에 관해 계속 동의하지 않는다. 그러므로 각각의 진술은 의견이다. 이것은 이런 진술 중 어느 하나가 거짓이라고 말하는 것이 아니라 둘 중 어느 쟁점도 합의되지 않았다고 말하는 것이다.

[정답] ①

07 하프 모의고사 해설

01 다음 밑줄 친 단어의 의미와 가장 가까운 것은?

> He was <u>exasperated</u> by the delay of the airplane.

① evacuated
② pacified
③ infuriated
④ threatened

[해설] exasperated [igzǽspərèitid] 혱 분노한 = infuriated
[영영] exasperated : greatly annoyed; out of patience
[어휘] evacuated 대피한 pacified 진정된 threatened 위협 당한
[해석] 그는 비행기의 지연에 매우 화가 났다.

[정답] ③

02 다음 빈칸에 들어갈 단어로 적절한 것을 고르시오.

> It is hard to say which _____ the above-mentioned factors is most responsible for the distortion and misunderstanding of his philosophy.

① by
② with
③ in
④ of

[해설] say의 목적절에서 주어로 쓰인 which는 의문대명사이다. which에는 한정된 대상에서 일부를 선택한다는 의미(~중에 어느 것)가 내포돼 있는데, 주어진 문장에서 빈칸 위의 the above-mentioned factors가 그 대상에 해당하므로, 빈칸에는 '부분', '일부'의 관계를 나타내는 전치사 of(~중에)가 들어가야 한다.
[어휘] above-mentioned 위에서 언급한 factor 요인, 요소 distortion (사실 등에 대한) 왜곡, 곡해
[해석] 위에서 언급한 요인들 중에 어느 것으로 인해 그의 철학에 대해 왜곡과 오해가 생겨나고 있는지를 말하기는 어렵다.

[정답] ④

03 다음 빈칸에 들어갈 말로 적절한 것을 고르시오.

> Ms. Kane was appointed head librarian because of her organizational abilities and her plans for improving the library's services. At first, the other staff members appreciated her ideas and enthusiasm. But after several weeks of working with her, they began to resent her frequent memos and meetings. The more they learned about her management style, the less the liked it. As one librarian said to another, familiarity breeds _____. The library staff welcomed Ms. Kane and her ideas at first, but after they got to know her better their respect for her changed to dislike and scorn.

① loyalty
② contempt
③ affinity
④ fraternity

[해설] 처음에는 새로 온 상사와 그 사람의 일처리 방식을 좋게 여겼지만, 시간이 흐른 뒤에 그것들을 안 좋게 여기는 쪽으로 바뀐 상황이므로, 빈칸에는 "친숙해지면 서로를 멸시하기 마련이다" 혹은 "익숙하면 얕보게 된다"는 의미가 되도록 ② contempt가 들어가는 것이 적절하다. ① 충성 ③ 친밀감 ④ 동포애

[어휘] **appoint** 지명하다, 임명하다, 지정하다 **organizational** 조직의, 조직상의, 기관의 **appreciate** 평가하다, 판단하다, 진가를 인정하다, 고맙게 여기다 **enthusiasm** 열심, 열중, 열광 **resent** 분개하다, 원망하다 **familiarity** 친밀, 친숙, 친밀한 사이, 익히 앎, 정통함 **breed** 기르다, 양육하다, 생기게 하다 **scorn** 경멸, 멸시, 냉소

[해석] 조직 운영 능력과 도서관 서비스 개선 계획 덕분에, 케인(Kene) 씨는 도서관장으로 임명되었다. 처음에는, 다른 직원들이 그녀의 생각과 열정을 높이 평가했다. 그러나 그녀와 함께 몇 주를 일하고 난 후에, 그들은 그녀의 잦은 메모와 회의를 불쾌하게 여기기 시작했다. 그녀의 일처리 방식에 대해 더 많이 알수록, 그들은 그것을 더 좋지 않게 여겼다. 도서관의 어느 직원이 다른 직원에게 말했듯이, 친숙해지면 서로를 멸시하기 마련이다. 도서관 직원들은 처음에는 케인 씨와 그녀의 생각을 환영했지만, 그녀에 대해 더 잘 알게 된 뒤에는 그녀에 대한 존경심이 혐오감과 경멸로 변해버렸다.

[정답] ②

04 다음 빈칸에 들어갈 알맞은 것은?

> One of the three shops the building contained was for rent; _____ was an all-night restaurant; the third was a garage.

① other   ② other thing   ③ the other   ④ another

[해설] 셋 중에 하나는 **one**, 다른 하나는 **another**, 마지막 남은 하나는 **the other**로 표현한다.

[어휘] **contain** ~을 포함하다, 수용할 수 있다, ~이 들어 있다 **garage** 차고; 자동차 수리 공장

[원팩더하기] **another**

1. 부정대명사 : 아직 남아 있는 다른 것들 중 특정하지 않은 다른 것(부정)을 가리키며 단수취급한다.
   * 'another of 한정사 + 복수명사'로 바꿀 수 있다.
   ⓔ A : These apples are delicious.
      B : Would you like another (of those apples)?
2. 부정형용사 : 단수가산명사만 수식한다.
   Would you like another sandwich?//sandwiches(X)
   ※ 예외 : 기수/few와 결합 시 복수가산명사 수식 가능
   ⓔ Another forty nurses are needed in hospitals.
3. A is one thing and B is another : A와 B는 별개이다
   Love is one thing and marriage is another.//the other.(X)
   사랑과 결혼은 별개의 문제이다.

[해석] 그 건물에 있는 세 가게 중 하나는 임대용으로 나와 있었고, 또 하나는 24시간 영업하는 식당이었고, 나머지 하나는 자동차 정비소였다.

[정답] ④

05 다음 우리말 영작이 올바르지 않은 문장을 고르시오.

① 이 식민지의 이야기는 그 이웃 식민지의 이야기보다 덜 흥미롭다.
 ⇨ The story of this colony is of less interest than that of the neighbor colony.

② 그러나 이것은 그들이 그 주식에 돈을 쏟아 붓는 것을 제지하지 못했다.
 ⇨ This, however, has deterred them from pouring money into the stock.

③ 그들은 다른 사람들이 당연하게 여기는 모든 것들을 그녀가 갖기를 원한다.
 ⇨ They want her to have everything other people take for granted.

④ 과거의 나쁜 행실을 거론하며 그 여자아이를 비난하는 것은 온당치 못하다.
 ⇨ It's not fair to hold the girl's past bad behavior by her.

[해설] ①에서 **of less interest**는 less interesting과 같은 의미이며, 비교대상을 동일하게 하기 위해 **than**뒤에 앞의 **the story**를 가리키는 대명사 **that**을 써서 표현했다. ②에서 '**deter + 목적어 + from ~ing**' 구문이 쓰였으며, '목적어로 하여금 ~하지 못하게 하다'라는 의미이다. **deter** 자리에 **keep, prevent, stop** 등을 써서 표현할 수도 있다. ③에서 **take ~ for granted**는 '~을 당연한 것으로 여기다'라는 의미이다. 주어진 문장에서 **everything** 뒤에는 목적격 관계대명사가 생략되어 있으며, 이것이 **take**의 목적어가 된다. ④에서 **hold ~ against …**는 '~를 이유로 …를 비난하다'라는 뜻이다. 따라서 **by her**를 **against her**로 고쳐야 한다.

[정답] ④

06 다음 글의 주제로 가장 적절한 것은?

> We argue that the ethical principles of justice provide an essential foundation for policies to protect unborn generations and the poorest countries from climate change. Related issues arise in connection with current and persistently inadequate aid for these nations, in the face of growing threats to agriculture and water supply, and the rules of international trade that mainly benefit rich countries. Increasing aid for the world's poorest peoples can be an essential part of effective mitigation. With 20 percent of carbon emissions from (mostly tropical) deforestation, carbon credits for forest preservation would combine aid to poorer countries with one of the most cost-effective forms of abatement. Perhaps the most cost-effective but politically complicated policy reform would be the removal of several hundred billions of dollars of direct annual subsidies from the two biggest recipients in the OECD — destructive industrial agriculture and fossil fuels. Even a small amount of this money would accelerate the already rapid rate of technical progress and investment in renewable energy in many areas, as well as encourage the essential switch to conservation agriculture.

① reforming diplomatic policies in poor countries
② increasing global awareness of the environmental crisis
③ reasons for restoring economic equality in poor countries
④ coping with climate change by reforming aid and policies

[해설] 탄소 배출에 의한 기후 변화에 대처하기 위해서 가난한 나라들에 대한 원조를 더 증가시키고, 선진국의 파괴적인 산업화 농업을 보존 농업으로 바꾸며 화석 연료의 사용을 줄이는 대대적인 정책 혁신이 필요하다고 주장하는 글이다. 따라서 주제로 가장 적절한 것은 ④ '원조와 정책의 개혁에 의하여 기후 변화에 대처하기'이다. ① 가난한 국가의 외교 정책 개혁 ② 환경의 위기에 대한 점증하는 세계적 의식 ③ 가난한 국가에서 경제적 평등을 복구하는 이유

[어휘] mitigation 완화 abatement 감소 subsidy 보조금 persistently 끈질기게 inadequate 부족한 in the face of ~에 직면하여 carbon emission 탄소 배출 deforestation 벌채 carbon credits 탄소 배출권, 탄소 상쇄권 reform 개혁 removal 제거 annual 해마다의, 연례적인 recipient 수혜 분야 accelerate 가속하다

[해석] 우리는 정의의 윤리적 원칙이 아직 태어나지 않은 세대와 가장 가난한 나라들을 기후 변화로부터 보호하기 위한 정책에 대한 근본적인 기초를 제공한다고 주장하는 바이다. 농업과 물 공급에 대한 점점 증가하는 위협과 주로 부유한 국가들에게만 이득을 주는 국제 무역의 규칙에 직면하여, 이 (가난한) 국가들을 위한 현재의 끈질기게 부족한 원조와 관련하여 연계된 문제들이 발생한다. 세계의 가장 가난한 국민들에 대한 원조를 증가시키는 것은 효과적인 (탄소 배출) 완화의 필수적인 부분이다. 탄소 배출량의 20%는 (대개 열대 지역의) 벌채로부터 오므로, 삼림 보존을 위한 탄소 배출권은 더 가난한 국가들에 대한 원조와 비용 효율성이 가장 높은 (탄소 배출) 감소의 형태 중의 하나와 결합시켜 줄 것이다. 아마 비용 효율성이 가장 높지만 정치적으로 가장 복잡한 정책 개혁은, OECD에서 두 가지의 가장 큰 수혜 분야, 곧 파괴적인 산업화 농업과 화석 연료로부터 오는 연간 수천억 달러의 직접적인 보조금을 없애는 일일 것이다. 이 돈의 적은 양이라도 보존 농업으로의 근본적인 변화를 촉진할 뿐만 아니라, 많은 지역에서 이미 빠르게 진행되고 있는 재생 가능한 에너지에 대한 기술적 진보와 투자를 가속할 것이다.

[정답] ④

07 주어진 글 다음에 이어질 글의 순서로 가장 적절한 것을 고르시오.

Clearly, schematic knowledge helps you — guiding your understanding and enabling you to reconstruct things you cannot remember.

(A) Likewise, if there are things you can't recall, your schemata will fill in the gaps with knowledge about what's typical in that situation. As a result, a reliance on schemata will inevitably make the world seem more "normal" than it really is and will make the past seem more "regular" than it actually was.

(B) Any reliance on schematic knowledge, therefore, will be shaped by this information about what's "normal." Thus, if there are things you don't notice while viewing a situation or event, your schemata will lead you to fill in these "gaps" with knowledge about what's normally in place in that setting.

(C) But schematic knowledge can also hurt you, promoting errors in perception and memory. Moreover, the types of errors produced by schemata are quite predictable: Bear in mind that schemata summarize the broad pattern of your experience, and so they tell you, in essence, what's typical or ordinary in a given situation.

① (C) – (B) – (A)
② (B) – (A) – (C)
③ (B) – (C) – (A)
④ (C) – (A) – (B)

[해설] 인간의 도식적 지식이 이해와 기억에 도움이 된다는 주어진 문장 다음에, 하지만 도식이 해가 될 수도 있다고 하면서 도식이 어떻게 작용하는지 설명한 (C)가 오고, 알아차리지 못해서 생기는 공백을 도식이 어떻게 채워주는지 설명한 (B)가 온 다음에, 마찬가지로 기억할 수 없어서 생기는 공백을 도식이 어떻게 채워주는지 설명한 (A)가 마지막에 오는 것이 가장 적절하다. 따라서 정답은 ①이다.

[어휘] **schematic** 도식적인 **schema** 도식, 스키마 (pl. **schemata**) **reliance** 의존 **promote** 조장하다, 촉진하다 **perception** 인식, 지각

[해석] 분명히, 도식적인 지식은 여러분의 이해를 이끌어주고 기억할 수 없는 것들을 재구성하게 하여 여러분에게 도움을 준다. (C) 하지만 도식적인 지식은 또한 인식과 기억에 오류를 조장하여 여러분에게 해를 끼칠 수 있다. 게다가, 도식에 의해서 발생하는 오류의 '유형'은 상당히 예측 가능하다. 도식이 여러분의 경험의 광범위한 유형을 요약하며 그래서 그것(도식)이 본질적으로 주어진 상황에서 무엇이 전형적이거나 평범한 것인지 여러분에게 말해 준다는 것을 명심하라. (B) 따라서, 도식에 대한 어떠한 의존이라 하더라도, 그것은 어떤 것이 '정상적'인 것인지에 대한 이러한 정보에 의해 형성될 것이다. 따라서 어떤 상황이나 사건을 보면서 여러분이 알아차리지 못하는 것이 있으면, 여러분의 도식이 그 상황에서 일반적으로 무엇이 어울리는지에 관한 지식으로 이러한 '공백'을 채우도록 여러분을 이끌어줄 것이다. (A) 마찬가지로, 여러분이 기억할 수 없는 것이 있으면, 여러분의 도식이 그 공백을 그 상황에서 어떤 것이 일반적인 것인지에 대한 지식으로 채워 줄 것이다. 결과적으로, 도식에 의존하는 것은 불가피하게 세상을 실제보다 더 '정상적인' 것으로 보이게 할 것이고, 과거를 실제보다 더 '규칙적인' 것으로 보이게 할 것이다.

[정답] ①

08 phainopepla nitens에 관한 다음 글의 내용과 일치하지 않는 것은?

Phainopepla nitens are medium-sized, crested birds with white wing patches that show in flight. Males are all black, and females and juvenile males are gray-brown. Both the male and the female have red eyes, but these are more noticeable in the female than the male. Phainopepla nitens leave the hot desert during the summer months, and return to Death Valley in October when the weather cools a bit. Around January, serious courting gets under way. During the courting time lasting for up to four months the male builds a nest. If the female likes his craftsmanship, the male and the female mate. Although phainopepla nitens eat insects, their most favorite food is the berry of the parasitic mistletoe that grows on the mesquite trees, so this is where the nesting usually takes place. The baby grows to be ready to leave the nest in five weeks. When the weather starts to warm up, these birds fly to a cooler climate where the courting, nest building, and egg laying start once again. * mistletoe: 겨우살이

① 암수 모두 빨간색 눈을 가지고 있다.
② 10월에 Death Valley 로 되돌아온다.
③ 가장 좋아하는 먹이는 곤충이다.
④ 태어난 지 5주가 지나면 새끼는 둥지를 떠날 준비가 된다.

[해설] 가장 좋아하는 먹이는 메스키트 나무에서 자라는 기생하는 겨우살이의 열매라고 했으므로 ③은 글의 내용과 일치하지 않는다. ① 암수 모두 빨간색 눈을 가지고 있다. ⇨ Both the male and the female have red eyes ② 10월에 Death Valley로 되돌아온다. ⇨ Phainopepla nitens leave the hot desert during the summer months, and return to Death Valley in October when the weather cools a bit. ④ 태어난 지 5주가 지나면 새끼는 둥지를 떠날 준비가 된다. ⇨ The baby grows to be ready to leave the nest in five weeks.

[어휘] **phainopepla nitens** 비단털여새(미국 서남부·멕시코산의 도가머리가 있는 검은 새) **noticeable** 뚜렷한 **craftsmanship** 솜씨 **parasitic** 기생하는

[해석] 비단털여새는 날 때 보이는 날개의 흰 부분이 있는 중간 크기의 볏을 가지고 있는 새이다. 수컷은 전체가 검정색이고, 암컷과 어린 수컷은 회갈색이다. 수컷과 암컷 모두 빨간색 눈을 가지고 있지만, 이것들은 수컷보다 암컷에서 더 뚜렷하다. 비단털여새는 하계 동안에는 뜨거운 사막을 떠나고, 날씨가 약간 선선해지는 때인 10월에 Death Valley로 되돌아온다. 1월경에 진지한 구애가 시작된다. 4개월까지 지속되는 구애 기간 동안에 수컷은 둥지를 짓는다. 만약 암컷이 수컷의 (둥지 짓는) 솜씨를 좋아한다면, 암수는 짝이 된다. 비록 비단털여새가 곤충을 먹기는 하지만, 그들이 가장 좋아하는 먹이는 메스키트 나무에서 자라는 기생하는 겨우살이의 열매여서, 보통 이곳은 둥지를 트는 곳이다. 새끼는 5주가 지나면 자라서 둥지를 떠날 준비가 된다. 날씨가 따뜻해지기 시작할 때 이 새들은 더 시원한 기후(의 곳으)로 날아가는데 그곳에서 구애, 둥지 짓기와 산란이 다시 한 번 시작된다.

[정답] ③

09 다음 빈칸에 들어갈 말로 가장 적절한 것을 고르시오.

> When a writer becomes an advocate for a particular point of view, he or she "selects" for reporting only the bits of evidence that support that position. This kind of selectivity involves an ignorance of evidence, either willful or unconscious, that favors opposing points of view. Ignoring evidence is not always willful, however; sometimes it is a product of limited awareness or limited resources, and thus is unintentional. For example, before the rise of feminist perspectives in the social sciences, many researchers did not see the pervasiveness of sexism in everyday life. Thus, evidence bearing on sexism was often missed in studies of a wide range of social relations. Many other forms of ignorance and unrecognized bias infect all research. While it would be great if every social scientist had some way to recognize the impact of such bias on his or her own research, there is no automatic safeguard. Social scientists are only human, and they can't designate evidence as relevant if _____.

① there's too little evidence to prove their argument
② other experts are strongly critical of their research
③ their unrecognized biases persuade them to ignore it
④ their findings are of considerable interest to investors

[해설] 어떤 견해를 뒷받침하는 증거를 묵살할 때 그것이 반드시 의도적인 것이 아니라 제한된 인식이나 자료로 인해 의도치 않게 무시되는 경우도 있다는 내용이므로, 빈칸에는 ③ '자신들이 인식하지 못한 편견이 증거를 무시하라고 자신을 설득하면'이 가장 적절하다. ① 주장을 입증하기에 증거가 너무나 빈약하다면 ② 다른 전문가들은 그들의 연구에 대해 강하게 비판한다면 ④ 그들의 발견은 투자자들에게 상당히 흥미롭다면

[어휘] **sexism** 성차별주의 **advocate** 옹호자 **willful** 의도[고의]적인 **pervasiveness** 만연함, 널리 퍼져 있음 **bear on ~**와 관련이 있다 **designate** 지정[지명]하다

[해석] 어느 글쓴이가 특정한 관점의 옹호자가 될 때, 그 사람은 그 입장을 뒷받침하는 약간의 증거만 보고하기로 '선택한다.' 이런 종류의 선별에는 의도한 것이든 무의식적이든 반대의 관점을 지지하는 증거에 대한 무시가 포함된다. 그러나 증거를 묵살하는 것이 항상 고의적인 것은 아닌데, 때로는 그것이 제한된 인식이나 제한된 자료의 산물이어서 의도치 않은 것이기도 하다. 예를 들어, 사회과학에서 여성주의적인 관점이 부상하기 이전에는 많은 연구자들이 일상생활에 만연한 성차별주의를 보지 않았다. 그래서 성차별주의와 관련이 있는 증거는 광범위한 사회적 관계에 관한 연구들에서 흔히 관심을 받지 못하고 지나쳤다. 많은 다른 형태의 무지와 인식하지 못한 편견이 모든 연구에 영향을 미친다. 만약 모든 사회과학자에게 그런 편견이 자신의 연구에 미치는 영향을 인식할 어떤 방법이 있다면 좋겠지만 자동적인 보호 장치는 없다. 사회과학자들은 인간일 따름이고 자신들이 인식하지 못한 편견이 증거를 무시하라고 자신들을 설득하면 그것을 유의미한 것으로 지정할 수 없다.

[정답] ③

10 다음 글의 내용과 일치하지 않는 것을 고르시오.

Think of how Wi-Fi has made computing so much more convenient. It has untethered users from troublesome cable connections to the internet, allowing them to wander around the home or office with laptop or tablet in hand, surfing the web, making free phone calls, sending files wirelessly to printers, video to television sets, and many more things. But what if Wi-Fi radio beams travelled not just a few hundred feet but stretched for several miles — and were unimpeded by trees, terrain and walls so that they could penetrate all the nooks and crannies within buildings? That is the promise of "white-space" wireless. "White-space" is technical slang for television channels that were left vacant in one city so as not to interfere with TV stations broadcasting on adjacent channels in a neighbouring city. In the early days of television, America's broadcasting authorities reserved 50 or so channels for TV stations. But because of worries about interference, no metropolitan area has ever come close to using all 50 channels at its disposal. In rural areas, vacant channels (ie, white-space) have frequently amounted to 70% or more of the total bandwidth available for television broadcasting. With the recent switch from analogue to digital television, much of this protective white-space is no longer needed. Unlike analogue broadcasting, digital signals do not "bleed" into one another — and can therefore be packed closer together. The attraction of white-space is that the frequencies used for television broadcasting (54MHz to 806MHz) were chosen in the first place for the distance they could travel and their ability to penetrate obstacles. They were also good at transmitting information quickly. Where Wi-Fi can shuttle data at 160–300 megabits per second, white-space can do so at 400–800 megabits per second.

① Wi-Fi is supported by many applications and devices as a wireless network technology.
② Wi-Fi allows an electronic device to send data wirelessly in the unlimited distances over a computer network.
③ Wi-Fi exchanges data over a computer network by using radio waves.
④ A device that can use Wi-Fi connects to a network resource such as the internet via a wireless network access point.

[해설] 와이파이(Wi-Fi)는 무선통신전파를 이용해서 데이터를 근거리에서 전달하는 무선네트워킹 기술이다. 그러므로 와이파이가 거리제한 없이 무선으로 자료를 전송한다는 ②는 본문의 내용과 일치하지 않는다.

[어휘] **untethered** 줄로 매지 않은 **troublesome** 귀찮은 **surf** 인터넷을 검색하다 **wireless** a. 무선의, 무선 전신의 **unimpeded** 방해하는 것이 없는 **terrain** 지형, 지역 **nook** 구석진 곳 **interfere with** 간섭하다 **broadcasting authorities** 방송국 **interference** 간섭, 방해, 혼선 **frequency** 주파수 **transmit** 전송하다

[해석] 와이파이(Wi-Fi)는 컴퓨터 사용을 더욱 편리하게 하고 있으며, 컴퓨터 사용자들을 인터넷에 연결된 성가신 전선으로부터 해방시켜 주었다. 사람들은 집이나 사무실에서 랩톱 컴퓨터나 태블릿 PC를 손에 들고 다니면서 인터넷 서핑을 하고 무료 인터넷 전화를 걸고 문서를 프린트로, 비디오 파일을 텔레비전으로 무선 전송하는 것과 같은 많은 일들을 전선에 매이지 않고 처리할 수 있다. 그러나 만약 와이파이 신호 전파가 수백 미터가 아니라 수 킬로미터까지 닿게 된다면, 그리고 나무와 지형 그리고 벽에 막히지 않고 뻗어나가 건물 안쪽의 구석진 곳과 틈새까지 닿게 된다면 어떻게 될까? 이것이 "화이트스페이스" 무선서비스의 약속사항이다. "화이트 스페이스"는 한 도시에서 인근 도시의 다른 TV채널 주파수와 충돌하지 않도록 사용하지 않고 비워놓은 채널 주파를 가리키는 기술 용어이다. 텔레비전 시대의 초창기에 미국의 방송당국은 TV방송국을 위해 50개의 채널을 확보해 두었다. 그러나 전파 간 충돌을 염려한 나머지 어떠한 주요 도시에서도 50개에 달하는 채널을 모두 자유롭게 사용할 수는 없었다. 외곽 지역에서는 그렇게 비어 있는 채널이 텔레비전 방송용 채널 전체 대역폭의 **70%**를 넘어가는 경우가 다반사였다. 최근 텔레비전 시스템이 아날로그에서 디지털로 전환되어감에 따라 그러한 방어용 화이트 스페이스는 더 이상 필요하지 않게 되었다. 아날로그 송출과 달리 디지털 신호는 다른 신호를 가해하지 않으며 따라서 서로 가까이 붙은 채로 함께 전송할 수 있었다. 결과적으로 현재의 화이트 스페이스가 주목 받고 있는 이유는 더 먼 송출거리와 방해물들을 관통하는 능력을 확보하고자 텔레비전 방송용으로 사용되던 주파수들(**54–806mhz**)을 첫 번째로 선택한다는 점이다. 또한 정보의 전송속도에서도 우위를 보인다. 와이파이를 통해 초당 **160–300메가비트**를 전송할 수 있는 반면에 화이트스페이스는 초당 **400–800메가비트**의 전송이 가능하다.

[정답] ②

08 하프 모의고사 해설

01 다음 밑줄 친 단어의 의미와 가장 가까운 것은?

> No one wants to be gulled by a sensational press, but the torrent of public figures who have been made to eat their own words on television erodes the very possibility of trust between the public and an individual reporter.

① decay
② upbraid
③ convert
④ deceive

[해설] gull [gʌl] 동 속이다 = deceive, take in
[영영] gull : ① make a fool or dupe of
[어휘] sensational 선정(煽情的)인 torrent 마구 쏟아짐[퍼부음], 빗발침 eat one's words 식언하다 (특히 부끄러움을 느끼면서) 한 말을 취소하다 erode 약화시키다, 좀먹다 decay 부패, 부패하다 upbraid 질책하다, 호되게 나무라다 convert 전환시키다[개조하다]
[해석] 어떤 사람도 선정적인 보도에 속게 되길 원치 않지만 텔레비전에서 식언을 해온 공인들이 넘침에 따라 대중들과 특정 리포터 사이의 신뢰의 가능성이 약화되고 있다.

[정답] ④

02 다음 빈칸에 들어갈 단어로 적절한 것을 고르시오.

> Luxury goods makers have long valued Chinese consumers not just because of their huge appetite for luxury goods but also for their willingness to pay more than their Western _____.

① cooperators
② conspirators
③ co-workers
④ counterparts

[해설] 중국 소비자와 서양 소비자를 비교해야 하므로, 빈칸에는 '서양에서 중국 소비자와 동일한 지위나 역할을 갖고 있는 사람들'의 의미를 나타낼 수 있는 표현이 들어가야 한다. 그러므로 '다른 장소나 상황에서 어떤 사람 혹은 사물과 동일한 지위가 기능을 갖는 상대', '대응 관계에 있는 사람이나 대상'이란 의미를 갖고 있는 ④ counterparts가 빈칸에 적절하다.
[어휘] cooperator 협력자, 협동조합원 conspirator 공모자 co-worker 동료, 함께 일하는 사람 counterpart 상대, 대응 관계에 있는 사람[것]
[해석] 사치품 제조업체들은 오랫동안 중국 소비자들을 가치 있게 여겨왔는데, 이는 중국 소비자들의 사치품에 대한 욕구가 대단히 클 뿐만 아니라 그들이 서양 소비자들 이상으로 기꺼이 많은 돈을 지불하려 하기 때문이다.

[정답] ④

03 다음 밑줄 친 부분 중 문법적으로 어색한 부분을 고르시오.

> It is terrific ① <u>that</u> generations ② <u>of</u> little girls will grow up, ③ <u>known</u> that women can ④ <u>run for</u> president.

[해설] ①에서는 명사절을 이끄는 접속사이며, 주어진 문장에서는 that절이 진주어, 문두의 it이 가주어다. ②에서는 generation이 어떤 사실을 직접 알게 되는 주체이므로, ③에 과거분사가 아닌 현재분사를 써야 한다. knowing으로 고친다. ④에서는 run은 '출마하다' '입후보하다'라는 의미로 쓰였으며, 출마하는 대상 앞에는 전치사 for를 쓴다.

[해석] 어린 소녀 세대가 여성이 대통령에 입후보할 수 있다는 것을 알면서 자라나는 것은 아주 좋은 일이다.

[정답] ③

04 다음 중 어법상 옳지 않은 문장을 고르시오.

① If I were you, I wouldn't return the call.
② However good a letter may express the thoughts of a writer, it cannot carry the full warmth of his personality.
③ She and her family have been here since 1993.
④ You'd better get your visa extended before it expires.

[해설] ①에서는 현재 사실의 반대를 가정하는 가정법 과거의 문장이며, 가정법 과거의 조건절에서 be동사는 주어의 수에 상관없이 were를 쓴다. ②에서는 동사 may express를 수식하는 역할을 해야 하므로 However 뒤에 위치한 형용사 good을 부사 well로 고쳐야 한다. ③에서는 '～로부터 지금까지'라는 의미를 가진 전치사 since가 쓰였으므로, 현재완료 시제의 문장을 썼다. ④에서는 '～하는 편이 낫다'라는 의미의 had better 뒤에는 동사원형이 오며, visa가 연장하는 행위의 대상이므로 수동을 나타내는 과거분사 extended를 쓴 것이다. 또한 접속사 before가 이끄는 절은 시간의 부사절이므로 현재시제로 미래를 나타낸다.

[해석] ① 만일 내가 너라면 그 전화에 답신을 하지 않을 텐데. ② 편지가 쓴 사람의 생각을 아무리 잘 나타낸다 하더라도, 그의 성격이 가진 따듯한 기운 모두를 옮기지는 못한다. ③ 그녀와 그녀의 가족들은 1993년 이래로 줄곧 이곳에 있어 왔다. ④ 너는 비자가 만기되기 전에 연장하는 편이 낫다.

[정답] ②

05 다음 중 문법적으로 옳지 않은 것은?

① Teenagers spend a lot of time thinking about what others think of them.
② The news that she was promoted was music to her husband's ears.
③ Women were looked upon as being housewives rather than breadwinners.
④ Her books have published in 15 languages and sold in over 20 countries.

[해설] ④에서 주어인 Her books와 동사 publish의 관계가 능동이 아닌 수동이므로 have published를 have been published로 해야 한다. ①에서 spend + 목적어 + v-ing의 구조가 옳다는 것과 그리고 what 이하가 불완전해야 한다는 것을 확인한다. 또한 이 문장에서는 think of와 함께 쓰인 what은 우리말로 '어떻게'라고 해석하는데 이로 인해 how로 전환하지 않도록 주의한다. ②에서 news는 단수 취급한다는 것을 확인한다. 즉 단수동사 was로 한 것이 옳다는 것을 확인한다. that절은 the news와 동격으로 사용되었다는 것도 확인한다. ③에서 look upon A as B(A를 B로 간주하다)가 수동이 되었다는 것을 확인한다. 이때 upon을 빼지 않도록 주의한다.

[어휘] breadwinner 한 가정의 벌이하는 사람 spend + 목적어 + v-ing ~을 ~하는데 시간, 돈을 보내다, 쓰다
look upon(regard, think of) A as B A를 B로 생각하다, 간주하다

[해석] ① 십대들은 남들이 자신에 대해 어떻게 생각할 지에 대해 생각하며 많은 시간을 보낸다. ② 승진했다는 소식이 남편에게는 기쁨이었다. ③ 여성들이 생계를 꾸려가는 사람이라기보다는 주부로 여겨졌다. ④ 그녀의 책은 15개의 언어로 출판되었고 20개국에서 판매되었다.

[정답] ④

06 다음 글의 빈칸 (A), (B)에 들어갈 말로 가장 적절한 것은?

Young people today lack self-confidence, which is evident in their awareness of appearance. Many young people wear brand-name clothes to boost their confidence. It is hard for them to feel good about themselves without those brand names. __(A)__, some girls believe they would look 10 pounds heavier in a pair of $15 jeans. A survey published by Boston Magazine showed that 31 out of 100 teen girls' clothes were all brand names. "They make me look thinner and give me confidence," was the common reason given. __(B)__, this belief in name brands actually contributes to the lack of self-confidence. According to Simon David Buckingham, who wrote Unorganization: Life Styles for the Next Millennium, when people buy designer goods, they can hide behind an image created by someone else, because these purchasers don't have the independence and originality to create their own lifestyle.

	(A)	(B)
①	In fact	In addition
②	In fact	However
③	Therefore	Accordingly
④	Therefore	Similarly

해설 (A) 다음에 앞의 내용이 사실이라는 것을 강조하는 내용이 뒤따르고 있으므로, **In fact**(사실은, 사실상)가 적절하다. (B)의 앞 내용과 뒤 내용은 대조·역접을 나타내고 있으므로, **However**(그러나)가 적절하다. ① 사실상(은) - 게다가 ③ 그러므로 - 그에 따라(따라서) ④ 그러므로 - 마찬가지로(비슷하게, 이와 같이)

어휘 self-confidence 자신감 boost 북돋다 originality 독창성

해석 오늘날의 젊은이들은 자신감이 없는데, 그것은 외모에 대한 그들의 인식에서 분명하게 나타난다. 많은 젊은이들이 자신들의 자신감을 키우기 위해 유명 상표의 옷을 입는다. 그러한 유명 상표가 없을 때 그들이 스스로에 대해 좋은 느낌을 갖기란 어렵다. 사실, 어떤 소녀들은 15달러짜리 청바지를 입을 때 체중이 10파운드는 더 나가 보일 거라고 믿는다. Boston Magazine에 발행된 한 조사는 100명 중 31명의 10대 소녀들의 옷이 모두 유명 상표였음을 보여주었다. "그것들이 나를 더 날씬하게 보이도록 해주고 나에게 자신감을 부여해줘요."라는 것이 보편적으로 제시되는 이유이다. 그러나, 유명 상표에 대한 이러한 믿음은 사실상 자신감 부족의 원인이 된다. Unorganization: Life Styles for the Next Millennium을 저술한 Simon David Buckingham에 따르면, 사람들이 (유명) 디자이너의 제품을 구입할 때 그들은 다른 사람들이 만들어낸 이미지 뒤에 숨을 수 있는 데, 이러한 구매자들은 자신만의 생활방식을 만들어낼 자립심과 독창성을 지니고 있지 못하기 때문이다.

정답 ②

07 (A), (B), (C) 각 빈칸 문맥에 맞는 말로 가장 적절한 것은?

> The Atitlán Giant Grebe was a large, flightless bird that had evolved from the much more widespread and smaller Pied-billed Grebe. By 1965 there were only around 80 birds left on Lake Atitlán. One immediate reason was easy enough to spot: the local human population was cutting down the reed beds at a furious rate. This __(A)__ was driven by the needs of a fast growing mat-making industry. But there were other problems. An American airline was intent on developing the lake as a tourist destination for fishermen. However, there was a major problem with this idea: the lake __(B)__ any suitable sporting fish! To compensate for this rather obvious defect, a specially selected species of fish called the Large-mouthed Bass was introduced. The introduced individuals immediately turned their attentions to the crabs and small fish that lived in the lake, thus __(C)__ with the few remaining grebes for food. There is also little doubt that they sometimes gobbled up the zebra-striped Atitlán Giant Grebe's chicks.

	(A)	(B)	(C)
①	accommodation	lacked	competing
②	accommodation	supported	cooperating
③	destruction	lacked	competing
④	destruction	supported	cooperating

[해설] (A) 인간들이 맹렬한 속도로 갈대밭을 베어 넘어뜨리는 행위를 대신하는 표현이 와야 하므로 '파괴'의 의미인 **destruction**이 적절하다. **accommodation**은 '적응, 조화, 화해'의 의미이다. (B) 관광지로서 호수가 가지고 있는 결함을 보충하기 위해 **Large-mouthed Bass**를 도입했다고 언급하고 있으므로 그 호수에는 스포츠용[낚시용] 물고기가 없었다는 것을 알 수 있다. 따라서 '없었다'의 의미인 **lacked**가 적절하다. **support**는 '지지[지원]하다'의 의미이다. (C) **Atitlá Giant Grebe**가 **Atitlá** 호수에서 생존에 어려움을 겪게 된 원인을 설명하고 있는 글이므로, 새로 도입된 **Large-mouthed Bass**가 먹이를 두고 **Atitlá Giant Grebe**와 경쟁하게 되었다는 것을 알 수 있다. 따라서 '경쟁하였다'의 의미인 **competing**이 적절하다. **cooperate**는 '협력하다'의 의미이다.

[어휘] **flightless** 날지 못하는 **evolve** 진화하다 **spot** 알아내다, 발견하다 **reed bed** 갈대밭 **furious** 맹렬한, 몹시 화가 난 **intent** 강한 관심을 보이는 **tourist destination** 관광지 **compensate for** ~을 보충[보상]하다 **obvious** 분명한 **defect** 결함 **chick** 새끼 새, 병아리 **reed** 갈대 **gobble up** 게걸스럽게 먹다

[해석] **Atitlá Giant Grebe**는 훨씬 더 널리 퍼져 있던 더 작은 **Piedbilled Grebe**(얼룩부리논병아리)에서 진화한 날지 못하는 큰 새였다. 1965년 무렵에는 **Atitlá** 호수에 약 80마리만이 남아 있었다. 한 가지 직접적인 원인은 알아내기 매우 쉬웠는데, 현지의 인간들이 맹렬한 속도로 갈대밭을 베어 넘어뜨리는 것이었다. 이런 파괴는 빠르게 성장하는 매트 제조 산업의 필요에 의해 추진되었다. 그러나 다른 문제들이 있었다. 한 미국 항공사가 그 호수를 낚시꾼들의 관광지로 개발하는 데 강한 관심을 보였다. 하지만 이 생각에 큰 문제가 있었는데, 그 호수에는 적절한 스포츠용[낚시용] 물고기가 없었다! 이런 다소 분명한 결함을 보충하기 위해 **Large-mouthed Bass**(큰입농어)라 불리는 특별히 선택된 물고기 종이 도입되었다. 그 도입된 개체는 즉시 그 호수에 사는 게와 작은 물고기에게 관심을 돌렸고, 이리하여 몇 마리 안 남은 논병아리와 먹이를 놓고 경쟁하였다. 또한, 가끔 그들[큰입농어들]이 얼룩말 줄무늬가 있는 **Atitlá Giant Grebe** 새끼들을 게걸스럽게 먹어치웠다는 데 의심의 여지가 거의 없다.

[정답] ③

08 다음 글의 내용과 일치하지 않는 것을 고르시오.

> Followers are a critical part of the leadership equation, but their role has not always been appreciated. For a long time, in fact, "the common view of leadership was that leaders actively led and subordinates, later called followers, passively and obediently followed." Over time, especially in the last century, social change shaped people's views of followers, and leadership theories gradually recognized the active and important role that followers play in the leadership process. Today it seems natural to accept the important role followers play. One aspect of leadership is particularly worth noting in this regard: Leadership is a social influence process shared among all members of a group. Leadership is not restricted to the influence exerted by someone in a particular position or role; followers are part of the leadership process, too.

① For a length of time, it was understood that leaders actively led and followers passively followed.
② People's views of subordinates were influenced by social change.
③ The important role of followers is still denied today.
④ Both leaders and followers participate in the leadership process.

[해설] ③ 네 번째 문장에서 오늘날에는 따르는 사람들의 중요한 역할을 받아들이는 것이 당연해 보인다고 언급했으므로, 따르는 사람들의 중요한 역할이 오늘날에도 여전히 부정되고 있다는 설명은 글의 내용과 일치하지 않는다. ① 두 번째 문장에서 리더십에 관한 공통적인 관점은 오랫동안 '리더들은 적극적으로 이끌고 따르는 사람들은 수동적으로 그리고 고분고분하게 따르는 것'이었다고 했으므로 글의 내용과 일치한다. ② 세 번째 문장에서 시간이 지나면서, 특히 지난 세기에 사회적 변화가 따르는 사람들에 대한 사람들의 관점을 형성했다고 했고, 두 번째 문장에서 종속자들이 이후에 따르는 사람들이라 불리게 되었다고 했으므로 종속자들 즉, 따르는 사람들에 대한 사람들의 관점이 사회적 변화에 의해 영향을 받았다는 설명은 글의 내용과 일치한다. ④ 여섯 번째 문장에서 리더십은 특정한 위치나 역할에 있는 누군가 즉, 리더에 의해 행사 되는 영향에만 국한되지 않고 따르는 사람들 역시 리더십 과정의 일부분이라고 했으므로 리더와 따르는 사람들 모두 리더십 과정에 참여한다는 설명은 글의 내용과 일치한다. ① 오랜 기간 동안 리더들은 적극적으로 이끌고, 따르는 사람들은 수동적으로 따르는 것으로 이해되었다. ② 종속자들에 대한 사람들의 관점은 사회적 변화에 의해 영향을 받았다. ③ 따르는 사람들의 중요한 역할은 오늘날에도 여전히 부정되고 있다. ④ 리더와 따르는 사람들 모두 리더십 과정에 참여한다.

[어휘] **equation** 방정식, 등식, 동일시, (여러 가지 요소들을 고려해야 하는) 상황 **appreciate** [사람·물건의] (가치를) 정당하게 평가하다, 이해하다; ~의 진가를 인정하다, 진가를 알다; [문학·예술 등을] 감상하다 **subordinate** 하위[하급]의; 열등한, 부차[보조]적인, ~에 지배된, 복종[종속]하는

[해석] 따르는 사람들은 리더십 방정식의 중요한 부분이지만, 그들의 역할이 항상 제대로 인식되어 온 것은 아니다. 오랫동안 사실 "리더십에 대한 공통된 관점은 리더들은 적극적으로 이끌고, 나중에 따르는 사람들로 불린 종속자들은 수동적으로 그리고 고분고분하게 따른다는 것이었다." 시간이 지나면서, 특히 지난 세기에 사회적 변화가 따르는 사람들에 대한 사람들의 관점을 형성했고, 리더십 이론들은 점차 따르는 사람들이 리더십 과정에서 수행하는 적극적이고 중요한 역할을 인식했다. 오늘날에는 따르는 사람들 하는 중요한 역할을 받아들이는 것이 당연해 보인다. 리더십의 한 측면은 이 점과 관련하여 특히 주목할 가치가 있다: 리더십은 한 그룹의 모든 구성원들 사이에서 공유되는 사회적 영향 과정이다. 리더십은 특정한 위치나 역할에 있는 누군가에 의해 행사되는 영향에만 국한되지 않는다; 따르는 사람들 역시 리더십 과정의 일부분이다.

[정답] ③

09 주어진 문장이 들어갈 위치로 가장 적절한 것은?

> The same thinking can be applied to any number of goals, like improving performance at work.

The happy brain tends to focus on the short term. (①) That being the case, it's a good idea to consider what short-term goals we can accomplish that will eventually lead to accomplishing long-term goals. (②) For instance, if you want to lose thirty pounds in six months, what short-term goals can you associate with losing the smaller increments of weight that will get you there? (③) Maybe it's something as simple as rewarding yourself each week that you lose two pounds. (④) By breaking the overall goal into smaller, shorter-term parts, we can focus on incremental accomplishments instead of being overwhelmed by the enormity of the goal in our profession.

[해설] 주어진 문장에 '그 같은 생각'이 '직장에서의 성과 향상'에도 적용될 수 있다는 내용이 있으므로, 이 '같은 생각'은 ④ 이전까지 설명된 장기적인 목표 달성을 위해 단기적인 목표를 세우는 것에 대한 체중 감량의 예시로 볼 수 있다. 또한 이것이 직장 또는 직업(profession)에서 적용된 결과가 ④ 이후에 설명되었으므로 주어진 문장은 ④에 들어가는 것이 자연스럽다.

[어휘] increment 증가, 증대, 증식; 증가량, 증액 rewarding 가치 있는, 보람이 있는 enormity 심각함, 영향력의 거대[막대]함, [범죄의] 무모함

[해석] 행복한 두뇌는 단기간에 집중하는 경향이 있다. 사정이 그렇다면, 결국 장기적인 목표를 달성하게 할 어떤 단기적인 목표를 우리가 달성할 수 있을지를 생각해 보는 것이 좋다. 예를 들어, 만약 당신이 6개월 안에 30파운드를 감량하기를 원한다면, 당신은 어떤 단기적인 목표를 여러분을 거기에 이르게 할 더 작은 무게의 증가량들을 감량하는 것과 연관 지을 수 있는가? 아마도 그것은 매주 2파운드를 감량할 때마다 당신 스스로에게 보상하는 것만큼 간단한 일일 것이다. 같은 생각이 직장에서의 성과를 향상시키는 것과 같은 어떤 목표에도 적용될 수 있다. 전체적인 목표를 더 작고 단기적인 부분으로 나눔으로서, 우리는 우리의 직업에서 목표의 거대함에 압도되는 대신 점진적인 성취에 초점을 맞출 수 있다.

[정답] ④

10 빈칸에 들어갈 말로 가장 적절한 것은?

About 20 years ago, a delicate seaweed named Caulerpa taxifolia was brought from its native habitat in the Pacific Ocean to a zoo in Germany, where it was used to decorate saltwater aquarium exhibits, a seemingly harmless action. The seaweed was such a success that samples were sent to other institutions, including the Oceanographic Museum in Monaco. Within about five years of its introduction there, an unfortunate accident took place. The seaweed was accidentally flushed into the Mediterranean when exhibit tanks were cleaned. This might seem harmless, but considering it so would ignore the tremendous power of the species to act as _____. Once freed in the Mediterranean, Caulerpa quickly changed its growth pattern and adapted to its new habitat. This may have occurred through a mutation or through hybridization with native seaweeds. Whatever the exact genetic explanation, today Caulerpa grows about six times larger in the Mediterranean than it does in its native Pacific Ocean. Over the past two or three years, Caulerpa has spread to the Adriatic, and it now appears to threaten the entire Mediterranean with its ability to choke out competing seaweeds. It grows on rocks, sand, and mud. It grows so widely and quickly that it blankets competing native seaweeds, excluding them and it appears to be toxic to local animals that feed on seaweeds.

① biological invaders
② trade barriers
③ germ carriers
④ protective filters

[해설] 외래종 해초가 유입되어 확산되는 것이 해롭지 않을 것이라고 생각하는 것은 그 종이 가진 생물학적 침입자로서의 힘을 무시하는 것이므로, 빈칸에는 ① '생물학적 침입자들'이 적절하다. ② 무역장벽들 ③ 세균 운반체 ④ 보호 필터

[어휘] flush 흘려보내다 mutation (돌연)변이 hybridization (이종)교배

[해석] 약 20년 전, Caulerpa taxifolia라는 이름을 가진 여린 해초가 태평양에 있는 본래 서식지에서 독일에 있는 동물원으로 가져와졌는데, 그곳에서 그 해초는 해수 수족관 전시회를 장식하는데 사용되었고, 이는 해롭지 않은 행위처럼 보였다. 그 해초는 매우 성공적이어서 표본들은 모나코에 있는 해양 박물관을 포함한 다른 기관들로 보내졌다. 그곳으로 해초가 유입된 지 대략 5년도 되지 않아 불행한 사고가 발생했다. 그 해초는 전시용 수조가 청소될 때 우연히 지중해로 흘러들어 갔다. 이는 무해한 것처럼 보일지 모르지만 그럴 것으로 생각하는 것은 생물학적 침입자로서의 역할을 할 수 있는 그 종의 엄청난 힘을 무시하는 것일 것이다. 일단 지중해로 흘러들어 가게 되자 Caulerpa는 자신의 성장 패턴을 빠르게 변화시켰고 새로운 서식지에 적응했다. 이러한 일이 변이 또는 토종 해초들과의 이종교배를 통해서 발생했을지도 모른다. 정확한 유전학적 설명이 무엇이든지 간에 오늘날 Caulerpa는 원산지인 태평양에서보다 지중해에서 약 6배 더 크게 자란다. 지난 2~3년에 걸쳐 Caulerpa는 아드리아 해로 퍼졌고, 이는 현재 경쟁 관계에 있는 해초들을 질식시키는 능력을 가지고 지중해 전체를 위협하고 있는 듯하다. 이 해초는 바위, 모래 그리고 진흙에서 자란다. 그것은 매우 넓고 빠르게 성장해서 경쟁 관계에 있는 토종 해초들을 몰아내고 완전히 덮어 버리고, 해초들을 먹고 사는 지역 동물들에게 해가 되는 것으로 보인다.

[정답] ①

09 하프 모의고사 해설

01 다음 밑줄 친 단어의 의미와 가장 가까운 것은?

> Riding a roller coaster can be a joy ride of emotions: the nervous anticipation as you're strapped into your seat, the questioning and regret that comes as you go up, up, up, and the sheer adrenaline rush as the car takes that first dive.

① utter
② scary
③ occasional
④ manageable

해설 sheer [ʃiər] 형 완전한, 순전한(= utter) 부 완전히(= quite); 똑바로(= directly)

영영 sheer : ① complete and without restriction or qualification; sometimes used informally as intensifiers ② not mixed with extraneous elements ③ very steep

어휘 joy ride 폭주 anticipation 기대 regret 후회 occasional 가끔 manageable 관리할 수 있는 scary 무서운, 겁나는 occasional 가끔의 manageable 관리할 수 있는

해석 롤러코스터를 타는 것은 감정의 드라이브일 수 있다: 당신이 좌석에 묶여 있을 때의 초조한 기대감, 위로, 위로 올라가고 또 올라가면서 오게 되는 의문과 후회, 그리고 기구가 첫 번째로 급강하할 때 솟구치는 순수한 아드레날린 같은 것이다.

정답 ①

02 밑줄 친 부분의 의미와 가장 가까운 것은?

> Justifications are accounts in which one accepts responsibility for the act in question, but denies the pejorative quality associated with it.

① derogatory
② extrovert
③ mandatory
④ redundant

해설 pejorative [pidʒɔ́ːrətiv] 형 경멸적인, 비난하는 의미의 = derogatory

영영 pejorative : expressing disapproval

어휘 justification 변명, 정당화 account 설명, 말 accept 받아들이다 responsibility 책임감 in question 논쟁 중인 deny 부정하다 quality 특성, 본질 associated with ~와 관련된 extrovert 외향적인 mandatory 의무적인 redundant 여분의

해석 변명이란 누군가 논쟁 중인 행위에 대한 책임은 인정하지만 그것과 관련된 경멸적인 본질을 부정하는 말이다.

정답 ①

03 (A), (B), (C) 빈칸의 문맥에 맞는 낱말로 가장 적절한 것은?

A broody hen, which sits on her eggs, needs to incubate her eggs for 21 days before they hatch. The eggs are protected under her against a featherless patch of skin on her breast called a brood patch. Though it is normally a feathered area on her body, the hormones of broodiness cause her to lose feathers on her belly, creating __(A)__ contact with the skin and acting to incubate the eggs. She turns the eggs several times each day so that the embryo inside the egg does not stick to the shell membrane. She will become very __(B)__, having her feathers stand on end and making a shrieking sound if approached too closely. Broody hens will leave the nest unattended for short periods of time only in search of food and water and to eliminate waste. Care should be taken not to position water and food too closely to the nest, as it could attract attention to the nest site and will __(C)__ her needed exercise.

	(A)	(B)	(C)
①	direct	protective	decrease
②	direct	protective	increase
③	direct	tolerant	decrease
④	indirect	tolerant	increase
⑤	indirect	tolerant	decrease

[해설] (A) 암탉의 배 부분에 깃털이 빠져서 알이 피부와 직접 접촉하게 된다고 하는 것이 글의 흐름상 자연스럽다. 그러므로 direct(직접적인)를 써야 한다. indirect는 '간접적인'이라는 뜻이다. (B) 누군가가 지나치게 가까이 접근하면 암탉이 깃털을 곤두세우고 날카로운 소리를 내는 것은 방어적인 자세를 취하는 것이므로 protective(방어적인)를 써야 한다. tolerant는 '관대한'이라는 뜻이다. (C) 물과 먹이를 둥우리에서 너무 가까운 곳에 놓으면 암탉의 운동량이 줄어들게 된다고 해야 하므로 decrease(줄이다)를 써야 한다. increase는 '늘리다'라는 뜻이다.

[어휘] broody 알을 품고 싶어 하는 incubate (알을) 품다 hatch 부화되다 brood patch 포란반(포란 중인 새의 복부에서 볼 수 있는 털이 없는 부분) shell (달걀) 껍질, 껍데기 protective 방어적인, 보호하려고 드는 tolerant 관대한, 아량 있는 shriek 날카로운 소리를 내다 in search of ~을 찾아서 eliminate 없애다 embryo 배아 membrane 막

[해석] 알을 품는 암탉은 알들이 부화될 때까지 21일 동안 품어야 한다. 알들은 '포란반(抱卵斑)'이라고 불리는 암탉 가슴의 깃털이 없는 피부 구역에 닿아 암탉의 몸 아래서 보호된다. 비록 그곳이 보통 때는 암탉의 몸 중 깃털이 난 부분이지만, 알을 품게 하는 호르몬이 암탉의 배에 난 깃털을 빠지게 하고 그리하여 피부와 직접적인 접촉을 하게 하여 알을 부화시키는 역할을 한다. 암탉은 알 속의 배아가 알 껍질막에 붙지 않도록 매일 몇 번씩 알을 굴린다. 암탉은 매우 방어적이 되어, 무엇인가가 지나치게 가까이 접근하면 깃털을 곤두세우고 날카로운 소리를 낸다. 알을 품는 암탉은 오직 먹이와 물을 찾기 위해서, 그리고 배변하기 위해서만 짧은 시간 동안 둥우리를 돌보지 않은 채 남겨둔다. 물과 먹이를 둥우리에서 너무 가까운 곳에 놓지 않도록 주의해야 하는데, 그렇게 하면 둥우리가 있는 지점에 대한 주의를 끌 수 있으며 암탉에게 필요한 운동량을 줄일 수도 있기 때문이다.

[정답] ①

04 밑줄 친 부분 중 어법상 가장 옳지 않은 것은?

> Inventor Elias Howe attributed the discovery of the sewing machine ① <u>for</u> a dream ② <u>in which</u> he was captured by cannibals. He noticed as they danced around him ③ <u>that</u> there were holes at the tips of spears, and he realized this was the design feature he needed ④ <u>to solve</u> his problem.

[해설] ①에서 'attribute A to B A를 B를 탓으로 돌리다(A를 B 때문이라고 생각하다)'는 의미의 표현이다. 재봉틀의 발견을 꿈의 탓으로 했다는 의미이므로 for는 to로 고쳐야 한다. for ⇨ to ②에서 관계절의 형태가 완전하므로 '전치사 + 관계대명사'의 형태가 바르다. 또한 which이하의 내용이 꿈속에서의 내용이므로 전치사 in의 사용 역시 바르다. ③에서 that은 명사절을 이끄는 접속사로 noticed의 목적어로 사용되었다. 뒤의 문장이 안전하므로 명사절 접속사 that이 바르게 쓰였다. as they danced around him은 부사절로 noticed와 that사이에 삽입된 것이다. ④에서 need는 to부정사를 목적어로 취하는 완전타동사로 to부정사가 need의 목적어로 바르게 쓰였다.

[어휘] sewing 재봉, 바느질, 봉제업 cannibal 식인종(의) spear 명 창, 죽창 형 찌르는 feature 명 두드러진 점, 특징, 요점 동 ~의 특징을 이루다, ~을 특집 기사로 다루다

[해석] 발명가 Elias Howe는 자신이 식인종에게 붙잡힌 꿈 때문에 재봉틀을 발견했다고 말했다. 그는 식인종들이 자신 주위에서 춤을 추면서 창끝에 구멍이 있다는 것을 알아차렸고, 이것이 자신의 문제를 해결하는 데 필요한 디자인적 특징이라는 것을 깨달았다.

[정답] ①

05 다음 우리말 영작이 올바른 문장을 고르시오.

① 그는 노파에게 공손하게 사과했다.
   ⇨ He politely apologized the old lady.
② 나의 한 친구는 이 소설을 읽는 것을 즐겼다.
   ⇨ A friend of mine enjoyed to read this novel.
③ 그녀는 부모님 댁을 격주로 주말에 방문한다.
   ⇨ She visits her parents every other weekends.
④ 운동을 하는 좋은 방법은 자전거를 타는 것이다.
   ⇨ A good means of exercise is riding a bicycle.

[해설] 명사 means는 '수단', '방법'이란 의미로 쓰인 경우에는 단수로 취급하며, '재산', '수입'이란 의미로 쓰인 경우에는 복수로 취급한다. 주어진 문장에서는 전자의 의미로 쓰였으므로, 동사로 is를 쓴 것은 옳은 표현이다. ①에서 apologize는 자동사이므로 사과하는 대상을 나타내는 표현 앞에 전치사를 써야 한다. 그러므로 apologized를 apologized to로 고쳐야 한다. ②에서 enjoy는 동명사를 목적어로 취하는 동사이므로, to read를 reading으로 고쳐야 한다. ③에서 격일, 격주, 격년 등을 표현할 때에는 every other 뒤에 단수 명사를 써서 every other day, every other week, every other year와 같이 해야 한다. 그러므로 every other weekends를 every other weekend로 고쳐야 한다.

[정답] ④

06 다음 글의 주제로 가장 적절한 것은?

As the digital revolution upends newsrooms across the country, here's my advice for all the reporters. I've been a reporter for more than 25 years, so I have lived through a half dozen technological life cycles. The most dramatic transformations have come in the last half dozen years. That means I am, with increasing frequency, making stuff up as I go along. Much of the time in the news business, we have no idea what we are doing. We show up in the morning and someone says, "Can you write a story about (pick one) tax policy/immigration/climate change?" When newspapers had once-a-day deadlines, we said a reporter would learn in the morning and teach at night—write a story that could inform tomorrow's readers on a topic the reporter knew nothing about 24 hours earlier. Now it is more like learning at the top of the hour and teaching at the bottom of the same hour. I'm also running a political podcast, for example, and during the presidential conventions, we should be able to use it to do real-time interviews anywhere. I am just increasingly working without a script.

① a reporter as a teacher
② a reporter and improvisation
③ technology in politics
④ fields of journalism and technology

[해설] 기술적 발전으로 인하여 언론계에서 발생하고 있는 변화들에 관해 자신의 경험을 토대로 설명하고 있는 글이다. 지문의 네 번째 문장인 That means I am with increasing frequency, making stuff up as I go along.을 이 글 전체의 주제문으로 볼 수 있는데, 기술적 발전으로 인해 뉴스가 이전과는 달리 즉흥적으로 콘텐츠를 창조하여 보도해야 하고 있음을 설명하고 있다. 아침에 배워 저녁에 글을 써야 했던 과거와는 달리 현재의 기자들은 어떤 시각이 시작할 때 배워 그 시각이 끝날 때 이미 그에 관해 보도를 해야 한다는 것이 그에 관한 예시이다 또한 자신의 정치 팟캐스트를 다른 예시로 들어 실시간 인터뷰를 위해 대본 없이 즉석에서 진행하는 일이 늘어나고 있음을 설명한다. 따라서 이 글의 주제로는 ②가 적합하다. ① 교사로서의 기자 ② 기자와 즉흥성 ③ 정치학에서의 기술 ④ 저널리즘과 기술의 분야들

[어휘] upend ~을 거꾸로 하다; [취미·의견·평판·조직에] 철저한[근본적인] 영향을 주다; ~을 뒤엎다 transformation 변화[탈바꿈], 변신 at the bottom of ~의 주요 원인[주모자]으로, ~의 밑바닥에 improvisation 즉석에서 한[지은] 것

[해석] 디지털 혁명이 전국의 뉴스룸에 근본적 변화를 일으키게 됨에 따라 여기 기자들에게 주는 내 조언들이 있다. 나는 25년 동안 기자였기 때문에, 여섯 번 정도의 기술적 라이프 사이클을 겪었다. 가장 극적인 변화들은 마지막의 6년간에 왔다. 이는 내가 더욱 잦은 빈도로 진행하면서 뭔가를 만들어가고 있음을 의미한다. 뉴스 업계에 있어 많은 시간 동안 우리는 우리가 하고 있는 것에 관해 모른다. 우리는 아침에 출근을 하고, 누군가는 "세금 정책/이민/기후변화에 관해 글을 써주실래요"라고 말한다. 기자들이 하루에 한 번씩 마감이 있었을 때, 우리는 기자들은 아침에는 배우고 밤에는 가르쳐야 한다고 말을 했다 —그 기자가 24시간 전에는 알지 못했던 주제에 관해 내일의 독자들에게 알려주는 기사를 쓰는 것 말이다. 이제 이것은 마치 정시에는 배우고 30분에는 가르치는 것과 같다. 예를 들면 나는 또한 정치 팟캐스트를 운영 중인데 대통령 정 중에 우리는 실시간 인터뷰를 하기 위해서 어디에서든 그것을 이용할 수 있어야만 한다. 나는 점점 더 대본 없이 일하고 있다.

[정답] ②

07 다음 빈칸에 들어갈 단어로 적절한 것을 고르시오.

> Nobel Prize-winning psychologist Daniel Kahneman changed the way the world thinks about economics, upending the notion that human beings are rational decision-makers. Along the way, his discipline-crossing influence has altered the way physicians make medical decisions and investors evaluate risk on Wall Street. In a paper, Kahneman and his colleagues outline a process for making big strategic decisions. Their suggested approach, labeled as "Mediating Assessments Protocol," or MAP, has a simple goal: To put off gut-based decision-making until a choice can be informed by a number of separate factors. "One of the essential purposes of MAP is basically to _____ intuition," Kahneman said in a recent interview with The Post. The structured process calls for analyzing a decision based on six to seven previously chosen attributes, discussing each of them separately and assigning them a relative percentile score, and finally, using those scores to make a holistic judgment.

① improve ② delay
③ possess ④ facilitate

[해설] Daniel Kahneman이 제시한 의사결정 방식에 대하여 설명하고 있는 글이다. 글의 앞부분에서 그가 기존의 의사결정 방식에 대한 사고를 뒤집었음을 언급하였고 글의 중반부 이하에서 그가 제시한 MAP이라는 이름의 의사결정 방식이 무엇인지를 설명하고 있다. 빈칸은 이러한 MAP의 핵심적 성격을 제시하는 부분에 있다. 빈칸 앞의 문장에서 MAP의 목표가 gut(직관, 배짱)에 의거한 결정을 지연(put off)시키는 것이라고 설명하므로 MAP이란 결국 직관을 유보하는 것임을 알 수 있다. 따라서 정답은 ②이다. 빈칸 뒤 문장에서도 MAP의 과정을 좀 더 자세히 설명하는데, MAP은 하나의 결정을 분석하고 각각을 평가하고 점수를 매겨 그것을 통해 총체적 판단을 내리는 것이라고 한다. 즉, 직관을 미루고 분석과 평가를 통해 총체적 판단을 한다는 것이다.

[어휘] upend ~을 거꾸로 하다. [취미·의견·평판·조직에] 철저한[근본적인] 영향을 주다; ~을 뒤엎다 along the way 그 과정에서 alter 변하다, 달라지다; 바꾸다, 고치다 label 라벨을 붙여 분류[명시]하다; ~을 (~이라고) 부르다(= designate) put off (시간·날짜를) 미루다 gut 명 직감, 배짱, 내장 통 (특히 화재로 건물방의) 내부[내용물]를 파괴하다 holistic 전체론의, 전체적인, 전체론적인

[해석] 노벨상 수상자인 심리학자 Daniel Kahneman은 인간이 이성적 의사결정자라는 개념을 뒤집으며 경제학에 관한 세계의 사고방식을 변화시켰다. 그 과정에서 그의 학문 전체에 걸친 영향력은 의사들이 의학적 결정을 내리는 방식, 그리고 투자가들이 월 스트리트에서의 위험을 평가하는 방식을 변화시켰다. 한 논문에서 Kahneman과 그의 동료들은 큰 전략적 결정을 내리기 위한 과정에 대한 개요를 제시했다. '조정 평가 프로토콜', 혹은 MAP이라고 이름 붙여진 그들이 제시한 접근법은 한 가지 간단한 목표를 갖는다: 하나의 선택이 다수의 개별적 요소들에 의해 설명될 때까지 배짱에 의거한 의사결정을 지연시키는 것이다. "MAP의 가장 중요한 목표 중에 하나는 기본적으로 직관을 유보하는 것이다"라고 Kahneman은 최근 〈포스트〉와의 인터뷰에서 말했다. 이러한 구조화된 과정은 이전에 선택된 여섯 개에서 일곱 개의 요소들에 의거하여 하나의 결정을 분해하고 각각을 개별적으로 논의한 후, 이들에게 상대적인 백분점수를 부여하고 마지막으로 총체적 판단을 위해 그 점수를 사용할 것을 요구한다.

[정답] ②

08 글의 흐름으로 보아, 주어진 문장이 들어가기에 가장 적절한 곳을 고르시오.

> Languages, too, have adapted over time to serve the needs of a particular population in their environment.

Language disappearance only superficially resembles species extinction. Animal species are complex, have evolved over long periods of time, possess unique traits, and have adapted to a specific ecological environment. (①) An extinct dodo bird can be stuffed by taxidermists and displayed in a museum after all its kind are dead and gone. (②) But a stuffed dodo is no substitute for a thriving dodo population. (③) They have been shaped by people to serve as repositories for cultural knowledge, efficiently packaged and readily transmittable across generations. (④) Like dodo birds in museums, languages may be preserved in dictionaries and books after they are no longer spoken. But a grammar book or dictionary is but a dim reflection of the richness of a spoken tongue in its native social setting.

[해설] ③ 뒤에 오는 문장에 있는 They가 languages를 가리키므로, 주어진 문장은 ③에 오는 것이 가장 적절하다.

[어휘] repository 저장소 stuff (동물을) 박제로 만들다 thriving (동식물이) 잘 자라는 reflection 그림자 no longer 더 이상 ~이 아닌, 이미 ~아니다 taxidermist 박제사

[해석] 언어 소멸은 피상적으로만 생물종의 멸종과 닮았다. 동물의 종은 복잡하고 오랜 기간 동안 진화해 왔으며 독특한 특성을 소유하고 있고 특정한 생태 환경에 적응해 왔다. 멸종된 도도새는 그 종이 모두 죽어 사라진 후에 박제사에 의해 박제되어 박물관에 전시될 수 있다. 그러나 박제된 도도새는 잘 자라는 도도새 개체의 대체물이 될 수 없다. 언어 역시 자기 환경에서 특정한 사람들의 필요에 기여하기 위해 오랜 기간 적응해왔다. 언어는, 세대 간에 효율적으로 포장되어 쉽게 전달될 수 있는 문화적 지식의 저장소 역할을 하기 위해 사람들에 의해 형성되어 왔다. 박물관에 있는 도도새처럼 언어도 더 이상 사용되지 않게 된 후에 사전과 책에 보존될 수 있다. 그러나 문법책이나 사전은 그 언어에 고유한 사회적 환경에서 말로 사용되는 언어의 풍부함에 대한 희미한 그림자에 불과하다.

[정답] ③

09 주어진 글 다음에 이어질 글의 순서로 가장 적절한 것을 고르시오.

Who could deny that the human body is a miracle? Imagine: each of us is safely housed within a bundle of blood, bone, and guts nurturing a little glow of life while suspended in a sea of constant change and danger.

(A) In other words, traditional housing approaches were specific to the culture, climate, and environment. Consider the igloo, a building using the thermal mass of ice to enclose heat and resist snow, or the ancient Egyptians' ventilation domes that produced interior cooling amid burning desert heat.

(B) Housing, likewise, originally developed slowly within particular human cultures and in response to specific climates and environments. Each culture around the world crafted a unique style of housing from the fabric of their surroundings.

(C) The miracle becomes even more amazing when you consider the long, slow, evolutionary process of give and take that produced the human body. Our bodies developed with nature, within it, as part of it, over time.

① (A) – (C) – (B)   ② (B) – (A) – (C)
③ (C) – (B) – (A)   ④ (C) – (A) – (B)

[해설] 인간의 몸이 생명을 유지할 수 있도록 구성되어 있다는 내용의 주어진 글 다음에, (C) 인간의 몸은 진화의 과정으로 발전했다는 내용이 오고, (B) 주택도 이와 마찬가지로 특정한 기후와 환경에 반응하며 발전했다는 내용이 이어지고, (A) 환경에 적응하여 발전한 전통적인 주택 방식의 예시 내용으로 이어지는 것이 자연스럽다.

[어휘] craft 만들다 fabric 구조 suspend 매달다, 걸다, 보류하다, 미루다; ~을 연기하다, 일시 정지[중지]하다, 정학[정직]시키다 thermal 형 열[온도]의, [의복이] 체온을 유지하는 명 상승 온난 기류 enclose 둘러싸다; [토지·건물 등을] [울타리로] 에워싸다, 두르다, 동봉하다 ventilation 통기, 환기; 통풍 상태, (자유로운) 토의, 토론; (감정의) 배출; 공표

[해석] 인간의 몸이 기적이라는 것을 누가 부정할 수 있겠는가? 상상해 보라. 우리 모두는 끊임없는 변화와 위험의 바다에 떠 있으면서, 생명의 작은 빛을 키워 주는 일단의 혈액, 뼈, 그리고 장기 내에 안전하게 보호된다. (C) 당신이 인간의 몸을 만들어 낸 상호 작용의 길고, 느린, 진화의 과정을 생각해 보면, 그 기적은 훨씬 더 대단한 것이 된다. 우리의 몸은 시간이 흐르면서 자연과 함께, 자연 안에서, 자연의 일부로서 발전했다. (B) 이와 마찬가지로, 주택은 특정한 인간 문화 내에서, 그리고 특정한 기후와 환경에 반응하면서 독창적으로 서서히 발전했다. 전 세계의 각 문화는 주변 환경의 구조로부터 독특한 주택 양식을 만들어냈다. (A) 다시 말해서, 전통적인 주택 방식은 문화, 기후, 그리고 환경에 고유한 것이었다. 열은 감싸고 눈은 견뎌내기 위해 얼음의 열질량을 이용한 건물인 이글루나, 타는 듯한 사막 열기 한 가운데에서 내부를 시원하게 해주는 고대 이집트인들의 통풍 돔을 생각해 보라.

[정답] ③

10 다음 글의 내용으로 적절한 것은?

> There are many different types of headaches. Tension or muscle headaches are experienced as a dull band of pain on both sides of the head. They may be caused by poor posture, eyestrain, or emotional conflicts such as grief or depression. Tension headache is the most common type of headache and is typically treated with over-the-counter medications. A migraine headache tends to produce a throbbing pain, often quite severe, and is generally localized on one side of the head. Often accompanied by nausea, vomiting, and dizziness, migraines affect more than 23 million people in North America. Women are three times more likely than men to have an attack. Migraines are associated with increased blood flow in the arteries and veins which surround the brain. About one-third of migraine sufferers will report the presence of an "aura" between five and 30 minutes before the migraine begins. This aura may involve visual experiences such as wavy lines or flashing lights or visual or auditory hallucinations. The presence of aura may indicate neurological problem, and you should seek medical attention.

① Women have more migraine headaches than men because they suffer more depression.
② Migraine headaches accompanied by an "aura" have the potential to be devastating.
③ Migraine headaches can be cured by taking over-the-computer medications.
④ One can relieve a migraine headache by rectifying a poor posture

[해설] '편두통 환자 가운데 일부는 이상감각을 경험하는데, 이는 뇌신경적 문제를 보여주는 것일 수 있기 때문에 병원에서 치료를 받아야 한다'는 지적에서, 이상감각을 동반하는 편두통이 큰 피해를 줄 수 있다고 유추할 수 있다. ① 여성들은 우울증을 앓기 때문에 남성보다 편두통이 더 심하다. ② "이상감각"을 동반하는 편두통은 파국적일 가능성이 있다. ③ 편두통은 일반 약국에서 파는 약을 복용해 치료할 수 있다. ④ 편두통은 자세를 바르게 교정해서 통증을 경감할 수 있다.

[어휘] **conflict** 싸움, 갈등 **depression** 의기소침, 우울, 불경기 **migraine** 편두통 **localize** 국한하다, 지방화하다 **throbbing** 두근거리는, 고동치는 **nausea** 메스꺼움 **vomiting** 구토 **dizziness** 현기증 **dull** 둔한, 둔감한 **severe** 가혹한, 위험한 **artery** 동맥 **aura** 위험한, 주위에 감도는 **hallucination** 환각, 망상

[해석] 두통에는 여러 가지 유형이 있다. 긴장형 두통, 즉 근육형 두통이 오면 머리 양쪽에서 일정 부위의 둔통을 느낀다. 이것은 바르지 못한 자세, 눈의 긴장, 슬픔과 우울 같은 정서적인 갈등으로 인해 생길 수 있다. 긴장형 두통은 가장 일반적인 유형의 두통인데, 이것은 약국에서 처방전 없이 판매하는 약으로 치료할 수 있다. 편두통은 종종 심하게 욱신거리는 통증과 한쪽 머리만 아픈 국부다. 가끔 메스꺼움, 구토, 그리고 현기증을 동반하는 편두통은 북아메리카 지역에만 2,300만 명 이상의 사람들이 겪고 있다. 여성이 편두통을 앓을 가능성은 남성의 세 배 이상이다. 편두통은 뇌를 둘러싸고 있는 동맥과 정맥의 혈압상승과 관련이 있다. 편두통 환자 가운데 약 1/3이상이 편두통이 오기 전에 5분에서 30분 정도의 '이상감각'을 경험한다고 한다. 이런 이상감각에는 구불거리는 선이나 섬광 같은 경험이나 시각적, 청각적 환각 현상들이 있다. 이상감각의 존재는 뇌신경적 문제를 보여주는 것일 수 있기 때문에 병원 진료를 받아야 한다.

[정답] ②

10 하프 모의고사 해설

01 다음 밑줄 친 단어의 의미와 가장 가까운 것은?

> Twenty years of Fascist talk of "Rome's fated hills" and "ineluctable destinies," of "unavoidable events" and "plows tracing furrows in the ground," have in the end left no trace in contemporary Italian.

① mutable
② inexorable
③ dismissive
④ potent

[해설] ineluctable [ìnilʌ́ktəbl] 형 피할 수 없는, 불가피한 = inexorable, inescapable, unavoidable
[영영] ineluctable : impossible to avoid or evade: "inescapable conclusion"
[어휘] Fascist 파시스트 신봉자, 독재자 fate 운명 지우다 plow 쟁기 furrow 밭고랑, 보습자리, 주름 mutable 변하기 쉬운, 변덕스러운 inexorable 무정한, 움직일 수 없는 dismissive 거부하는, 경멸적인 potent 강력한
[해석] 파시스트 신봉자들이 20 년간 얘기했던 "로마의 운명 지워진 언덕 (운명적인 흥망성쇠)"과 "불가피한 운명", 그리고 " 땅 위의 밭고랑을 따라가는 쟁기 (운명을 그대로 따르게 되는 것)"와 같은 얘기들은 현대 이탈리아인들에게 어떤 흔적도 남기지 못했다.

[정답] ②

02 다음 빈칸에 들어갈 표현으로 적절한 것을 고르시오.

> He had been elected by a wide margin, promising to _____ the imbalances of an ever more economically divided city.

① stimulate
② preserve
③ rectify
④ agitate

[해설] 그가 많은 격차로 당선되었다고 했으므로, 공약으로 내세운 것은 도시의 경제적 격차를 바로 잡는 일이라고 볼 수 있다. 따라서 빈칸에는 ③이 적절하다.
[어휘] rectify (잘못된 것을) 바로잡다 stimulate 자극하다 preserve 보전하다, 유지하다 agitate 동요시키다, 선동하다
[해석] 그는 더욱더 경제적으로 큰 격차를 보이는 도시의 불균형을 바로잡을 것을 약속하면서 많은 표차로 당선되었다.

[정답] ③

03 다음 빈칸에 들어갈 표현으로 적절한 것을 고르시오.

> The Yazoo Basin _____ the finest agricultural land in Mississippi, but floods and poor drainage have always caused problems in this area.

① contains
② contains of
③ containing
④ containing of

[해설] but이 두 문장을 연결하고 있기에 앞 문장의 동사가 필요하며, contain은 타동사라 전치사 없이 곧 바로 목적어를 취한다. 반면에, consist는 전치사 of나 in을 동반하는 자동사이다.

[해석] 야주 분지에는 미시시피에서 가장 훌륭한 농토가 포함되어 있지만, 홍수와 부실한 배수로가 언제나 이 지역에서 문제를 야기 시켰다.

[정답] ①

04 다음 우리말을 영어로 바꾼 것 중 잘못된 것은?

① 우리는 보다 나은 해결책을 찾고 있는 John을 격려했다.
  ⇨ We have encouraged John committed to finding a better solution.
② 그는 부모의 반대에도 불구하고 꿈을 결코 포기하지 않았다.
  ⇨ He never ever gave up his dream despite his parents' objection.
③ 그가 예전에 일을 했던 것처럼 지금도 열심히 일을 하면 좋을 것 같다.
  ⇨ I wish he were working now as hard as he did before.
④ 너희들은 농구를 하는 거보다 등산을 하는 편이 더 나을 것 같다.
  ⇨ You may as well climb the mountains than play basketball.

[해설] ①에서 be committed to ~ing ~에 열중하다, ~에 헌신하다 ③에서 I wish 가정법 과거이고 현재(now) 사건을 가정(= 반대로 나타내는 것)하므로 가정법 과거가 된다. ④에서 may[might] as well A as B = B보다 A가 더 나을 것이다. than ⇨ as

[정답] ④

05 (A), (B), (C)의 각 네모 안에서 어법에 맞는 표현으로 적절한 것은?

> Exactly how, when, why, and where the first maps came to be created is difficult to discover. Much of what was drawn in prehistoric and early historical times (A) [has/have] not survived, so what we find today may not be wholly representative of what was once there. There are other problems for the modern observer. Maps (B) [make/made] in prehistoric times cannot be accompanied by a title that explains the meaning of the drawing or that describes its content. However, we may be sure that in early times, just like today, maps were created for a variety of purposes and (C) [took/taken] a variety of forms. It may also be clear that, contrary to popular belief, of all the purposes to which maps have been put through the ages, the least important single purpose has been to find the way. Sea charts did not come into existence until the European Middle Ages, and topographical maps were not normally carried about by land travelers until the 18th century.

① have – make – taken
② have – made – took
③ has – made – taken
④ has – made – took

해설 (A) 주어는 much이므로 동사는 단수가 되어야 한다. (B) 동사가 이미 나와 있는 상태이므로 maps뒤에 나오는 동사는 명사를 수식하는 분사다. 전치사가 이어지므로 수동의 의미인 made를 써야 한다. (C) 병렬구조 – 앞 문장이 과거이므로 and뒤에 이어지는 동사도 과거가 되어야 하며, 뒤에 목적어가 있으므로 능동이 되어야 한다.

어휘 exactly 정확히, 틀림없이 prehistoric 선사시대의 wholly 완전히, 전적으로 representative of ~을 대표하는 observer 관찰자; 목격자 be accompanied by ~을 동반하다 contrary to ~와는 정반대로 put through to 연결하다 sea chart 해도(海圖) come into existence 생기다 topographical map 지형도 normally 보통 carry about 지니고 다니다

해석 정확히 어떻게, 언제, 왜 그리고 어디에서 최초의 지도가 만들어지게 되었는지는 발견하기가 어렵다. 선사시대와 초기 역사 시대에 그려진 많은 것들이 남아있지 않기 때문에 오늘날 우리가 발견하는 것은 한 때 존재했었던 것을 전적으로 대표하지 못할 수 있다. 현대 관찰자들에게는 다른 문제들이 있다. 선사시대에 만들어진 지도는 그림의 의미를 설명하거나 그 내용물을 묘사하는 제목을 가지고 있을 수 없다. 하지만, 우리는 오늘날과 마찬가지로 옛날에 지도가 다양한 목적을 위해 만들어 졌으며 여러 가지 형태를 가지고 있었다고 확신할 수 있다. 통념과는 정반대로 지도가 그 시대와 연결된 모든 목적들 중에서, 가장 덜 중요한 하나의 목적은 길을 찾는 것이다. 해도는 유럽의 중세시대가 되어서야 생겨났고, 지형도는 18세기가 되어서야 육상 여행자들이 평소에 지니고 다녔다.

정답 ④

06 (A), (B), (C) 각 빈칸 문맥에 맞는 말로 가장 적절한 것은?

I noticed that the wavelike motion of fish's fins and bodies was similar to the twisting patterns of seaweeds. Seaweeds can be quite __(A)__ if you pull on them. I discovered this when I caught hold of their stalks while snorkeling near reefs or rocks. As a surge from a wave washed me away from where I wanted to be, I grabbed on to seaweeds to anchor myself. Often they broke. Yet even in the wildest storms, these same weeds were able to stay __(B)__ and survive. The surge of huge waves couldn't break or dislodge most plants from their grip on the ocean floor. It became apparent to me that they were adapting their shapes to the path of least resistance to __(C)__ the onrush of water. Although at first it appeared that the weed fronds were moving chaotically, long observation showed me that all the plants were generally bending to a particular swirling pathway.

	(A)	(B)	(C)
①	sturdy	afloat	check
②	sturdy	intact	relieve
③	fragile	afloat	check
④	fragile	intact	relieve

해설 (A) 필자가 자신의 몸을 정지시키기 위해 해초를 움켜쥐었을 때 보통 해초가 망가졌다는 뒤의 문맥으로 보아 해초를 잡아당기면 손상되기 쉽다고 할 수 있다. 따라서 '쉽게 손상되는(fragile)'이 적절하다. *sturdy: 튼튼한, 견고한 (B) 거대한 파도에도 망가지지 않고 해저에 단단히 붙어 있을 수 있었다는 뒤의 문맥으로 보아 거친 파도에 온전한 상태를 유지할 수 있었다고 볼 수 있다. 그러므로 '(손상되지 않고) 온전한(intact)'이 적절하다. *afloat: (물에) 뜬 (C) 해초가 최소 저항의 방향으로 자신의 모양을 적응시키고 있었다는 앞의 문맥과 소용돌이 경로로 구부려서 밀려오는 파도에 적응한다는 뒤의 문맥으로 보아 해초가 돌진해오는 바닷물의 힘을 완화하려 한다고 볼 수 있다. 따라서 '완화하다(relieve)'가 적절하다. *check: 저지하다, 방해하다

어휘 frond (해조류의) 길게 갈라진 잎 motion 움직임, 운동 fin (물고기의) 지느러미 catch hold of ~을 붙잡다 stalk (식물의) 줄기, 대 reef 암초 surge (갑자기) 밀려듦, 큰 파도 grab 움켜쥐다 anchor 고정하다, 닻으로 정박시키다, 머무르게 하다 dislodge 뜯어내다, 강제로 옮기다 grip 단단히 붙잡음 apparent 분명한 adapt 맞추다, 적응시키다 path 방향, 길 onrush 돌진, 돌격 chaotically 무질서하게, 혼란스럽게 observation 관찰 pathway 경로, 좁은 길

해석 나는 물고기 지느러미와 몸체의 물결 같은 움직임이 해초가 비틀리는 형태와 유사하다는 것을 알게 되었다. 잡아당기면 해초는 아주 쉽게 손상될 수 있다. 암초나 바위 근처에서 스노클링을 하는 동안 해초의 줄기를 붙잡았을 때 나는 이것을 알게 되었다. 파도가 갑자기 밀려와 내가 있고 싶은 곳으로부터 나를 쓸어 갈 때, 나는 자신을 고정시키기 위해 해초를 움켜쥐었다. 자주 해초는 부러졌다. 하지만 가장 거친 폭풍우에서조차 이 동일한 해초들은 온전한 상태를 유지하여 살아남을 수 있었다. 거대한 파도가 밀려들어도 해저에 단단히 붙어 있는 대부분의 (해양) 식물을 부러뜨리거나 뜯어낼 수 없었다. 해초가 돌진하는 바닷물(의 힘)을 완화하기 위해 저항이 가장 적은 방향으로 자신의 모양을 맞추는 것이 나에게는 분명해 보였다. 처음에 해초의 길게 갈라진 잎들이 무질서하게 움직이는 것 같았지만, 오랜 관찰로 나는 그 모든 (해양) 식물들이 보통 특정한 소용돌이 경로로 구부리는 것을 보게 되었다.

정답 ④

07 다음 글의 내용으로 가장 적절한 것은?

> From Boston to Los Angeles, from New York City to Chicago to Dallas, museums are either planning, building, or wrapping up wholesale expansion programs. These programs already have radically altered facades and floor plans or are expected to do so in the not-too-distant future. In New York City alone, six major institutions have spread up and out into the air space and neighborhoods around them or are preparing to do so. The reasons for this confluence of activity are complex, but one factor is a consideration everywhere—space. With collections expanding, with the needs and functions of museums changing, empty space had become a very precious commodity. Probably nowhere in the country is this more true than at the Philadelphia Museum of Art, which has needed additional space for decades and which received its last significant facelift ten years ago. Because of the space crunch, the Art Museum has become increasingly cautious in considering acquisitions and donations of art, in some cases passing up opportunities to strengthen its collections. Deaccessing—or selling off—works of art has taken on new importance because of the museum's space problems. And increasingly, curators have been forced to juggle gallery space, rotating one masterpiece into public view while another is sent to storage. Despite the need for additional gallery and storage space, however, "the museum has no plan, no plan to break out of its envelope in the next fifteen years", according to Philadelphia Museum of Art's president.

① 대부분의 박물관들이 더 많은 공간을 필요로 하는 이유는 Changing needs 때문이다.
② 대부분의 박물관들이 더 많은 공간을 필요로 하는 이유는 More curators 때문이다.
③ 대부분의 박물관들이 더 많은 공간을 필요로 하는 이유에 Changing functions 때문이다.
④ 대부분의 박물관들이 더 많은 공간을 필요로 하는 이유에 Enlarged collections 때문이다.

[해설] ①, ③, ④는 본문의 5번째 문장에서 언급이 되고 있다. 그러나 ②에 대해서는 본문 어디에도 언급이 없다.

[어휘] **wrap up** 매듭을 짓다, 결론을 내리다, ~을 크게 망치다 **wholesale** 도매의, 대규모의 **radically** 근본적으로, 본래가(= naturally) 완전히, 철저하게(= thoroughly) 과격하게 **confluence** 합류, 합류점, 모임, 집합, 군중 **facelift** 얼굴의 주름을 없애는 성형수술, 개조, 개축, 신형화 **deaccessing** 매각, 처분, 양도 **curator** 관리자, 감독, 지배인 **juggle** 마술을 부리다 **rotate** ~을 회전시키다, 선회시키다, 교대시키다 **masterpiece** 걸작, 명작, 대작 **gallery** 화랑, 미술품 진열실, 베란다, 발코니

[해석] Boston에서 Los Angeles까지, 또 New York시에서 Chicago, Dallas에 이르기까지 박물관들은 대규모의 확장 계획들을 입안하고 수립하거나 마치고 있는 중이다. 이러한 계획들은 이미 정면도와 평면도들을 근본적으로 변화시켰거나 혹은 멀지 않는 미래에 그렇게 할 것이라고 계획되고 있다. 오직 New York 시에서만도 여섯 개의 주요한 기관들이 그들 주위 부근과 공간의 위와 밖을 향해 확장해오고 있거나 또는 그럴 준비를 하고 있는 중이다. 이러한 합류 활동의 이유들은 복잡하지만, 그러나 한 가지 사실은 모든 곳에서의 고려사항인 공간 때문이다. 소장품들이 늘어가고, 박물관의 필요와 기능이 변화함에 따라 공간 은 매우 귀중한 상품이 되었다. 아마도 **Philadelphia** 미술박물관 보다 더 이러한 것이 사실인 곳은 전국 어느 곳에도 없을 것인데, 그곳은 수십 년 동안이나 추가 공간을 필요로 해 왔고, 그리고 **10**년 전에 주목할 만 한 마지막

수선을 받았다. 공간의 위기 때문에 미술박물관은 어떤 경우에는 그곳의 소장품들을 늘릴 수 있는 기회들을 놓쳐가면서까지 미술품을 수집하거나 기부하는 일에 점차적으로 신중해졌다. 박물관의 공간문제 때문에 미술 작품들을 양도하거나 매각하는 것은 새로이 중요성을 띠어가고 있다. 그리고 점차적으로 박물관장들에게는 다른 작품들이 창고에 보내진 동안 하나의 작품을 대중들에게 보이는 식으로 교환시켜가며 전시 공간으로 요술을 부릴 것이 강요되고 있다. 그러나 추가적인 전시공간이나 저장 공간의 부족에도 불구하고 Philalephia 미술박물관의 관장에 따르면 "박물관은 앞으로 15년 내에는 그 외형을 깨뜨릴 아무런 계획도 없다"고 한다.

정답 ②

08 다음 글의 빈칸 (A), (B)에 들어갈 말로 가장 적절한 것은?

> Before language develops, emotions and touch are the primary means by which parent and child communicate. __(A)__, it would not be surprising if preverbal infants had some basic understanding of other people's emotional, nonverbal communications, which research has indicated is indeed the case. For example, infants as young as 14 months understand that emotions are often "about" a particular event (e.g., someone is scared of a dog) and are very adept at identifying what a person is emoting about. In addition, by 18 months, infants begin to appreciate that two people can have a different emotional response about the exact same object (e.g., you like peas, but I hate them). __(B)__, 14-month-old infants are still highly egocentric and assume that everyone has the same emotional responses to a particular object or event.

	(A)	(B)		(A)	(B)
①	Consequently	In contrast	②	Consequently	Similarly
③	Nevertheless	Similarly	④	Nevertheless	For instance

해설 '아기의 주요 의사소통 수단이 감정과 접촉이므로 이에 대한 기본 지식을 갖추고 있는 것은 당연하다'와 같이 전후 내용이 인과 관계에 있으므로, Consequently가 들어가는 것이 적절하다. (B) 18개월경의 아기들이 가진 특정한 감정에 대한 이해 능력을 언급한 다음에, 14개월 된 아기들은 그런 능력이 없다는 것을 대조적으로 설명하고 있으므로, In contrast가 들어가는 것이 적절하다.

어휘 adept 능숙한 preverbal 말을 할 수 있기 전의 infant 아기, 영아 be scared of ~을 무서워하다 emote 감정을 (과장되게) 드러내다 pea 완두콩 egocentric 자기중심적인

해석 감정과 접촉은 언어가 발달하기 전에 부모와 아이가 의사소통하는 주요 수단이다. 따라서 말을 할 수 있기 전의 아기가 다른 사람들의 감정적, 비언어적 의사소통을 어느 정도 기본적으로 이해한다고 해도 놀라운 것이 아니며, 그것이 정말 사실이라는 것을 연구가 보여 주었다. 예를 들면, 14개월 정도 된 어린 아기는 감정이 흔히 특정 사건에 '대한' 것(예를 들면, 누군가가 개를 무서워한다)이라는 것을 이해하고 한 사람이 무엇에 대해 감정을 드러내고 있는지를 식별하는 데 매우 능숙하다. 또한 18개월 무렵에 아기들은 두 사람이 정확히 동일한 사물에 대하여 상이한 감정적 반응을 할 수 있다는 것(예를 들면, 너는 완두콩을 좋아하지만, 나는 그것을 싫어한다)을 인식하기 시작한다. 대조적으로 14개월 된 아기들은 여전히 매우 자기중심적이며 모든 이가 특정 사물이나 사건에 동일한 감정적 반응을 보인다고 생각한다.

정답 ①

09 빈칸 (A), (B)에 들어갈 말로 가장 적절한 것은?

When you hear someone tell you outright that they need help after just informing you of her tendency toward seizures, it is a bit hard to imagine that you wouldn't notice or be aware that she was in trouble. Nevertheless, the presence of others can prevent us from helping. This is because of a powerful effect that groups can have on us, known as diffusion of responsibility. For a victim to receive help, someone needs to decide that it will be his or her responsibility to act. When you are responsible, the moral thing to do is to help. When you are the only witness, the burden clearly rests on your shoulders. But when others are present, it is easy to imagine that someone else should or has already taken action. In fact, even being primed to think about being part of a group can make people feel less personally accountable and less likely to donate money or stay to help out an experimenter.

If there are multiple ___(A)___ in a situation where help is needed, the likelihood of them feeling responsible for taking action ___(B)___.

	(A)	(B)		(A)	(B)
①	victims	diminishes	②	victims	disappears
③	witnesses	increases	④	witnesses	diminishes

[해설] 도움이 필요한 상황이 발생할 때 목격자가 다수이면, 다른 목격자가 피해자를 돕기 위한 조치를 취할 것이거나 이미 취했다고 생각하기 쉬워서 조치를 취할 책임감을 느낄 가능성이 줄어든다는 내용의 글이다. 그러므로 요약문의 빈칸에 들어갈 말로 (A)에는 '목격자(witnesses)'가, (B)에는 '줄어든다(diminishes)'가 가장 적절하다. ① 피해자 … 줄어든다 ② 피해자 … 사라진다 ③ 목격자 … 증가한다

[어휘] seizure 발작 diffusion 분산, 확산 prime 미리 알리다, 준비시키다 outright 터놓고, 솔직히 tendency 성향, 경향 notice 알아차리다, 주목하다 victim 피해자, 희생자 witness 목격자 burden 부담, 짐 rest on ~ 위에 놓여[얹혀] 있다 take action 조치를 취하다 accountable 책임이 있는

[해석] 어떤 사람이 자신이 발작하는 성향이 있다는 정보를 여러분에게 막 알린 후에 도움이 필요하다고 터놓고 여러분에게 말하는 것을 들을 때, 여러분은 그 사람이 곤경에 처했다는 것을 알아차리지 못하거나 인지하지 못할 것이라고 생각하기는 다소 어렵다. 그럼에도 불구하고, 다른 사람들의 존재는 우리가 돕지 못하도록 막을 수 있다. 이것은 '책임의 분산'으로 알려진, 집단이 우리에게 미칠 수 있는 하나의 강력한 영향력 때문이다. 피해자가 도움을 받기 위해서는 행동을 취하는 것이 자신의 책임일 것이라고 누군가가 결정할 필요가 있다. 여러분이 책임이 있을 때, 해야 할 도덕적 행위는 돕는 것이다. 여러분이 유일한 목격자일 때, 그 부담은 분명히 여러분 어깨 위에 놓여 있다. 그러나 다른 사람들이 존재할 때, 다른 누군가가 조치를 취할 것이거나 이미 취했다고 생각하기 쉽다. 사실 한 집단의 일부라고 생각하도록 미리 귀띔을 받는 것도 사람들을 개인적으로 책임감을 덜 느끼게 하고 돈을 기부하거나 실험자를 돕기 위해 남아 있을 가능성을 더 적게 만들 수 있다.

⇨ 도움이 필요한 상황에 다수의 목격자가 있을 때, 그들이 조치를 취할 책임감을 느낄 가능성이 줄어든다.

10 다음 빈칸에 들어갈 말로 가장 적절한 것은?

About ten thousand years ago, farming was discovered and proved to be a more efficient and dependable way to provide calories than the nomadic lifestyle of hunter-gatherers. For the first time, a few individuals were able to accumulate surplus food, and with it possessed the resources to hire others to do their bidding. Instead of having to roam across the landscape in search of nutrition, farmers could settle in villages and then cities, accumulating property. It was agriculture that made the division of labor possible, and thus created the conditions for civilized living. The downside has been that it also made possible the exploitation of labor. This pattern has repeated itself throughout history whenever a new technological development has allowed some enterprising individuals to get an edge over the rest of the population. It happened again in the Middle Ages when a few knights arrayed in expensive armor were able to force defenseless farmers to share their produce. It happened when the first factories using mechanical looms put thousands of independent cottage industries out of business, and then hired the unemployed weavers as factory hands. In each case, a minority who happened to be well positioned to exploit the new way of doing things was able to benefit, and as a result opened a wide gap in the ownership of resources. The minority in power then used political and legal means to institutionalize and protect its predominance — until a new political or technological revolution came along to challenge solid _____.

① myths
② prejudices
③ inequalities
④ hypotheses

해설 시대마다 새로운 기술을 가진 소수가 그렇지 못한 다수를 착취하고 자신들의 우위를 제도화하고 보호하려 했다는 내용이므로, 빈칸에는 ③이 가장 적절하다. ① 근거 없는 믿음 ② 편견 ④ 가설

어휘 loom 베틀 nomadic 유목민의 accumulate 축적하다 do one's bidding ~의 명령대로 하다 roam 떠돌아다니다 downside 부정적인 면 exploitation 착취 enterprising 진취적인, 야망이 있는 array 옷을 잘 차려 입히다 cottage industry 가내 수공업 predominance 우위, 우세

해석 약 만 년 전 농업이 발견되고 수렵과 채집을 하는 유목민 생활방식보다 농업이 칼로리를 제공하기에 더 효율적이고 믿을 수 있는 방법이라는 것이 증명되었다. 처음으로 몇 명의 개인들은 잉여 식품을 축적할 수 있었으며, 그것을 가지고 자신들의 명령대로 할 다른 사람들을 고용할 자원을 소유했다. 음식물을 찾아 지역을 떠돌아다녀야만 하는 대신에 농부들은 재산을 축적하면서 마을에 그다음엔 도시에 정착할 수 있었다. 노동의 분업을 가능케 만들어서 문명화된 삶의 조건을 만든 것은 바로 농업이었다. 부정적인 면은 그것이 또한 노동의 착취를 가능하게 만들었다는 점이었다. 이러한 패턴은 새로운 기술적인 발전이 일부 진취적인 개인들이 나머지 사람들보다 우위를 점령하는 것을 가능케 했을 때마다 역사가 진행되는 내내 반복되었다. 그러한 일은 값비싼 갑옷으로 잘 차려입은 몇 명의 기사들이 무방비의 농부들이 그들의 농산물을 공유하도록 강제했던 중세시대에 다시 일어났다. 그러한 일은 기계 베틀을 사용하는 공장들이 수천 개의 독립적인 가내 수공업을 파산시킨 다음 실직한 직물업자들을 공장의 일손으로 고용했을 때 벌어졌다. 각각의 경우에 있어 일을 하는 새로운 방식을 이용하도록 자리를 잘 잡은 소수는 이득을 볼 수 있었고, 결과적으로 자원의 소유권에 있어 커다란 차이를 벌렸다. 그때 권력을 가지고 있는 소수는 정치적이고 법률적인 수단을 이용해서 자신의 우위를 제도화하고 보호했는데, 이런 일은 새로운 정치적 혹은 기술적 혁명이 굳어진 불평등에 도전하기 위해 나타날 때까지 계속되었다.

정답 ③

11 하프 모의고사 해설

01 다음 밑줄 친 단어의 의미와 가장 가까운 것은?

> Your <u>insouciant</u> attitude indicates that you do not understand the seriousness.

① indifferent
② sarcastic
③ impeccable
④ impassioned

[해설] insouciant [insúːsiənt] 휑 무관심한, 태평한 = indifferent, apathetic, uninterested
[영영] insouciant : marked by blithe unconcern
[어휘] sarcastic 빈정대는 impeccable 나무랄 데 없는 impassioned 열정적인 playful 장난스러운
[해석] 너의 무관심한 나타낸다./네가 이해하지 못하고 있다는 것을/(무엇을? 심각성(seriousness)을

[정답] ①

02 다음 빈칸에 들어갈 단어로 가장 적절한 것은?

> Alcoholics Anonymous takes its name from the fact that it's a _____ group — people use only their first names and do not identify one another as members of the group.

① obstinate
② advisory
③ remedial
④ confidential

[해설] Alcoholics Anonymous의 이름을 어디서 따왔는지에 대한 사실을 that 이하에서 설명하고 있는데 대시(—)이하에서 사람들이 자신의 이름을 제대로 밝히지 않음을 알 수 있다. 따라서 anonymous와 유사한 뜻의 ④ confidential이 빈칸에 적절하다.
[어휘] Alcoholics Anonymous 단주회, 알코올 중독자 갱생회 take one's name from ~에서 이름을 따다 confidential 기밀의, 비밀의 obstinate 완고한 advisory 권고의 remedial 치료하는, 교정하는
[해설] 알코올 중독자 갱생회는 그것이 비밀 그룹이라는 사실, 즉 사람들이 성을 빼고 이름만 사용하고 그룹의 일원으로써 서로 신원을 확인하지 않는다는 사실에서 그 명칭을 따왔다.

[정답] ④

03 다음 빈칸에 들어갈 표현으로 가장 적절한 것은?

> If you think about the calories of the cake, you _____ the cake.

① will regret to eat
② regret eating
③ will regret eating
④ regret to eat

[해설] if절이 가정법 현재이므로, 주절에는 '조동사 + 동사원형'이 와야 한다. 따라서 ②와 ④는 빈칸에 들어갈 수 없다. 문맥상 케이크를 '먹었던' 것에 대해 후회할 것이므로 과거에 했던 일을 후회하는 'regret ~ing' 형태가 와야 한다. 따라서 ③ will regret eating이 빈칸에 적절하다.
[해석] 만일 당신이 그 케이크의 칼로리를 생각한다면, 당신은 그 케이크를 먹었던 것을 후회할 것이다.

[정답] ③

04 다음 문장에서 문법적으로 어색한 부분을 고르시오.

> The magicians, ① having discovered Minecoo Aniello's great wealth, concretely ② laid a plan ③ of robbing him ④ of his good fortune.

[해설] plan은 to부정사만을 동격어구로 하는 명사이므로 ③을 to rob으로 고쳐야 한다.
[해석] Minecoo Aniello의 막대한 재산을 알아낸 그 마법사들은 그의 상당한 재산을 그에게서 빼앗을 계획을 구체적으로 세웠다.

[정답] ③

05 다음 우리말 영작이 올바르지 않은 문장을 고르시오.

① 공식적인 반대가 없어서, 휴가를 허락받았다.
  ⇨ There being no official objection, leave was granted.
② 바로 떠나면, 당신은 그 기차를 잡을 수 있다.
  ⇨ Leaving immediately, the train can be caught for you.
③ 팔짱을 낀 채, 그녀는 화난 목소리로 말했다.
  ⇨ She spoke in an angry voice, with her arms folded.
④ 그들의 치아로 판단해 볼 때, 그들은 다양한 음식을 먹었다.
  ⇨ Judging from their teeth, they had a variety of diets.

[해설] ②에서 분사구문의 주어가 주절의 주어와 같을 경우, 분사구문의 주어는 생략하므로, ②는 분사구문의 주어가 the train이 되는데, "기차가 즉시 떠나면 기차를 잡을 수 있다"라는 말이 되어 어색하다. 문맥상 떠나는 주체가 you가 되므로, 주절을 you can catch the train으로 고쳐야 한다.

[정답] ②

06 다음 글의 빈칸 (A), (B)에 들어갈 말로 가장 적절한 것은?

> Some people are more susceptible to pain than others. For example, women experience painful stimuli more intensely than men. These gender differences are associated with the production of particular hormones. ___(A)___, certain genes are linked to the experience of pain, so that we may inherit our sensitivity to pain. However, the experience of pain is not determined by biological factors alone. For example, women report that the pain experienced in childbirth is moderated to some degree by the joyful nature of the situation. ___(B)___, even a minor stimulus can produce the perception of strong pain if it is accompanied by anxiety like a visit to the dentist. Clearly, then, pain is a perceptual response that depends heavily on our emotions and thoughts.

	(A)	(B)
①	In addition	In contrast
②	In addition	As a result
③	Therefore	Similarly
④	Nevertheless	In contrast

[해설] (A) 뒤의 문장은 앞 문장에 대한 추가적인 내용을 기술하고 있으므로 (A)에는 In addition이 적절하다.
(B) 뒤의 문장은 앞 문장과 역접의 관계에 있으므로 (B)에는 In contrast가 적절하다.

[어휘] **susceptible** 민감한, 영향을 받기 쉬운 **intensely** 심하게, 강렬하게 **inherit** 물려받다 **moderate** 누그러뜨리다, 완화하다 **perceptual** 지각의

[해석] 어떤 사람들은 다른 사람들보다 통증에 더 민감하다. 예를 들어, 여자는 남자보다 통증을 주는 자극을 더 강하게 겪는다. 이런 성 차이는 특정 호르몬의 생산과 관련이 있다. 게다가 어떤 유전자는 통증의 경험과 관련이 있어서 우리는 통증에 대한 민감성을 물려받은 것일지도 모른다. 그러나 통증의 경험은 생물학적 요인에 의해서만 결정되지 않는다. 예를 들어, 여자들은 분만할 때 겪는 통증이 그 상황의 기쁜 특성 때문에 어느 정도 완화된다고 보고한다. 이와 대조적으로 치과 방문과 같이 걱정이 수반되면 심지어 작은 자극조차 강한 통증의 인식을 만들어 낼 수 있다. 그렇다면 통증은 감정과 생각에 많이 달려 있는 지각 반응인 것이 분명하다.

[정답] ①

07 다음 빈칸에 들어갈 말로 가장 적절한 것은?

> Bees have their choice of flora according to color. Lord Avenbury once made an experiment to see if the color of flowers attracted bees. Placing honey on slips of paper of different shades, he found that the insects which visited them seemed to have a marked preference for blue, after which came white, yellow, red, green and orange. This finding should be considered for our beekeeping planning. If pollination is the prime consideration of taming bees and if the crop is identified, the color of other floras in the vicinity should be considered while planning. Let us consider beekeeping near a mustard field. Mustard gives tiny yellow flowers full of nectar and pollen. For better yield of mustard seeds, pollination is necessary. But if there is plenty of blue-colored wild flora in the vicinity, bees may prefer the blue flowers to mustard. Although we shall get honey and other products, the objective for pollination of mustard may be _____.

① defeated
② disclosed
③ protected
④ promoted

[해설] 겨자밭 근처에 벌들이 가장 좋아하는 색인 청색 꽃들을 피우는 식물들이 많이 있다면 벌들은 겨자 꽃보다는 주변 식물들의 꽃을 더 많이 찾아갈 것이다. 그렇게 되면 겨자 꽃의 꽃가루받이는 실패할 것이므로 빈칸에는 ① '좌절될'이 가장 적절하다. ② 드러날 ③ 보호받을 ④ 촉진될

[어휘] **flora** 식물군 **shade** 색조 **preference** 선호 **pollination** 꽃가루받이, 수분 **prime** 주된, 가장 중요한 **tame** 길들이다 **vicinity** 근처, 가까운 곳 **mustard** 겨자 **nectar** 화밀, (꽃의) 꿀 **pollen** 꽃가루 **yield** 수확(량); 생산하다 **objective** 목적, 목표

[해석] 벌들에게는 색깔에 따라 선호하는 식물군이 있다. Avenbury 경은 꽃의 색깔이 벌들을 유인하는지 알아보기 위해 실험을 한 적이 있었다. 다양한 색조의 종이쪽지에 꿀을 발라 놓았을 때, 그것들을 찾아 온 그 곤충들이 청색을 두드러지게 더 좋아하는 것처럼 보였으며, 그다음으로 흰색, 노란색, 빨간색, 녹색, 주황색이 뒤따른다는 것을 그는 발견했다. 이 발견은 우리가 양봉 계획을 하는 데 고려되어야 한다. 벌을 길들이는 데 있어서 주된 고려 사항이 꽃가루받이이고 그 농작물이 확인되면, 계획을 세울 때에 근처에 있는 다른 식물군들의 색깔이 고려되어야 한다. 겨자밭 근처에서 양봉을 한다고 생각해 보자. 겨자는 화밀과 꽃가루가 가득 찬 아주 작은 노란 꽃을 피운다. 더 많은 겨자씨 수확을 위해서는 꽃가루받이가 필수적이다. 하지만 근처에 청색 야생 식물군이 많이 있다면, 벌들은 겨자보다 청색 꽃들을 더 좋아할 수 있다. 비록 우리는 꿀과 다른 생산품들을 얻기는 하겠지만, 겨자 꽃가루받이의 목적은 좌절될 수 있다.

[정답] ①

08 다음 글의 내용으로 가장 적절하지 않은 것은?

> Genetic research has produced both exciting and frightening possibilities. Scientists are now able to create new forms of life in the laboratory due to the development of gene splicing. On one hand, the ability to create life in the laboratory could greatly benefit mankind. For example, because insulin is very expensive to obtain from natural sources, scientists have developed a method to manufacture inexpensively in the laboratory. Another beneficial application of gene splicing is in agriculture. Scientists foresee the day when new plants will be developed using nitrogen from the air instead of from fertilizer; therefore food production could be increased. In addition, entirely new plants could be developed to feed the world's hungry people. Not everyone is excited about gene splicing, however. Some people feel that it could have terrible consequences. A laboratory accident, for example, might cause an epidemic of an unknown disease that could wipe out humanity. As a result of this controversy, the government has made rules to control genetic experiments. Still many people feel that these rules are not strict enough even though the scientific community may feel that they are too strict.

① Food production capacity with gene splicing is sufficient to meet the demands.
② Nitrogen in the atmosphere may be used for expediting the growth of plants in future.
③ The regulations of gene splicing are relevant to risks associated with the fall of mankind.
④ It is possible to produce insulin chemically identical to the naturally produced form.

[해설] 유전자 접합 기술을 응용한 새로운 식물이 개발된다면 굶주린 사람들을 먹여 살릴 수도 있다고 했지만 현재 이 기술로 식품생산능력이 수요를 맞추기에 충분한 것은 아니므로 ①은 이 글을 통해 추론할 수 없다.

[어휘] laboratory 실험실 gene splicing 유전자 접합 benefit ~에게 이롭다, ~의 이득이 되다 manufacture 제조하다 application 적용, 응용 foresee 예견하다 nitrogen 질소 fertilizer 비료 feed 먹이다 terrible 끔직한, 소름끼치는 epidemic 전염병 wipe out 파괴하다

[해석] 유전연구는 흥미와 우려라는 두 가지 가능성을 불러일으켰다. 이제 과학자들은 유전자 접합의 발달 덕분에 실험실에서 새로운 형태의 생명을 만들어낼 수 있다. 실험실에서 생명을 창조할 수 있는 능력이 한편으로는 인류에게 상당히 이로울 수 있을 것이다. 예를 들어, 인슐린은 자연으로부터 구하기엔 비용이 너무 많이 들기 때문에 과학자들이 실험실에서 싼 값으로 인슐린을 만들어 낼 수 있는 방법을 개발해 냈다. 유전자 접합의 또 다른 유익한 적용은 농업에서 이루어지고 있다. 과학자들은 비료 대신에 공기로부터 질소를 이용하는 새로운 식물이 개발 될 때가 있을 것이며, 그로 말미암아 식량 생산량이 늘어날 수 있게 되리라고 예견하고 있다. 게다가 이 세상에 있는 굶주린 자들을 먹여 살릴 수 있는 전혀 다른 새로운 식물을 개발할 수도 있을 것이라고 한다. 그러나 모든 사람들이 이 유전자 접합에 대해 흥미롭게 생각하는 것은 아니다. 혹자는 그것이 무서운 결과를 초래할 수도 있다고 생각한다. 예를 들어 실험실사고가 인류를 멸망시킬 수도 있는 어떤 알려지지 않는 전염병의 발생을 초래할 수도 있을 것이다. 이런 반론 때문에 정부는 유전 실험을 통제하는 규정을 만들게 되었다. 그럼에도 불구하고 많은 사람들은 비록 과학계에선 그런 제한이 너무 심하다고 여길지라도 이 규정만으로는 충분하지 못하다고 생각한다.

[정답] ①

09 다음 글의 밑줄 친 부분 중, 문맥상 낱말의 쓰임이 적절하지 않은 것은?

Laughter resulting from humor shows itself when people find themselves in an ① <u>unfavorable</u> situation, for which they generally would have felt anger and/or fear, and the detection of incongruent elements allows them to watch it from a different perspective. In this instance, thus, laughter comes from the release of energies generally associated with negative feelings, but that in the specific situation, thanks to the ② <u>consistency</u> of perspective, can be expressed as laughter of relief. Humor, in this perspective, represents a defense mechanism that allows people to ③ <u>better</u> handle difficult and stressful life situations. Freud even describes this humor as "the highest of the defense mechanisms." This self-defense mechanism — differently from the ability to understand jokes, which is very widespread — does not ④ <u>present</u> itself in every human being. Actually, some individuals are able to see the funny and positive side of a certain situation, while others, even in the same circumstances, react showing negative feelings.

[해설] 유머는 좋지 않은 상황에서 웃음을 통해 부정적인 상황을 긍정적으로 승화시키는 최상위 방어기제로서 이때 웃음은 부정적인 감정과 관련 있지만, 관점의 변화 덕분에 안도의 웃음으로 표현된다는 내용이므로 ②의 **consistency**를 **change**와 같은 단어로 고쳐야 한다.

[어휘] **result from** ~에서 나오다, 기인하다 **unfavorable** 좋지 않은, 불리한 **detection** 감지, 간파, 발견 **perspective** 관점, 시각 **release** 방출, 해방, 석방 **associated** 관련된, 연관된 **relief** 안도, 안심, 위안 **defense mechanism** 방어기제 **incongruent** 일치하지 않는

[해설] 유머로부터 나오는 웃음은 사람들이 자신이 보통 분노, 그리고/또는, 두려움을 느꼈을 좋지 않은 상황에 있음을 알게 될 때 나오는데, 그 일치하지 않는 요소를 감지함으로써, 사람들은 그것을 다른 관점에서 볼 수 있다. 따라서 이러한 경우, 웃음은 일반적으로 부정적인 감정과 관련된 에너지의 방출로부터 나오는 것이지만, 그 특정 상황에서 그것은 관점의 일관성(→ 변화) 덕분에 안도의 웃음으로 표현될 수 있다. 이러한 관점에서 유머는 사람들이 힘들고 스트레스를 주는 생활환경을 더 잘 다루게 해 주는 방어기제를 나타낸다. **Freud**는 심지어 이러한 유머를 '최상위의 방어기제'라고 기술한다. 이러한 자기방어기제는, 매우 널리 퍼져 있는 농담 이해 능력과는 달리, 모든 인간에게서 나타나지는 않는다. 사실상, 어떤 사람들은 특정 상황에서 재미있고 긍정적인 측면을 볼 수 있는데, 반면에 다른 사람들은 심지어 똑같은 상황에서도 부정적인 감정을 드러내는 반응을 보인다.

[정답] ②

10 주어진 글 다음에 이어질 글의 순서로 가장 적절한 것은?

A mnemonic device that uses imagery is known as 'the method of place.' Here you form an association between something you want to remember and a particular location on a familiar walk.

(A) You continue in this manner until you have developed an image connecting each point in your speech to a landmark. Then, When it's time to present the speech, you simply imagine that you're taking that familiar walk.

(B) As you pass the first familiar landmark on that walk, you develop an image that somehow connects that familiar landmark to the first point in your speech. For example, the image of a tree with a nest of baby birds could help you remember that you have to begin providing healthy foods when children are young.

(C) Let's say that you have to present a speech about healthy eating habits in one of your classes and that your speech consists of seven main ideas. You simply imagine yourself taking a very familiar walk.

① (A) – (C) – (B) ② (B) – (A) – (C)
③ (B) – (C) – (A) ④ (C) – (B) – (A)

[해설] 장소의 방법으로 기억을 돕는 방법이 있다는 주어진 글 다음에 이야기를 한다는 사례로 상황 제시가 시작되는 (C)가 이어지고 익숙한 지형지물인 나무에 첫 번째 이야기의 요지를 연결시키는 방법을 보여주는 (B)가 이어지며 이런 식으로 계속 해서 장소를 매개로 내용을 기억하는 방법이 도움이 된다는 (A)가 이어지는 것이 적절하다. 그러므로 가장 자연스러운 글의 순서는 ④ '(C) – (B) – (A)'이다.

[어휘] mnemonic 기억을 돕는 imagery 심상(心像) device 방법, 방책 association 연관, 연상 landmark 지형지물 nest 둥지 provide 제공하다, 주다 eating habit 식습관 consist of ~로 구성되다

[해석] 심상을 이용하는 기억법은 '장소의 방법'으로 알려져 있다. 이 방법에서는 기억하고 싶은 것과 익숙한 산책길에 있는 특정한 위치를 연관시킨다. (C) 어느 수업 시간에 건강한 식습관에 관한 이야기를 해야 하는데, 그 이야기가 일곱 개의 주요 개념으로 구성되어 있다고 하자. 아주 익숙한 산책을 하고 있다고 상상하기만 하면 된다. (B) 그 산책길에서 첫 번째 익숙한 지형지물을 지날 때 그 익숙한 지형지물을 이야기의 첫 번째 요점과 어떻게든 연결시키는 이미지를 만든다. 예를 들어, 새끼 새들의 둥지가 있는 나무의 이미지는 아이들이 어릴 때부터 몸에 좋은 음식을 주기 시작해야 한다는 것을 기억하는 데 도움이 될 수 있다. (A) 이야기의 각 요점을 지형지물에 하나씩 연결시키는 이미지를 다 만들 때까지 이런 방식으로 계속한다. 그런 후 이야기를 할 때가 되면, 그 익숙한 산책을 하고 있다고 상상하기만 하면 된다.

[정답] ④

하프 모의고사 해설

01 밑줄 친 단어의 의미와 가장 가까운 것은?

> Don's few personal <u>effects</u> were in a suitcase under the bed.

① belongings
② outcomes
③ influences
④ impacts

[해설] effect [ifékt] 명 영향, 결과, 효과, 소지품 = belongings
[어휘] personal effects 소지품 outcome 결과 impact 충돌, 영향
[해석] 돈(Don)의 몇 개 안 되는 개인 소지품들은 침대 아래 여행 가방에 들어있었다.

[정답] ①

02 다음 밑줄 친 단어의 의미와 가장 가까운 것은?

> What companies will ultimately choose is still <u>up in the air</u>, but for now the technology is being tested to demonstrate its viability.

① uncertain
② approachable
③ complicated
④ meticulous

[해설] up in the air 아직 미정인 = uncertain
[영영] up in the air : Not yet resolved, finished, answered, decided or certain.
[어휘] viability 실행 가능성 approachable 이해하기 쉬운 접근 가능한 meticulous 매우 신중한, 소심한
[해석] 회사들이 궁극적으로 무엇을 선택할지는 아직 미정이지만, 현재로서는 그 기술의 실현가능성을 증명하기 위한 실험이 진행되고 있다.

[정답] ①

03 다음 빈칸에 들어갈 단어로 가장 적절한 것은?

> Named after Vulcan, the Roman god of fire, volcanoes are best known for their _____ power. But they can also be havens for life, as _____ for plants and animals during ice ages.

① blazing – obstacles
② proficient – heritages
③ destructive – refuges
④ beneficial – charms

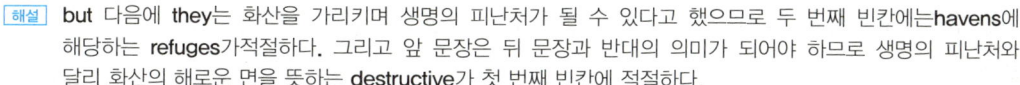

[해설] but 다음에 they는 화산을 가리키며 생명의 피난처가 될 수 있다고 했으므로 두 번째 빈칸에는 havens에 해당하는 refuges가 적절하다. 그리고 앞 문장은 뒤 문장과 반대의 의미가 되어야 하므로 생명의 피난처와 달리 화산의 해로운 면을 뜻하는 destructive가 첫 번째 빈칸에 적절하다.

[어휘] **destructive** 파괴적인 **haven** 안식처 **blazing** 불타는 듯한 **proficient** 숙달된, 능숙한 **heritage** 유산, 전통 **charm** 매력

[해석] 로마의 불의 신인 불카누스에서 이름을 따온 화산은 파괴적인 힘으로 잘 알려져 있다. 그러나 화산은 또한 빙하기 동안 식물과 동물의 은신처인 생명의 피난처일 수 있다.

[정답] ③

04 다음 빈칸에 들어갈 표현으로 가장 적절한 것은?

> Other possible contributors to the increased suicide _____ economic hardship and isolation.

① is risk
② risk is
③ being risk
④ risk are

[해설] 빈칸에는 주어에 대한 동사가 들어가야 하는데, 주어가 the increased suicide가 아니라 Other possible contributors이므로 is가 쓰인 ①과 ②는 빈칸에 들어갈 수 없으며, 절이 와야 하므로 동사가 아닌 ③도 빈칸에 적절하지 않다. Other possible contributors에 대한 동사로 are가 적절하게 왔으며, risk는 빈칸 앞의 suicide와 합성명사를 이루므로 ④의 risk are가 정답이다.

[해석] 자살위험이 증가하는 다른 가능한 원인들은 경제적 궁핍 및 고립이다.

[정답] ④

05 다음 문장에서 문법적으로 어색한 부분을 고르시오.

> You will not always ① <u>get along with</u> everyone that you ② <u>encounter</u>, but it is imperative that you ③ <u>are able to tolerate</u> each other and ④ <u>focus on</u> the common goal.

[해설] imperative(필수적인)와 같이 '이성적 판단'을 뜻하는 형용사 다음에 that절이 오면, 그 that절의 동사는 '(should) 동사원형'이 와야 한다. 따라서 ③을 (should) be able to로 고쳐야 한다.

[해석] 당신은 만나는 모든 사람과 언제나 잘 어울리지는 못할 것이지만, 당신이 서로를 용인하고 공통된 목표에 매진할 필요가 있다.

[정답] ③

06 (A), (B), (C)의 각 네모 안에서 어법에 맞는 표현으로 가장 적절한 것은?

> After physicist Richard Feynman won a Nobel prize for his work, he visited his old high school and looked up his records. He was surprised to find that his grades were not as good as he had remembered (A) [them/it] and that his IQ was 124, not much above average. Dr. Feynman saw that winning the Nobel prize was one thing, but winning it with an IQ of only 124 was really something. Most of us would assume that the winners of Nobel prizes have exceptionally high IQs. Feynman confided that he always assumed that he (B) [did/was]. If Feynman had known he was just a bit above average in the IQ department, he would not have launched the unique research experiments (C) [that/what] would win him the greatest recognition the scientific community can give.

	(A)	(B)	(C)
①	them	did	that
②	them	did	what
③	it	was	that
④	it	did	what

[해설] (A) 가리키는 내용이 문맥상 his grades이므로, them이 맞다. (B) 노벨상 수상자들은 유난히 높은 IQ를 가지고 있고(have ~), 더불어 자신도 과거에 그러했다고 생각했다는 문맥이므로, did가 맞다. (C) the unique research experiments를 수식할 관계절이 필요하므로, 관계대명사 that이 맞다.

[어휘] confide 털어놓다 physicist 물리학자 assume ~가 당연하다고 생각하다, 가정하다 exceptionally 유난히, 특별히 department 부문, 과 launch 시작하다, 개시하다 unique 독특한 recognition 인정 community ~계, 지역 사회

[구조분석] He was surprised to find [that his grades were not as good as he had remembered them] and [that his IQ was 124, not much above average].: find의 목적어로 두 개의 that절이 병렬을 이루고 있다.

[해석] 물리학자 Richard Feynman은 그의 연구 덕에 노벨상을 수상한 후에, 자신의 옛 고등학교를 방문해서 자신의 기록을 찾아보았다. 그의 성적은 자신이 그것들을 기억하고 있었던 것만큼 좋지 않았으며 그의 IQ는 평균보다 많이 높지 않은 124였다는 것을 알고 그는 놀랐다. Feynman 박사는 노벨상을 수상하는 것은 특별한 일이지만 겨우 124의 IQ를 가지고 그것을 수상하는 것은 정말로 대단한 일이라는 것을 알았다. 우리 대부분은 노벨상 수상자들이 유난히 높은 IQ를 가지고 있는 것이 당연하다고 생각할 것이다. Feynman은 자신이 그러했다(유난히 높은 IQ를 가지고 있었다)고 생각했다고 털어놓았다. Feynman이 자신이 IQ 부문에서 평균의 약간 위에 있을 뿐이라는 것을 알았더라면 그는 과학계가 줄 수 있는 가장 위대한 인정을 얻게 해 줄 독특한 연구 실험을 시작하지 않았을 것이다.

[정답] ①

07 글의 흐름으로 보아, 주어진 문장이 들어가기에 가장 적절한 곳은?

As the heart begins beating, the head of the chicken is moved up and down in a manner that mimics the movement that will be used later for pecking the ground.

It was for quite some time thought that when chickens hatched and immediately began pecking the ground for food, this behavior must have been instinctive. In the 1920s, a Chinese researcher named Zing-Yang Kuo made a remarkable set of observations on the developing chick egg that overturned this idea. (①) He found that rubbing heated Vaseline on a chicken egg caused it to become transparent enough so that he could see the embryo inside without disturbing it. (②) In this way, he was able to make detailed observations of the chick's development, from fertilization to hatching. (③) One of his observations was that in order for the growing embryo to fit properly in the egg, the neck is bent over the chest in such a way that the head rests on the chest just where the developing heart is encased. (④) Thus the "innate" pecking behavior that the chicken appears to know miraculously upon birth has, in fact, been practiced for more than a week within the egg.

[해설] 이 글은 병아리가 태어나자마자 먹이를 쪼는 행동을 하는데 이것이 달걀 안에서 연습된 행동이라는 것을 중국의 한 연구자가 관찰 했다는 것이다. 주어진 문장에서 병아리의 심장이 고동치기 시작하면서 병아리가 먹이 쪼기 행동에 필요한 동작과 닮은 머리를 위와 아래로 움직이는 행동을 하게 된다고 했는데 이는 ④ 앞의 병아리의 머리가 심장을 감싸고 있는 가슴 위에 놓이게 된다는 내용과 연결된다. 따라서 주어진 문장의 위치로 가장 적절한 곳은 ④이다.

[어휘] embryo 배아 fertilization 수정 beat 고동치다 mimic 흉내 내다 peck 쪼다 hatch 부화하다 immediately 즉시 behavior 행동 instinctive 본능적인 remarkable 주목할 만한 observation 관찰 chick 병아리, 새 새끼 overturn 뒤집다, 뒤엎다 rub 문지르다 transparent 투명한 disturb 방해하다, 교란하다 properly 적절하게 rest on ~에 놓이다 encase 감싸다, 둘러싸다 innate 선천적인, 타고난 miraculously 기적적으로

[해석] 병아리들이 부화하여 바로 먹이를 찾기 위해 땅바닥을 쪼기 시작할 때의 행동은 본능임이 틀림없다고 상당히 오랜 시간 동안 생각되었다. 1920년대에 Zing-Yang Kuo라는 중국의 연구자가 이 생각을 뒤집은, 발달하고 있는 병아리의 알에 대한 주목할 마나한 일련의 발견을 했다. 그는 달걀에 가열된 바셀린을 문지르면 안에 있는 배아를 방해하지 않고 볼 수 있도록 달걀이 충분히 투명해진다는 것을 알게 되었다. 이런 방식으로는 그는 수정에서 부화까지 병아리의 발달 과정을 자세하게 관찰할 수 있었다. 그의 관찰 중의 하나는 자라고 있는 배아가 달걀 속에 제대로 자리를 잡기 위해서는 발달하는 심장을 감싸고 있는 바로 그 가슴 위에 머리가 놓이는 방식으로 목이 가슴 위로 굽어진다는 것이었다. 심장이 고동을 치기 시작함에 따라 병아리의 머리는 나중에 땅바닥을 쪼는 데 사용되게 될 동작을 흉내 내는 형태로 위아래로 움직여지게 된다. 그리하여 병아리가 태어나자마자 기적같이 아는 것처럼 보이는 '선천적인' 쪼는 행동이 사실은 달걀 안에서 1주일이 넘게 연습되었던 것이다.

[정답] ④

08 빈칸 (A)와 (B)에 들어갈 말로 가장 적절한 것은?

Psychologist Michelene Chi asked physics professors and some Ph.D. students from the physics department and several undergraduate students to solve several physics problems. As expected, the professors and Ph.D. students were better at solving the physics problems than were the undergraduates. Interestingly, however, the physics experts were not necessarily faster than the undergraduates. Sure, once the professors and Ph.D.s got going on a problem, they were quicker to compute a solution. But Chi also found that the professors and Ph.D.s were slower than the undergraduates to begin to solve the problems. The experts paused before they ever put pencil to paper. They spent a few moments assessing the underlying structure of the problem and figuring out the best physics principle to use. The undergraduates, on the other hand, jumped right into problem-solving, which often got them in trouble. By rushing to start the problem, the undergraduates got distracted by irrelevant problem details, which led them astray.

⬇

The above experiment indicates that a big difference between success and failure in difficult problem-solving situations is the ___(A)___ taken to think about a problem at the ___(B)___ stage.

	(A)	(B)		(A)	(B)
①	time	final	②	time	initial
③	perspective	halfway	④	perspective	initial

[해설] 물리학 교수들과 물리학과 박사 과정 학생들이 학부 재학생들보다 물리 문제를 잘 풀기는 했지만, 항상 더 빠르게 문제를 풀지는 못했는데, 그 이유는 교수들과 박사 과정 학생들이 문제를 푸는 초기 단계에서 문제의 기저 구조를 가늠하고 적용할 수 있는 최선의 물리 법칙을 생각하면서 잠시 시간을 보냈지만, 학부 재학생들은 문제 풀이로 바로 들어갔기 때문이다. 이로 인해 교수들과 박사 과정 학생들은 일단 문제를 풀기 시작하면 빨리 해결했지만, 학부 재학생들은 문제와 무관한 지엽적인 것으로 산만해져서 문제 풀이에 어려움을 겪게 되었다는 내용의 글이다. 따라서 빈칸 (A)와 (B)에는 각각 time(시간)과 initial(초기의)이 들어가야 하며, 정답은 ②이다.

[해석] 심리학자 Michelene Chi는 물리학 교수들과 일부 물리학과 박사과정 학생들, 그리고 몇몇 대학 학부 재학생들에게 물리 몇 문제를 풀어 달라고 요청했다. 예상대로, 교수들과 박사 과정 학생들이 학부재학생들보다 물리 문제를 더 잘 풀었다. 하지만, 흥미롭게도 물리학 전문가들이 학부 재학생들보다 반드시 더 빠른 것은 아니었다. 물론, 일단 교수들과 박사 과정 학생들이 문제를 풀기 시작하면, 해결책을 처리하는 데 더 빨랐다. 하지만 Chi는 교수들과 박사 과정 학생들이 문제를 풀기 시작하는 데에는 학부 재학생들보다 더 느렸다는 것도 알게 되었다. 전문가들은 항상 연필을 종이에 대기 전에 잠시 멈추었다. 그들은 문제의 기저 구조를 가늠하고 이용할 수 있는 최선의 물리 법칙을 생각해 내면서 잠시 시간을 보냈다. 반면, 학부 재학생들은 문제 풀이에 바로 뛰어들었는데, 이것이 보통 그들을 곤란에 처하게 했다. 문제를 급히 서둘러 시작해서, 학부 재학생들은 문제와 무관한 지엽적인 것으로 인해 산만해졌고, 이것이 그들을 헤매게 했다.

⇨ 위의 실험은 어려운 문제 풀이 상황에서 성공과 실패 사이의 큰 차이가 초기 단계에서 문제에 관해 생각하는 데 쓴 시간이라는 것을 보여 준다.

[정답] ②

09 다음 글의 내용으로 가장 적절하지 않은 것은?

> Narcissistic individuals feel superior to others, fantasize about personal successes, and believe they deserve special treatment. When they feel humiliated, they often lash out aggressively or even violently. Unfortunately, little is known about the origins of narcissism. Such knowledge is important for designing interventions to curtail narcissistic development. We demonstrate that narcissism in children is cultivated by parental overvaluation: parents believing their child to be more special and more entitled than others. In contrast, high self-esteem in children is cultivated by parental warmth: parents expressing affection and appreciation toward their child. These findings show that narcissism is partly rooted in early socialization experiences, and suggest that parenttraining interventions can help curtail narcissistic development and reduce its costs for society.

① Narcissistic children may have difficulty in socializing with other children.
② The parental attention to their children is not always harmful to the life of children.
③ Thanks to the parental intervention, all narcissistic children can become normal.
④ Making children narcissistic depends on the parenting method of parents.

해설 부모의개입이 자기도취증 발달을 줄여준다고 했을 뿐, 모든 아이들이 부모의 개입으로 정상으로 돌아올 수 있다는 것은 아니므로 ③이 정답이다.

어휘 narcissistic 자기도취증에 빠진 feel superior to 우월감을 갖다 deserve ~을 받을 만하다 humiliated 굴욕적인 lash out 맹렬히 비난하다 intervention 개입 curtail 줄이다 cultivate 기르다 entitled ~을 받을 자격이 있는 self-esteem 자존감 be rooted in ~에 원인이 있다

해설 자기도취증에 빠진 개인들은 다른 사람들보다 우월하다고 느끼고, 개인적인 성공에 대해 환상을 갖고 있으며, 그들이 특별한 대우를 받을 만하다고 믿는다. 이들이 굴욕감을 느낄 때, 그들은 종종 공격적으로, 또는 심지어 맹렬히 비난한다. 안타깝게도, 자기도취증의 원인에 관해 알려진 것은 거의 없다. 그런 자기도취증의 원인에 관해 알고 있는 것은 자기도취증 발달을 줄이기 위한 개입을 계획하는데 있어 중요하다. 우리는 아이의 자기도취증이 부모의 과대평가, 즉 그들의 자녀들이 다른 자녀보다 더 특별하고 더 자격이 있다고 믿는 부모들에 의해 생긴다는 것을 입증한다. 이와 대조적으로, 아이의 높은 자존감은 부모의 온정, 즉 자녀에게 애정과 고마움을 표현하는 부모들에 의해 생긴다. 이러한 연구결과는 자기도취증이 부분적으로 이른 시기의 사회화 경험에 원인이 있음을 보여주며, 부모 훈련이라는 개입이 자기도취증 발달을 줄여주고 자기도취증의 사회비용을 감소시켜 주는 데 기여할 수 있음을 시사해준다.

정답 ③

10 다음 빈칸에 들어갈 말로 가장 적절한 것은?

I was counseling a man who had been in a long and painful relationship with a woman who constantly found fault with him and laid the blame for her unhappiness. "She is not doing it to you," I suggested to him, "She is doing it for you." "How's that?" he asked. "You 'hired' your girlfriend to magnify every self-hating thought you have had about yourself and play it back to you in such an intense and obvious way that you would have to examine your self-worth until you recognize and practice it," I told him. If others are continually annoying you with criticism, do not fight back or run away. Instead, say "thank you" to them. They are your best teachers, not because they are correct in their fault-finding, but because they are serving as a mirror of your own internal critic. They have come to show you how hard you are on yourself so that you can begin to love yourself and heal a long pattern of internal self-abuse. Criticism cannot disturb you unless you agree with it. If you are clear and confident about who you are and what you do, negative feedback will not be a big factor in your psyche. If you harbor internal doubts about yourself or your abilities, _____, someone will likely voice those doubts. If you argue or seek revenge, you have missed the gift of the experience. If you look inside and ask yourself, "Is this really true?," then you are on your way to higher ground. If it is true, you can correct it. If not, you can forget it. Your critic is your friend. Do not fight with your critic.

① most of all
② however
③ therefore
④ similarly

해설 빈칸을 중심으로 바로 앞부분과 바로 다음 부분이 상반되는 내용을 기술하고 있으므로, 빈칸에 들어갈 말로 역접의 연결사 however가 가장 적절하다. ① 무엇보다도 ③ 따라서 ④ 마찬가지로

어휘 pollster 여론조사 요원 find fault with ~를 비판하다 intense 극심한, 강렬한 criticism 비판 fight back 강력히 맞서다, 반격하다 serve as ~의 역할을 하다 be hard on ~을 심하게 대하다[나무라다] self-abuse 자학, 자기 비난 psyche 마음, 정신 harbor 〈계획·생각 등을〉 품다 revenge 보복

해석 나는 끊임없이 그를 비난하고 그녀의 불행에 대해 책임을 지운 한 여자와의 길고도 고통스러운 관계를 맺었던 한 남자를 상담하고 있었다. "그녀는 그것을 당신에게 하고 있는 것이 아닙니다."라고 나는 그에게 제안했다. "그녀는 당신을 위해 그것을 하고 있습니다." "그것이 어떻게 그렇지요?라고 그가 물었다. "당신은 당신이 당신 자신에 대해 가지고 있었던 모든 자신을 미워하는 생각을 확대해서 당신이 그것을 깨닫고 그것을 실천할 때까지 당신의 자아 존중감을 조사해야 할 그러한 강력하고 명백한 방식으로 당신에게 그것을 다시 틀어 들려주기 위해 당신의 여자 친구를 '고용한' 것입니다."라고 나는 그에게 말했다. 만약 다른 사람들이 비판으로 당신을 끊임없이 짜증나게 하고 있다면, 강력히 맞서거나 도망가지 말라. 대신에 그들에게 '고맙다'고 말하라. 그들은 그들의 흠집 찾기가 정확해서가 아니라 그들이 당신 자신의 내부의 비판자라는 거울 역할을 하고 있기 때문에 당신의 가장 훌륭한 교사이다. 그들은 당신이 자신을 사랑하기 시작하고 오래된 유형의 내부의 자기 비난을 고칠 수 있기 위해서 당신이 스스로 얼마나 심하게 대하는지를 당신에게 보여주기 위해 왔다. 비판은 만약 당신이 그것에 동의하지 않는다면 당신의 마음을 어지럽힐 수 없다. 만약 당신이 누구인지 그리고 당신이 무엇을 하는지에 관해 분명하고 확신에 차 있다면, 부정적인 피드백은 당신의 마음에서 큰 요인이 되지 않을 것이다. 하지만, 만약 당신 스스로나 당신의 능력에 대해 내적 의심을 하고 있다면, 누군가가 아마도 그러한 의심을 말로 나타낼 것이다. 만약 당신이 논쟁하거나 보복을 찾는다면 당신은 그 경험이 주는 선물을 놓치게 된다. 만약 당신이 자신의 내부를 들여다보고 "이것이 정말로 사실인가?"라고 자문한다면, 그렇다면 당신은 더 높은 곳으로 가고 있다. 만약 그것이 사실이라면 당신은 그것을 고칠 수 있다. 만약 그렇지 않다면 당신은 그것을 잊을 수 있다. 당신의 비판자는 당신의 친구이다. 당신의 비판자와 싸우지 말라.

정답 ②

13 하프 모의고사 해설

01 다음 밑줄 친 단어의 의미와 가장 가까운 것은?

> Brown and his wife are always bickering.

① hugging ② dancing ③ joking ④ arguing

[영영] bicker : a quarrel about petty points
[어휘] bicker [bíkər] 통 말다툼하다, 언쟁하다 명 언쟁 = argue
[해석] 브라운과 그의 아내는 늘 말다툼한다.

[정답] ④

02 다음 빈칸에 알맞은 것은?

> We tried everything to _____ him, but the injured man remained unconscious.

① rectify ② mitigate ③ resuscitate ④ freeze

[해설] but은 역접관계이므로 unconscious와 대비되는 내용이 와야 한다.
[어휘] injure 부상을 입히다 unconscious 의식이 없는 rectify 수정하다, 개정하다 mitigate 완화하다, 누그러뜨리다 resuscitate 소생시키다, 부활시키다 freeze 얼다
[해석] 우리는 그를 소생시키려고 온갖 시도를 했지만, 부상당한 남자는 여전히 의식불명이었다.

[정답] ③

03 다음 빈칸에 들어갈 표현으로 적절한 것을 고르시오.

> Even though the giraffe is very tall, this coloring _____ when it stands on the shade of a tree. Thus it is protected from enemies.

① makes hard to see
② makes it hard to see
③ making easy to see
④ makes it easy to see

[해설] 문두의 Even though의 양보접속사를 통해 blank에는 '보는 것이 어렵다'의 문맥이 들어가야 한다는 것을 알 수 있다. 또한, make와 목적보어 hard 뒤의 to see는 진목적어로 이와 같이 진목적어 자리에 to부정사나 that절 등이 올 때 make와 형용사 사이에는 가목적어 it을 써야 한다. 따라서 ②가 적절한 정답이 된다.
[해석] 비록 기린은 매우 키가 크지만, 기린의 색깔 때문에 나무 그늘에 서 있게 되면 잘 보이지 않는다. 그래서 기린은 적으로부터 보호받는다.

[정답] ②

04 다음 중 옳은 문장을 고르시오.

① It is difficult that we master English in one or two years.
② Social competence is a skill we often take it for granted.
③ All you have to do now is recover from the operation.
④ He has given me many useful advices on my study.

[해설] ①에서는 **difficult**는 난이형용사로 It ~ of ~ to 동사원형/It ~ that절로 쓰지 않으며, 'It ~ for ~ to 동사원형'으로 쓴다. 따라서 **that we master**를 **for us to master**로 고친다. ②에서는 **a skill we**은 명사 + 명사가 나란히 온 형태인데 의미전달이 되지 않는 것으로 보아 **a skill**과 **we** 사이에 목적격관계대명사가 생략되어 있다. **take**의 목적어는 생략되어 있는 관계대명사이므로, 대명사 **it**이 있는 경우 목적어가 중복된다. 따라서 **it**을 삭제해야 한다. ③에서는 **do** 혹은 **did**가 들어가는 주어부의 표현에 **what**이나 **all** 등이 있는 경우, 보어의 자리에는 **to**부정사와 원형부정사 둘 다 가능하다. ④에서는 **advice**는 셀 수 없는 산명사이므로 복수형으로 쓸 수 없고 **many**로 수식할 수도 없다. **many useful advices**를 **many useful advice**로 고친다.

[해석] ① 우리가 1, 2년 안에 영어를 마스터하는 것은 어렵다. ② 사회적 역량은 우리가 흔히 그것을 당연하게 여기는 기술이다. ③ 이제 수술에서 회복하기만 하면 된다. ④ 그는 나의 연구에 대해 많은 유익한 조언을 해주었다.

[정답] ③

05 다음 우리말 영작이 올바르지 않은 고르시오.

① 당신은 단지 많은 채소를 먹는 것만으로도 당신이 건강을 유지할 수 있다고 생각할지도 모른다.
  ⇨ You might think that just eating a lot of vegetables will keep you perfectly healthy.
② 학문적 지식이 늘 당신이 옳은 결정을 하도록 이끌어 주진 않는다.
  ⇨ Academic knowledge isn't always that leads you to make right decisions.
③ 다치는 것에 대한 두려움은 그가 무모한 행동에 가담하는 것을 막지 못했다.
  ⇨ The fear of getting hurt didn't prevent him from engaging in reckless behaviors.
④ Julie의 주치의는 그녀에게 가공식품을 많이 먹는 것을 멈추라고 말했다.
  ⇨ Julie's doctor told her to stop eating so many processed foods.

[해설] ②에서 동사 다음에 쓰이는 **that**절은 명사절의 **that**이고 위 문장에선 보어로 쓰였다. 명사절 접속사 **that**은 완전한 절을, 명사절 접속사 **what**은 주어, 목적어, 보어 중 하나가 빠진 불완전한 절을 이끌어야 하므로 **that**은 **what**으로 고쳐야 옳다. **that** ⇨ **what** // 전체를 나타내는 표현 **always**와 부정어 **not**이 함께 쓰여 '언제나 ~인 것은 아니다'를 나타내는 부분부정은 옳게 쓰였다. ①에서 동사 **keep**의 목적보어로 형용사 형태인 **healthy**가 바르게 쓰였다. 부사 **perfectly**는 형용사 **healthy**를 수식하고 있다. 참고로 부사와 추상명사는 목적보어로 쓰지 못한다. ③에서 "~가 ~하는 것을 막다, 금지하다"의 의미로 '**prevent** + 목적어 + **from** ~ing'가 바르게 쓰였다. ④에서 '말하다' 동사 **tell**은 3, 4, 5형식으로 쓰인데 위 문장에서 5형식으로 쓰인 것으로 **to**부정사를 목적보어로 갖는다.

[어휘] **academic knowledge** 학문적 지식 **engage in** 가담하다, 참여하다 **reckless** 무모한 **processed food** 가공식품

[정답] ②

06 다음 글의 제목으로 가장 적절한 것은?

The public plays almost no expressive or even approving role in selecting "big pictures" of photojournalism (the exception being some contests to name "photo of the year"). Editors do not poll the public before displaying images of the day's news and selecting those worthy of more extensive coverage and comment. The Pulitzer Prize, too, is voted upon by journalistic elites. Photographers and journalists (through prize committees), editors (through selection), and political and editorial elites (through notation and commentary) impose greatness and thus fame on images. Historians and textbook companies, by reemploying or "quoting" such images for discussion or simply illustration, reaffirm that they are "great." Obviously, after repeatedly viewing and absorbing such observations, members of the public are likely to agree with this verdict, even if they may be less than susceptible to the pictures' affecting their beliefs or actions. Elites, thus, largely set the agenda of greatness and establish the criteria for which images are judged great.

① Elites Determine Great Images
② The Prized Picture: Making Sense out of Life
③ Fearless Photographers Take Big Pictures
④ Spoken Image: Photography and Language

[해설] 포토저널리즘에서 '중요한 사진'을 선택할 때 대중은 의견을 표현하거나 찬성하는 역할을 거의 하지 않으며, 이미지에 위대함, 그리하여 명성을 부여하는 사람들은 엘리트라는 내용이므로, 글의 제목으로 가장 적절한 것은 ① '엘리트가 위대한 이미지를 결정한다'이다. ② 중요한 사진: 삶을 이해하기 ③ 두려움 없는 사진작가들이 중요한 사진을 찍는다 ④ 구두(口頭)의 이미지: 사진 촬영술과 언어

[어휘] photojournalism 포토저널리즘, 사진 보도 extensive 광범위한 coverage 보도 comment 논평 editorial 논설의, 사설의 notation 주석, 메모 impose 부여하다, 부과하다 quote 인용하다 illustration 삽화 reaffirm 재확인하다 observations (관찰) 정보[결과] less than 조금도[결코] ~ 아닌 agenda 의제 verdict 결정, 평결 susceptible to ~에 흔들리기 쉬운

[해석] 대중은 포토저널리즘에서 '중요한 사진'을 선택할 때 (자신의 의견 등을) 표현하거나 혹은 심지어 찬성하는 역할을 거의 하지 않는다. (예외는 '올해의 사진'이라고 부르는 일부 대회임). 편집자들은 그날의 뉴스 이미지를 보여 주기 전에, 그리고 더 광범위한 보도와 논평의 가치가 있는 것들(이미지들)을 선택하기 전에 대중에게 여론 조사를 하지 않는다. 퓰리처상 역시 저널리즘의 엘리트들에 의해 표결에 붙여진다. 사진작가들과 저널리스트들(수상 위원회를 통해), 편집자들(선택을 통해), 그리고 정치와 논설 엘리트들(주석과 논평을 통해)이 이미지에 위대함을 부여하고, 그리하여 명성을 부여한다. 역사가들과 교과서 회사들은 논의 혹은 단지 삽화용으로 그러한 이미지를 재사용 하거나 '인용'함으로써 그것들이 '훌륭하다'는 것을 재확인한다. 분명히, 그러한 정보를 반복적으로 보고 받아들인 이후에 대중의 구성원은, 비록 그 사진들이 그들의 믿음이나 행동에 영향을 미치는 것에 자신은 조금도 흔들리지 않을 수 있다 하더라도, 이러한 결정에 동의하기 쉬울 것이다. 그러므로 엘리트들은 대개 위대함이라는 의제를 설정하고 이미지가 위대하다고 판단되는 기준을 마련한다.

[정답] ①

07 다음 글에서 전체 흐름과 관계없는 문장은?

I have met several art therapists and doctors who can pinpoint illnesses people have by asking patients to draw how they see themselves and how they feel about their life. ① Folding a sheet of paper twice to make four quarters, these doctors and therapists have the patients use colored pencils to draw and color in their face, body, family, and anything else that they feel is relevant on different parts of the page. ② This can give an experienced health practitioner information about their patients' lives, what emotions they are dealing with, and what tests may need to be done, as well as the possible causes of a patient's "dis-ease." ③ In counselling, the relationship between the therapist and client is extremely important as this helps to facilitate the process of change and can enable clients to reach a greater understanding of themselves. ④ The different quarters can also relay information about the patient's past, present, and future. This kind of intuitive drawing technique is particularly powerful with children, as it also gives them an opportunity to express themselves and understand what is going on in their lives.

[해설] 이 글은 의사와 미술 치료사들이 환자들에게 종이 위에 그림을 그리게 함으로써 환자가 가진 질병의 원인, 환자의 삶에 대한 정보 등을 알아내는 기법에 관해 설명하고 있는데, ③은 상담에서 치료사와 내담자 사이의 관계가 중요하다는 것을 말하고 있어서 글의 흐름에서 벗어난다.

[어휘] therapist 치료사 quarter 4분의 1 color in A A를 색칠하여 넣다 relevant 관련된, 타당한 practitioner (의사·변호사 등) 전문직 종사자 client 내담자, 고객 facilitate 촉진하다, 조장하다 relay 전달하다, 중계하다 intuitive 직관적인 powerful 효과가 큰 pinpoint 정확히 찾아내다

[해석] 나는 환자들에게 자신을 어떻게 보는지 그리고 자신의 삶에 대해 어떻게 느끼는지를 그리도록 요청함으로써, 사람들이 가진 질병을 정확히 찾아낼 수 있는 몇 명의 미술 치료사와 의사들을 만난 적이 있다. 이 의사들과 치료사들은, 종이 한 장을 두 번 접어 네 등분으로 만들어서, 환자들이 색연필을 사용하여 자신들의 얼굴, 몸, 가족, 그리고 그 밖에 관련 있다고 느끼는 것이면 무엇이든지 그 종이의 서로 다른 부분에 그려서 색을 칠해 넣게 한다. 이것은 경험 많은 건강 전문가에게 환자의 '질병(편안하지 않은 상태)'의 있을 수 있는 원인뿐만 아니라, 환자의 생활, 그들이 어떤 감정을 다루고 있는지, 그리고 어떤 검사가 이루어져야 하는지에 관한 정보를 줄 수 있다. (상담을 할 때 치료사와 내담자 사이의 관계는 대단히 중요한데, 그 이유는 이것이 변화 과정을 촉진하는 데 도움을 주고, 내담자들이 자신을 더 잘 이해할 수 있게 해 줄 수 있기 때문이다.) 4등분된 서로 다른 조각은 또한 환자의 과거, 현재, 미래에 대한 정보를 전달할 수 있다. 이러한 종류의 직관적인 그림 그리기 기법은 특히 아이들에게 효과가 큰데, 그 이유는 그것이 또한 아이들에게 자신을 표현하고 자신의 삶에서 일어나고 있는 일을 이해할 수 있는 기회를 주기 때문이다.

[정답] ③

08 다음 글의 내용과 일치하는 것은?

Soils of farmlands used for growing crops are being carried away by water and wind erosion at rates between 10 and 40 times the rates of soil formation, and between 500 and 10,000 times soil erosion rates on forested land. Because those soil erosion rates are so much higher than soil formation rates, that means a net loss of soil. For instance, about half of the top soil of Iowa, the state whose agriculture productivity is among the highest in the U.S., has been eroded in the last 150 years. On my most recent visit to Iowa, my hosts showed me a churchyard offering a dramatically visible example of those soil losses. A church was built there in the middle of farmland during the 19th century and has been maintained continuously as a church ever since, while the land around it was being farmed. As a result of soil being eroded much more rapidly from fields than from the churchyard, the yard now stands like a little island raised 10 feet above the surrounding sea of farmland.

① A churchyard in Iowa is higher than the surrounding farmland.
② Iowa's agricultural productivity has accelerated its soil formation.
③ The rate of soil formation in farmlands is faster than that of soil erosion.
④ Iowa has maintained its top soil in the last 150 years.

[해설] ① 글 마지막 문장에서 교회 부지보다 주변의 농지의 토양이 더 빠르게 침식되었기 때문에 처음에는 동일한 위치에 있었던 교회 부지가 주변의 농지보다 지금은 **10피트**(약 3미터) 더 올라간 상태라고 설명한다. 따라서 글의 내용과 일치한다. ② 아이오와의 농업 생산성과 토양 형성의 가속은 본문에서 연관되어 언급되지 않았다. ③ 두 번째 문장에서 토양의 침식속도가 생성속도보다 더 높다고 했으므로 글의 내용과 일치하지 않는 내용이다. ④ 세 번째 문장에서 아이오와 주 표면 토양의 약 절반이 지난 **150**년간 침식되었다고 언급되어 있으므로 글의 내용과 일치하지 않는다. ① 아이오와 교회 부지는 주변 들판보다 더 높다. ② 아이오와의 농업 생산성은 토양 형성을 가속시켰다. ③ 농지의 토양 생성률은 토양 침식률보다 더 빠르다. ④ 아이오와는 지난 **150**년 동안 표면 토양을 유지했다.

[해설] 농작물 재배에 사용되는 농지의 토양은 토양 형성 속도의 **10**배에서 **40**배, 그리고 산림지에서 토양 침식율의 **500**배에서 **10,000**배 사이로 물과 바람의 침식에 의해 휩쓸려 나가고 있다. 이러한 토양 침식의 속도는 토양 생성의 속도보다 훨씬 높기 때문에 토양의 순손실을 의미한다. 예를 들어, 미국에서 농업 생산성이 가장 높은 아이오와 주 표면 토양의 약 절반이 지난 **150**년간 침식되었다. 최근에 아이오와를 방문했을 때, 나의 호스트들은 나에게 토양 손실이 극적으로 눈에 띄는 예를 보여주는 한 교회 부지를 보여주었다. 교회는 **19**세기에 농지의 한가운데에 지어졌으며 이후로 교회가 계속 유지되고 주변의 땅은 경작되었다. 교회 부지보다 농지에서 토양이 훨씬 더 빠르게 침식된 결과, 교회 부지는 농지의 바다 위로 **10피트** 더 올라간 작은 섬처럼 서 있다.

[정답] ①

09 빈칸 (A)와 (B)에 들어갈 말로 가장 적절한 것은?

> International maritime codes specify that more maneuverable vessels must keep out of the way of less maneuverable vessels. The captains of more maneuverable vessels, such as power-driven boats, are responsible for avoiding less steerable vessels, such as sailing ships, and ships engaged in fishing, and vessels not under command. It is easier for powerboats to avoid hitting sailing ships than vice versa. Aviation codes are based on the same principle. The right of way of the sky ranks craft in order of the ease with which they can be controlled. Airplanes in normal operation, which are the most easily maneuvered aircraft, have the lowest priority in right of way. Airplanes refueling other aircraft, which are less easily maneuvered, have a greater right of way than airplanes in normal operation. Balloons, which are still less maneuverable than airplanes refueling other aircraft, have a higher priority right of way. Finally, aircraft in distress have the highest priority right of way of all, since an aircraft in distress is very difficult or impossible to control.

↓

> On the sea or in the sky, the responsibility of giving way usually falls on the party who has less difficulty in ___(A)___ the vehicle because it is easier for that party to ___(B)___ an accident.

	(A)	(B)		(A)	(B)
①	controlling	report	②	controlling	avoid
③	leaving	investigate	④	leaving	report

해설 해양법과 항공법에 따르면 통제하기가 더 쉬운 선박이나 비행기가 사고를 피하기 위한 조치를 취하기가 더 쉬우므로 양보의 책임이 그쪽에 돌아간다는 내용의 글이다. 그러므로 요약문의 빈칸에 들어갈 말로 (A)에는 '통제하는(controlling)'이, (B)에는 '피하다(avoid)'가 가장 적절하다. ① 통제하는 … 신고하는 ③ 떠나는 … 조사하는 ④ 떠나는 … 신고하는

어휘 specify 명시하다 vessel 선박, 배 steerable 조종할 수 있는 vice versa 반대의 경우 aviation code 항공법 the right of way 우선 통행권 craft 항공기 priority 우선순위 balloon 열기구 풍선 maritime code 해양법 maneuverable 조종할 수 있는 in distress 조난 사고를 당한

해석 국제해양법은 조종하기가 더 어려운 선박에게 조종하기가 더 쉬운 선박이 길을 비켜 주어야 한다고 명시한다. 동력으로 움직이는 배와 같은 조종하기가 더 쉬운 선박의 선장은 범선, 낚시를 하고 있는 배, 조종 불능선과 같은 조종하기가 더 어려운 선박을 피하는 것에 대한 책임이 있다. 동력선이 범선과 충돌하는 것을 피하는 것이 그 반대의 경우보다 더 쉽다. 항공법도 이와 동일한 원칙에 기초한다. 하늘에서의 우선 통행권은 조종되기 쉬운 순서로 항공기의 순위를 매긴다. 가장 쉽게 조종되는 정상적으로 운행되고 있는 비행기는 우선 통행권에 있어서 가장 낮은 우선순위를 갖는다. 조종하기가 덜 용이한, 다른 항공기에 연료를 재급유하고 있는 비행기는 정상적으로 운행되는 비행기보다 더 큰 우선 통행권을 갖는다. 다른 항공기에 연료를 재급유하고 있는 비행기보다 훨씬 더 조종하기가 어려운 열기구 풍선은 더 높은 우선 통행권을 갖는다. 마지막으로 조난 사고를 당한 항공기는 모든 것들에 앞서서 가장 높은 우선 통행권을 갖는데, 왜냐하면 조난 사고를 당한 항공기는 통제하기가 매우 어렵거나 불가능하기 때문이다.

⇨ 바다나 하늘에서 양보의 책임은 운송수단을 통제하는 데 있어서 더 적은 어려움을 겪는 쪽에서 사고를 피하는 것이 더 쉽기 때문에 대개 그쪽에 (책임이) 있다.

정답 ②

10 다음 빈칸에 공통으로 들어갈 말로 가장 적절한 것은?

A San Francisco-based polygrapher told me about a polygraph exam he had given to a 45-year-old bank vice-president who was a suspect in an embezzlement investigation. When initially run through the polygraph exam, the bank vice-president's heart rate, blood pressure, and other physiological levels were quite high. This is normal for both innocent and guilty people, because such an exam is almost always threatening. _____, the polygrapher suspected that the bank vice-president was lying or holding back information, because his physiological levels went even higher when he was asked about some of the details of the embezzlement. With repeated questions, the vice-president finally broke down and confessed to embezzling $74,000 over a 6-month period. In line with standard procedures, after the bank vice-president had signed a written confession, he was then polygraphed again to be certain that his confession was itself not deceptive. When connected to the monitoring device the second time, his overall physiological levels were extremely low. His hands were no longer sweaty. His heart rate and blood pressure were extraordinarily low. You can appreciate the irony of this situation. This man had come into the polygrapher's office a free man, safe in the knowledge that polygraph evidence was not allowed in court. _____, he confessed. Now, his professional, financial, and personal lives were on the brink of ruin. He was virtually assured of a prison term. Despite these realities, he was relaxed and at ease with himself. Indeed, when a policeman came to handcuff and escort him to jail, he warmly shook the polygrapher's hand and thanked him for all he had done.

① Moreover
② Therefore
③ As a result
④ Nevertheless

[해설] 첫 번째 빈칸의 앞에서는 테스트의 결과가 누구에게나 자연스러운 결과라고 했으므로, 뒤 문장은 그럼에도 불구하고 검사관이 의심했다고 이어지는 것이 자연스럽다. 두 번째 빈칸이 이어주는 부분은, 테스트 결과가 법정에서 증거로 채택되지 않는데도 남자가 자백했다고 이어지는 것이 자연스럽다. 그러므로 빈칸에 공통으로 들어갈 말로 가장 적절한 것은 ④ '그런데도(Nevertheless)'이다. ① 더욱이 ② 그러므로 ③ 그 결과

[어휘] suspect 용의자, 의심하다 investigation 수사, 조사 innocent 죄가 없는, 무죄의 guilty 죄가 있는, 유죄의 threatening 위협적인 hold back 숨기다, 비밀로 하다 break down 무너지다, 허물어지다 confess 자백하다 in line with A A에 따라, A와 함께 standard 표준의 confession 자백(서) deceptive 믿을만하지 않은, 속이는 evidence 증거 court 법정 on the brink of A A의 직전에 prison term 형기 at ease with A A에 마음을 놓은 handcuff 수갑을 채우다 escort 연행하다, 호송하다 polygraph 거짓말 탐지기, 거짓말 탐지기로 조사하다 embezzlement 횡령 physiological 생리학적인, 생리학상의

[해석] 샌프란시스코에 근거지를 둔 한 거짓말 탐지 검사관이 한 횡령 사건 수사에서 용의자였던 45세의 은행 부사장에게 실시했던 거짓말 탐지기 테스트에 관해 나에게 이야기해주었다. 처음에 거짓말 탐지기 테스트를 거쳤을 때, 은행 부사장의 심장박동 수, 혈압, 그리고 다른 생리학적인 수치는 상당히 높았다. 그런 테스트는 거의 항상 위협적이기 때문에 이것은 죄가 없는 사람이나 죄가 있는 사람 모두에게 자연스러운 일이었다. 그런데도, 그가 횡령의 몇몇 세부적인 사실에 관해 질문을 받았을 때 그의 생리학적 수치가 훨씬 더 올라갔기 때문에 거짓말 탐지 검사관은 그 은행 부사장이 거짓말하고 있거나 정보를 숨기고 있다고 의심했다. 반복되는 질문에, 그 부사장은 마침내 무너졌고 6개월의 기간에 걸쳐 74,000달러를 횡령한 것을 자백했다. 그 은행 부사장이 서면 자백서에 서명한 뒤에 표준 절차에 따라, 그는 그 뒤에 그의 자백이 그 자체로 믿을만한 것인지 확인하기 위해 다시 거짓말 탐지기 테스트를 받았다. 모니터링 장치에 두 번째로 연결되었을 때, 그의 전반적인 생리학적 수치는 극히 낮았다. 그의 손은 더 이상 땀으로 축축하지 않았다. 그의 심장박동 수와 혈압은 이례적으로 낮았다. 이 상황의 아이러니를 여러분은 이해할 수 있을 것이다. 이 남자는 거짓말 탐지기 증거가 법정에서 받아들여지지 않는다는 사실을 알고 안심하며, 거짓말 탐지 검사관의 사무실에 자유인으로 들어왔었다. 그런데도, 그는 자백했다. 이제 그의 직업적인, 재정적인, 그리고 개인적인 삶은 파탄 직전에 있었다. 그는 형기에 대해서도 거의 확신하고 있었다. 이런 현실에도 불구하고, 그는 자신에 대해 편안하게 느끼고 마음을 놓고 있었다. 실제로, 경찰관이 그에게 수갑을 채우고 감옥으로 연행해 가려고 왔을 때, 그는 거짓말 탐지 검사관과 따뜻하게 악수를 하고 그가 한 모든 일에 대해 감사를 표했다.

[정답] ④

14 하프 모의고사 해설

01 밑줄 친 단어의 의미와 가장 가까운 것은?

> She owes her election to having tapped deep public disillusionment with professional politicians.

① drained   ② utilized   ③ struck   ④ extracted

[해설] tap [tæp] 통 가볍게 두드리다, 이용하다 = utilize
[영영] tap : draw from; make good use of
[어휘] owe 빚지고 있다 extract 뽑다, 추출하다 strike 세게 부딪치다
[해석] 그녀의 당선은 직업 정치인들에 대한 대중의 깊은 환멸을 이용한 덕분이다.

[정답] ②

02 다음 밑줄 친 표현과 의미와 가장 가까운 것은?

> She is on the fence about going to see the Mona Lisa at the Louvre Museum.

① anguished   ② enthusiastic   ③ apprehensive   ④ undecided

[해설] on the fence 결정하지 못한, 애매한 태도를 취하는 = undecided, uncommitted
[영영] on the fence : undecided; wavering in one's opinion
[표현더하기] on the fence는 '울타리(fence) 위에 앉은'이라는 말로, 사람들이 모여 논의할 때 멀찍이 떨어져 앉아 자기 의견을 정하지 않고 있는 것을 뜻한다.
[어휘] anguish 괴로운 enthusiastic 열정적인 apprehensive 걱정되는, 불안한
[해석] 그녀는 루브르 박물관에 있는 모나리자를 보러갈 것인지 아직 결정하지 못했다.

[정답] ④

03 다음 빈칸에 들어갈 말로 적절한 것을 고르시오.

> The seasoned burglars were extremely careful not to leave any footprints, but this time they _____ and were immediately apprehended.

① missed out   ② broke through   ③ slipped up   ④ backed off

[해설] careful과 상반된 의미가 되어야 하므로 '실수를 하다'는 뜻을 갖는 ③번의 slipped up이 적절하다.
[어휘] seasoned 노련한 burglar 강도 miss out 기회를 놓치다 break through ~을 헤치고 나아가다, 위반하다 slip up 미끄러지다, 실수하다 back off 뒤로 물러서다, 주장을 굽히다
[해석] 그 노련한 강도들은 발자국 하나라도 남기지 않기 위해 극도로 조심했지만, 이번에는 실수를 해서 즉시 체포되었다.

[정답] ③

04 다음 글의 밑줄 친 부분 중, 어법상 어색한 것은?

When people face real adversity — disease, unemployment, or the disabilities of age — affection from a pet takes on new meaning. A pet's continuing affection becomes crucially important for ① those enduring hardship because it reassures them that their core essence has not been damaged. Thus pets are important in the treatment of ② depressed or chronically ill patients. In addition, pets are ③ used to great advantage with the institutionalized aged. In such institutions it is difficult for the staff to retain optimism when all the patients are declining in health. Children who visit cannot help but remember ④ what their parents or grandparents once were and be depressed by their incapacities. Animals, however, have no expectations about mental capacity. They do not worship youth. They have no memories about what the aged once ⑤ was and greet them as if they were children. An old man holding a puppy can relive a childhood moment with complete accuracy. His joy and the animal's response are the same.

[해설] ①에서 대명사 those: '~하는 사람들'의 의미로 뒤에 분사구, 형용사구, 전치사구, 관계절 등의 수식어구가 온다. enduring hardship이라는 분사구의 수식을 받는다. ②에서 '우울증을 겪는, 우울한'의 의미로 chronically ill과 or로 연결되어 patients를 수식하고 있다. ③에서 pets가 사용하는(use) 행위의 주체가 아니라 대상을 나타내므로 수동태 are used가 쓰인다. ④에서 what은 remember의 목적어인 절을 유도하며 절 안에서 were의 보어 역할을 하는 의문사이다.(*"What is he? – "He is a teacher.") ⑤에서 [the + 형용사]는 '~한 사람들'이라는 뜻으로 복수로 취급된다. 따라서 주어 the aged (=aged people)에 일치하는 술어 동사는 were가 되어야 한다.

[어휘] disability 장애 age (많은) 나이, 오래됨 affection 애정 chronically 만성적으로 to advantage 유익하게, 유리하게 institutionalized 시설에 수용되어 있는 retain 유지하다 optimism 낙관주의 incapacity 무능력, 불능 worship 숭배하다 relive 회상하다, 다시 체험하다 accuracy 정확성

[해석] 사람들이 질병, 실직, 혹은 노령으로 인한 장애와 같은 실질적인 역경에 직면할 때, 애완동물로부터의 애정은 새로운 의미를 띠게 된다. 애완동물의 지속적인 애정은 그들의 핵심(가장 중요 한) 본질이 손상되지 않았음을 그들에게 확신시켜 주기 때문에 어려움을 견디어 내는 사람들에게 대단히 중요해진다. 그러므로 애완동물은 우울증이 있거나 만성질환이 있는 환자들의 치료에 중요하다. 뿐만 아니라, 애완동물은 시설에 수용되어 있는 노인들에게 매우 유익하게 이용된다. 그런 시설에서는 모든 환자들의 건강이 쇠퇴한다는 것을 감안하면 직원들이 낙관적인 태도를 유지하기가 어렵다. 방문하는 자녀들은 부모님이나 조부모님이 한때 어떤 사람이었는지를 기억하고서는 그분들이 정상 생활이 어려운 것에 대해 의기소침해질 수밖에 없다. 그러나 동물들은 정신적 능력에 대한 기대를 갖지 않는다. 그들은 젊음을 숭배하지 않는다. 그들(동물들)은 노인들이 과거에 어떤 사람이었는지에 대한 기억이 전혀 없으며 그들(노인들)이 마치 어린이들인 것처럼 그들을 반긴다. 강아지를 안고 있는 노인은 완벽하게 어린 시절의 순간을 다시 체험 할 수 있다. 그의 기쁨과 그 동물의 반응은 (어린 시절과) 똑같다.

[정답] ⑤

05 다음 중 옳은 문장을 고르시오.

① I found my wife laying unconscious beside the kitchen table.
② The rent for our new apartment is higher than our old apartment.
③ Last week, Fred has had a broken leg and a sprained wrist.
④ As a parent, I can imagine how hard it is for him to see his son die slowly.

[해설] ①에서는 5형식 문장에서 목적어와 목적보어의 관계는 주어와 술어의 관계이다. 주어진 문장에서 my wife와 동사 lay가 주어와 술어의 관계인데, 타동사 lay의 목적어가 주어져 있지 않으므로 laying을 쓴 것은 적절하지 않다. 따라서 이것을 자동사 lie의 현재분사인 lying으로 고쳐야 한다. ②에서는 새 아파트의 집세와 이전 아파트의 집세를 비교해야 하므로 비교 대상을 같게 하기 위해 our old apartment를 that of our old apartment로 고쳐야 한다. ③에서는 현재완료 시제는 과거시점을 명확히 나타내는 yesterday, last week, in 1997 등의 표현과는 함께 쓰지 않는다. 따라서 has had를 과거시제 had로 고쳐야 한다. ④에서는 imagine 이하는 의문사절로서 'how + 형용사 + 주어 + 동사'의 어순으로 쓰였으며, 이때 it은 가주어이며 to see 이하가 진주어이다. 지각동사 see의 목적보어로 동사원형 die가 왔다.

[해석] ① 나는 내 아내가 식탁 옆에 의식을 잃은 채로 누워 있는 것을 발견했다. ② 우리 새 아파트의 집세가 이전 아파트의 집세보다 더 비싸다. ③ 지난주에 프레드는 다리가 부러졌고 손목을 삐었다. ④ 부모로서 나는 그가 자신의 아들이 천천히 죽어가는 것을 보는 것이 얼마나 힘든지 상상할 수 있다.

[정답] ④

06 다음 우리말 영작이 올바른 문장을 고르시오.

① 그 경기는 비 때문에 연기되었다.
  ⇨ The game was postponed on account of rain.
② 제시가 많이 도와줬기 때문에 나는 가까스로 그 경기에서 승리했다.
  ⇨ With a lot of help from Jesse, I managed winning the game.
③ 바쁘지 않으면 기꺼이 너를 도와줄 텐데.
  ⇨ I would help you willingly but that I was busy.
④ 나는 너와 그것에 대해 논의하고 싶다.
  ⇨ I want to discuss about it with you.

[해설] ①에서는 postpone은 '~을 연기하다'라는 의미의 타동사로, 주어인 The game이 postpone의 대상이 되므로 수동태 문장으로 썼다. on account of는 '~ 때문에'라는 의미이다. ②에서는 manage 뒤에 to부정사가 와야 한다. managed to win으로 고친다. ③에서는 '가정법 주절 + but (that) + 직설법 문장'의 형태가 되어야 한다. 주절이 가정법 과거의 문장이므로, but that 이하는 직설법 현재가 되어야 한다. was를 am으로 고친다. 이 문장은 I would help you willingly if I were not busy와 같은 의미이다. ④에서는 discuss는 타동사이므로 뒤에 전치사 about이 필요하지 않다.

[정답] ①

07 다음 글의 주제로 적절한 것은?

> Forget splashy news articles about initial public offerings, the latest tech gizmo, Google buses or ever-climbing real estate prices. For San Francisco, that was so 2014. So far, the city's biggest news stories in 2015 have read like one unbelievable horror story come to life. There were nine homicides in January, including four young men gunned down in a car in Hayes Valley and a mother killed by a stray bullet in front of her three children in broad daylight in the Bayview. Last weekend saw a spate of home invasions — none of them believed to be related. In one, an assailant forced her way into an Ocean View home, covered the head of a 26-year-old woman with a towel and then tied her up with extension cords. The assailant made off with jewelry, cell phones and money. Masked men rammed a sport utility vehicle into a museum at the site of the original Wells Fargo Bank and fled with Gold-Rush era nuggets. Then there was a shocking discovery made by kayakers in Lake Merced: a mysterious decomposing body found floating facedown among the reeds. T. S. Eliot, in his poem The Waste Land, wrote that "April is the cruelest month", but it's hard to imagine a month more cruel in San Francisco than January.

① News articles reflect the ways in which a society has changed.
② San Francisco has witnessed an unprecedented number of horrible crimes so far this year.
③ It is clear that there is a growing disrespect for life in San Francisco.
④ T. S. Eliot should have written that the cruelest month is January, not April.

해설 이 글은 2015년 1월 한 달 동안 샌프란시스코에서 발생한 강력범죄 사건을 예로 들고 있다. 글 첫머리의 2014년에 대한 언급과 끝머리의 T. S. Eliot에 대한 언급은 2015년 들어 샌프란시스코에서 전개된 상황을 부연 설명하는 역할을 한다. 이 글의 주제로 ②가 정답이다.

어휘 splashy 눈에 확 띄는 initial public offering 기업공개(IPO) gizmo 장비 come to life 살아나다, 갑자기 움직이기 시작하다 실현되다 homicide 살인 gun down ~을 쏘아죽이다 stray bullet 유탄(목표물에서 빗나간 탄환) assailant 가해자 force one's way into 침입해 들어가다 tie ~ up ~을 단단히 묶다 make off 달아나다 ram ~을 ~에 들이받다 nugget 천연금괴 facedown 얼굴을 숙이고 겉을 아래로 하고

해석 기업공개(IPO), 최신 첨단기술 장비, 구글 버스, 또는 계속해서 오르는 부동산 가격에 관한 눈에 띄는 뉴스기사들은 잊어라. 샌프란시스코에게는 그것은 너무나 2014년처럼 느껴지는 뉴스기사들이다. 2015년 지금시점까지, 샌프란시스코의 최대 뉴스기사들은 믿기지 않은 공포소설이 현실이 된 것처럼 읽힌다. 1월에 아홉 건의 살인사건이 있었는데, 그 중 네 명의 젊은이들은 헤이즈 밸리(Hayes Valley)에서 누군가가 쏜 총에 맞아 차안에서 죽었으며, 베이뷰(Bayview)에서 어떤 세 아이의 엄마는 밝은 대낮에 아이들이 보는 앞에서 빗나간 총탄에 맞아 목숨을 잃었다. 지난 주말에는 일련의 가택침입사건들이 있었는데, 그중 어느 것도 서로 관련이 없는 것으로 여겨졌다. 한 가택침입사건에서, 어떤 가해자는 바다가 보이는 전망 있는 어떤 가정에 침입해, 26세의 어떤 여성의 머리를 수건으로 가린 다음 연장용 전선으로 그녀를 단단히 묶었다. 그 가해자는 보석, 휴대폰 그리고 돈을 챙겨 달아났다. 복면을 한 남자들은 원래 웰스파고 은행이 있던 부지에 위치한 한 박물관을 스포츠 유틸리티 차량(SUV)으로 들이받아 골드러시 시대의 천연금괴를 가지고 달아났다. 그리고 레이크 메르세드(Lake Merced)에서는 카약을 타던 사람들이 충격적인 것을 발견을 하였는데, 그것은 바로 부패되고 있는 의문의 시신으로, 갈대숲 사이에 얼굴이 호수 속에 잠겨 떠 있는 채 발견되었다. T. S. 엘리엇은 그의 시 황무지에서 "4월은 가장 잔인한 달이다."라고 말했다. 그러나 샌프란시스코에서는 1월보다 더 잔인한 달을 상상하기는 힘들다.

정답 ②

08 다음 글의 내용으로 가장 적절한 것은?

Unlike many other real assets, such as farmland or property, art is movable, which is handy for buyers who do not plan to tell the taxman about it. It can be a relatively discreet way of investing, too: Christie's arranged $916m of private purchases in 2014, compared with just $266m in 2009. Even so, the risks of investing in art are high. Prices are volatile and the market is idiosyncratic — no two pieces are interchangeable. "Especially at the top it's based on the passions and whims of a small group of collectors," says Orlando Rock from Christie's. The most popular genres and the most expensive pieces skew art's overall performance as an asset. Last year 0.5% of transactions accounted for nearly half the value of all fine art sold at auction. According to Arts Economics, a research firm, the value of works of art that cost more than €200,000 is growing five times faster than the cheaper stuff. And although contemporary art has had a great year, prices for Old Masters are stagnant and Chinese decorative art is losing value.

① Rising prices of art in recent years must have scared off lots of speculators.
② The works of art are difficult to hide from tax collectors.
③ The demand for art works can vary depending on their genre.
④ The more expensive the works of art are, the faster they decrease in value.

[해설] 미술품의 가격이 불안정한 것이 위험 요소로 설명하고 있는데 마지막에서 현대 미술은 좋은 한 해를 보냈지만, 옛 거장의 작품의 가격은 정체되어있고, 중국 장식미술은 가치가 하락하고 있다고 밝혔다. 이를 다른 말로 표현해 보면 어떤 시기에는 현대 미술이 안 좋을 때도 있었고, 중국 장식 미술이 좋은 대접을 받았던 시기도 있었을 것이다. 따라서 미술품에 대한 수요는 장르에 따라 다를 수 있으므로 ③은 추론할 수 있다.

[어휘] real assets 부동산 movable 움직일 수 있는 〈법률〉 토지에 정착되지 않은, 동산의 taxman 세무당국, 세무관리 discreet 신중한, 조심스러운 volatile (가격·정세 따위가) 심하게[끊임없이] 변동하는, 불안정한 idiosyncratic 특이한, 색다른 interchangeable 교환할 수 있는 whim 일시적인 생각, 변덕 skew 왜곡하다

[해석] 농장 또는 소유지와 같은 다른 많은 부동산과 달리 예술품은 움직일 수 있는 재산(동산)이며 이것은 예술품을 구입하는 것에 대해 세무 당국에게 알리지 않을 계획을 가진 구매자들에게 도움이 되는 것이다. 그것은 또한 비교적 조심스러운 투자의 한 방법일 수 있다. 크리스티스 경매회사는 2009년 2억6천6백만 달러와 비교해서 2014년에는 9억1천6백만 달러어치의 개인 구매를 성사시켰다. 그렇기는 하지만, 예술품 투자의 위험은 높다. 가격은 불안정하며 어떤 두 작품도 상호교환 할 수 없기 때문에 이 시장은 독특하다. "특히 최고 작품들의 경우 소수의 수집가들의 열정과 변덕에 기반을 둔다."라고 크리스티스 경매 회사의 올랜도 락(Orlando Rock)은 말한다. 가장 인기 있는 장르와 가장 비싼 작품들은 자산으로서 예술의 전반적인 기능을 왜곡시킨다. 작년에 거래된 작품들 중 0.5%가 경매에서 팔린 모든 예술품의 가치의 거의 절반을 차지했다. 리서치 회사인 Arts Economics에 따르면 가격이 2십만 유로가 넘는 예술품의 가치는 보다 저렴한 예술품보다 5 배나 빠르게 상승하고 있다고 한다. 그리고 현대미술은 근사한 한해를 보내왔지만, 옛 거장의 작품의 가격은 정체되어 있고, 중국 장식 미술은 가치가 하락하고 있다.

[정답] ③

09 빈칸 (A)와 (B)에 들어갈 말로 가장 적절한 것은?

"Why, in country after country that mandated seat belts, was it impossible to see the promised reduction in road accident fatalities?" John Adams, professor of geography at University College London, wrote in one of his many essays on risk. "It appears that measures that protect drivers from the consequences of bad driving encourage bad driving. The principal effect of seat belt legislation has been a shift in the burden of risk from those already best protected in cars, to the most vulnerable, pedestrians and cyclists, outside cars." Adams started to group these counterintuitive findings under the concept of risk compensation, the idea that humans have an inborn tolerance for risk. As safety features are added to vehicles and roads, drivers feel less vulnerable and tend to take more chances. The phenomenon can be observed in all aspects of our daily lives. Children who wear protective gear during their games have a tendency to take more physical risks. Hikers take more risks when they think a rescuer can access them easily.

⬇

According to John Adams, the phenomenon that safety measures __(A)__ careless driving may be accounted for by the notion that a greater sense of security __(B)__ people to take more risks.

	(A)	(B)
①	contribute to	tempts
②	contribute to	forbids
③	discourage	tempts
④	discourage	forces

[해설] 운전자들은 안전장치가 추가될수록 위기의식을 덜 느끼게 되어 더 많은 모험을 무릅쓰는 경향이 있다는 내용의 글이다. 따라서 (A)에는 contribute to(~의 원인이 되다, ~에 도움이 되다), 그리고 (B)에는 tempts (부추기다, 유혹하다)가 적절하다.

[어휘] mandate 명령[위임]하다 fatality 사망자(수), 참사 measures 수단, 방책 legislation 입법, 법률 제정 vulnerable 상처를 입기 쉬운, 공격 받기 쉬운 counterintuitive 직관에 반하는 finding 연구 결과, 발견 compensation 보상, 배상 safety 안전(장치) chance 위험, 모험

[해석] 왜 안전벨트를 의무화한 나라들에서 도로상의 사고로 인한 사망자 수가 기대한 만큼 감소하는 것을 보는 것이 불가능한가? 런던대학의 부속 단과대학 지리학교수인 John Adams는 위험에 관한 자신의 많은 글들 중 하나에 (다음과 같이) 썼다. "운전자들을 잘못된 운전의 결과로부터 보호하는 수단들이 바람직하지 않은 운전을 조장하는 것처럼 보인다. 안전벨트 법률 제정의 주요 효과는 차량 안에서 이미 가장 잘 보호받고 있는 사람들로부터 가장 취약한 사람들, 즉, 차 밖에 있는 보행자들과 자전거를 타는 사람들로 위험에 대한 부담이 옮겨가는 것이었다." Adams는 '위험 보상', 즉 인간은 위험에 대해 타고난 내성이 있다는 생각에 의거하여 이러한 직관에 반한 연구 결과들을 정리하기 시작했다. 두드러진 안전장치들을 차량이나 도로에 추가할수록,

운전자들은 위기의식을 덜 느끼게 되고 더 많은 모험을 하는 경향이 있다. 그러한 현상은 우리의 일상적인 삶의 모든 면에서 관찰될 수 있다. 게임을 하는 동안 보호 장구를 착용한 어린이들은 더 많은 신체적인 위험을 무릅쓰는 경향이 있다. 도보 여행을 하는 사람들은 구조자가 자신들에게 쉽게 접근할 수 있다고 생각할 때 더 위험을 무릅쓴다.

⇨ John Adams에 따르면, 안전장치들이 부주의한 운전에 원인이 되는 현상은 더 큰 안전감이 사람들로 하여금 더 많은 위험을 감수하도록 부추긴다는 생각으로 설명될 수 있을 것이다.

[정답] ①

10 다음 빈칸에 들어갈 말로 가장 적절한 것을 고르시오.

It turns out that the brain is modular, its neurons wired together into circuits that perform complex tasks. Some regulate heart rate and body temperature, and others enable us to write poetry or figure out Sudoku puzzles. Blocked into different regions of the brain, every circuit seems to _____. As a child grows, certain brain structures associated with particular functions have periods of intense activity and development, while others remain relatively quiet. Then the quiet structures awaken and begin to develop rapidly, while previously active structures hit the end of their growth spurts. In the middle of a growth spurt, the brain's various structures are like a room full of preschoolers. While two in one corner drift to sleep, three in another will act up. When those three go to sleep, others will wake up and fuss.

① be similar in function
② have its own timetable
③ have different components
④ be connected to one another

[해설] 뇌의 모든 회로는 여러 개로 나뉘어져 있어도 함께 연결되어 있는 모듈식의 구조를 가지고 있지만, 각각 활동하고 발달하는 시기는 서로 다르다는 내용이 빈칸 다음에 이어지고 있으므로, 빈칸에 들어갈 말로 ② '그것 자체의 시간표를 가지고 있는'이 가장 적절하다.

[어휘] modular 모듈식의 circuit 회로 body temperature 체온 growth spurt 급성장 preschooler 미취학 아동 drift to sleep 서서히 잠들다 act up 버릇없이 굴다 fuss 호들갑을 떨다

[해석] 뇌는 모듈식, 즉 뇌의 신경 세포는 복잡한 과제를 수행하는 회로로 함께 연결되어 있다는 것이 밝혀졌다. 어떤 회로는 심박동 수와 체온을 조절하고, 다른 어떤 회로는 우리로 하여금 시를 쓰거나 스도쿠 퍼즐을 해결할 수 있게 한다. 뇌의 다양한 지역에 차단된 모든 회로는 그것 자체의 시간표를 가지고 있는 듯하다. 아이가 자라면서, 특정한 기능과 연관된 어떤 뇌 구조물은 강렬한 활동과 발달의 시기를 가지고 있는 반면에, 또 다른 어떤 뇌 구조물은 비교적 조용한 채로 남아 있다. 그리고 나서 조용한 구조물이 깨어나 빠르게 발달을 시작하는 반면에, 이전에 활동적이었던 구조물이 급성장을 끝낸다. 급성장하는 도중에, 뇌의 다양한 구조물은 미취학 아동으로 가득 찬 방과 같다. 구석 한 쪽에 있는 두 아동(구조물)이 서서히 잠드는 동안, 또 다른 쪽 구석의 세 아동은 버릇없이 굴 것이다. 이 세 아동이 잠들 때, 다른 아이들이 깨서 호들갑을 떨 것이다.

[정답] ②

하프 모의고사 해설

01 밑줄 친 단어의 의미와 가장 가까운 것은?

> The elegant Princess ingrid has long complained about Duchess Sarah Norton's <u>common</u> accent.

① vulgar
② recognizable
③ trivial
④ frequent

[해설] 기품 있는 사람이 다른 사람의 말투에 대해 불평했다면, 이는 그 사람의 말투가 자신의 기준에 미치지 못했기 때문일 것이다. 따라서 common이 '기품 있는'과 반대되는 의미로 쓰였음을 알 수 있으므로 '저속한'이란 의미의 ①이 정답이다.

common [kámən] 형 공통의(= (public), 일반적인, 평범한, 비속한 = vulgar

[Comment] common은 좋은 의미 혹은 나쁜 의미 양쪽으로 쓰임. popular, familiar는 좋은 의미로만, notorious는 나쁜 의미로만 쓰임.

[Remark] ① common 일반적인 것·특별하지 않은 것. 특히 사람에 쓰일 경우는 경멸의 뜻을 담고 있음. ② ordinary 보통 표준치, 또는 평균 내지는 그 이하의 것. ③ vulgar 서민에 속하거나 서민 특유의 것을 가리키지만 저속·조잡·무식함의 경멸적인 뜻이 내포되어 있음.

[어휘] recognizable 인지할 수 있는 알아볼 수 있는 trivial 하찮은 사소한 평범한 frequent 자주 일어나는 빈번한 상습적인

[해석] 기품 있는 잉그리드 공주는 사라 노튼 공작부인의 저속한 말투에 관해 오랫동안 불평해 왔다.

[정답] ①

02 다음 밑줄 친 표현의 의미와 가장 가까운 것은?

> He never takes responsibility for his problems and always tries to <u>pass the buck</u>.

① foot the bill
② break even
③ ignore others
④ blame someone else

[해설] pass the buck 남에게 책임을 전가하다; 다른 사람에게 ~에 대한 비난을 퍼붓다; 다른 사람에게 ~에 대한 책임을 전가하다 = blame someone else

[영영] pass the buck : refuse to accept responsibility for a mistake, an accident, an important decision, etc. and try to get another person, organization, etc. to accept responsibility for it instead

[어휘] takes responsibility for ~에 책임을 지다 foot the bill 계산을 하다 break even 수입액이 지출액과 맞먹다, 손익분기점에 도달하다

[해석] 그는/책임을 전혀 지지 않고/자기 문제에 대해/항상 책임을 전가하려 한다.

[정답] ④

03 다음 빈칸에 들어갈 표현으로 가장 적절한 것은?

> The asteroid that occurred in what is now the Yucatan at the end of the Cretaceous period, 66 million years ago, was probably 10km or more across. That impact is widely thought to have brought with it a _____ which killed off well over half the species on the planet.

① natural selection
② genetic diversity
③ mass extinction
④ global warming

[해설] 소행성의 직경이 10km가 넘는다고 했으며, 이 소행성의 충돌로 인해 지구에 살고 있던 종의 절반 이상이 전멸되었다고 했으므로 소행성 충돌은 ③ 대량멸종을 야기했다고 볼 수 있다.

[어휘] asteroid 소행성 Cretaceous 백악기(紀)의 kill off 전멸시키다 natural selection 자연선택 genetic diversity 유전적 다양성

[해석] 6천 6백만 년 전 백악기말에 현재의 유카탄 반도인 곳에 있었던 소행성은 직경이 아마도 10km이상 이었을 것이다. 그 소행성의 충돌로 지구에 존재한 종의 절반이상을 사망케 한 대량멸종이 초래 되었던 것으로 널리 여겨지고 있다.

[정답] ③

04 다음 문장들 중 어법상 가장 적절한 것은?

① It is much more easy to edit document on a word processor than on a typewriter.
② The students were all obedient and did what the teacher had told them to do.
③ The computer has made it possible the phenomenal leap in human proficiency.
④ It is Mr. Brown's responsibility of maintenance all computer files on current projects.

[해설] ①에서는 easy는 단음절이므로 그 비교급은 more easy가 아니라 easier이다. 이때 much는 비교급을 강조하는 어구이다. ②에서는 did의 목적어는 선행사를 포함하고 있는 관계대명사 what이 이끄는 절이며, tell은 'tell + 목적어 + to부정사'의 형태로 쓰므로 옳은 표현이다. ③에서는 made는 목적어 the phenomenal leap in human proficiency이므로, 대명사 it이 있으면 목적어의 중복이 된다. 따라서 it을 삭제해야 하며, 목적어의 길이가 길어서 목적보어 뒤로 보낸 문장으로 이해하면 된다. 여기서 it을 가목적어라고 착각해서는 안 된다. it이 가목적어로 사용되는 경우는 진목적어가 to부정사나 that절 등일 경우이며, 명사(구)를 진목적어로 받을 수 없다. ④에서는 maintenance는 명사이므로 목적어를 취할 수 없음에도 불구하고, maintenance 다음에 all computer files라는 목적어가 주어져 있다. it을 가주어로 보고 to부정사를 이용하여 '가주어-진주어' 구문으로 만들어, 진주어 to maintain이 all computer files를 목적어로 받는 구조로 바꾸면 된다. of maintenance를 to maintain으로 고친다.

[해석] ① 타자기보다 워드 프로세서로 문서를 편집하는 것이 훨씬 더 쉽다. ② 그 학생들은 모두 말을 잘 들었고 선생님이 그들에게 시킨 일을 하였다. ③ 컴퓨터로 인해 인간의 능률이 비약적으로 신장했다. ④ 현행 프로젝트에 관한 모든 컴퓨터 파일을 관리하는 것은 브라운 씨의 책임이다.

[정답] ②

05 다음 우리말을 영어로 옮긴 것 중 틀린 것을 고르시오.

① 그를 설득하지 못한다면 정보를 얻을 수 없을 것이다.
  ⇨ Unless you persuade him, you won't get information.
② 그는 누가 들을까봐 내게 작은 소리로 말했다.
  ⇨ He talked to me in whispers lest he should be heard.
③ 나는 그를 도울 수도 없고, 또한 돕고 싶지도 않다.
  ⇨ I cannot help him, and I don't want to help him, too.
④ 잘못을 저지르지 않는 사람은 하나도 없다.
  ⇨ There is no one but commits errors.

해설 ③에서 too는 긍정 동의에 쓰는 '또한'이고, either는 부정 동의에 쓰이는 '또한'이다. too ⇨ either ①에서 unless가 속해 있는 절에는 절대 not을 쓸 수 없고 unless는 if ~ not과 같다. 그리고 unless이하는 조건표시부사절로 현재가 미래를 대신 한다. ②에서 lest는 부정 목적 접속사(~하지 않도록)로 lest절에서는 동사를 동사원형 또는 (should) 동사원형으로 쓰는 것이 원칙이다. ④에서 There is no one[man, person] but~ 구문에서 but은 부정 의사 관계대명사(~하지 않는)로 이하에 재차 not을 쓰면 중복 부정이 되어 틀린 표현이다. = There is no one who[that] doesn't commit errors.

정답 ③

06 주어진 글 다음에 이어질 글의 순서로 가장 적절한 것은?

Some teachers are eager to make immigrant students blend in with others as quickly as possible. They rarely consider the transitional phase these children and families experience while struggling to adjust to the new environment.

(A) Some Muslim girls in the local school wore the traditional headscarves(hijab), while others did not. Some girls expressed to their teachers their wish that they could remove their headscarves like their friends. The teachers encouraged them to remove their scarves at school, suggesting they could replace them before returning home.

(B) Rather than accelerating the mainstreaming process, this overzealous approach of the teachers can sometimes have the opposite result. An example of such a negative outcome occurred during the conduct of one set of workshops, which included several Muslim families.

(C) Shortly thereafter, some of the girls who removed their headscarves were no longer in school. Hence the teachers' eagerness to accelerate the acculturation process only served to abolish the opportunity completely.

① (C) – (B) – (A)   ② (B) – (A) – (C)
③ (B) – (C) – (A)   ④ (C) – (A) – (B)

[해설] 이민 온 학생들이 새로운 환경에 적응하는 이행 단계를 고려하지 않는 것에 대해 지적한 주어진 글 다음에 문화적 적응을 가속화하려다가 부정적인 결과를 초래한 사례가 있다고 언급한 내용인 (B)가 이어지고, 그 사례로 이슬람 여학생에게 전통적인 머리 스카프를 학교에서는 착용하지 말라고 권유한 교사에 대해 언급한 (A)가 이어지며, 결국 머리 스카프를 착용하지 않았던 여학생의 일부가 학교에 나오지 않게 되었다는 결과를 보여주는 (C)가 이어지는 것이 적절하다. 그러므로 가장 자연스러운 글의 순서는 ②'(B) – (A) – (C)'이다.

[어휘] eager 간절한, 열심인 blend in with ~와 어울리다 transitional phase 이행 단계[시기] adjust to ~에 적응하다 headscarf 머리 스카프 (pl. headscarves) replace 다시 착용하다, 원래 위치에 두다 accelerate 가속화하다 mainstreaming process 주류 사회에 편입하는 과정 outcome 결과 conduct 수행 eagerness 열의 serve 기여하다 abolish 없애다 overzealous 과도하게 열성적인 acculturation 문화적 적응

[해석] 일부 교사들은 이민 학생들이 가능한 한 빨리 다른 학생들과 어울리게 만들고 싶어 한다. 그들은 이 아이들과 가족들이 새로운 환경에 적응하려고 애쓰는 동안 경험하는 이행 단계에 대해 거의 고려하지 않는다. (B) 그 교사들의 이렇게 과도하게 열성적인 접근 방법은 주류 사회에 편입하는 과정을 가속화하기는커녕, 때로는 정반대의 결과를 가져올 수도 있다. 그런 부정적인 결과의 한 사례가 일련의 워크숍을 수행하는 도중에 나타났는데, 그것은 몇몇 이슬람계 가족을 포함했다. (A) 그 지역 학교에서 일부 이슬람 여학생들은 전통적인 머리 스카프(hijab)를 착용한 반면 다른 학생들은 하지 않았다. 일부 여학생들은 자신들의 교사에게 자기들도 친구들처럼 머리 스카프를 착용하지 않으면 좋겠다는 소망을 표현했다. 교사들은 그들에게 집으로 돌아가기 전에 다시 착용할 수 있으니 학교에서는 (머리) 스카프를 착용하지 말라고 권유했다. (C) 그 후 얼마 지나지 않아 머리 스카프를 착용하지 않았던 그 여학생들 중 일부는 더 이상 학교에 나오지 않았다. 그래서 문화적 적응 과정을 가속화하려는 교사의 열의가 그 기회를 완전히 없애는 데 기여했을 따름이었다.

[정답] ②

07 다음 빈칸에 들어갈 말로 가장 적절한 것은?

> Life has rules and only the foolish person refuses to follow these rules at all. However, sometimes we expand this "rule" approach to life to such a degree that we get locked into patterns that are no longer applicable to life and our creative juices get squeezed out. Therefore, one way to enhance our creativity is to challenge the rules. In the movie IQ, Walter Matthau played the part of Einstein. Meg Ryan was Einstein's niece. At one point in the movie, Einstein said to his niece, "Question everything!" That's good advice. Every advance in history came from someone who challenged the rules. Columbus discovered America because he challenged the rules of navigation. Martin Luther started the Reformation because he challenged the rules of the church. Einstein discovered the theory of relativity because he challenged the rules of Newtonian physics. Sometimes creativity arises out of the awareness that we do not have to _____.

① imagine a future without any form of conflict
② be under pressure to improve our own creativity
③ be a genius to make valuable contributions to science
④ do things in the same way they have always been done

[해설] 기존의 규칙에 대해 의심하고 도전해보는 것이 창의력을 높이는 한 방법이고 역사의 진보는 그렇게 한 사람들에게서 나왔다는 것을 Columbus, Martin Luther, Einstein의 예를 들어 보여주는 내용이므로 빈칸에는 ④ '늘 해오던 것과 같은 방식으로 일들을 할'이 가장 적절하다. ① 어떠한 형태의 갈등도 없는 미래를 상상할 ② 우리 자신의 창의성을 향상시키라는 압박을 받을 ③ 과학에 가치 있는 기여를 할 천재가 될

[어휘] **refuse** 거부하다, 거절하다 **expand** 확장하다 **approach** 접근(법) **get locked into** ~에 갇히다 **applicable** 적용할 수 있는 **creative juices** 창의력 **squeeze out** 모두 짜내다 **enhance** 고양하다 **challenge** 도전하다 **navigation** 항해, 운항 **the theory of relativity** 상대성 이론 **arise** 생기다 **awareness** 인식 **conflict** 갈등 **contribution** 기여, 공헌 **the Reformation** 종교 개혁

[해석] 삶에는 규칙이 있고 어리석은 사람만이 이 규칙들을 따르는 것을 아예 거부한다. 그러나 우리는 가끔, 삶에 더 이상 적용될 수 없는 형태에 갇혀서 창의력이 모두 짜내어져 없어질 정도까지, 이러한 삶에 대한 '규칙'의 접근 방식을 확대한다. 그러므로 우리의 창의력을 고양하는 한 방법은 규칙에 도전하는 것이다. 'IQ'라는 영화에서 Walter Matthau가 Einstein의 역을 했다. Meg Ryan이 Einstein의 조카딸 역을 했다. 그 영화의 한 시점에서 Einstein은 자기의 조카딸에게 "모든 것을 의심하라!"라고 말했다. 그것은 좋은 충고이다. 역사에서 모든 진보는 규칙에 도전하는 사람에게서 나왔다. Columbus는 항해의 규칙에 도전했기 때문에 아메리카를 발견했다. Martin Luther는 교회의 규칙에 도전했기 때문에 종교 개혁을 시작했다. Einstein은 Newton의 물리학의 규칙에 도전했기 때문에 상대성 이론을 발견했다. 때로는 창의성은 늘 해오던 것과 같은 방식으로 일들을 할 필요가 없다는 인식에서 생긴다.

[정답] ④

08 다음 글의 빈칸에 들어갈 말로 가장 적절한 것은?

Contemporary Western athletes speak in their own terms about time _____. Tennis great Jimmy Connors has described transcendent occasions when his game rose to a level where he felt he'd entered a "zone." At these moments, he recalls, the ball would appear huge as it came over the net and seem suspended in slow motion. In this rarified air, Connors felt he had all the time in the world to decide how, when, and where to hit the ball. In truth, of course, his seeming eternity lasted only a fraction of a second. Basketball chatter is also laced with mystical-sounding references to "getting into zones" where time stands still. Players describe unexplainable occasions when everyone around them seems to move in slow motion. During these moments they report a feeling of being able to move around, between, and through their opponents at will.

① limit
② waste
③ pressure
④ expansion

[해설] 테니스에서 공이 네트를 넘어올 때 느린 동작으로 일시 정지한 것처럼 보이고 농구에서 선수들 주위의 모든 사람이 느린 동작으로 움직이는 것처럼 보인다는 내용의 글이다. 그러므로 빈칸에 들어갈 말은 ④ '확장'이 가장 적절하다. ① 한계 ② 낭비 ③ 압박

[어휘] **transcendent** 초월적인, 탁월한 **contemporary** 현대의, 동시대의 **recall** 회상하다 **suspend** 일시 정지시키다, 매달다 **all the time in the world** 아주 많은 시간 **eternity** 영원 **a fraction of a second** 1초의 몇 분의 1 **chatter** 이야기, 잡담 **be laced with** ~이 가미되어 있다, ~이 짜 넣어져 있다 **mystical-sounding** 신비스럽게 들리는 **reference** 언급, 참고, 문의 **opponent** 상대, 반대자 **at will** 마음대로 **rarified** 심원한, 고상한

[해석] 현대 서구의 운동선수들은 시간 확장에 대하여 자신들의 용어로 말한다. 테니스계의 거인 Jimmy Connors는 자신의 경기가 자신이 '경지'로 들어갔다고 느끼는 수준으로 상승한 초월적인 때를 묘사했다. 이런 순간에는 공이 네트를 넘어올 때 거대해 보이고 느린 동작으로 일시 정지한 것처럼 보이곤 한다고 그는 회상한다. 이런 심원한 분위기에서 Connors는 자신에게 공을 어떻게, 언제, 그리고 어디서 칠지를 결정할 아주 많은 시간이 있다고 느꼈다. 사실, 물론 그의 외견상의 영원한 시간은 고작 1초의 몇 분의 1 동안 지속되었다. 농구와 관련된 이야기에도 또한 시간이 정지해 있는 '경지로 들어가는 것'에 대한 신비스럽게 들리는 언급들이 가미된다. 선수들은 자신들 주위의 모든 사람이 느린 동작으로 움직이는 것처럼 보이는 설명할 수 없는 경우를 묘사한다. 이런 순간에 그들은 마음대로 자신들의 상대 선수들 사이를 헤집고 돌아다닐 수 있다는 느낌을 말한다.

[정답] ④

09 다음 글의 빈칸 (A), (B)에 들어갈 말로 가장 적절한 것은?

The principle of distinctiveness suggests that we make attributions about people based on whether their particular characteristics and actions are associated with specific outcomes unique to the situation. Distinctiveness is the extent to which things occur only with each other and not with other things. ___(A)___, if a student, who has a habit of submitting his assignments late, seems well liked by peers and professors but is clearly treated harshly by one of the professors, then the student seems to cause a distinctive reaction from this professor. If the professor in question is consistently harsh with many other students, then the behavior is not distinctive to the late-assignment student; rather it is low in distinctiveness, and you will tend to consider the professor a harsh person. If, ___(B)___, you see this professor being friendly with all students except the student with the late assignments, then the student seems to be unique or distinctive in eliciting this response from the professor. In this case, the professor's behavior is high in distinctiveness and you are more likely to attribute the cause to the late student having done something to upset this professor.

	(A)	(B)		(A)	(B)
①	For example	instead	②	For example	consequently
③	On the contrary	instead	④	On the contrary	consequently

[해설] (A) 어떤 결과를 가져오도록 서로 특이하게 관련이 있는 것들을 가리키는 개념을 소개한 다음 과제를 늦게 제출한 학생과 그 학생을 가혹하게 다루는 교수의 반응을 사례로 제시하고 있으므로 '예를 들어(For example)'가 가장 적절하다. (B) 그 교수가 과제를 늦게 제출한 학생뿐만 아니라 모든 학생에게 가혹하다면 교수의 그런 반응은 교수의 탓이 된다는 내용 다음에 이와 반대로 그 교수가 다른 학생들에게는 친절한데 과제를 늦게 제출한 학생에게만 가혹했다면 교수의 그런 반응은 해당 학생의 탓으로 돌아간다는 내용이므로 '그 대신에(instead)'가 가장 적절하다. ② 예를 들어 … 그 결과로 ③ 그와는 반대로 … 그 대신에 ④ 그와는 반대로 … 그 결과로

[어휘] elicit (반응을) 끌어내다 principle of distinctiveness 특이성의 원리 characteristic 특성 associated with ~와 연관된 outcome 결과 unique 독특한 extent 정도 assignment 과제 peer 동료, 또래 harshly 가혹하게 consistently 일관되게 upset 화나게 하다 attribution (사회심리학에서) 귀인(歸因), 행동의 원인 찾기

[해석] 특이성의 원리는, 사람들의 특별한 특성과 행동이 그 상황에 고유한 특정 결과와 연관되어 있는지에 근거해서, 우리가 사람들에 관해 귀인(歸因) 분석을 한다는 점을 보여준다. 특이성은 어떤 일들이 다른 것과 관련해서가 아니라 서로 간에만 관련해서 일어나는 정도를 말한다. 예를 들어, 과제를 늦게 제출하는 습관이 있는 어느 학생이 동료들과 교수들에게는 매우 호감을 얻는 것 같지만 그 교수들 중의 한 명에게서는 가혹한 대우를 받는 것이 분명하다면, 그 학생은 이 교수에게서 특이한 반응을 불러일으키는 것으로 보인다. 문제의 그 교수가 많은 다른 학생들에게도 일관되게 가혹하다면 그 행동은 과제를 늦게 제출한 학생에게 특이한 것이 아니라 오히려 특이성의 정도는 낮고 그 교수를 가혹한 사람이라고 여기는 경향이 있을 것이다. 만약 그 대신에, 이 교수가 과제를 늦게 제출한 학생을 제외한 모든 학생에게 친절한 것을 본다면 그 학생은 그 교수에게서 이런 반응을 이끌어내는 데 있어서 독특하거나 특이한 것으로 보인다. 이 경우에 그 교수의 행동은 특이성의 정도가 높은데, 여러분은 그 원인이 과제를 늦게 제출한 학생이 이 교수를 화나게 하는 행동을 했다는 데 있다고 생각할 가능성이 더 많다.

[정답] ①

10 다음 글의 주제로 가장 적절한 것은?

A chef does not turn off the oven when the meal is half done. Even microwaves take some time to cook. Far too often we lose patience with the process and quit too soon, missing out on what we could have gained. In these fast times, we run the risk of cutting the harvest short. Watching the corn grow can be a very anxious process. We want it safely in the barn now. Yesterday would be even better. Our lives are one big hurry. We rush through our childhood, red lights, and a courtship as if channel surfing. We speed-read directions, come late to and leave early from meetings, and choose a church because its worship service is precisely one hour long. Our addiction to speed gets us things we'd not have without it, but it also guarantees we'll never see things we long for most. For example, going into debt to purchase a car, clothes, and vacation can keep us from qualifying for a house or the kind of home we dream about. Haste in a relationship can ruin long-term fulfillment, because we go too fast too soon or wind up with someone who is less than our dreams. The unwillingness to persevere with an organization through its trying times can cut us out of potential rewards when the tide changes. Waiting for the harvest is not fun for most of us, but when we plant seed and then run off to some other plot of ground without reaping our harvest, we've wasted a portion of our lives.

① ways to cure shopping addiction
② myths that waste energy in the kitchen
③ disadvantages of moving too fast in life
④ effects of late-life debt use on quality of life

[해설] 우리는 인생을 살아가면서 지나치게 서두르는 경향이 있고 수확을 기다리지 못하는 이러한 성급함으로 인해 우리가 가장 바라는 것들을 얻지 못하게 된다는 내용이므로, 글의 주제로 가장 적절한 것은 ③ '인생에서 너무 서두르는 것의 단점'이다. ① 쇼핑 중독을 치유하는 방법 ② 주방에서 에너지를 낭비하게 하는 그릇된 사회 통념들 ④ 노년에 부채의 사용이 삶의 질에 미치는 영향

[어휘] **miss out on** ~을 놓치다 **cut ~ short** ~을 갑자기 끝내다, ~을 도중에 그만두다 **rush through** 서둘러[신속히] 처리하다 **addiction** 중독 **guarantee** 확실히 하다, 보장[약속]하다 **qualify** 자격[자격증]을 얻다[취득하다] **fulfillment** 성취 **wind up with** 결국~을 가지게 되다, 결국~한 상황에 처하다 **unwillingness** 자발적이 아님, 반항적임 **trying** 괴로운, 힘든 **tide** 흐름, 조수 **reap** 거둬들이다, 수확하다 **courtship**(결혼 전의)교제

[해석] 주방장은 음식이 절반 정도 됐을 때 오븐을 끄지 않는다. 심지어 전자레인지도 요리하는 데 얼마간의 시간이 필요하다. 너무 지나치게 자주 우리는 과정에 대한 인내심을 잃고 너무도 빨리 그만두어, 우리가 얻을 수 있었던 것을 놓쳐 버린다. 이 빠른 시대에, 우리는 수확을 갑자기 끝내 버리는 위험을 무릅쓴다. 옥수수가 자라는 것을 지켜보는 일은 매우 조마조마하게 하는 과정일 수 있다. 우리는 지금 그것이 안전하게 곳간에 들어 있기를 바란다. 어제라면 훨씬 더 좋을 것이다. 우리의 삶은 하나의 큰 서두름이다. 우리는 마치 채널을 자주 돌리듯이 우리의 어린 시절, 빨간 신호등, 그리고 교제를 급하게 지나쳐 버린다. 우리는 설명서를 빠르게 읽고, 모임에 늦게 와서 빨리 떠나고, 그리고 예배가 정확하게 한 시간 걸린다는 이유로 교회를 선택한다.

속도에 대한 중독은, 그것이 없다면 가지지 못할 것들을 우리에게 가져다주지만, 또한 우리가 가장 열망하는 것들을 우리는 결코 보지 못할 것이라는 점을 확실하게 한다. 예를 들어 자동차, 옷, 휴가를 갖기 위해 빚을 내면, 주택이나 우리가 꿈꾸는 종류의 가정을 가지는 자격을 얻지 못할 수도 있다. 관계에서의 성급함은 장기간에 걸친 성취를 망칠 수 있는데, 이는 우리가 너무 빨리 너무 급하게 서두르거나 혹은 우리의 이상형에 못 미치는 사람에게 정착해 버리기 때문이다. 조직이 힘든 시기에 조직에 대해 인내 하기를 꺼려함으로써 그 흐름이 바뀔 때 우리는 잠재적인 보상으로부터 제외될 수 있다. 수확을 기다리는 것이 대다수의 우리에게 즐거운 일은 아니지만, 우리가 씨앗을 뿌리고 나서 수확을 거둬들이지 않고 다른 밭으로 급히 갈 때, 우리는 우리 삶의 일부를 낭비해 버린 것이다.

정답 ③

16 하프 모의고사 해설

01 다음 밑줄 친 단어의 의미와 가장 가까운 것은?

> They all failed to understand my gestures; some were simply stolid, some thought it was a jest and laughed at me.

① tremulous
② apathetic
③ wayward
④ diffident

[해설] stolid [stάlid] 무감각한, 무딘, 멍청한 = apathetic
[영영] stolid : having or revealing little emotion or sensibility
[어휘] jest 농담 tremulous 떨리는, 진동하는 apathetic 무관심한, 무감각한 wayward 제멋대로의, 변덕스러운 diffident 소심한, (자신감이 부족하여) 조심스러운
[해석] 그들 모두 내 제스처를 이해하는데 실패했다. 일부는 무덤덤했고, 일부는 농담이라고 생각하고 날보고 웃었다.

[정답] ②

02 다음 밑줄 친 부분과 의미와 가장 가까운 것은?

> This sort of thing will cut no ice the international market.

① back
② have no influence
③ advocate
④ support

[해설] cut no ice 효과가 없다, 쓸모가 없다, (~에게) 아무런 소용[효과]이 없다 = have no influence
[영영] cut no ice : not impress or influence somebody
[어휘] back, advocate, support 도와주다, 지지하다
[해석] 이런 종류의 상품은 국제시장(international market)에 내놔도 별 효과가 없다.

[정답] ②

03 다음 문장에서 문법적으로 어색한 부분을 고르시오.

> Just as a planet ① circling the sun cannot help ② following Kepler's laws, so a program ③ obeying an invariant cannot help but ④ behaving in a predictable way.

[해설] 동명사의 관용구를 묻고 있다. cannot help 다음에는 동명사가 나오는 반면, cannot help but 다음에는 동사원형이 온다. 따라서 ④를 behave로 고쳐야 한다.
[해석] 태양을 공전하는 행성이 케플러의 법칙을 따르지 않을 수 없듯이, 불변식을 따르는 프로그램은 예상할 수 있는 방식으로 작용하지 않을 수 없다.

[정답] ④

04 다음 빈칸에 들어갈 단어로 가장 적절한 것은?

> Videotape was not new in 1963, but the technology was unwieldy, and the machines were huge, neither terribly reliable nor easily _____.

① portable
② noticeable
③ vulnerable
④ reversible

[해설] **the machines**는 비디오 기계이며 부피가 컸다고 했으므로 당연히 휴대하기 어려웠을 것이다. **neither A nor B**는 'A나 B 둘 다 아닌'의 뜻이므로 '휴대할 수 있는'이라는 뜻의 ① **portable**이 빈칸에 적절하다.

[어휘] **unwieldy** (크기·모양·무게 때문에) 다루기 불편한 **noticeable** 눈에 띄는 **vulnerable** 약점이 있는 **reversible** 거꾸로 할 수 있는

[해석] 1963년에 비디오테이프는 새로운 것이 아니었지만, 그 기술은 다루기 어려웠으며, 그 기계들은 부피가 컸고, 대단히 신뢰할 만 하지도 휴대가 쉽지도 않았다.

[정답] ①

05 다음 우리말을 영어로 옮긴 것 중 틀린 것을 고르시오.

① 나는 그처럼 아량 있는 사람을 본 적이 없다.
  ⇨ I've never met such an understanding man as him.
② 무엇 때문에 너는 공무원이 되기로 결심을 했느냐?
  ⇨ What made you decide to become a public servant?
③ 인간이 항상 환경의 지배를 받는 것은 아니다.
  ⇨ Men are not always influenced by environment.
④ Brian은 자신의 건강이 좋지 않다고 주장하고 있다.
  ⇨ Brian insist that his health be in bad shape.

[해설] ①에서 such + a(n) + 형 + 명 = so + 형 + a(n) + 명 ②에서 사역 동사 **make + O + R**(원형부정사) ④에서 **insist that**절의 내용이 미래의 일, 현재 입장에서 하지 않은 일, 앞으로 해야 할 일이면 **should + 동사원형**을 쓰고 과거의 일이나 했던 일, 한 일이거나 단순 사실의 내용이므로 주절의 시제와 일치시켜야 한다. **be ⇨ is**

[어휘] **understanding** 이해심 있는 **in (good) shape** 건강한

[정답] ④

06 다음 글의 주제로 가장 적절한 것은?

Robert Schuman's works for the piano are acknowledged as brilliant masterworks. However, his large scale orchestral works have always suffered by comparison to those of contemporaries such as Mendelssohn and Brahms. Perhaps this is because Schuman's works should be measured with a different yardstick. His works are often considered poorly orchestrated, but they actually have an unusual aesthetic. He treats the orchestra as he does the piano: one grand instrument with a uniform sound. This is so different from the approach of most composers that, to many, it has seemed like a failing rather than a conscious artistic choice.

① The greatness of Schuman's piano works
② The difference between piano works and orchestral music
③ The reassessment of Schuman's musical works
④ The influence of Schuman's performances

[해설] 이 글에서 Robert Schuman의 오케스트라의 곡이 그와 동시대의 작곡가들의 오케스트라 곡들과 비교해서 고통을 받는다고 언급하면서 그 이유를 Robert Schuman의 작품은 다른 척도를 가지고 평가되어져야 한다고 말하고 있다. 이 부분이 글의 주제문으로 Schuman의 작품에 대한 재평가가 글의 주제로 가장 적합하다.
① Schuman의 피아노곡 작품들의 위대함 ② 피아노 작품들과 오케스트라 음악의 차이 ③ Schuman의 음악 작품들의 재평가 ④ Schuman 공연의 영향

[어휘] masterwork 걸작 orchestral 오케스트라의 suffer 고통 받다, 시달리다 comparison 비교 yardstick 척도 orchestrate 오케스트라용으로 편곡하다 aesthetic 심미적, 미학적 conscious 의식하는, 자각하는 artistic 예술의, 예술적인 reassessment 재평가 performance 공연

[해석] Robert Schuman의 피아노곡 작품들은 뛰어난 걸작으로 알려져 있다. 그러나 그의 대규모의 오케스트라 작품들은 Mendelssohn and Brahms 같은 동시대인의 작품들과의 비교에 의해 시달림을 겪는다. 아마도 그것은 Schuman의 작품들이 다른 척도로 평가되어야만 하기 때문일 것이다. 그의 작품들은 종종 오케스트라용으로는 형편없다고 여겨진다. 그러나 실제로는 특이한 미적 특징이 있다. 그는 오케스트라를 그가 피아노를 다루는 것처럼 다룬다. 즉, 하나의 통일된 소리를 가진 거대한 악기로 다룬다. 이것은 대부분의 작곡자들의 접근법과는 너무 달라서 많은 사람들에게 이것이 의식적인 예술적인 선택이라기보다는 실패작처럼 보인다.

[정답] ③

07 글의 흐름으로 보아, 주어진 문장이 들어가기에 가장 적절한 곳은?

> Only a few analysts noted the large number of "undecided" respondents a week before the election.

Public opinion polls are snapshots of opinions and preferences at a specific moment in time and as expressed in response to a specific question. Given that definition, it is fairly easy to understand situations in which the polls are wrong. (①) For example, opinion polls leading up to the 1980 presidential election showed President Jimmy Carter defeating challenger Ronald Reagan. (②) Those voters shifted massively to Reagan at the last minute, and Reagan won the election. (③) The famous photo of Harry Truman showing the front page of the newspaper that declared his defeat in the 1948 presidential election is another tribute to the weakness of polling. (④) Again, the poll that predicted his defeat was taken more than a week before Election Day. Truman won the election with 49.9 percent of the vote. *tribute 증거

[해설] 주어진 문장의 the large number of "undecided" respondents 는 마음을 정하지 못했다가 선거 마지막 순간에 대규모로 Reagon 쪽으로 이동한 유권자들을 의미하므로 주어진 문장의 적절한 위치는 ②이다.

[어휘] analyst 분석가 note 주목하다, 알아차리다 respondent 응답자 poll 여론조사 snapshot 단편적인 정보 preference 선호, 선택 presidential election 대통령 선거 defeat 이기다, 패배시키다, 패배 challenger 도전자 massively 대규모로 declare 공표하다, 선언하다 predict 예측하다

[해석] 여론조사는 시간상 특정 순간의, 그리고 특정 질문에 대한 응답에 나타나 있는 의견과 선호를 보여주는 단편적인 정보이다. 그 정의를 고려하면, 여론조사가 틀린 상황을 이해하는 것은 상당히 쉽다. 예를 들어, 1980년 대통령 선거 이전에 있었던 여론조사들은 Jimmy Carter 대통령이 도전자인 Ronald Reagan을 이기고 있다는 것을 보여주었다. 선거 일주일 전 단지 몇몇 분석가만이 '결정하지 못한' 다수의 응답자에 주목했다. 그 유권자들은 마지막 순간에 대규모로 Reagan 쪽으로 이동했고 Reagan이 당선되었다. 1948년 대통령 선거에서 자신의 패배를 공표한 신문의 첫 페이지를 Harry Truman이 보여주는 유명한 사진은 여론조사의 취약성에 대한 또 다른 증거이다. 이번에도, 그의 패배를 예측했던 여론조사는 선거일을 일주일 넘게 앞두고 시행되었다. Truman은 총투표수의 49.9퍼센트를 득표하며 당선되었다.

[정답] ②

08 다음 빈칸에 들어갈 말로 가장 적절한 것을 고르시오.

What does curiosity mean, and why is it so important? We think of curiosity as exploration: being inquisitive, seeking to learn and understand. Some associate curiosity with being nosy. After all, aren't we being nosy if we are curious about another person, asking personal questions? We believe there is a difference between the two. Nosy people ask questions and proceed to weigh the answers provided. Their intention is not to learn about the other person, but to compare, perhaps wanting to determine who is better or worse. In contrast, true curiosity _____. It is about exploring and learning with the goal of greater understanding, which is free from setting values. When curious people ask a question, their only intention is to better understand, whether it is another person, an idea, a place, an origin, or anything that creates an interest in further exploration.

① grows with age
② overcomes fear
③ holds no judgment
④ comes from confidence

[해설] 진정한 호기심은 참견을 좋아하는 것과는 달리 대상을 비교하거나 가치를 정하지 않는다는 내용을 통해 빈칸의 내용을 추론할 수 있다. ① 나이가 먹어감에 따라 ② 두려움을 극복하다 ④ 자신감에서 나오는

[어휘] inquisitive 호기심이 많은 nosy 참견하기 좋아하는

[해석] 호기심은 무엇을 의미하고, 왜 그것은 그렇게 중요한가? 우리는 호기심을 탐구로 생각하는데, 즉 배우고 이해하려고 하면서 알고 싶어 하는 것이다. 어떤 사람들은 호기심을 참견하기 좋아하는 것과 연관시킨다. 결국, 만약 우리가 다른 사람에 대해서 호기심이 있다면, 개인적인 질문들을 하며 우리가 참견을 하게 되지 않는가? 우리는 그 둘 사이에는 차이가 있다고 믿는다. 참견하기 좋아하는 사람들은 질문을 하고 이어서 주어진 답변들에 대해 저울질을 시작한다. 그들의 의도는 다른 사람에 대해 배우는 것이 아니라, 아마 누가 더 낫거나 못한지를 결정하기를 원하면서 비교하는 것이다. 반면에 진정한 호기심은 어떠한 판단도 내포하지 않는다. 그것은 더 큰 이해라는 목표를 가진 탐구와 배움에 관한 것으로 가치를 정하는 것이 없다. 호기심 많은 사람이 질문을 할 때면 그들의 유일한 의도는 더 깊이 탐구하는 가운데 흥미를 자아내는 것이 다른 사람, 생각, 장소, 기원 혹은 그 어떤 것이든 간에 이해를 더 잘하는 것이다.

[정답] ③

09 주어진 글 다음에 이어질 글의 순서로 가장 적절한 것을 고르시오.

Mass customization is a strategy that allows manufacturers or retailers to provide individualized products to consumers. Today's apparel supplier must look for new ways to offer customers top-quality goods at highly competitive prices.

(A) The customer then receives the finished product in a very short time. This technological strategy is used today by some fashion firms. This type of customization is often limited, however, to a small number of customers.

(B) Based on the exact image, body scanning software then defines and captures all the measurements necessary for actually producing the garment or shoe. This data is forwarded online to the manufacturer, whose production technologies ensure an exact fit.

(C) Consumers desire products that can be personalized through fit preferences, color selection, fabric choices, or design characteristics. A solution to the fit preference is a body or foot scanner that takes a customer's measurements digitally, creating what is referred to as digital twin.

① (A) – (C) – (B)   ② (B) – (A) – (C)
③ (B) – (C) – (A)   ④ (C) – (B) – (A)

어휘 apparel 의류 mass customization 대량 주문 제작 strategy 전략 manufacturer 제조업자 retailer 소매상 individualize 개인의 요구에 맞추다 supplier 공급 회사 top-quality 최고 품질의 competitive 경쟁력 있는 measurement 치수, 측정(된 것) capture 입력하다 garment 옷, 의복 forward 전송하다 personalize (개인의 필요에) 맞추다 preference 선호(도) fabric 직물 characteristic 특징 be referred to as ~로 불리다, ~로 언급되다

해설 대량 주문 제작은 제조업자나 소매상이 개개인의 요구에 맞추어 만든 제품을 소비자들에게 제공할 수 있게 하는 전략이다. 오늘날의 의류 공급 회사는 고객들에게 최고 품질의 상품을 매우 경쟁력 있는 가격으로 제공하는 새로운 방법을 찾아야 한다. (C) 소비자들은 크기나 모양에 대한 선호도, 색상 선택, 직물 선택, 혹은 디자인 특성을 통해 개인의 요구에 맞추어 질 수 있는 상품을 원한다. 크기나 모양에 대한 선호도에 대한 한 가지 해결책은 디지털 방식으로 고객의 치수를 측정하는 전신 스캐너 혹은 발 스캐너인데, 이것은 디지털 쌍둥이라고 불리는 것을 만들어낸다. (B) 그 정확한 이미지에 기초하여, 신체를 스캔하는 소프트웨어가 그 다음으로 실제로 옷이나 신발을 제조하는 데 필요한 모든 치수를 확정하고 (그 자료를) 입력한다. 이 자료는 제조업자에게 온라인으로 전송되는데, 제조업자의 제조 기술이 몸에 꼭 들어맞게 해 준다. (A) 그러면 고객은 이내 곧 완성된 제품을 받는다. 오늘날 일부 패션 회사들은 이러한 기술 전략을 사용한다. 그러나 이러한 종류의 주문제작은 흔히 소수의 고객들에게 한정되어 있다.

정답 ④

10. 다음 글의 내용으로 가장 적절한 것은?

If You're Bitten, Trap the Spider

In the rare case you do get bitten, it's a good idea to trap the spider so you can identify the species in case treatment is needed. Isolate your leggy little tourist — along with fruit, if that's where you found it — in a plastic bag or container. Put that package in the fridge to slow the cold-blooded arachnid down. This makes it easier to brush it into a jar or other container, wearing rubber gloves if you like. "Do this quickly and with confidence." If you're too uncomfortable, you can put the whole shebang in the freezer, which will kill the spider, leaving an intact specimen for identification. If you're bitten, an ice pack on the area will usually suffice for treatment, but experts suggest seeking medical attention if you experience symptoms such as "increasing pain, nausea, vomiting, sweating, dilated pupils, uncontrollable muscle spasms, and loss of consciousness." If a Spider Is in Your Food, Don't Set It Free. In case the spider is a non-native species that got into your house via your food, don't release it outside. The animal could harm the native environment. If you found the spider elsewhere in your house, you can put it outside. If the spider did arrive in your food, "although it pains me to say this [as an arachnologist], the best course of action is to probably to kill the eight-legged cargo," the experts say.

* arachnid 거미류의 절지동물 ** arachnologist 〈동물〉 거미학자

① It is not necessary to treat a spider as dangerous until you know better.
② Alien spiders in your imported fruits may disturb the local ecosystem.
③ Most of the known spiders are venomous enough to be harmful to humans.
④ It is important to receive immediate medical attention when you're bitten by spiders.

17 하프 모의고사 해설

01 밑줄 친 단어의 의미와 가장 가까운 것은?

> This isn't terribly important and maybe I'm just a bit <u>dense</u>, but if someone could clarify, I'd really appreciate it.

① crowded
② heavy
③ opaque
④ stupid

[해설] dense [dens] 형 dense 밀집한, 조밀한, 밀도가 높은, 아둔한, 어리석은 = stupid, dim, dull, dumb, obtuse, slow
[영영] dense : slow to learn or understand; lacking intellectual acuity
[어휘] crowded 붐비는, 혼잡한, 꽉 찬, 만원의 opaque 불투명한, 통과시키지 않는
[해석] 이것은 대단히 중요한 게 아니고 아마도 제가 조금 아둔한 것일 수도 있습니다만, 누군가 명확하게 밝혀주시면 정말 감사하겠습니다.

[정답] ④

02 다음 빈칸에 들어갈 단어로 가장 적절한 것은?

> Snapchat's primary value proposition is a _____ mobile message that disappears after a few seconds to protect message privacy.

① transient
② ubiquitous
③ tailored
④ bilateral

[해설] that 이하에서 프라이버시를 보호하기 위해서 메시지가 몇 초 후에 사라진다고 했으므로 스냅챗의 모바일 메시지를 수식하는 형용사로 '일시적인'이라는 뜻의 ① transient가 적절하다.
[어휘] value proposition 가치제안 transient 일시적인 ubiquitous (동시에) 도처에 있는 tailored (특정한 개인·목적을 위한) 맞춤의 bilateral 쌍방의
[해석] 스냅챗의 주된 가치 제안은 메시지의 프라이버시를 보호하기 위해 몇 초 후에 사라지는 일시적인 모바일 메시지이다.

[정답] ①

03 다음 빈칸에 들어갈 단어로 가장 적절한 것은?

> Impulsive children interrupt others, are impatient about waiting their turn, blurt out answers before hearing the entire question, or _____ other people's conversations.

① butt in on
② listen in on
③ stand up for
④ look up to

[해설] 충동적인 아이들의 특징이 or에 의해 병치되고 있다. 다른 사람을 방해하고 차례를 기다리지 못하는 아이들이라면 다른 사람들이 대화하고 있을 때도 끼어들 것이다.

[어휘] impulsive 충동적인 interrupt 방해하다 blurt out 무심결에 말하다, 불쑥 말하다 butt in on (대화 중에) 불쑥 끼어들다, 참견하다 listen in on ~을 엿듣다 stand up for ~을 지지하다 look up to ~을 존경하다

[해석] 충동적인 아이들은 다른 사람들을 방해하거나, 자신들의 차례를 기다리지 못하고, 전체 질문을 듣기 전에 답을 불쑥 말하거나, 다른 사람들의 대화중에 불쑥 끼어든다.

[정답] ①

04 다음 빈칸에 들어갈 표현으로 적절한 것을 고르시오.

> Our news is free of charge, but just as the popularity of our news grows, _____.

① so too have our costs of operation
② our costs of operation do so too
③ so too do our costs of operation
④ our costs of operation have so too

[해설] '~하는 것처럼, 그렇게 ~하다'는 구문인 'just as + 주어1 + 동사1, so + 주어2 + 동사2'에서 so 이하는 도치가 가능하다. 따라서 빈칸에는 원래 so our costs of operation grow too가 와야 하는데, 반복되는 grow는 대동사인 do로 바꿀 수 있으며(즉, so our costs of operation do too), so 이하는 도치가 가능하므로 so do our costs of operation too가 되며, too는 부사이므로 부사인 so 다음에 와도 상관없다. ③의 so too do our costs of operation이 정답이다.

[해석] 우리가 제공하는 뉴스는 무료이다. 그러나 우리가 제공하는 뉴스의 인기가 증가하는 것처럼, 우리의 운영비도 증가한다.

[정답] ③

05 (A), (B), (C)의 각 네모 안에서 어법에 맞는 표현으로 가장 적절한 것은?

Like life in traditional society, but unlike other team sports, baseball is not governed by the clock. A football game is comprised of exactly sixty minutes of play, a basketball game forty or forty-eight minutes, but baseball has no set length of time within which the game must be completed. The pace of the game is therefore leisurely and (A) [unhurried/unhurriedly], like the world before the discipline of measured time, deadlines, schedules, and wages paid by the hour. Baseball belongs to the kind of world (B) [which/in which] people did not say, "I haven't got all day." Baseball games do have all day to be played. But that does not mean that they can go on forever. Baseball, like traditional life, proceeds according to the rhythm of nature, specifically the rotation of the Earth. During its first half century, games were not played at night, which meant that baseball games, like the traditional work day, (C) [ending/ended] when the sun set.

	(A)	(B)	(C)
①	unhurried	in which	ended
②	unhurried	which	ending
③	unhurriedly	which	ended
④	unhurriedly	which	ending

[해설] (A) 주격 보어가 와야 하므로 형용사 unhurried를 써야 한다. unhurriedly는 부사이므로 쓸 수 없다. (B) 뒤에 주요 구성 성분을 모두 갖춘 절이 왔으므로 in which를 써야 한다. (C) that ~은 meant의 목적어 역할을 하는 명사절이므로 동사의 과거형 ended를 써야 한다.

[어휘] govern 좌우하다, 지배하다 be comprised of ~으로 구성되다 leisurely 여유로운 unhurried 느긋한, 서두르지 않는 discipline 규율 measured 정확히 잰 belong to ~에 속하다 proceed 진행하다 rotation 자전, 회전

[해석] 전통 사회의 삶과 마찬가지로, 그러나 다른 팀 스포츠와는 달리, 야구는 시계에 의해 좌우되지 않는다. 미식축구 경기는 정확히 60분 경기로 구성되고, 농구 경기는 40분이나 48분으로 이루어지지만, 야구는 경기가 끝나야 하는 정해진 시간의 길이가 없다. 따라서 정확히 잰 시간, 마감 시간, 일정, 시간 단위로 지급되는 임금 같은 규율이 있기 이전의 세상과 마찬가지로 경기의 속도가 여유롭고 느긋하다. 야구는 사람들이 "저는 시간이 많지 않아요."라고 말하지 않았던 그런 종류의 세상에 속해 있다. 야구 경기는 '정말로' 온종일 경기가 이루어진다. 그러나 그것이 그 경기가 영원히 계속 될 수 있다는 것을 의미하는 것은 아니다. 야구는 전통적인 삶과 마찬가지로 자연의 리듬, 구체적으로 말해 지구의 자전에 따라 진행된다. 그것(야구)의 첫 반세기 동안 경기가 밤에는 이루어지지 않았는데, 그것은 야구 경기가 전통적인 근무일처럼 해가 질 때 끝난다는 것을 의미했다.

[정답] ①

06 다음 글의 요지로 적절한 것을 고르시오.

> Some health-screening efforts have gone too far. A recent study found that yearly mammograms do not prolong the lives of low-risk women ages 40 to 59. Following more than 89,000 women for 25 years in a randomized controlled trial (the gold standard of science), the study is methodologically impressive. As hard as it is for our pro-screening culture to believe, the data are clear. We are taxing far too many women not only with needless and sometimes humiliating X-rays but also with unnecessary follow-up surgery. In this era of rising medical prices, cutting waste should be the top priority, especially when that waste pulls doctors away from the important work of caring for sick patients. A 2012 Institute of Medicine report concludes that Americans spend as much as one-third of their health care dollars on tests, medicine, procedures and administrative burdens that do not improve health outcomes. Reducing overdiagnosis and overtreatment will require broadening medicine's focus beyond hunting and killing disease to sound research and education on appropriate care.

① Excessive screening can cause unintended harm, stress and waste.
② Advances in modern medicine will help reduce growing healthcare costs.
③ A health-screening test used to detect tumors is rarely problematic.
④ The risks of chasing indolent diseases can only be detected by a screening test.

[해설] 첫 문장에서 검진 노력이 도를 넘었다고 했고, 의학적인 검사들이 실제 건강을 향상시키지 못하며 의료낭비로 인한 부작용에 대해 언급하고 있으므로 이 글의 요지로는 ①이 적절하다.

[어휘] health-screening 검진 go too far 도를 넘다 mammogram 유방조영상(유방암 검진용 X선 촬영) prolong 연장시키다 tax 무거운 짐을 지우다 humiliate 창피를 주다, 굴욕을 주다 follow-up 후속 조치 pull away from ~에서 떼어놓다[구해내다]

[해석] 일부 검진 노력들은 도를 넘었다. 최근 연구에 따르면 해마다 받는 유방암 검진은 40세에서 59세에 이르는 저위험군 여성들의 수명을 늘이지 못하는 것으로 나타났다. 무작위로 통제된 실험에서(과학의 신뢰할 수 있는 기준) 25년 동안 8만 9천명 이상의 여성들을 대상으로 한 그 연구는 방법론적으로 인상적이다. 의학적인 검사를 찬성하는 우리의 문화로서는 믿기 어렵겠지만 그 자료는 분명하다. 우리는 불필요하면서도 때때로 굴욕감을 주는 엑스선 사진들로 너무나 많은 여성을 혹사시키고 있을 뿐만 아니라 불필요한 후속 수술들로 부담을 주고 있다. 오늘날과 같이 의료비용이 치솟는 시대에 (의료) 낭비를 줄이는 것은 최우선이 되어야 한다. 특히 그 낭비가 의사들이 아픈 환자를 돌보는 중요한 업무를 하지 못하게 할 때 그렇다. 2012년 의학 연구소의 보고서는 미국인들이 건강상의 결과를 향상시키지 않는 검사, 약, 수술절차와 행정적인 비용에 그들의 건강관리 비용의 1/3이나 소비한다고 결론짓고 있다. 과잉 진단과 과잉 치료를 줄이려면 병을 발견하고 없애는 것을 뛰어넘어 적절한 치료에 대한 철저한 연구와 교육으로까지 의학의 주안점을 넓혀야 할 필요가 있을 것이다.

[정답] ①

07 다음 빈칸에 들어갈 말로 가장 적절한 것을 고르시오.

> If we can't have everything we want today, what do we do? We are forced to make choices. We must choose some goods and services and not others. Sometimes this kind of choosing can be visibly painful. Have you ever watched children in a toy store with a gift certificate in hand? It can take them all day before they make a choice. And instead of bubbling with excitement over the toy they bought, they usually appear frustrated over not being able to walk away with everything! Life is like that. _____ governs us. Because we cannot have everything all at once, we are forever forced to make choices. We can use our resources to satisfy only some of our wants, leaving many others unsatisfied.

① Scarcity
② Morality
③ Knowledge
④ Reputation

[해설] 모든 것을 다 가질 수 없으므로 결국 무언가를 선택해야 하는 상황에 놓인다는 내용을 통해 빈칸의 내용을 추론할 수 있다.

[어휘] visibly 분명히

[해석] 만약 우리가 오늘 원하는 모든 것을 가질 수 없다면, 우리는 무엇을 하는가? 우리는 선택을 할 수밖에 없다. 우리는 다른 것들이 아닌 어떤 재화와 서비스를 선택해야 한다. 때때로 이런 종류의 선택하기는 분명히 고통스러울 수 있다. 당신은 장난감 가게에서 손에 상품권을 쥐고 있는 아이들을 본 적이 있는가? 그들은 선택하기까지 온종일이 걸릴 수 있다. 그리고 그들이 산 장난감을 두고 흥분으로 잔뜩 들떠 있는 것 대신, 그들은 모든 것을 가지고 가지 못하는 것에 대해 대개는 좌절하는 것처럼 보인다! 인생은 그와 같다. 부족이 우리를 지배한다. 우리가 한꺼번에 모든 것을 가질 수 없기 때문에 우리는 영원히 선택할 수밖에 없다. 우리는 많은 다른 원하는 것들을 충족되지 않은 상태로 두고, 우리가 원하는 것들의 일부만을 충족시키기 위해 우리의 자원을 활용할 수 있다.

[정답] ①

08 다음 글의 제목으로 가장 적절한 것은?

Trish and Andrea enjoyed a good relationship as business partners until Andrea began to feel victimized by the amount of time she needed to devote to a project. Overwhelmed by the prospect of what lay ahead, she sent Trish an e-mail demanding a larger share of the profits. Trish was shocked and hurt by the message and by the impersonal way it was delivered. Rather than let herself become overwhelmed by hurt and disappointment, she reminded herself that she and Andrea were friends and that she didn't understand what was so troubling. Trish made an appointment to discuss the matter leisurely with Andrea in a comfortable setting that favored communication. When the two met, Trish was relaxed and genuinely interested in knowing why Andrea felt resentful when she hadn't in the past. Face to face, with Trish showing genuine interest and regard, Andrea relaxed and was able to tell Trish that their project had become more than she could handle. Andrea felt reassured by Trish's support and their interaction as they discussed possible solutions that would enable Andrea to continue working on the project. The discussion ended with each feeling greater excitement about working together and more appreciation for one another.

① Emotionally Intelligent Communication Turns Mad into Glad
② Nonverbal Cues That Convey Confidence at Work
③ How to Peacefully Break Up with Your Business Partner
④ Leaving a Never-Ending Conversation Without Being Rude

[해설] 동업자 관계인 Trish와 Andrea가 갈등을 겪자, Trish가 편안하게 소통할 수 있는 환경에서 얼굴을 마주하고 대화를 나누며 진심 어린 관심과 배려를 보였고, 이를 통해 해결책을 도출하고 상호 간에 더 좋은 감정을 갖게 되었다는 내용의 글이므로, 글의 제목으로 가장 적절한 것은 ① '감성적으로 지능적인 소통은 화를 기쁨으로 변화시킨다.'이다. ② 직장에서 자신감을 전달하는 비언어적 신호들 ③ 여러분의 동업자와 평화롭게 헤어지는 방법 ④ 무례하지 않게 끝없는 대화 중지하기

[어휘] victimize 부당하게 괴롭히다, 희생시키다 devote 기울이다, 쏟다, 헌신하다 overwhelmed 압도된 prospect 예상, 가능성, 가망 impersonal 비인격적인, 인간미 없는 leisurely 느긋하게, 여유롭게 genuinely 진정으로, 성실하게 resentful 분해하는, 분개하는 reassured 안심하는 appreciation 감사, 감탄, 감상

[해석] Trish와 Andrea는 Andrea가 자신이 프로젝트에 기울여야 하는 시간으로 인해 희생당한다고 느끼기 시작했을 때까지 동업자로서 좋은 관계를 누렸다. 앞으로 전개될 일에 대한 예상에 압도되어, 그녀는 Trish에게 수익의 더 많은 몫을 요구하는 이메일을 보냈다. Trish는 그 메시지와 그것이 전달된 비인격적인 방식에 충격과 상처를 받았다. 자기 자신이 상처와 실망에 압도되도록 두기보다는, 그녀는 자기와 Andrea가 친구였고 무엇이 그렇게 힘들었는지를 자기가 이해하지 못한다는 것을 스스로에게 상기시켰다. Trish는 소통에 도움이 되는 편안한 환경에서 Andrea와 느긋하게 그 일을 논하기 위해 약속을 잡았다. 그 둘이 만났을 때, Trish는 편안했고 Andrea가 이전에는 그렇지 않았는데 왜 화가 났는지를 아는 데 진심으로 관심을 가졌다. 얼굴을 마주하고, Trish가 진심 어린 관심과 배려를 보여 주자, Andrea는 긴장을 누그러뜨렸고 Trish에게 그들의 프로젝트가 자기가 처리할 수 있는 정도를 넘어섰다고 말했다. Andrea가 계속해서 그 프로젝트 작업을 할 수 있도록 해 주는 가능한 해결책들을 그들이 논하면서, Trish의 지지와 그들의 상호 작용이 Andrea를 안심시켰다. 그 논의는 각자가 함께 일하는 것에 대해 더 큰 흥분감과 서로에 대한 더 많은 감사를 느끼면서 끝났다.

[정답] ①

09 다음 글의 내용으로 가장 적절한 것은?

> The general tendency is away from conflicts that are clearly one side against the other toward multiplayer conflicts in which several groups, ranging from the local to the international, kaleidoscopically compete against one another as much as they participate in a two-way fight. Fragmentation is not new, but its effects are radically catalyzed by the speed and interconnectivity of contemporary globalization driven by the information revolution. The information revolution encourages fragmentation because it simultaneously has the power to bring powerful networks together and to break them up. Consider the Arab Spring, in which a disparate range of people and of interests were drawn together by the simple and powerful desire to rise up against oppressive regimes. But, once formed, the information revolution catalyzed the fragmentation of those networks once they started to disagree with one another, thus reforming new groups. Look at how the Arab Spring became the Arab Winter; comrades in arms have been split by factional and religious differences. Fragmentation profoundly affects any armed conflict that may well start as a relatively polarized fight, as people are drawn together under one cause — be it toppling Bashar Assad in Syria or Moammar Gadhafi in Libya — but soon fight among each other as much as with the original enemy. These confusing, complex, multilayered patterns are replicated by each of the factions' regional and international backers. The convoluted evolution of who backs whom with the mutating factions in Syria over the past three years, and now in Iraq, makes that clear.

① Libyans and Syrians had a clear enemy to be defeated at the beginning of the revolution.
② The consequences of the Arab Spring differ depending on the forms of political systems.
③ The people who participated in the Arab Spring fought for constitutional monarchy to protect minorities.
④ The group which was firmly in control of networks took absolute power in the Middle East.

[해설] 세 번째 단락 첫 문장에서 시리아와 리비아의 사람들이 독재자를 몰아내기 위해 하나의 명분아래 뭉쳤다고 했으므로 ① '리비아인과 시리아인은 혁명의 초기에 패배할 분명한 적이 있었다.'은 이 글과 관련하여 추론할 수 있다. ② 아랍의 봄의 결과는 정치체제의 형태에 따라 다르다. ③ 아랍의 봄에 참여한 사람들은 소수민족을 보호하기 위해 입헌군주제를 위해 싸웠다. ④ 네트워크를 확고히 장악하고 있던 집단이 중동에서 절대 권력을 장악했다.

[어휘] **kaleidoscopically** 만화경 같이, 변화무쌍하게 **fragmentation** 분열, 단편화 **catalyze** 촉진하다, 자극하다 **disparate** (본질적으로) 다른, 공통점이 없는 **rise up against** ~에 대항하여 들고 일어나다 **polarize** (당파 등을) 양극화하다 **topple** 전복시키다 **replicate** 반복하다 재생하다 **convoluted** 복잡한

[해석] 명확히 한편이 다른 한편에 대항하는 전쟁에서 탈피해 다자간의 전쟁으로 발전하는 것이 일반적인 추세이다. 다자간의 전쟁에서는 지역단체에서 국제적인 단체에 이르는 다양한 세력들이 쌍방의 전쟁에 가담하는 것만큼 서로에 대항하여 변화무쌍하게 싸운다. 단편화는 새로운 것이 아니지만, 그것의 영향은 정보혁명이 가져다주는 현대 세계화의 속도와 상호연결성에 의해 급격히 촉진된다. 정보혁명이 단편화를 부추기는데 정보혁명은 강력한 네트워크를 결집시킬 수 있으며 동시에 네트워크를 해체할 수 있는 힘을 갖고 있기 때문이다. 아랍의 봄을 생각해보라. 아랍의 봄에서 본질적으로 공통점이 없는 다양한 사람들과 이해집단들이 압제정권에 대항하여 들고 일어나고자 하는 단순하고 강한 욕구에 의해 함께 단결됐다. 그러나 일단 형성된 정보혁명은 그 네트워크 사이에서 서로 불화가 시작되자 그 단합된 네트워크의 단편화를 촉진시켜 새로운 집단들을 다시 형성됐다. 아랍의 봄이 아랍의 겨울로 변해버린 과정을 살펴보라. 전우들이 당파적이고 종교적인 차이들로 분열되었다. 단편화는 무력분쟁에 지대한 영향을 미친다. 그 무력 분쟁은 비교적 양극화된 싸움으로 시작되는 것이 당연한데 시리아의 바샤르 아사드(Bashar Assad)를 몰아내든, 리비아의 무아마르 카다피(Moammar Gadhafi)를 전복시키든 사람들은 하나의 명분 아래 함께 뭉치기 때문이다. 그러나 곧 원래의 적과 싸우는 만큼 같은 편에서도 서로 싸우기 시작한다. 이런 혼란스럽고 복잡하며, 다층적인 패턴은 각 파벌의 지역적, 국제적 후원세력에 의해 되풀이된다. 지난 3년에 걸쳐 시리아에서, 그리고 지금 이라크에서 진화하는 파벌들이 복잡하게 얽히고설키는 상황이 그것을 확실하게 보여주고 있다.

[정답] ①

10 다음 빈칸에 들어갈 말로 가장 적절한 것은?

The "hygiene hypothesis," which proposes that kids today live in overly sanitized environments thanks to things like bleach and hand sanitizers, has been long used to explain the rise in children's allergies. The thought was that urban immune systems do not get exposed to enough bacteria and other microbes that prepare the immune system to be _____. This hypothesis is partly based on studies showing that children raised on farms have fewer allergies and asthma attacks. Playing outside, digging for worms, planting vegetables, and essentially coming into contact with plenty of dirt and livestock are actually good things. Not just good — essential! Bacteria, viruses, parasites, and fungi play a critical role in developing and maintaining a healthy gut and immune system. Another explanation for the rise in allergies has been called the "old friends hypothesis," because allergic children lack a diversity of these friendly microbes in their guts. To evaluate these theories, scientists compared microbial samples from an urban apartment to those from a rural farm. Shockingly, they found that the two environments actually had similar numbers of microbes. What differed, however, was the diversity of bacteria. The microbial sample from the urban apartment was limited, while the microbial sample from the farm was rich with varied microbes. A study of an Amazonian indigenous tribe free of chronic illness — isolated entirely from modern life — revealed the most diverse number of microbes ever documented in humans. A healthy gut is filled with diverse microbes: the more kinds, the better. Biodiversity makes the difference between balance and dysregulation.

① healthy
② infected
③ changed
④ inefficient

[해설] 도시는 지나치게 위생적인 환경을 제공해 오히려 알레르기가 증가하고 농장에서 양육된 아이들은 더 적은 알레르기를 보인다고 했으므로 도시에서의 면역 체계가 건강한 상태로 작동하지 못하고 있음을 알 수 있다. 따라서 빈칸에 들어갈 말로 가장 적절한 것은 ① '건강한'이다. ② 오염된 ③ 변경된 ④ 비효율적인

[어휘] bleach 표백제 dysregulation 조절 장애 hygiene 위생 overly 지나치게 sanitize 위생 처리하다, 살균하다 microbe 미생물 asthma attack 천식 발작 parasite 기생충 fungus 곰팡이류 (pl. fungi) maintain 유지하다 gut 장 indigenous 토착의 chronic 만성의 isolated 고립된 documented 문서로 기록된 biodiversity 생물 다양성

[해석] 오늘날 아이들이 표백제와 손 세정제 같은 것들로 인해 지나치게 위생적인 환경에서 산다고 제안하는 '위생 가설'은 아이들의 알레르기 증가를 설명하는데 오랫동안 사용되어 왔다. 그것은 도시에서 의 면역 체계는 면역 체계가 건강해지도록 준비시키는 박테리아와 다른 미생물들에 충분히 노출되지 못한다는 생각이었다. 이 가설은 농장에서 양육된 아이들이 더 적은 알레르기와 천식 발작을 일으킨다는 것을 보여 주는 연구에 부분적으로 기초하고 있다. 야외에서 놀고, 벌레를 찾으려고 땅을 파며, 채소를 심고, 기본적으로 많은 흙과 가축을 접촉하게 되는 것은 실제로 좋은 것이다. 단지 좋은 정도가 아니라 필수적이다!

박테리아, 바이러스, 기생충, 그리고 곰팡이류는 건강한 장과 면역 체계를 발전시키고 유지하는데 결정적인 역할을 한다. 알레르기 증가의 또 다른 설명은 '오래된 친구 가설'이라고 불리어 왔는데, 그 이유는 알레르기가 있는 아이들은 자신의 장에 이 우호적인 미생물의 다양성이 부족하기 때문이다. 이 이론들을 평가하기 위해 과학자들은 도시 아파트에서 가져온 미생물 샘플과 시골 농장에서 가져온 미생물 샘플을 비교하였다. 놀랍게도 그들은 두 환경이 실제로 유사한 수의 미생물을 가지고 있음을 발견했다. 그러나 다른 점은 박테리아의 '다양성'이었다. 도시 아파트에서 가져온 미생물 샘플은 제한적이었지만, 농장에서 가져온 미생물 샘플은 다양한 미생물이 풍부했다. 현대생활과 완전히 고립되어 있고 만성 질환이 없는 아마존강 유역의 토착 부족에 대한 연구는 인간에게 있는 지금까지 문서로 기록된 것 중 가장 다양한 수의 미생물을 드러내 보였다. 건강한 장은 다양한 미생물로 가득 차 있다. 즉 종류가 많을수록 더 좋은 것이다. 생물 다양성은 균형과 조절 장애 사이의 차이를 만든다.

[정답] ①

18 하프 모의고사 해설

01 다음 밑줄 친 단어의 의미와 가장 가까운 것은?

> The flowers delivered yesterday have already withered.

① wilted ② wavered
③ wandered ④ writhed

[해설] wither [wíðər] 동 시들다, 쇠퇴시키다, 위축시키다, 활기를 잃다 = wilt, disappear, shrivel up, fade, shrink
[영영] wither : ① wither, as with a loss of moisture ② lose freshness, vigor, or vitality
[어휘] waver 흔들리다 wander 배회하다 writhe 고뇌
[해석] 그 꽃들은/(어떤? 어제 배달된/이미 시든 상태였다.

[정답] ①

02 다음 빈칸에 들어갈 표현으로 가장 적절한 것은?

> Natural instincts are either disregarded or treated as nuisances, as _____ traits to be suppressed or at all events to be brought into conformity with external standards. Since conformity is the aim, what is distinctively individual in a young person is _____ or regarded as a source of mischief or anarchy.

① obnoxious – brushed aside ② beneficent – bottled up
③ profane – sanctified ④ ghastly – encouraged

[해설] 타고난 본능, 선천적 특성을 해악시하는 사회의 풍조를 지적하고 있다. 타고난 본능을 '성가신 것'으로 보고 그것을 억압해야 할 대상 혹은 외부의 기준에 순응시켜야 할 것으로 본다면, 그것을 '불쾌한, 고약한(obnoxious)' 것으로 간주한다고 말할 수 있다. 한편, 순응을 목표로 하는 상황에서는, '특징적으로 개인적인 것, 즉 개성적인 것(what is distinctively individual)'은 '무시될(brushed aside)' 것이다.
[어휘] natural instinct 타고난 본능 nuisance 성가신 존재, 귀찮음, 불쾌 suppress 억누르다 conformity 순응 distinctively 특징적으로, 독특하게 mischief 해악, 장난 anarchy n. 무정부 상태, 무질서 obnoxious 아주 불쾌한, 고약한 brush aside 털어내다, 무시하다 beneficent 인정 많은 bottle up 억누르다, 봉쇄하다 profane 불경스러운, 신성모독의 sanctify 신성하게 하다, 축성하다 ghastly 섬뜩한
[해석] 타고난 본능은 무시되거나 혹은 성가신 것, 억압되거나 여하튼 외부의 기준에 순응되어야 할 불쾌한 것으로 취급된다. 순응이 목적이기 때문에, 젊은이 각자의 개성은 무시되거나, 혹은 해악이나 무질서의 원천으로 간주된다.

[정답] ①

03 다음 빈칸에 들어갈 표현으로 적절한 것을 고르시오.

> This is to confirm our understanding and agreement in regard of the long-term lease by us of one refrigerator truck from you. If you are at one with our understanding, as attached, please confirm _____.

① by letter, fax or email
② by a letter, a fax or an email
③ by a letter, fax or email
④ by a letter, fax, or an email

[해설] 교통(by car, by air, on foot, on horseback)이나 통신 수단(by letter, by fax, by email)을 나타내는 말 앞에서는 관사(a, an, the)가 생략된다.

[해석] 이것은 당신의 냉동 트럭을 우리에게 장기 임대하는 것에 대한 우리의 이해와 합의를 확인하기 위한 것이다. 첨부된 것과 같이 당사가 이해한 내용과 같은지 편지, 팩스 또는 이메일로 확인하여 주기 바란다.

[정답] ①

04 다음 빈칸에 들어갈 표현으로 적절한 것을 고르시오.

> Relationship is more valuable than money; ___(A)___ may give us more comfort in life, but ___(B)___ gives us satisfactions which no amount of money can buy.

	(A)	(B)
①	this	that
②	that	this
③	these	those
④	those	these

[해설] 의미상 (A)는 money를 지칭하고 (B)는 relationship을 지칭한다. 따라서 위치상 가까운 것을 지칭하는 (A)에는 this(후자)가, 먼 것을 지칭하는 (B)에는 that(전자)이 적합하다.

[해석] 대인 관계는 돈보다 더 가치 있다. 후자는 인생에 있어서 우리에게 더 큰 편안함을 제공하지만 전자는 우리에게 돈으로 살 수 없는 만족감을 준다.

[정답] ①

05 다음 중 어법상 어색한 문장을 고르시오.

① When questioned, she denied being a member of the group.
② Allowed unusual privileges, the prisoner seemed to enjoy his captivity.
③ Through now frail, they were quit capable of looking after themselves.
④ Considering works of art, the collections of china were admitted into the country without customs duties.

해설 ④에서 도자기 수집품이 미술 작품으로 여겨지는 것이므로 수동의 의미인 과거분사 **Considered**가 와야 맞다. ①에서 질문을 받은 것이므로, 수동의 의미인 과거분사가 사용되었고 시간의 의미를 강조하기 위해 접속사 **when**을 생략하지 않은 분사구문이다. ②에서 죄수가 허락을 받았다는 수동의 의미이므로, 과거분사가 사용된 분사구문이다. ③에서 **Though they are now frail**이 분사구문으로 전환되어 **Though being now frail**이 된 후, **being**이 생략된 형태이다. **frail**은 '허약한'을 의미하는 형용사이다.

해석 ① 그녀는 질문을 받자 자기가 그 그룹의 구성원임을 부인했다. ② 흔치 않은 특혜가 허용되자 그 죄수는 감금을 즐기는 듯 했다. ③ 비록 그들이 지금 허약하지만, 그들 자신을 아주 잘 돌볼 수 있었다. ④ 도자기 수집품이 미술 작품으로 여겨져서 관세 없이 그 나라로 들어올 수 있었다.

정답 ④

06 다음 우리말 영작이 올바르지 않는 문장을 고르시오.

① 구독자에게 제공된 이 보고서에 들어 있는 그 어떤 정보도 개인에 맞춘 재정 자문을 포함하고 있지 않다
⇨ None of the information contained in these reports provided to the subscribers constitute personalized financial advice.
② 가격이 오르고 있는 치즈와 밀가루 비용 때문에 돈이 궁한 피자 제조업자에게는 자금이 힘든 때이다.
⇨ It is a tough time for pizza makers, who are strapped by rising cheese and flour costs.
③ 치솟는 석유 가격이 가장 큰 석유 소비국인 미국의 수요 붕괴의 원인이 되고 있다.
⇨ The surging oil price is leading to demand destruction in the largest consumer of oil – the United States.
④ 나는 이 집과 지금 이후로 이 집에서 살게 될 모든 사람들에게 신의 은총이 내리기를 하늘에 기도한다.
⇨ I pray heaven to bestow the vest of blessing on this house and all that shall hereafter inhabit it.

해설 ①에서는 주어는 None of the information이고, contained와 provided는 앞의 명사를 수식하는 역할을 하는 과거분사이며, 전체 문장의 동사는 constitute로 주어져 있는 형태의 문장이다. 'none of + 불가산명사'는 단수로 취급하므로 동사 constitute를 constitutes로 고쳐야 옳은 문장이 된다. ②에서는 전치사 by 뒤에 위치한 rising은 동명사가 아니라 현재분사임에 유의한다. 즉, 전치사 by의 목적어는 rising cheese and flour costs 전체이다. ③에서는 lead to ~는 '~의 원인이 되다' '결국 ~이 되다'라는 의미인데, 이때 to는 전치사이며 그것의 목적어로 명사구 demand destruction이 왔다. ④에서는 bestow A on B는 'A를 B에게 주다'라는 의미이며, that은 '모든 사람들'이란 의미로 쓰인 all을 선행사로 하는 관계대명사이다. inhabit은 타동사이므로 뒤에 전치사 없이 바로 목적어를 취하며, it은 this house를 지칭한다.

정답 ①

07 다음 글의 제목으로 가장 적절한 것은?

On the national level of culture, we assume that people of the same national background share many things that bind them in a common culture: language, values, norms, and traditions. Thus, we expect Germans to differ from Hmong based on differing national cultures. However, cultures can be formed on other levels, such as generation, gender, race, and region, among others. For example, in many parts of the country, regionalisms exist. People who live in the middle of the United States (in states such as Kansas, Illinois, Iowa, Nebraska, Indiana, and Wisconsin) are often referred to as "Midwesterners." People who live in Vermont, New Hampshire, Maine, Massachusetts, Rhode Island, and Connecticut are called "New Englanders." Both Midwesterners and New Englanders have their own unique way of looking at things, but the two regions also share a great deal in common — namely, pragmatic thinking and an independent spirit.

① Culture Is Multilayered
② Culture Shapes Our Behavior
③ Diversity Makes Us Stronger
④ We Are All the Same Within!

해설 서로 특징을 공유하는 국가적 층위의 문화 속에 다양한 층위에서 각기 특유한 문화가 존재한다는 내용의 글이므로, 글의 제목으로 가장 적절한 것은 ① '문화는 다층적이다'이다. ② 문화가 우리의 행동을 구체화한다 ③ 다양성은 우리를 더 강하게 만든다 ④ 우리는 속으로는 모두 같다!

어휘 Hmong 몽족(베트남의 소수민족) pragmatic 실용적인 assume (당연한 일로) 생각하다, 추정하다 bind 묶다 norm 규범 differ from ~과 다르다 regionalism 지역주의 be referred to as ~이라고 불리다

해석 국가적 층위의 문화에서 우리는 동일한 국적의 사람들은 그들을 공통의 문화 속에 묶어 주는 많은 것, 즉 언어, 가치, 규범, 전통을 공유한다고 생각한다. 따라서 우리는 서로 다른 국가 문화에 근거해서 독일인은 몽족과 다를 것이라고 예상한다. 하지만 문화는 특히 세대, 성, 인종, 지역 같은 그 밖의 다른 층위에서 형성될 수 있다. 예를 들어 전국의 많은 지역에는 지역주의가 존재한다. 미국의 중부(Kansas, Illinois, Iowa, Nebraska, Indiana, Wisconsin 같은 주)에 사는 사람들은 흔히 '중서부인'이라고 불린다. Vermont, New Hampshire, Maine, Massachusetts, Rhode Island, Connecticut 주에 사는 사람들은 '뉴잉글랜드인'이라고 불린다. 중서부인과 뉴잉글랜드인 모두 사물을 바라보는 자기 자신의 특유한 방식을 가지지만, 그 두 지역은 또한 많은 것, 즉 실용적 사고와 독립적인 정신을 공통으로 공유한다.

정답 ①

08 다음 빈칸에 들어갈 말로 가장 적절한 것은?

Here's a curious paradox. If perfection is a state beyond improvement, then isn't every moment, by definition, perfect? After all, any given "now," any given moment of reality is what it is in the sense that it cannot be anything other than what it is. Take this moment, right now: this moment is already here, and, as such, as theoretically imperfect as it may be, it is — at present — beyond any _____. While you could take the lessons of this moment and try to make the next moment better, this very moment is beyond improvement. It is too late to add anything to this moment to make it better. And if this moment, this slice of reality, is beyond improvement, then it's the only way it can be (the best it can be — perfect).

① doubt
② argument
③ evaluation
④ modification

[해설] 지금 이 순간은 개선이 불가능하며 현재 그대로의 상태가 그것이 될 수 있는 유일한 방식이자 최선이라는 내용의 글이므로, 빈칸에 들어갈 말로 가장 적절한 것은 ④ '수정'이다. ① 의심 ② 논쟁 ③ 평가

[어휘] **paradox** 역설 **perfection** 완벽, 완전 **improvement** 개선, 향상 **by definition** 당연히, 의미상 **theoretically** 이론(상)으로 **imperfect** 불완전한, 결함이 있는

[해석] 여기에 호기심을 끄는 역설이 있다. 만약 완벽이 개선을 할 수 없는 상태라면, 그러면 당연히 매 순간은 완벽하지 않은가? 어쨌든 간에 결국 그 어떤 '지금'도, 그 어떤 현실의 순간도, 그것이 그것 그대로의 상태 외에는 그 어떤 것도 될 수 없다는 의미에서 그것 그대로의 상태이다. '이' 순간, '지금 당장'을 예로 들어보자. 이 순간은 이미 여기에 있고, 그렇기 때문에, 그것이 이론상으로 불완전 할지라도, 그것은 현재 그 어떤 수정도 할 수 없다. 여러분이 이 순간의 교훈들을 얻고 다음 순간을 더 낫게 만들려고 노력할 수는 있겠지만, 바로 이 순간은 개선을 할 수 없다. 이 순간을 더 좋게 만들기 위해 그것에 어떤 것이라도 더하기에는 너무 늦었다. 그리고 만약 이 순간이, 이 현실의 단면이, 개선을 할 수 없다면, 그러면 그것은 그것이 될 수 있는 유일한 방식이다(그것이 될 수 있는 최선의 상태이고, 즉 완벽하다).

[정답] ④

09 빈칸 (A)와 (B)에 들어갈 말로 가장 적절한 것은?

Martin Buber taught that there are two kinds of relationships: I–Thou and I–It. As an example of the difference between the two, imagine heading to work on a daily route that includes a stop at one of the corporate coffee chain stores. You place the same order each morning, get the same stuff, throw down the money and pick up the change. This automatic, mechanical, "It's early! I'm sleepy!" interaction with the person behind the counter is the kind of relationship Buber would call I–It. Then, one day, instead of a muffin, you order a whole wheat bagel with no-fat cream cheese. The barista smiles and comments, "On a diet?" and you are taken by surprise, to the point of embarrassment. Here you thought that the counter clerk did not even recognize you, let alone remember what you eat. The dull routine has broke; you discover that, unbeknownst to yourself, your presence makes a difference. Leaving the shop, instead of dragging with fatigue as usual, you realize your mood has lifted a little, thanks to the reaction you received. Buber would say that this exchange was I–Thou.

The kind of relationship Martin Buber would call I–It is characterized by __(A)__ interaction, and in the kind of relationship he would call I–Thou, we feel we are perceived as a(n) __(B)__.

	(A)	(B)
①	informal	loyal customer
②	informal	authoritative figure
③	symbolic	stereotypical image
④	impersonal	particular person

[해설] 주어지는 사례로 보건대 상대를 어떤 과정의 일부로 볼 뿐 얼굴 없는 존재로 여기는 '나와 그것'의 관계와 달리, '나와 너'의 관계에서는 상대를 특정한 사람으로 인식한다는 내용이므로 (A)에는 '몰개성적인(impersonal)'이, (B)에는 '특정한 사람(particular person)'이 가장 적절하다. ① 격식에 얽매이지 않는 – 충직한 고객 ② 격식에 얽매이지 않는 – 권위 있는 인물 ③ 상징적인 – 전형적인 이미지

[어휘] thou 너, 당신 unbeknownst to ~도 모르게 head (특정 방향으로) 가다[향하다] route 길, 경로 corporate 기업의 place an order 주문하다 mechanical 기계적인 whole wheat 통밀 taken by surprise 깜짝 놀란 embarrassment 당황, 당혹 let alone ~하기는커녕 drag (몸을 끌듯) 힘들게 움직이다 fatigue 피로 exchange 대화

[해석] Martin Buber는 '나와 너' 그리고 '나와 그것'이라는 두 가지 종류의 관계가 있다고 가르쳤다. 그 둘 사이의 차이를 보여주는 사례로, 기업형 커피 체인점 한 곳을 들르는 일상적인 출근길을 상상해 보라. 매일 아침 같은 주문을 하고 같은 것을 받고 돈을 내려놓고 거스름돈을 집어 든다. 계산대 뒤에 있는 사람과 이렇게 습관적이고 기계적으로 "이른 시간이네요! 졸리네요!"라고 말하는 정도의 상호작용이 Buber가 '나와

그것'이라고 부를 관계의 유형이다. 그러다가 어느 날 머핀 대신에 무지방 크림치즈가 들어간 통밀 베이글을 주문한다. 바리스타가 미소를 지으면서 "다이어트 중이세요?"라고 말하고 여러분은 당황할 정도로 깜짝 놀란다. 여기서 여러분은 계산대 담당 직원이 여러분이 무엇을 먹는지 기억하기는커녕 여러분을 알아보지도 못할 거라고 생각했다. 지루한 일상의 틀이 깨졌으며, 자신도 모르게 여러분의 존재가 중요하다는 것을 알게 된다. 그 가게를 나서면서 여느 때처럼 피로 때문에 힘들게 몸을 움직이는 대신 여러분이 받은 반응 덕분에 기분이 조금 나아졌음을 알게 된다. **Buber**는 이런 대화가 '나와 너'라는 관계라고 말할 것이다.

> **Martin Buber**가 '나와 그것'이라고 부르는 종류의 관계는 몰개성적인 상호작용이 특징이고, 그가 '나와 너'라고 부르는 관계의 유형에서 우리는 특정한 사람으로 인식된다고 느낀다.

정답 ④

10 다음 글의 내용으로 가장 적절한 것은?

The zoo is not a window on nature but rather a prism that bends the light according to the culture it is set in. And our view of nature accords us a clearer view of ourselves. We have always defined man in comparison to other animals. We thought we were the only tool users, but Jane Goodall and others dispelled that notion. Today, our place as the only true language users is being questioned. But human beings are not defined by what we do with our hands or our vocal cords but by what we do with our hearts. Arguments can be made for preserving nature because it may hold medical and technological secrets that could cure cancer or provide more efficient solar energy. Arguments can be made that we must preserve the fragile web of life because changing one small thread could alter the whole world. But the best argument for putting so much energy into preserving nature is for the sheer, breathtaking, poetic beauty of the diversity of life. This is an argument that is at once selfish and altruistic. Throughout history, zoos have entertained and educated; now they have a staggering opportunity before them: to tip the global balance back in favor of nature. To work toward the restoration of harmony in the living world. Zoos, which have provided so much joy to people, can now breathe life back into moribund populations of wild creatures.

① It is worthwhile to preserve nature if only for the sake of the diversity of life itself.
② Human beings are unquestionably the only species that can use language, if not tools in general.
③ Nature must be studied mainly because it will certainly yield knowledge we can use for our well-being.
④ Confining wildlife in zoos for entertainment and education is now facing adamant objections.

[해설] 필자는 "자연을 보존하는 데 그 많은 에너지를 쏟아야 한다는 주장 중 최고의 것은, 생명의 다양성이 지닌 그 순수하고, 숨이 멎을 듯하고, 시적인 아름다움을 위해서 그래야 한다는 것이다."라고 말함으로써, 자연 보존의 당위성을 '자연이 지닌 생명의 다양성과 그 아름다움을 보존'하는 것에서 찾고 있다. 따라서 ①의 추론은 타당하다. 한편, 필자는 오락과 교육의 역할을 제공하는 데 한정되었던 동물원 앞에 '어마어마한 기회(a staggering opportunity)'가 펼쳐지고 있다고 말하면서, 그것은 바로 '생명의 다양성을 보존하기 위해 멸종 위기에 처한 야생동물들을 복원시키는 데 일조하는 것'이라고 역설하고 있다. 기존 동물원의 역할에서 '생명 다양성 보존, 자연 보존' 쪽으로 중점을 옮기자는 주장일 뿐, 기존 동물원의 존재와 역할을 '단호히 반대(adamant objections)'하는 내용은 본문에서 명시되거나 암시된 적이 없으므로 ④는 추론으로 적절치 않다. ① 생명의 다양성 그 자체만을 위해서라도 자연을 보존하는 것은 가치 있다. ② 인간은 일반적 의미에서 도구를 사용하는 유일한 종은 아닐지라도 언어를 사용할 수 있는 유일한 종임이 분명하다. ③ 자연은 우리의 복지를 위해 활용할 수 있는 지식을 확실히 제공할 것이라는 주된 이유로 연구되어야 한다. ④ 오락과 교육을 위해 야생동물을 동물원에 가두는 것은 이제 단호한 반대에 직면하고 있다.

[어휘] prism 프리즘, 분광기 bend 구부리다, 굴절시키다 accord 주다, 수여하다 dispel 일소하다, 쫓아버리다 vocal cords 성대 argument 논거, 주장 fragile 망가지기 쉬운, 허약한 thread 실, 섬유 alter 바꾸다 sheer 순수한, 순전한, 완전한 breathtaking (아름다워서) 숨이 멎을 듯한 altruistic 이타주의적인 staggering 충격적인, 믿기 어려운 tip (어떤 것이 어느 방향으로 가도록) 살짝 건드리다 restoration 회복, 복구, 부흥 moribund 소멸[절멸] 직전의, 빈사 상태의 layout 배치 for the sake of ~ 때문에, ~를 위해서 confine 가두다 adamant 요지부동의, 단호한

[해석] 동물원은 자연을 향해 나 있는 하나의 창이 아니라 그 동물원이 놓여 있는 문화에 따라 빛을 굴절시키는 하나의 프리즘이다. 그리고 자연에 대한 우리의 견해는 우리에게 우리 자신에 대한 더 선명한 시각을 제공한다. 우리는 언제나 다른 동물들과 비교하여 인간을 정의해왔다. 우리는 인간만이 유일한 도구 사용자라고 생각했지만, 제인 구달(Jane Goodall)과 다른 이들은 이런 생각을 일소해버렸다. 오늘날 유일한 진짜 언어 사용자로서의 인간의 지위도 의문시되고 있다. 그러나 인간은 손이나 성대로써 우리가 행하는 바에 따라 정의되는 것이 아니라, 우리의 마음으로 행하는 바에 따라 정의된다. 암의 치료나 더 효율적인 태양에너지 제공과 같은 의학적, 기술적 비밀을 간직하고 있을 수도 있다는 이유 때문에 자연을 보존해야 한다는 주장을 할 수도 있다. 작은 실 하나를 변화시킴으로써 전체 세계를 변화시킬 수도 있으므로 깨지기 쉬운 생명의 망을 보존해야 한다는 주장을 할 수도 있다. 그러나 자연을 보존하는 데 그 많은 에너지를 쏟아야 한다는 주장 중 최고의 것은, 생명의 다양성이 지닌 그 순수하고, 숨이 멎을 듯하고, 시적인 아름다움을 위해서 그래야 한다는 것이다. 이러한 주장은 이기적인 것인 동시에 이타적인 것이다. 역사를 통틀어, 동물원들은 즐거움을 제공하는 역할과 교육하는 역할을 해왔다. 이제 그들 앞에 어마어마한 기회가 놓여 있다. 그것은 세계의 균형을 자연을 위하는 쪽으로 되돌리는 것이다. 생명 세계의 조화를 회복시키기 위해 노력하는 것이다. 사람들에게 그토록 많은 즐거움을 제공해온 동물원들은 이제 전멸 직전의 야생동물 개체군들에게 생명의 숨결을 다시 불어넣어 줄 수 있을 것이다.

[정답] ①

19 하프 모의고사 해설

01 밑줄 친 단어의 의미와 가장 가까운 것은?

> One goal of this symposium is to canvass modern scientific thought and research approaches regarding the three main categories of selection that Darwin addressed during his career.

① scrutinize
② portray
③ emulate
④ represent

[해설] canvass [kǽnvəs] 图 상세히 조사하다(= scrutinize) 유세하다, 점검하다; ~을 철저히 검토하다, 토론하다 (= discuss)

[어휘] regarding ~에 관해서 address 주소를 적다, 다루다 portray 그리다, 묘사하다

[해설] 이번 토론회의 목적은 다윈이 활동한 기간 동안 다루었던 세 가지 주된 선택 범주에 관한 현대 과학 사상과 연구 접근법들을 자세히 조사하는 것이다.

[정답] ①

02 다음 밑줄 친 부분의 풀이가 잘못된 것을 고르시오.

① The arrest of their leader touched off a riot. [= stopped]
② Bill takes the part of his sister. [= supports]
③ They are ready to meet us halfway. [= compromise with]
④ Her good advice is lost on him. [= doesn't influence]

[해설] touch off 야기 시키다(= cause, give rise to, bring on, trigger) take the part of ~을 지지하다(= support) meet + 사람 + halfway 타협하다(= make terms with, compromise with) be lost on ~에게 영향을 주지 않다

[해설] ① 그들 지도자의 체포가 폭동을 유발시켰다. ② 빌은 여동생을 지지했다.(여동생의 마음과 같다.) ③ 그들은 타협할 준비가 되어있다. ④ 그녀의 괜찮은 조언은 그에게 영향을 주지 않았다.

[정답] ①

03 다음 빈칸에 들어갈 표현으로 가장 적절한 것은?

Pressure to publish in leading academic journals encouraged researchers to cut corners and pursue trendy fields of science instead of doing more important work. The problem was _____ by editors who were not active scientists but professionals who _____ studies that were likely to make a splash.

① exacerbated – favored
② ameliorated – preferred
③ obscured – snubbed
④ remedied – misrepresented

[해설] 문제 해결의 가장 커다란 열쇠는 **cut corners**와 **make a splash**라는 표현인데, 전자는 '원칙이나 절차를 무시하다', 후자는 '큰 인기를 끌다'는 의미이다. 주요 학술지에 발표해야 한다는 압박감을 느껴 학술지 발표 가능 여부나 일정에 신경쓰다보니 연구실험의 원칙이나 절차를 무시하기 일쑤이고 학문적 중요성은 생각지 않고 최신 유행 분야만 연구하게 된다는 것이다. 그리고 이런 문제는 학문적 중요성을 아는 현역 과학자가 학술지를 만들지 않고 인기 있는 연구를 '선호하는' 전문 편집인들이 학술지를 만들다보니 '악화된다는' 것이다.

[어휘] **cut corners** 절차를 무시하다 **trendy** 최신 유행의 **make a splash** 많은 관심을 모으다 **exacerbate** 악화시키다 **ameliorate** 개선하다 **obscure** 모호하게 하다 **snub** 모욕하다 **remedy** 개선하다 **misrepresent** 잘못 표현하다

[해석] 주요 학술지에 발표해야 한다는 압박감은 연구자들로 하여금 절차를 무시하도록 그리고 좀 더 중요한 연구를 하는 대신 최신 유행의 과학 분야만을 추구하도록 부추겼다. 그 문제는 편집자들이 현역 과학자들이 아니라 큰 인기를 끌 것 같은 연구를 선호하는 전문가들이라는 점에 의해 악화되었다.

[정답] ①

04 다음 문장들 중 어법상 가장 적절한 것은?

① The virus that caused several hundred cases of flu is similar with one that causes a flu-like illness in swine.

② In opposition to President Carter's Foreign policy was the House Majority Leader and the Chairman of the Ways and Means Committee.

③ We have, in fact, two kinds of morality side by side: one which we preach but do not practice and another which we practice but do not preach.

④ Many of the old plantation gardens around Chalreston were planted a century or more ago and have been carefully tended and improved ever since.

해설 ①에서는 '~와 유사하다'라는 의미의 표현은 **be similar to**이다. 전치사 **with**를 **to**로 고친다. **one**은 **virus**를 의미하는 것이므로 옳게 쓰였다. ②에서는 부사구가 문두에 위치하여 주어와 동사가 도치되어 있는 문장이며, 주어부에서 핵심 표현을 추리면 **Leader**와 **Chairman**이 된다. 주어가 복수이므로 **was**를 **were**로 고쳐야 한다. ③에서는 둘 가운데 하나는 **one** 나머지 하나는 **the other**로 표현한다. **another**를 **the other**로 고친다. ④에서는 **many of** 뒤에는 '한정사+명사'의 형태가 오며, **ever since**는 '그 이후 지금까지'의 뜻이므로 현재완료시제와 호응한다. 따라서 ④는 옳은 문장이다.

정답 ④

05 다음 우리말 영작이 올바르지 않은 문장을 고르시오.

① 난민들은 식량도 쉴 곳도 없다.
  ⇨ The refugees had neither food nor shelter.

② 그는 용감함에도 불구하고 그 일을 하는 데 머뭇거렸다.
  ⇨ Brave man as he was, hesitated to do it.

③ 네가 시키는 대로 해라, 그렇지 않으면 벌을 받을 것이다.
  ⇨ Do what you are told, or you will be punished.

④ 모형 비행기는 제어 전선 혹은 무선 송신기 둘 중 하나에 의해 조종될 수 있다.
  ⇨ Model airplanes can be guided both by control wires or by radio transmitters.

해설 ④에서 **both**와 **or**가 함께 사용되는 것은 적합지 않다. **both A and B** 또는 **either A or B**의 형태 중 선택해야 한다. 문맥상 'A와 B 둘 중 하나'를 의미하는 **either A or B**가 적합하다. ①에서 **neither A nor B**는 'A도 B도 아니다'의 뜻이다. ②에서 「형용사+(명사)+as+주어+동사」는 '비록 ~이지만'이라는 의미의 양보의 표현이다. ③에서 **be told**는 수동태로서 **hear**와 같은 뜻이다. 또한 명령문 뒤에 **or**가 오면 '~해라, 그러지 않으면'의 의미를 나타낸다.

정답 ④

06 다음 글의 요지로 가장 적절한 것을 고르시오.

> Circumstantial evidence is evidence not drawn from the direct observation of a fact. If, for example, there is evidence that a piece of rock embedded in a wrapped chocolate bar is the same type of rock found in the candy factory, and that rock of this type is found in few other places, then there is circumstantial evidence that the stone found its way into the candy during manufacture and suggests that the candy-maker was negligent even though there is no eyewitness evidence that this is true. Despite a popular notion to look down on the quality of circumstantial evidence, it is of great usefulness if there is enough of it and if it is properly interpreted. Each circumstance, taken singly, may mean little, but a whole chain of circumstances can be as conclusive as direct evidence.

① A manufacturer's negligence can be shown by direct evidence only.
② Enough circumstantial evidence is as persuasive as direct evidence.
③ Circumstantial evidence can be very useful in science.
④ Circumstantial evidence can be accepted by the court.

해설 첫 문장에서 정황증거를 정의하고 있다. 마지막문장에서는 충분한 정황증거는 직접증거만큼 설득력이 있다는 것을 진술하고 있다. 제조업자의 태만을 증명하는 내용은 예로 사용된 사항일 뿐이다.

어휘 **observation** 관찰 **evidence** 증거 **embed** 깊숙이 박다, 끼워 넣다 **in the vicinity of** ~의 부근에, 근처에 **negligent** 태만 **interpret** 해석하다, 이해 해다 **conclusive** 결정적인, 단호한

해석 상황증거는 한 사실을 직접 관찰한 것으로부터 얻어지지 않는 증거이다. 예를 들어, 만일 포장된 초콜릿 안에 들어있는 돌이 사탕 공장 주변에서 발견되는 돌과 똑같은 종류이고, 이런 종류의 돌이 다른 곳에서는 거의 발견되지 않는다는 증거가 있다면, 이 돌이 제조 과정 중에 이 사탕에 들어갔다는 상황증거가 되는 것이고, 비록 이것이 사실이라는 목격자 증거가 없을지라도 사탕 제작자가 태만했다는 것을 나타낸다. 그 가치를 경시하려는 일반적 견해에도 불구하고 상황증거는 일단 증거의 양이 많고 올바르게 해석만 된다면 매우 유용하다. 각각의 상황은 하나씩 보면 거의 의미가 없지만, 전체 상황을 연결해 놓고 보면 직접적인 증거만큼 결정적일 수 있다.

정답 ②

07 다음 빈칸에 들어갈 말로 가장 적절한 것을 고르시오.

> Security should be thought of as an art; it cannot be accomplished through the old "tools and techies" model. An organization should not believe itself to be secure simply because it spends millions on security devices every year. The fact is that having an infinite budget and a large variety of security resources can often be more of a detriment than a benefit in many organizations. Organizations with vast resources at their command are very likely to try to solve security problems by implementing new security toys. I use the word "toy" because a security device, no matter how expensive or complex, is nothing more than a toy if it does not function within a greater security framework. Security cannot be handled exclusively through expensive equipment, as many of us have been led to believe. Security is not a technology; it is a thought process and a methodology. Security within our technologies is nothing until security is _____.

① in danger
② made simple
③ up to standard
④ within our minds

[해설] 이 글은 보안이란 오로지 값비싼 장비를 통해서만 다루어질 수는 없는 것으로 기술이 아니라 사고의 과정이고 방법론이라는 내용으로 빈칸에는 이를 포괄적으로 표현할 수 있는 말이 들어가야 한다. 그러므로 빈칸에 들어갈 말로 가장 적절한 것은 ④ '우리의 마음속에 있는'이다. ① 위험에 처한 ② 단순해진 ③ 기준에 부합하는

[어휘] security 보안 be thought of as ~으로 간주되다 accomplish 이루다, 성취하다 techie 기술 전문가 organization 기관, 조직체 device 장치 infinite 막대한, 무한한 budget 예산 more of ~ than ~이라기보다는 ~ at one's command ~의 마음대로 사용할 수 있는 implement 실행하다, 이행하다 framework 체계, 구조 exclusively 오로지 ~만 detriment 손해 methodology 방법론

[해석] 보안은 예술로 간주되어야 하는데, 왜냐하면 그것은 예전부터 있던 '도구와 기술 전문가' 모델을 통해서는 이루어질 수 없기 때문이다. 어떤 기관은 그것이 매년 수백만 달러를 보안 장치에 지출한다는 이유만으로 그 자체가 보안이 유지된다고 믿어서는 안 된다. 사실 막대한 예산과 아주 다양한 보안 재원을 가지고 있다는 것은 많은 기관들에서 흔히 이익이라기보다는 손해이다. 마음대로 사용할 수 있는 막대한 재원을 지니고 있는 기관들은 새로운 보안 장난감을 실행함으로써 보안 문제를 해결하고자 할 가능성이 매우 크다. 나는 '장난감'이라는 단어를 사용하는데, 왜냐하면 보안 장치라는 것은 아무리 비싸거나 복잡하더라도 그것이 더 큰 보안 체계 내에서 기능을 하지 않는다면 장난감에 지나지 않기 때문이다. 보안은 우리들 중 많은 이들이 믿게 되었던 것처럼 오로지 값비싼 장비를 통해서만 다루어질 수는 없다. 보안은 기술이 아니라 사고의 과정이고 방법론이다. 우리의 기술 속에 있는 보안은 (보안이) 우리의 마음속에 있을 때 가치가 있다.

[정답] ④

08 주어진 글 다음에 이어질 글의 순서로 가장 적절한 것은?

Prior to the Second World War, nation-states regulated their economic and fiscal affairs primarily as domestic matters; however, in the post-war era we have witnessed a huge expansion and intensification of economic interdependence.

(A) The resulting destabilization of these national economies hastened the 'Asian Economic Crisis' and sparked a global recession. Increasingly, national institutions cannot handle emerging economic, political, and social problems; this has prompted an urgent call for effective international regulatory institutions.

(B) As a result, the global economy is acutely vulnerable to disruption by the malfunction of any single nation-state's fiscal-political system; a serious malfunction can trigger a chain reaction known commonly as the 'domino effect.'

(C) Such a disruptive event occurred in 1997 when Thailand, with a relatively small national economy, suffered a financial collapse which touched off sufficient uncertainty among investors that they pulled their money out of neighbouring Malaysia, Indonesia, and South Korea.

① (C) - (B) - (A) ② (B) - (A) - (C)
③ (B) - (C) - (A) ④ (C) - (A) - (B)

해설 주어진 글에서 제2차 세계대전 이후에 경제적 상호 의존이 크게 확대되고 심화되었다고 했으며 이어서 (B)에서 그것에 대한 결과로 한 국가가 재정적으로나 정치적으로 제 기능을 못하면 세계 경제에 연쇄반응을 일으킨다고 말했다. (C)에서 예로 태국의 재정적 붕괴가 다른 국가에도 파급된 것을 설명하였고 마지막으로 (A)에서 이러한 국가들의 경제 불안정화가 아시아 경제의 위기를 재촉했고 세계적인 불황을 촉발했기 때문에 효과적인 국제 규제 기관이 긴급하게 필요하게 되었다는 순서로 글이 전개되고 있다. 그러므로 주어진 글 다음에 이어질 글의 순서로 가장 적절한 것은 ③ '(B) - (C) - (A)'이다.

어휘 nation-state 민족국가, 국민국가 regulate 규정하다, 통제하다 post-war era 전후 시대 witness 목격하다 expansion 확대, 확장 intensification 심화, 격화 interdependence 상호 의존 hasten 재촉하다 spark 촉발하다 recession 불황, 침체 institution 기관, 제도 prompt 유발하다, 자극하다 urgent 긴급한 regulatory institution 규제 기관 acutely 극도로, 대단히, 몹시 vulnerable 취약한, 영향을 받기 쉬운 disruption 혼란, 파멸 malfunction 기능 불량 trigger 유발하다 collapse 붕괴, 와해 touch off A A를 촉발하다 sufficient 충분한 fiscal 재정(상)의 destabilization 불안정화

해석 제2차 세계대전 이전에 민족국가들은 경제와 재정 문제를 주로 국내 문제로 규정했다. 그러나 전후 시대에 우리는 경제적 상호 의존의 엄청난 확대와 심화를 목격해 왔다. (B) 그 결과 세계 경제는 어떤 하나의 민족국가의 재정적·정치적 시스템의 기능 불량에 의한 혼란에 극도로 취약하다. 심각한 기능 불량은 흔히 '도미노 효과'라고 알려진 연쇄 반응을 일으킬 수 있다. (C) 그러한 파멸적인 사건은 1997년에 발생했는데, 그 당시 비교적 경제 규모가 작았던 태국은, 인접한 말레이시아, 인도네시아 그리고 한국으로부터 투자자들이 자신들의 돈을 빼낼 정도로 투자자들 사이에 충분한 불확실성을 촉발한 재정적인 붕괴를 겪었다. (A) 그 결과로 초래된 이러한 국가 경제의 불안정화는 '아시아의 경제 위기'를 재촉했으며, 세계적인 불황을 촉발했다. 점점 더 국가 기관은 부상하고 있는 경제적, 정치적 그리고 사회적인 문제를 다룰 수 없으며, 이것은 효과적인 국제적 규제 기관의 긴급한 필요성을 유발하였다.

정답 ③

09 글의 흐름으로 보아, 주어진 문장이 들어가기에 가장 적절한 곳을 고르시오.

> To meet what it needs, a solution adopted by psychologists was not to attempt to examine the mind's workings.

One of the major obstacles in getting psychology recognized as a branch of science was the abstract nature of the mind. (①) In order to establish its scientific credentials, psychologists needed to adopt scientific methodology, including observation and experimentation. (②) Because we only have direct access to our own minds, our observation of mental processes is introspective and necessarily subjective, but science demands an objective approach. (③) Instead, it was to observe how they manifest themselves in behavior. (④) Not only can behavior of humans be watched, but the behavioral response of a human being to a specific situation can be examined under strict laboratory conditions. Thanks to this objective scientific approach, behaviorism and its theories of stimulus and response dominated experimental psychology until the mid-20th century.

[해설] 과학이 필요로 하는 것을 충족시키기 위해서 심리학자들이 마음이 하는 일들을 조사하려고 시도했다는 주어진 문장은 과학이 요구하는 것이 무엇인지 언급한 내용 다음에 위치해야 한다. 따라서 주어진 문장은 ③에 들어가는 것이 가장 적절하다.

[어휘] **branch** 분야 **credentials** 자격(증) **methodology** 방법론 **introspective** 자기 성찰의 **manifest** 나타내다

[해석] 심리학을 과학의 한 분야로 인정받게 하는 데 가장 큰 장애물 중의 하나는 마음의 추상적인 본질이었다. 마음의 과학적인 자격을 확고히 하기 위해서, 심리학자들은 관찰과 실험을 포함한 과학적인 방법론을 채택할 필요가 있었다. 우리 자신의 마음에 대해서는 우리만 직접적으로 다가갈 수 있기 때문에, 정신 과정에 대한 우리의 관찰은 자기 성찰적이고 필연적으로 주관적이지만, 과학은 객관적인 접근을 요구한다. 과학이 필요로 하는 것을 충족시키기 위해서, 심리학자들이 채택한 방법은 마음이 하는 일들을 조사하려고 시도하는 것이 아니었다. 대신에 그 방법은 마음이 하는 일들이 어떻게 행동에서 나타나는지 관찰하는 것이었다. 인간의 행동은 관찰될 수 있을 뿐만 아니라, 특정한 상황에서 인간의 행동 반응 또한 엄격한 실험실 조건에서 조사될 수 있다. 이러한 객관적인 과학적 접근 덕분에, 행동주의와 자극과 반응에 대한 그 이론들이 20세기 중반까지 실험 심리학을 지배했다.

[정답] ③

10 다음 글의 내용과 일치하지 않은 것은?

Within the context of the overall murder rate, the death penalty cannot be said to be widely or routinely used in the United States; in recent years the average has been about one execution for about every 700 murders committed, or 1 execution for about every 325 murder convictions. It is noted that the death penalty is sought and applied more often in some jurisdictions, not only between states but within states. A 2004 Cornell University study showed that while 2.5% of murderers convicted nationwide were sentenced to the death penalty, in Nevada 6% were given the death penalty. Texas gave only 2% of murderers the death sentence, less than the national average. Texas, however, executed 40% of those sentenced, which was about 4 times higher than the national average. California had executed only 1% of those sentenced. Only 1.4% of those executed since 1976 have been women. African-Americans make up 42% of death row inmates while making up only 12% of the general population. On the other hand, others note that this is lower than the 50% of the total prison population which is African-American and that whites are in fact twice as likely as African-Americans to receive the death penalty, and are also executed more quickly after sentencing.

① The percentage of those sentenced to the death penalty based on area
② The percentage of death row inmates based on race
③ The percentage of those sentenced to the death penalty based on occupation
④ The percentage of those executed based on gender

[해설] 지역별(Nevada, Texas, California), 인종별(African-Americans, whites), 성별(women) 비율은 나와 있으나, 직업별(occupation) 비율은 나와 있지 않다.

[어휘] context 문맥, 전후관계, 정황, 환경 overall 전부의, 전반(면)적인, 종합적인 death penalty 사형 execution 집행, 실행 commit 위탁, 위임하다 conviction 유죄판결, 유죄선고, 확신·신념 jurisdiction 사법권·재판권(이 미치는 범위), 관할권(한) sentence 형을 판결(선고)(하다) make up 구성하다, (이야기 따위를) 날조하다, 꾸며내다, 화장하다 death row 사형수 감방 inmate 재소자

[해석] 전반적인 살인율의 정황에서 볼 때, 사형이 미국에서 널리 또는 통상적으로 이용되고 있다고 할 수 없으며; 최근 그 평균은 매 저질러지는 살인의 700건 정도에 한건 처형하거나 매 325건의 살인 유죄판결에 대해 한 건의 처형이었다. 주간 뿐 아니라 주 자체 내에서 일부 관할지역에서는 사형이 보다 빈번히 모색되고 적용되고 있다는 점이 주목된다. 2004년 코넬대학의 한 연구결과 전국적으로 유죄판결을 받은 살인자들중 2.5%는 사형선고를 받은 한편 네바다 주에서는 6%가 사형을 언도받았던 것으로 나타났다. 텍사스 주는 살인자들 중 2%에게만 사형을 선고했는데 이것은 전국평균보다 낮다. 하지만 텍사스 주는 선고를 받은 대상자의 40%를 처형했는데 이것은 전국평균의 4배 이상이 된다. 캘리포니아는 선고를 받은 대상자 중 1%만을 처형했다. 1976년 이래 처형된 살인자들 중 1.4%만 여성이었다. 흑인이 사형수 감방 재소자들의 40%를 구성하고 있는 한편 전체인구의 12%만을 차지하고 있다. 반면, 다른 이들은 이 수치가 흑인 전체 총 인구의 50%보다는 낮으며 백인은 사실 사형을 선고받는 흑인의 두 배이며 또한 선고가 있고 난 다음 보다 신속히 처형된다는데 주목하고 있다.

[정답] ③

20 하프 모의고사 해설

01 다음 밑줄 친 단어의 의미와 가장 가까운 것은?

> Cloth which is diaphanous is very fine or thin.

① sheer ② consensus
③ sensible ④ sagacious

[해설] diaphanous [daiǽfənəs] 형 투명한, 내비치는, 아주 얇은 = sheer, transparent
[영영] diaphanous : so thin as to transmit light
[어휘] consensus 일치, 합의 sensible, sagacious 현명한, 느낄 수 있는
[해석] 투명한 옷은 매우 곱거나 얇다.

[정답] ①

02 다음 밑줄 친 표현과 의미가 가장 가까운 것은?

> He goes off the deep end about the unexpected result.

① falls from the cliff ② feels disheartened deeply
③ loses his self-restraint ④ acts with consideration

[해설] go off the deep end 버럭 화를 내다; (감정이) 욱[울컥]하다, 자제력을 잃다 = lose one's self-restraint
[영영] go off the deep end : suddenly become very angry or emotional
[해석] 그는 자제력을 잃어버린다./예기치 않은(unexpected) 결과에 대해서는

[정답] ③

03 다음 빈칸에 들어갈 표현으로 가장 적절한 것은?

> Our society has developed a taboo against the use of words associated with group hatred, as a way to _____ said hatred.

① unfetter
② ennoble
③ transfuse
④ stigmatize

[해설] 금기란 당혹스럽거나, 불쾌한 언급을 회피하도록 사회적 관습으로 강제하는 것을 말한다. 특정 표현을 '금기시'하는 것은 그 대상이 나쁘거나, 수치스러운 것이라고 규정하는 것인데, 결국 '낙인을 찍는' 하나의 방편이 된다고 말할 수 있다.

[어휘] **taboo** 금기 **a taboo against** ~에 대한 금기 **hatred** 증오 **said** 앞에서 말한 **unfetter** ~을 자유롭게 하다 **ennoble** 귀족에 봉하다 **transfuse** 수혈하다 **stigmatize** 오명을 씌우다

[해석] 우리 사회는 집단 증오에 대해 낙인찍는 방편으로 집단 증오와 관련된 표현의 사용에 대한 금기를 발달시켜왔다.

[정답] ④

04 다음 빈칸에 들어갈 표현으로 가장 적절한 것은?

> Good medical practice is always characterized by _____ and diagnostic elegance, aimed not at saving money but at what would be best for the patient, since too much testing and treating can be harmful.

① pharmaceutical innovation
② emotional reservations
③ intellectual rigor
④ therapeutic parsimony

[해설] 훌륭한 의료행위는 '진단상의 간결함을 특징으로 한다.', '과도한 검사와 치료는 해롭다' 등의 진술을 종합적으로 고려하면, 환자를 위해 '치료적인 절제'를 실천하는 의료행위가 바람직하다고 말하고 있음을 알 수 있다.

[어휘] **medical practice** 의료행위 **be characterized by** ~로 특징지어지다 **diagnostic** 진단의 **elegance** 우아함 **pharmaceutical** 약학의 **innovation** 혁신 **reservation** 예약 **rigor** 엄함 **therapeutic** 치료의 **parsimony** 인색

[해석] 훌륭한 의료행위는 비용 절감을 목표로 삼는 것이 아니라 환자에게 가장 좋은 치료를 목표로 하는, 치료적 절제와 진단적 간결함으로 항상 특징지어진다. 과도한 검사와 치료는 오히려 해로울 수 있기 때문이다.

[정답] ④

05 다음 문장들 중 어법상 적절하지 않은 것은?

① With the blood flowing form the wound, he shouted to us to come on.
② Nobody thought he would last 15 rounds, but he went the full distance.
③ Three years of seesaw fighting, in which many civilians died, resulted in a stalemate.
④ Whether happiness is relative or absolute depends on if it is about money or mentality.

해설 ①에서는 콤마 앞부분은 이유를 나타내는 'with 분사구문'을 이루고 있으며, the blood가 flow의 주체이므로 능동관계를 나타내는 현재분사 flowing을 썼다. ②에서는 주절의 과거시제 thought에 맞춰 종속절의 시제를 would last로 썼다. go the full distance는 '마지막 라운드 까지 싸워내다'라는 의미이다. ③에서는 result in은 '~을 초래하다'라는 뜻이다. 삽입된 관계대명사절에서 '전치사+관계대명사', 즉 in which 다음에 완전한 문장이 왔으므로 옳은 표현이다. ④에서는 whether절은 전치사의 목적어가 될 수 있지만, if절은 그렇지 못하다. depends on 다음의 if를 whether로 고쳐야 한다.

해설 ① 피가 상처 부위에서 흘러나와서, 그는 우리에게 오라고 소리를 질렀다. ② 아무도 그가 15파운드를 버틸 것으로 생각하지 않았지만, 그는 끝까지 싸웠다. ③ 많은 민간인들이 죽었던 3년간의 엎치락뒤치락하는 전투는 교착 상태를 가져왔다. ④ 행복이 상대적이냐 절대적이냐 하는 것은 그것이 돈에 관한 것이냐 정신에 관한 것이냐에 달려 있다.

정답 ④

06 다음 우리말 영작이 올바르지 않는 문장을 고르시오.

① 요즈음 자동차가 많아져서 대도시에서는 어떤 때는 걷는 것이 빠를 때가 있다.
  ⇨ Nowadays motorcars are so numerous that in a large city it sometimes takes less time to walk than to ride.
② 사람들은 흔히 책이 너무 비싸다고 불평하는데, 책값은 다른 물건만큼 오르지 않았다.
  ⇨ People often complain that books are too expensive, but their prices have not risen as much as other commodities.
③ 아무리 부유해도 행복을 살 수는 없다.
  ⇨ No matter how rich he is, he can't buy happiness.
④ 영어를 배우는 목적은 단지 그 말을 배우는 것뿐만 아니라, 영미의 문화를 이해하는 것이다.
  ⇨ The purpose of studying English is not only to learn the language itself, but to understand English and American culture.

해설 ②에서 as ~ as의 원급비교문장에서 비교대상은 반드시 일치해야 한다. 책의 가격을 다른 물건의 가격과 비교하기 때문에 other commodities가 아니라 those of other commodities로 써야 옳다. 이때 those는 명사인 prices를 대신하는 지시대명사이다. ①에서 so ~ that 용법과 "it takes+시간+to동사원형"의 구조가 사용된 올바른 문장이다. ③에서 '아무리 ~해도'라는 양보의 표현은 「No matter how+형용사/부사+주어+동사」로 쓴다. ④에서 not only A but (also) B 의 구조가 사용된 문장이다. but also에서 also 가 생략되어 사용될 수 있다. A 와 B가 병렬관계를 이루어 to부정사로 표현되고 있다.

정답 ②

07 다음 글의 주제로 가장 적절한 것은?

In organizations, there is no simple cause-and-effect relationship between introducing a management technique and getting an improved business result. This contrasts with other spheres of activity where simple causal relationships do seem to operate. Hit the nail with the hammer, and it goes into the wood. Show a dog food, and it salivates. This kind of simple cause-and-effect logic can be misleading if applied to the complex world of organizations, where it is difficult to trace single effects to single causes. Uncontrollable outside factors can sink a wonderfully designed team (a hurricane just swept the entire inventory out to sea) or rescue one whose design was so bad that failure seemed assured (the firm that was competing for the contract just went belly-up). In organizations, multiple causes are operating at the same time and interacting with each over an extended period of time.

① complex causal relationship in organizations
② benefits of a fair relationship in organizations
③ strategies to maximize profits of organizations
④ new technologies introduced to manage a business

[해설] 조직 내에서는 통제할 수 없는 외적 요인이 작용하거나 여러 원인들이 동시에 오랜 기간에 걸쳐 상호작용하기 때문에 경영 기법과 사업 실적 사이에 단순한 인과 관계가 적용되지 않는다는 내용의 글이므로, 이 글의 주제로 가장 적절한 것은 ① '조직 내에서의 복잡한 인과 관계'이다. ② 조직 내에서 공정한 관계의 장점 ③ 조직의 수익을 극대화하는 전략 ④ 기업을 운영하기 위해 도입된 새로운 기술들

[어휘] organization 조직, 기관 cause-and-effect relationship 인과 관계 contrast with A A와 대조를 이루다 sphere 영역, 구(球) causal 인과 관계의 misleading 오해를 일으키는 apply 적용하다 trace 추적하다 factor 요인, 요소 inventory 재고(품), 물품 목록 assured 확실한, 자신감 있는 compete 경쟁하다 contract 계약 extended 장기간의, 광범위한 salivate 침을 흘리다 belly-up 파산한

[해석] 조직에서 경영 기법을 도입하는 것과 향상된 사업 실적을 얻는 것 사이에는 어떤 단순한 인과 관계도 없다. 이것은 단순한 인과 관계가 정말로 작용하는 것처럼 보이는 다른 활동 영역들과 대조를 이룬다. 망치로 못을 치면, 못은 나무로 들어간다. 개에게 음식을 보여 주면, 개는 침을 흘린다. 이런 종류의 단순한 인과 논리가 조직이라는 복잡한 세상에 적용되면, 그것은 오해를 일으킬 수 있는데, 거기서는 단 한 가지 결과를 단 한 가지 원인으로 거슬러 올라가 추적하기 어렵다. 통제할 수 없는 외부 요인이 훌륭하게 계획된 팀을 망칠 수 있거나(허리케인이 모든 재고품을 막 바다로 휩쓸어 갔다) 또는 계획이 너무 볼품없어서 실패가 확실해 보인 팀을 구할 수도 있다(계약을 놓고 경쟁하던 회사가 막 파산했다). 조직에서는 복합적인 원인들이 동시에 작용하고 있으며 오랜 시간에 걸쳐 서로 상호작용하고 있다.

[정답] ①

08 빈칸 (A)와 (B)에 들어갈 말로 가장 적절한 것은?

Gift giving is one of the most mysterious areas of shopping. Irrational behavior is almost the norm in this area of consumer spending and it is tolerated, expected, and even encouraged. Gift giving is less about shopping and more about the emotions of the shopper. This helps to explain the extreme nature of gift shopping and the illogical nature of the whole process. From the consumer's point of view, shopping for gifts is an emotional process that one gets caught up in. It is an area where the laws of supply, demand, and price go out the window as anxious shoppers do their utmost to bring pleasure to another person, and thereby, to themselves. The shopper shopping for gifts is the most susceptible of all shoppers. Smart retailers are ready to take advantage of the defenseless and emotionally vulnerable gift buyer. Meanwhile, the shopper knows he is vulnerable, but he is also unwilling to defend himself. Pleasing the recipient and conveying the intended emotional message are often more important than the price.

⬇

When shopping for gifts, consumers exhibit a(n) __(A)__ consumption pattern because they are driven usually by __(B)__.

	(A)	(B)		(A)	(B)
①	strategic	supply	②	strategic	demand
③	unreasonable	emotion	④	unreasonable	supply

해설 이 글의 중심 생각은 선물을 사기 위해 쇼핑하는 것은 받는 사람을 기쁘게 하려는 감정적 요인에 영향을 받아 비이성적인 소비 패턴을 보인다는 것이다. 그러므로 요약문의 빈칸 (A)에는 **unreasonable**이, (B)에는 **emotion**이 가장 적절하다. ① 전략적인 - 공급 ② 전략적인 - 수요 ④ 비이성적인 - 공급

어휘 the norm 일반적인 것 point of view 관점 go out the window 쓸모없게 되다 do one's utmost 전력을 다하다 thereby 그렇게 함으로써 retailer 소매상 take advantage of ~을 이용하다 vulnerable 취약한 recipient 받는 사람, 수령인 susceptible 쉽게 영향을 받는

해석 선물을 주는 것은 쇼핑의 가장 설명하기 힘든 분야 중의 하나이다. 이러한 소비자 지출의 분야에서는 비합리적인 행동이 거의 일반적인 것이며 그것은 용인되고, 기대되며, 심지어 권장된다. 선물을 주는 것은 쇼핑보다 쇼핑객의 감정과 더 관련이 있다. 이것은 선물 쇼핑의 극단적인 특성과 전체 과정의 비논리적인 특성을 설명하는 데 도움이 된다. 소비자의 관점에서 보았을 때, 선물을 위한 쇼핑은 사람이 휘말려 들어가는 감정적 과정이다. 그것은 열심인 쇼핑객이 다른 사람에게 기쁨을 주려고, 그리고 그럼으로써 자신에게도 기쁨을 주려고 전력을 다하기 때문에 공급, 수요, 그리고 가격의 법칙이 쓸모없게 되는 영역이다. 선물을 (사기) 위해 쇼핑하는 쇼핑객은 모든 쇼핑객 중에서 가장 쉽게 영향을 받는다. 똑똑한 소매상은 무방비한 그리고 감정적으로 취약한 선물 구매자를 이용할 준비가 되어 있다. 한편 쇼핑객은 자신이 취약하다는 것을 알면서도 자신을 방어하기를 꺼린다. 받는 사람을 기쁘게 하고 의도된 감정적 메시지를 전달하는 것이 흔히 가격보다 더 중요하다.

⇨ 선물을 위한 쇼핑을 할 때, 소비자들은 감정에 의해 대체로 이끌리기 때문에 비이성적인 소비 패턴을 보인다.

정답 ③

09 다음 빈칸에 들어갈 말로 가장 적절한 것은?

> A point to keep in mind when thinking about paranormal, supernatural, and pseudo-scientific beliefs is that letting go of them is not necessarily a _____. Not only can thinking skeptically be safer and more economical over the course of a lifetime, it doesn't have to be any less fun, either. Whatever I may have lost by not believing in things like astrology and ghosts, I am confident that I more than make up for it by embracing reality with great enthusiasm. All scientific discoveries to date and all the mysteries still to be solved excite me, and I find plenty of reason for optimism and hope, even amid harsh realities. I understand that it may feel comforting or stabilizing to believe that invisible forces influence us, but it can also be comforting and stabilizing to realize that as humans we are smart enough and strong enough to face up to the universe as it really is and get on with our lives.

① must ② reality
③ sacrifice ④ pleasure

[해설] 점성술이나 유령 같은 것에 의지하는 것보다 인간이 충분히 강하며 현명하다는 것을 깨닫는 것이 더 안전하고 더 경제적이라는 본문의 내용으로 보아, 첫 문장이 '초자연적이며 유사 과학적 믿음을 버리는 것은 어떤 것을 포기하거나 잃어버리는 것이 아니다'는 내용을 나타낼 수 있도록 빈칸에 ③ '희생'이 들어가는 것이 적절하다는 것을 알 수 있다. ① 꼭 해야 하는 것 ② 현실 ④ 즐거움

[어휘] **supernatural** 초자연적인 **let go of A** A를 놓아버리다 **skeptically** 회의적으로 **economical** 경제적인 **astrology** 점성술 **confident** 확신하는 **make up for A** A를 만회하다 **embrace** 받아들이다, 껴안다 **enthusiasm** 열정 **to date** 지금까지의 **optimism** 낙관주의 **harsh** 가혹한 **stabilizing** 안정감을 주는 **face up to A** A를 직시하다 **get on with one's life** 삶을 계속해 나가다 **paranormal** 불가사의한 **pseudoscientific** 유사 과학적인 **amid** ~ 속에서

[해석] 불가사의하고 초자연적이며 유사 과학적인 믿음에 대해 생각할 때 명심할 점은 그런 믿음을 놓아버리는 것이 반드시 희생은 아니라는 것이다. 회의적으로 생각하는 것은 평생에 걸쳐 더 안전하고 더 경제적일 수 있을 뿐만 아니라, 그것이 조금도 덜 재미있을 리도 없다. 점성술과 유령 같은 것을 믿지 않음으로써 내가 무엇을 잃었든 상관없이, 큰 열정을 가지고 현실을 받아들임으로써 그것(잃어버린 것)을 만회하는 것 이상의 일을 한다고 나는 확신한다. 지금까지의 모든 과학적인 발견과 아직 해결되어야 할 모든 신비가 나를 흥분시키며, 가혹한 현실 속에서도 낙관주의와 희망에 대한 충분한 이유를 나는 발견한다. 보이지 않는 힘이 우리에게 영향을 준다고 믿는 것이 위로가 되거나 안정감을 준다고 느껴질 수 있다는 것을 나는 이해하지만, 우주를 실제 있는 그대로 직시하고 우리의 삶을 계속할 만큼 인간으로서 우리는 충분히 현명하고 충분히 강하다는 것을 깨닫는 것도 위로가 되고 안정감을 줄 수 있다.

[정답] ③

10 다음 글의 내용과 일치하지 않는 것은?

> For decades, Ebola haunted rural African villages like some mythic monster that every few years rose to demand a human sacrifice and then returned to its cave. It reached the West only in nightmare form, a Hollywood horror that makes eyes bleed and organs dissolve and doctors despair because they have no cure. But 2014 is the year an outbreak turned into an epidemic, powered by the very progress that has paved roads and raised cities and lifted millions out of poverty. This time it reached crowded slums in Liberia, Guinea and Sierra Leone; it traveled to Nigeria and Mali, to Spain, Germany and the U.S. It struck doctors and nurses in unprecedented numbers, wiping out a public-health infrastructure that was weak in the first place. One August day in Liberia, six pregnant women lost their babies when hospitals couldn't admit them for complications. Anyone willing to treat Ebola victims ran the risk of becoming one.

① Ebola has not been an intimidating epidemic in Africa for a long time.
② The dangers of Ebola were unjustifiably exaggerated in the West.
③ Ebola became a threatening epidemic as poverty was widespread in Africa.
④ Some Liberian women miscarried their babies as hospitals were unable to admit them.

저자 ··· 권혁민

[현]
- 김승봉 경찰팀 경찰영어 전임

[전]
- 윌비스 경찰팀 영어 강의
- 한교고시학원 경찰영어 강의
- 이투스 외국어영역 강의

[저서]
- One-Pack(원팩) 권혁민 문법 기출지문 총정리 OX
- One-Pack(원팩) 기출어휘 & 이디엄 1500
- 기출문장으로 익히는 직독직해 & 해석공식
- One-Pack(원팩) 문법적용공식zip
- One-Pack(원팩) 권혁민 기출영어 story
- One-Pack(원팩) 권혁민 HALF 모의고사
- One-Pack(원팩) 권혁민 FINAL 복·생·이

권혁민 하프 모의고사

2020년 7월 30일 초판 1쇄 인쇄·발행

저 자·권혁민 발행인·김성권 발행처·도서출판 웅비
주　소·서울시 강남구 강남대로 136길 5-4, 301호(논현동, 정빌딩)
교재문의·www.woongb.co.kr
Tel 02) 2264-4543 / 070-8740-5900
Fax 02) 2264-4544

본서의 無斷轉載·複製를 禁함
본서의 무단전재·복제행위는 저작권법 제136조 제1항에 의거 5년 이하의 징역 또는 5,000만 원 이하의 벌금에 처하거나 이를 병과할 수 있습니다.

파본은 구입처에서 교환하시기 바랍니다.
ISBN 979-11-5506-574-7 (13740)

정가 21,000원